LESBIAN STUDIES
Present and Future

Other Works by the Same Author

The Lesbian Path
Thomas Babington Macaulay

LESBIAN STUDIES
Present and Future

Margaret Cruikshank

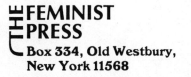
THE FEMINIST
PRESS
Box 334, Old Westbury,
New York 11568

Library of Congress Cataloging in Publication Data
Main entry under title: Lesbian studies.
    Bibliography: p. 237.
    Includes index.
    1. Lesbians—Biography.   2. Lesbianism—Study and
teaching.   3. Women's studies.   I. Cruikshank, Margaret.
HQ75.3. L48   306.7'663'07   82-4972
ISBN 0-935312-06-4 (cloth)   AACR2
ISBN 0-935312-07-2 (paper)

First edition
Manufactured in the USA

We gratefully acknowledge permission to reprint the following material:

"Dyke in Academe (II)," by Paula Bennett, was presented at the panel "The
Second Sex in Academia: Stress, Anger and Energy" during the Modern Language
Association Convention in Houston, December 27-30, 1980.

"'Out' at the University: Myth and Reality," by Toni A. H. McNaron, is reprinted
from Women's Studies Newsletter 8, no. 4 (Fall/Winter 1980).

"'Kissing/Against the Light': A Look at Lesbian Poetry," by Elly Bulkin, was
originally published in the Radical Teacher 10 (December 1978), and is reprinted
with permission. It also appears as the introduction and afterword to Lesbian
Poetry: An Anthology, edited by Elly Bulkin and Joan Larkin (Watertown, Massachusetts, Persephone Press, 1981).

A shorter version of "Who Hid Lesbian History?," by Lillian Faderman appeared in
Frontiers: A Journal of Women's Studies 4, no. 3 (Fall 1979).

"Lesbian Biography, Biography of Lesbians," by Frances Doughty, first appeared in
Frontiers: A Journal of Women's Studies, 4, no. 3 (Fall 1979).

An earlier version of "Is Feminist Criticism Really Feminist?" by Becky Birtha
originally appeared in Sojourner, The New England Women's Journal of News,
Opinions and the Arts 6 no. 2 (October 1980).

"Love Between Women in Prison," by Karlene Faith, is adapted from a book in
progress. Another version of the material, edited by Robin Linden, appeared in
Sinister Wisdom 16 (1981).

Lesbian Perspective of Women's Studies by Marilyn Frye originally appeared in
Sinister Wisdom 14 (Summer 1980).

Text design: Lea Smith

Contents

Contents

Acknowledgments

I wish to thank several women for their important contributions to this book. My committee of "auxiliary editors" read submissions, proposed revisions, and helped me decide which essays best illustrate lesbian studies: Jane Gurko, Kathy Hickok, Madeline Davis, Bonnie Zimmerman, and Nancy Manahan.

I am especially grateful to Nancy for the actual editing of several essays. Her writing and editing talents have shaped other books besides this one.

Three authors of *Lesbian Studies* read a draft of the Introduction and made many helpful comments: Ida VSW Red, Clare Potter, and Matile Poor. I owe special thanks to my editors at the Feminist Press, Liz Phillips, Elsa Dixler, and Jo Baird, and to Lyndall MacCowan, who prepared the bibliography and typed the manuscript.

Finally, I thank Matile for her loving support of all my work.

—Margaret Cruikshank

Introduction

Twelve years ago the founders of women's studies spoke confidently about the radical changes the new discipline would bring as it re-examined the university curriculum in the light of the women's movement. But few feminists then would have predicted the rise of *lesbian* feminism or the *public* lesbian life of the 1980s. Even in 1977, at the first lesbian caucus of the New National Women's Studies Association,[1] it would have been hard to imagine lesbian-feminist scholarship as it exists today, when *Matrices: A Lesbian-Feminist Research Newsletter* lists hundreds of subscribers from several countries; when lesbians of color are publishing numerous books and articles; when the current edition of *The Lesbian in Literature* contains more than seven thousand entries; and when lesbian archives and history projects are starting or expanding in New York, San Francisco, Washington, Buffalo, and other cities.

All of this work might have sprung up independently, but the national lesbian-feminist network begun by NWSA has certainly encouraged its growth. By creating a climate in which some academic women could come out as lesbians, women's studies has allowed us to find each other, explore common concerns, and support each other's work. Another precondition for the development of our projects and studies was the outpouring of books by and about lesbians in the 1970s and early 1980s. Historical studies, novels, collections of poetry and short fiction, anthologies of autobiographical writing, sociology and interviews all celebrate our survival. Today it seems hard to believe that only rarely before 1970 (and not often before 1975) did books present positive images of lesbians.

Despite all these recent publications the concept of "lesbian studies" is still fairly new. It means both the grassroots cultural work which tells us who we are and the more formally organized *courses* on lesbians which now exist in a few women's studies programs and in women's centers. Examples are a three-part "lesbian perspectives" program at the Women's Building in Los Angeles (see the Resources section of this book) and courses on "Lesbian Culture" at the University of Wisconsin; "Twentieth-Century Lesbian Novels" at Nebraska; "The Lesbian Novel" at California

State, Long Beach; "Lesbian Literature and Feminism" at San Francisco State University; and "Lesbian Literature" at the University of Massachusetts, Boston (see Appendix for course outlines). In all of these a feminist point of view is assumed.

Usually "lesbian studies" means studies *about* us, but certain books and essays have so pronounced a lesbian perspective that they can be considered part of lesbian studies, even though they focus on other subjects: for instance, Adrienne Rich's *Of Women Born; This Bridge Called My Back: Writings by Radical Women of Color*, edited by Cherríe Moraga and Gloria Anzaldúa; Audre Lorde's *Cancer Journals*; and *Gyn/Ecology* by Mary Daly. Examples in this anthology are Becky Birtha's critique of feminist literary criticism and Clare Bright's response to a perennial question in women's studies classes, "But what about men?" Theoretically, a work by anyone which offers information about lesbianism or about attempts to suppress it might be construed as "lesbian studies," but with rare exceptions the term means studies that we ourselves undertake.[2]

While the following essays offer no formal definitions, they show by example the meaning of lesbian studies. They clarify its origins, characteristics, goals, and assumptions, at least in this early stage of its development. A single book cannot presume to speak for all lesbian researchers, however. Representing significantly more white women than women of color, this anthology cannot claim to be comprehensive. But it will add a new political dimension to women's studies by implicitly demanding that lesbian-feminist issues be taken more seriously than they have been so far. Less isolated than we were a few years ago and better organized, we are no longer grateful for tokenism—for a reference to *Rubyfruit Jungle*, a footnote on lesbians, an allusion to women who were lovers, or an appearance of a guest lesbian speaker in a college class. Even the phrase "lesbian studies" shows our determination to take up more space in the field of women's studies.

For me, one of the chief characteristics of the lesbian-feminist educational movement is simply the euphoria of the women involved in it. This is due partly to emergence from the closet and recognition of our sheer numbers. The emotional high women experience when we feel for the first time a passionate connection between our lives and our work is hard to describe to someone who has not directly felt it. Academic lesbians typically find that our teaching takes on a whole new dimension when we can be ourselves. Several writers comment on this transformation in the essays published here. The euphoria of lesbian students, teachers, and administrators has perhaps been most intense and most obvious at the annual conventions of NWSA, although we now meet in other professional groups as well, including the Modern Language Association and the Berkshire Conference on the History of Women.

High spirits would not carry us very far, of course, if we did not have serious and challenging work to do. Unfortunately, some teachers of women's studies have deplored its large lesbian contingent and have stayed away from conferences where our numbers and our exuberance have drawn attention to us. But our goal, like theirs, is to re-examine traditional ways of thinking and to replace ignorance with knowledge. The contributors to *Lesbian Studies* believe that our past invisibility has been harmful not only to us, but to all students and teachers, to anyone, in fact, who trusts education to "lead out" to comprehensive views and a tolerance for diversity.

Thus one purpose of this anthology is to show what lesbian academics and lesbian cultural workers have been thinking and writing recently so that everyone involved in feminist education can better grasp the implications of lesbian visibility for the women's movement as a whole and especially for women's studies. Courses and books by lesbian feminists will demonstrate that we have been pursuing work of our own, the scope of which cannot be known from an occasional article, one or two lectures in a semester course, or a few titles on a supplementary reading list. Just as feminist courses were taught before books on "women's studies" were available, courses on lesbians have preceded a book titled *Lesbian Studies*. A new educational movement exists which ought now to be formally documented.

Another purpose of the book is to explore the consequences of our exclusion from the university curriculum. A measure of our invisibility is our absence from the tables of contents and indexes of college texts, even in the field of women's studies. Lesbians are omitted from the indexes of such seemingly comprehensive works as, for example, the 1979 titles: *Women United, Women Divided: Comparative Studies of Ten Contemporary Cultures* and *Women's Studies: A Recommended Core Bibliography*. We are also frequently missing from books purporting to treat homosexuality, for example, *Homosexuality in Literature, 1890–1930.*[3] More thorough documentation of our exclusion from women's studies is provided here in the essays on textbooks by Kathy Hickok and Bonnie Zimmerman. The especially damaging exclusion of lesbians of color from women's studies is a theme of the dialogue between Cherríe Moraga and Barbara Smith, "Teaching Third World Lesbian Literature: A Practical Ethical Vision."

A third reason for producing this anthology is to record part of our history. We feel a special urgency about the work of lesbian studies because so much of our past has been lost. Sometimes editors and biographers hid the truth, and sometimes families destroyed evidence of lesbian relationships. Several of the most interesting documents in the Lesbian Herstory Archives were actually rescued from trash cans on New York City sidewalks. Worst of all has been the obliteration of our past by our own hands. Edith Lewis's destruction of Willa Cather's letters is one example.[4]

A perplexing question for us is exactly how to define lesbianism, especially in history and biography. Emphasizing the sexual dimension of lesbianism can lead to distortions and oversimplifications, but playing it down can be misleading, too. As Joanna Russ has said, our homophobic culture encourages a tendency to regard homosexuality as "affection or politics or companionship or anything you like but *not sex*," as well as an "impulse to reduce homosexual people to *nothing but* sexual activity. . . . "[5] Faced by these extremes of confusion we need many collections of lesbian studies to illustrate *our* ways of seeing ourselves.

This work is especially needed because the study of the past has been marked by "the historial denial of lesbianism."[6] Certain misconceptions contribute to its persistence. Some Woolf scholars assume, for example, that a woman who remains married cannot be considered a lesbian. Similarly, biographers have often concluded that lesbianism is a private matter, an eccentric pursuit not needing any elucidating comment. Even when the evidence of a passionate relationship between two notable women has been too obvious to be entirely suppressed, scholars have still been able to dodge the question of lesbianism.

The recovery of our past carries implications for everyone's study and teaching of history. As more lesbian feminists study American history, we may discover that many progressive movements besides the feminist revival of the recent past have been fueled by lesbian energy. The hypothesis that our influence has been disproportionate to our numbers is one we must test ourselves. As Frances Doughty says in her essay, lesbian historians are better equipped than others to recognize the codes which in the past served as our survival techniques. Other issues for biographers and historians are discussed in *Lesbian Studies* by Estelle Freedman and Lillian Faderman.

Generalizations about lesbians are necessarily based on women open enough to be found by researchers, women who are usually white and middle class, like the researchers themselves. About the vast number of closeted women we can only speculate, although our own past lives give us some clues. For these reasons, we must retain some skepticism about how widely our generalizations can be applied.

One way to understand the need for lesbian studies is to consider some analogies to the arguments often presented in the last decade to legitimate women's studies. Just as women have been neglected by traditional college courses supposedly dealing with human kind, lesbians have been overlooked in courses about women. The feminist curriculum challenged the sexist myth of the woman as other, but left unexamined the idea of the lesbian as other. Most courses called "Psychology of Women," for example, still assume that all women relate sexually to men, and the same false assumption underlies sociology courses in the changing roles of women. Conceptual flaws in the traditional curriculum have been easier for women's studies professors to identify than conceptual flaws in the feminist curriculum.

To justify special courses, women's studies proponents say that women have a right to be the center of study and that a feminist perspective is essential for understanding the condition of women. Now that a few courses on lesbians exist, both inside and outside the university, it is clearer than before that we deserve a special focus. Lesbian issues ought to be significantly included throughout the curriculum. And we must teach the material ourselves. As Cherríe Moraga notes in her conversation with Barbara Smith, there is "nothing like a passionately lived connection when you're teaching a subject." The need for our own lesbian-feminist perspective in the classroom is a theme of several essays here, including those by Doris Davenport, Toni McNaron, Marilyn Frye, Nancy Manahan, Jane Gurko, and Coralyn Fontaine.

Analogous to the terms "misogny" and "sexism" are the less familiar terms "homophobia" and "heterosexism," the irrational fear of homosexuals and the belief in the superiority of heterosexual behavior. Doris Davenport observes that "lesbophobic" is a more accurate term than "homophobic" to describe anti-lesbian attitudes. In her book *Surpassing the Love of Men*, Lillian Faderman speaks of "heterocentric" perspectives. And other phrases suggest the viewpoint of one who is excluded, ignored, or put in second place—Adrienne Rich's "compulsory heterosexuality" and Sarah Hoagland's "totalitarian heterosexuality."[7]

Courses devoted partly or entirely to lesbianism can help to correct the heterosexist bias we have all been conditioned to accept as truth. It is important to recognize that, as one linguist points out, heterosexism is more than a prejudice; it is the "dominant perspective" of our culture.[8] Thus "the lesbian who grounds her identity in her outcast status challenges the most basic assumptions" about society, that women need men, for example, and that heterosexual experience is universal.[9] The outcast sees that male supremacy has been perpetuated not only by sex role conditioning and inequalities in pay and professional opportunity, but also by the institution of heterosexuality itself.[10] In addition, the depth of women hatred in our culture seems to be better illustrated by the work of lesbian scholars than by the work of non-lesbian researchers.

As long as lesbian issues are kept at the fringe of women's studies or treated in a fragmentary, cursory way, none of us in the field will understand the constraints imposed on us by heterosexist thinking. The problem is that most teachers of women's studies do not *see* heterosexism as a point of view. If they recall explaining to nonfeminist colleagues the pervasiveness of sexism, they can perhaps take one more step and confront heterosexism. A good starting point would be to assign in every class the article "Heterosexism and Women's Studies" in which Elly Bulkin proposes anti-heterosexism CR groups and offers questions for them.[11]

A lesbian perspective will be construed in different ways, of course, depending on the individual teacher's cultural and political experiences, both inside and outside the lesbian community. Contributors to this book may not agree, for example, on separatism, on the degree to which integration into the mainstream is an appropriate goal for lesbian feminists, on strategies for influencing women's studies programs and conferences, or even on the wisdom of getting Ph.D.s, university jobs, and tenure. But those of us writing in this anthology do share certain beliefs.

One is that racism is only beginning to be confronted in our women's studies programs, the white feminist press, and white feminist communities. We do not want "lesbian studies" to mean studies by and about white, middle-class women, which unconsciously take them to be the norm. Although several articles in *Lesbian Studies* focus on women of color, the material is still filtered through the consciousness of white editors and surrounded by work which may be racist. The importance of context is shown by *This Bridge Called My Back: Writings by Radical Women of Color*, in which the individual woman of color is not alone, not a variation of the main theme: instead, her own themes reverberate in all the other poems and essays. Karlene Faith's article on lesbians in prison is included in this anthology to demonstrate that working class women and women of color, who are far more likely to be imprisoned than white middle-class women, are as important to lesbian studies as university women. For every lesbian who gets a grant, writes a book, or finishes a Ph.D., there are many others who stand outside the circle of privilege. To be effective, our work will have to include us all.

Second, we believe that lesbian studies is essentially a grassroots movement. Archives and history projects aim to return their work to their own community. Although some lesbian cultural workers have formal training in such fields as history and library science, our work does not depend on university support. Further, many contributors to this book would probably not favor university status for lesbian studies, even if it could be achieved. Our integrity, in the root meaning of wholeness, would be lost if we followed the example of some women's studies coordinators and shaped our goals on the need to win approval from male administrators. Some individuals will choose to become fully integrated into the academic system, but as practitioners of lesbian studies, we must remain apart; our scholarship cannot flourish in isolation from our communities. The freedom to create our own culture has been too painfully won to be entrusted to university sanction or control.

At the same time, we believe that the university is an important forum for us, especially now that our community exists partly within it. Women's studies programs often provide the first shared workplace for heterosexual women and those who call themselves lesbians. *Lesbian Studies* has been prepared with women's studies classes in mind—it can be used as a text for introductory courses, for the integrative seminar that concludes many major and minor programs, and for the course sometimes called "Feminist Ideologies." It can provide supplementary reading for any course on women. But as Bonnie Zimmerman warns, lesbian studies classes should not become "ghettoized" with women's studies or any other discipline.[12] Our ideas must filter through to philosophy, history, literature, sociology, and psychology. Although the number of courses specifically about lesbians may increase, it is unlikely, given the homophobia of the university and the limited resources of women's studies programs, that *programs* called lesbian studies will come to life. For this reason, we believe, the work of bringing lesbian issues into the curriculum must be carried on by all feminist educators.

Fear of being mistaken for a lesbian, of saying the wrong thing, or of putting the emphasis in the wrong place may prevent some of our heterosexual colleagues from incorporating material on lesbians into their courses. Others may find it impossible to break the taboo by simply mentioning our existence. We believe that a teacher need not be a lesbian to inform her women's history class, for example, that the suppression of lesbian material in the past gives special importance to the discovery and preservation of contemporary evidence of our lives or to explore with her students some ramifications of anti-lesbian bias within the women's movement. A student need not be a lesbian to learn from the stories and essays in *Sinister Wisdom* or *Conditions* (see Resources).

When I first began seeking material for this anthology, I looked for articles from women in many different fields. Most of the work here, however, comes from the humanities, and over half of the writers are in English. Nearly all the sample syllabi sent to me were for literature courses. If lesbian studies has been largely the work of women in the humanities, the reason may be simply our numbers, compared to the numbers of women in disciplines such as psychology or anthropology. Just as courses on women writers were among the first in higher education to show a feminist perspective, they are now beginning to reflect lesbian-feminist influence.

The first five essays in *Lesbian Studies* describe what it feels like to be a lesbian in the academic world. Both closeted women and those who have come out at work tell about their professional lives. Women fired from university jobs have formed a support group, the Fired Lesbians Caucus. Their stories belong here too.[13] In an essay in progress titled "How I Lost My Innocence in Academia," Rosemary Curb, now on the faculty of Rollins College in Florida, tells how she was forced to resign from a teaching job at her former college when her lesbianism became known.[14]

A separate section on the classroom is an integral part of *Lesbian Studies* because, as Elly Bulkin observes in her essay, very little has been written about the experience of introducing lesbian issues in the classroom. This is a conspicuous gap in pedagogical literature, considering all that has been written about teaching women's studies (an exception is issue number 17 of *The Radical Teacher*).

The third section of the book, "New Research/New Perspectives," may not prove to the satisfaction of everyone in women's studies that a uniquely lesbian perspective on the study of women exists, but it indicates that certain questions will not be asked unless lesbian scholars ask them. Jane Gurko's article, "Sexual Energy in the Classroom" and JR Roberts's bibliographical essay on Black lesbians are good examples. In addition, our perspectives on older lesbians, lesbians in sports, and lesbians in science can shed light on all women in those categories. The Lesbian Periodical Index is an especially good example of the grassroots intellectual work which lesbians are now pursuing. Even traditional reference tools can be useful to us, as Ida VSW Red shows, by revealing changing attitudes towards lesbians.

Other examples of new research and perspectives can be found in the Resources section, which includes addresses so that readers can obtain more information about the various projects and studies described. Course outlines from 1972 to 1981 are included in the Appendix. The Bibliography should be a useful tool for developing future women's studies courses, not only those focusing specifically on lesbians.

The range of subjects that might fit under the heading of "lesbian studies" is suggested by the essays presented here, but they are only a beginning. A comprehensive list of other areas of investigation might indicate that lesbian studies presents a test of identity for women's studies. If she is to become, in Adrienne Rich's phrase, a "dutiful daughter" of the academy, then there will be very little room for the work of lesbian students and teachers. If, on the other hand, women's studies lives up to her early promise of radical challenges to the traditional curriculum, to her crone/hag/spinster potential, then our work will be central to her development and our existence will be assumed rather than denied. Lesbian studies can help all women in the academy recover a sense of the deep bonds among us, which come before alliances with men and allegiance to their universities.

My own visibility as a lesbian academic came as recently as 1977, at a Minnesota Women in Higher Education conference. I felt free to discuss the newly created lesbian caucus of NWSA only because I was soon to leave Minnesota. At that time, I would not have guessed that within a few years, the phrase "lesbian studies" would sound as natural as "women's studies," or that, having taught a women's literature course in 1975 without once having said the word "lesbian," I would propose this anthology.

My internalized homophobia, shown by my silence in the literature class and my silence in Minnesota Women in Higher Education until my bags were packed, suggests that one aim of lesbian studies must be to root out lies of inferiority, sickness, and sinfulness that in some degree many of us have accepted about ourselves. Having seen our lesbianism denied, and having sometimes denied it ourselves, we know that lesbian studies is more than a discipline or an intellectual pursuit—it is an instrument of our survival.

At a time when a state law in Oklahoma closes the teaching profession to us, when an increasing number of lesbians are fired from their university jobs, when the anti-gay McDonald amendment easily passes the U.S. House of Representatives,[15] and when a few extremists even justify killing us, it may be dangerous to reveal in this book who and where we are, the work we do, and the attitudes common among us. But a return to the silence and invisibility of the past would be even more dangerous. Some of us keep two résumés, one "straight" and one including all lesbian and gay publications. Others change titles so that the the world "lesbian" is replaced by "woman." While such strategies can easily be justified in the name of survival in a hostile environment, there is always a lingering suspicion that altering or omitting titles to "pass" involves some residual shame about our lesbian identity.

Many of the contributors to this book have been punished for being lesbians. If the right-wing backlash results in outright persecution, our concern for lesbian studies within the university will be short-lived, for our work will go underground. But as long as our numbers grow, we will argue that everyone is educationally disadvantaged until more material about a wide range of lesbian issues is taught. Aware of the harm inflicted on us all by heterosexist bias, we will no longer accept anthologies on women in literature which neglect lesbian writers, courses in women and society which ignore lesbian culture, sexuality courses which do not consider *our* sexuality, or any course which presumes to be about *human* experience but merely covers heterosexual experience. Lesbians have come a long way since the first years of women's studies, but until the elimination of heterosexist bias is a widely accepted goal of our courses and programs, we will not have come far enough. If *Lesbian Studies* challenges academic feminists to re-examine their teaching and research and provides them with new material for their classrooms, it will achieve its purpose.

Notes

[1] A historic moment for lesbian academics came during one of the general sessions of the founding convention of 1977. To support a statement on ending discrimination against them a large number of lesbians stood up to show who they were and how many of them were attending the session.

[2] Several gay men influenced by feminism have done valuable work, for example, Jonathan Katz in *Gay American History* (New York: Crowell, 1976); and Allan Berube in slide shows about women who passed as men and about World War II experiences of lesbians and gay men.

[3] Esther Stineman and Catherine Loeb, *Women United* (Littlejohn, Colorado: Libraries Unlimited, 1979); Patricia Caplan and Janet N. Bujra, *Women's Studies* (Bloomington: University of Indiana Press, 1979); and Jeffrey Meyers, *Homosexuality in Literature 1890-1930* (London: Athlone Press, 1977).

[4] Cather would have had good reason to fear damage to her literary reputation if her lesbianism were widely known. Her longtime companion Edith Lewis wrote a biography called *Willa Cather Living: A Personal Record*, first published in 1953 and reissued in paperback by the University of Nebraska Press, 1976. Lewis is so reticent about her life with Cather that the subtitle of the biography is misleading.

[5] Judith Schwarz, ed., "Questionnaire on Issues in Lesbian History," *Frontiers* 4 (Fall 1979): 5. (Special issue on lesbian history)

[6] Blanche Cook, "The Historical Denial of Lesbianism," *Radical History Review* 20 (Summer 1979) p. 60. See also Cook's article, "Women Alone Stir My Imagination: Lesbianism in the Cultural Tradition," *Signs: Journal of Women in Culture and Society* 4 (Summer 1979): 718-739.

[7] Lesbophobia, "The Pathology of Racism," *This Bridge Called My Back*, eds. Moraga and Anzaldúa (Watertown, Massachusetts: Persephone Press, 1981), p. 90; Faderman, *Surpassing the Love of Men* (New York: Morrow, 1981), passim; "Compulsory Heterosexuality and Lesbian Existence," *Signs: Journal of Women in Culture and Society* 4 (Summer 1980): 631-660; totalitarian heterosexuality, "Lesbian Ethics," *Lesbian Inciter* 2 (January 1981): 9.

[8] Julia Penelope (Stanley), "The Articulation of Bias: Hoof in Mouth Disease" (paper delivered to the Annual Convention of the National Council of Teachers of English, November 1979), p. 4.

[9] Julia Penelope, "The Lesbian Perspective: Pedagogy and the Structure of Human Knowledge" (paper presented to the National Council of Teachers of English, November 1976), p. 7.

[10]The connections between male supremacy and institutionalized heterosexuality are drawn by Cheryl Clarke in "Lesbianism: An Act of Resistance," *This Bridge Called My Back*, eds. Moraga and Anzaldúa, p. 130; by Lucia Valeska in "The Future of Female Separatism," *Building Feminist Theory* (New York: Longman, 1981),pp. 28–29; and by Charlotte Bunch in "Not for Lesbians Only," *Building Feminist Theory*, p. 68.

[11]"Heterosexism in Women's Studies," *The Radical Teacher* 17 (Spring 1981): 25–31. This excellent special issue on Black women's studies and lesbian studies also includes articles by Judith McDaniel, Marilyn Frye, JR Roberts, and Bonnie Zimmerman.

[12]"Lesbianism 101," *The Radical Teacher* 17: 22.

[13]The Fired Lesbians Caucus was founded at the 1981 conference of the NWSA at the University of Connecticut. Some of us in the caucus are not sure whether our lesbianism or simply our feminism cost us our jobs, but all of us believe we were not fired because of any specific actions we took or failed to take.

[14]The Educational Testing service in Princeton confirmed that someone in the administration changed hundreds of Curb's students' evaluations so that favorable replies became unfavorable. The altered scores were used as a pretext for not renewing Curb's contract.

[15]The McDonald amendment denies low-income lesbians and gay men access to free legal aid. See *Gay Community News*, 4 July 1981, p. 1. The so-called "Family Protection Act" would prevent the use of federal money for legal action on our behalf and would deny federal funds to any organization that presents homosexuality in a positive light.

Lesbians in the Academic World:
The Personal/Political Experience

We have been silent for too long; we have been silenced for too long. For the first time in centuries, we can now hear the music of other Lesbian voices.

Julia Penelope Stanley and Susan J. Wolfe
The Coming Out Stories

For us, the process of naming and defining is not an intellectual game, but a grasping of our experience and a key to action. The word lesbian *must be affirmed because to disregard it is to collaborate with silence and lying about our very existence; with the closet-game, the creation of the* unspeakable.

Adrienne Rich
On Lies, Secrets and Silence

Dyke in Academe (II)

Paula Bennett

I take as my theme the first five lines of Muriel Rukeyser's "To Be a Jew in the Twentieth Century":

> To be a Jew in the twentieth century
> Is to be offered a gift. If you refuse,
> Wishing to be invisible, you choose
> Death of the spirit, the stone insanity.
> Accepting, take full life.
>
> *(Complete Poems)*

Before describing what it is like to be a lesbian in twentieth-century academe, I would like to explain what it was once like for me to have been a Jew—and invisible.

I grew up during the Second World War when Hitler and anti-Semitism were daily news. Like the three little black boys who play chain gang in Toni Morrison's *Sula*, I and my little Jewish friends played concentration camp. We used a laundry court, as I remember, and strung each other up from the lines. We had been raised in a neatly kept, middle-class Jewish suburb outside Boston. To my knowledge, none of us had ever been directly subjected to anti-Semitism. But Jew-hating was part of our reality, just as chain gangs were part of black reality, and like Morrison's three Dewies, we acted out our reality in our games.

When I was eleven, my parents took me out of the predominantly Jewish public school I was attending and sent me to a private girl's school in the city. I and two other Jewish children, neither of whom were in my class, had been accepted on a trial basis to see if assimilation would take in what was then a largely Episcopalian sanctuary. My parents had never been particularly observant nor had they done much to bolster my sense of pride in being Jewish. Their chief concern was the quality of my education. Problems of assimilation were beyond them. The one thing my mother said to prepare me for any anti-Semitism I might encounter, was that since Christians looked down on Jews, it was up to me to prove we were as good as anybody else by being better. It was, she said—and I'll never forget this—"the cross I would have to carry."

Filled with fears I could not express, I chose to hide instead. As luck would have it, the first book we read that year was *Oliver Twist*. When one girl, out of bland curiosity I am sure, asked if there were any Jews in Winsor, I did not answer. I had become invisible, a closet Jew. And since I did not look Semitic or bear a "Jewish" last name, it was, unfortunately, possible for me to pass. I told only one or two close friends of my religious background and lived in almost daily terror that the rest of my classmates would find out the truth. Never very good in groups anyway, I pulled more and more into myself, isolated by my lie and by the hostile suspiciousness that it engendered in me. Eventually, the hostility and isolation—not to mention self-betrayal—took their toll, as they were bound to do, and at the end of my freshman high-school year, I flunked out.

The most significant aspect of this story is that during the three years I spent at Winsor, I never once heard an anti-Semitic remark or witnessed an anti-Semitic act. Given the time period and the makeup of the school population, I am sure there was anti-Semitism, but if there was, it lived solely in what people thought, not what they said. They said nothing. Jews, as far as most Winsorites were concerned, simply didn't exist, or if they did exist, aside from an occasional query or two, their existence was not a matter worth discussing. For the rest, it was silence.

Looking back at this incident now, I am overwhelmed by how much I contributed to my own defeat. I have no way of knowing, of course, what my real reception would have been, had I "come out." But it is fairly easy to guess. Some students would have befriended me just because I was Jewish. Others, for the same reason, would have steered clear. But most, I believe, would have gotten over their initial surprise and discomfort at my difference and would have judged me for myself. I never gave them the chance. Unable to deal with or talk about my fears, I hid until hiding became too painful. Then I dropped out.

My experience at Winsor colors everything I have to say about being a lesbian in academe or anywhere else where one cannot feel free to be fully and publicly oneself. It is the experience of the closet, of a void created by fear on one side and silence on the other. It produces a form of oppression that comes not from the things people do, *but what they do not do.* At best, this experience leads to feelings of anger and alienation. At worst, it produces an attitude of apathy and indifference. For some it is a stone insanity, for others, a living hell of self-hate and self-betrayal.

I do not wish to suggest that all gay academics are miserable. A goodly number of them obviously are not. They are sound, whole individuals, well respected by their departments and profession, who have been able to fuse their public and private lives in an integrated and productive manner.

Nor would I suggest that colleges and universities are especially bad places to be if you are gay. Over the past ten years in particular, many college departments and administrations have shown themselves warmly, even enthusiastically, supportive of their gay faculty and staff. And there are now, as we know, quite a number of "happy" coming-out stories, stories which suggest that at least in particular cases many of our worst fears about coming out may prove unfounded.

The problem is that most of us do not dare to find out whether our fears are unfounded or not. Since most academic institutions maintain silence on this issue, the onus for discovering whether one will be accepted or not lies with the individual gay. For most gay academics, even the tenured, this is, apparently, too great a risk to take. Overwhelmed by fears which may or may not be justified, unable to find out simply and without risk whether their fears are justified or not, the vast majority of gay and lesbian teachers remain, however unwillingly, in the void I have described, victims of their own anxiety and a social situation which through their silence they have helped perpetuate as well as create.

Caught between silence on one side and fear on the other, the typical closeted gay academic spends his or her professional life in a state of constant duplicity, internally and externally divided by a lie that is not spoken, by an act of deception that is never acted out. Even the most mundane or natural aspects of human interaction and communication are distorted by the invisible presence of the void such duplicity creates. Talk about nights out, living arrangements, vacations, lovers, divorces is carefully censored to control how much real information is given out. Sometimes the ability to communicate on both sides becomes warped beyond recognition. Then the failure to speak becomes in itself another form of oppression. A friend of mine at Northeastern told me this story.

Joe had lived with his lover of twelve years in a house outside the city. Their relationship was well known to many of Joe's colleagues although technically speaking Joe was not "out" to his department at the time. When the relationship ended, Joe moved back into the city, sharing an apartment with a graduate student. His colleagues would then ask the graduate student how Joe was doing. They did not ask Joe directly, although it was apparent to everyone that he was going through a period of deep stress and mourning. Like Joe's colleagues, most of us are naturally reluctant to bring up private matters unless we have, in effect, been given permission to do so; but what kept Joe, who desperately wanted comfort, from giving permission was the closet, and it was the closet that prevented his colleagues in turn from showing their sincere interest and concern.[1]

There is no way to put a statistical number on this "act of oppression," because no act has occurred. No act occurs when two gay members of the same department or university can know each other for several years—as Joe and I did at Northeastern—and never share one of the single most important facts about themselves, that they are gay. No act occurs when a gay teacher, seeing a gay student at a gay bar, turns on his or her heel and walks away. The warmth, support, and human kindness lost in such cases is as intangible as it is incalculable. It cannot be measured; it can only be weighed by the heart that has felt it.

To live in the closet, in this void, is to be constantly aware of what one is *not* saying, is *not* doing, is *not* experiencing or receiving, because you are afraid to be fully, publicly yourself. In the classroom, it often means avoiding authors or themes that might cast you as a teacher or student in a questionable light. I know, for example, some lesbian teachers who will not touch Stein or Barnes because they are too obvious. I know others who will treat these writers but who will either avoid the subject of their sexual orientation or mention it only in passing. I know only a few lesbian teachers for whom teaching "out" writers is simply a matter of course, producing neither anxiety or second thoughts. For myself, I have never been able to teach lesbian writers without feeling an enormous sense of inner division over the kind of deception such teaching involves when I myself have not come out.

Where writers themselves are not open about their sexual preference (and most are not), the closeted lesbian or gay teacher confronts an even more painful dilemma: do you say what you know or believe about Emily Dickinson, Sarah Orne Jewett, Virginia Woolf, Willa Cather, Amy Lowell, Lorraine Hansberry, May Sarton, Elizabeth Bishop, and risk the appearance of a special interest, or do you suppress the information that you have and help perpetuate the conspiracy of silence which distorts our reading of these and so many other authors. Either way, for the closeted teacher, it is a no win situation. For the students and for scholarship, it is also a dead loss.

The consequences of the closet on research and writing are just as pernicious, affecting both the quality and the quantity of the scholarship produced. Gay and lesbian teachers are obviously suited to research on gay writers. They are sensitive to the issues. They understand the problems, having lived through them. They are more likely because of their sensitivities to recognize encoding when encoding occurs and to respect the complex validity of such hidden expression. And finally, of course, they care. But the fear of being stigmatized disables the gay or lesbian teacher in a way that straight scholars are not. At a recent meeting of the Boston Gay Academic Union, Monica McAlpine discussed her excellent article on Chaucer's "Pardoner's Tale," (*PMLA*, January, 1980). Almost the first question from the audience after the presentation was "weren't you afraid someone would take you for a lesbian?" (Ms. McAlpine is both married and straight.) The question may sound naíve, but it was clearly on everyone's mind since a ten minute discussion followed on the perils and possibilities of research for the homosexual scholar. The tenor of the discussion was far from encouraging.

Even without the fear of stigmatization, however, gay research appears to many gay and lesbian teachers a dead end. True, it is a largely unexplored area, filled, if you look at the list of nondeclared writers, with all kinds of exciting possibilities. The fact is that like women's studies and ethnic studies, gay studies, such as they are, are an academic stepchild. They weigh less heavily toward promotion and tenure, and they are taken less seriously by scholars-at-large. Teachers committed to such areas risk being labeled and treated as second class, that is, too "narrow" in their interest and too far outside the academic mainstream to be considered full-fledged members in good standing of their departments. The caste/class system of the universities, based on white male patriarchal models, dominates research and demands that teachers who wish to advance, give most of their interest and energy to topics that carry the patriarchal imprimatur. Thus a friend of mine now bucking for tenure at a prestigious eastern university has given up a book on Amy Lowell for one on Emerson and Hawthorne instead. Her heart may be with the lesbian poet, but her head and her pocketbook tell her to stick with what she knows will be well received.

That such decisions represent the suppression of knowledge goes, I believe, without saying. Again, no one has moved deliberately to limit the freedom of speech or inquiry of the gay scholar—there is no "act of oppression" that one can name—but oppression has occurred, from within and without, and the loss to our community is one we can ill afford.

When weighed together, the various effects of the closet—on human communication, on teaching and research—have a profound effect on the gay or lesbian herself. In an article in *Concerns*, [reprinted in this book] Toni McNaron describes with moving honesty what she calls the "hypocrisy and ill health" of her position before coming out to her department (see p. 13). It was a period when she struggled with weight, alcohol, and constant anxiety over exposure. In my own article, "Dyke in Academe," in *Concerns*, I described similar bouts I had, not with food and drink, but with self-hate and Freudian therapy, for much the same reason as Toni: it was the best way I knew to make the price of hiding or having to hide clear.

I do not want to repeat the arguments of that paper here. Suffice it to say that it is no easy matter to maintain self-esteem when, in order to preserve your job, you feel it necessary to betray yourself in a variety of major and minor ways: from not treating authors or ideas that might open you to question to not speaking out when one of your colleagues tells an offensive joke. To suffer an injustice without protest is, in my opinion, far more destructive in its consequences than the original injustice itself, since the self-betrayal silence involves eventually rots away the inner person. To betray oneself in this way for a job is certainly not a price worth paying. Yet it is a price asked constantly of lesbians and gays in our society, and having had to pay it, to any degree, makes me angrier than I can say.

Anger is not a pleasant emotion, but as I suggested in the original "Dyke in Academe" essay, it can be a preserving one. Over the years, my anger has helped me learn how to insulate myself against the worst effects of not being able to come entirely out (I am an untenured part-timer and, therefore, permanently vulnerable). I have learned not to go places where I do not feel comfortable (such as the English Department offices) and not to do things that would force me to betray myself (such as write on authors I do not care for). I spend most of my free time working for those things I believe in: gay rights and lesbian literature. But this is not the kind of arrangement most academics can afford to make. Only the fringe nature of my job gives me the latitude to go so much my own way. Succinctly, since I am not asking for tenure, what I do, or do not do, does not really matter. As far as my department is concerned, I barely exist. In a curiously ironic way, the "invisibility" of the outsider remains the price I pay for my freedom.

To be an outsider, as Rukeyser suggests, can be a gift. Certainly one can achieve in alienation a degree of autonomy, a sense of choice, a clarity of vision hard to obtain in any other way. But it is a gift which to yield "full life" must be fully and completely accepted, fully and completely used. Promotion, tenure, respect, collegiality, self-esteem, human warmth, and kindness should not depend upon sexual preference any more than they should depend upon matters of race, religion, or sex. Yet because of the silence and fear that distorts outlives, they do.

We are not free, nor will we be, until this silence at last is ended and we are invisible no more.

Notes

The original "Dyke in Academe" appeared in *Concerns*, the newsletter of the Women's Caucus of the Modern Languages, Spring 1980, pp. 12-4. "Dyke in Academe (II)" was presented at the panel "The Second Sex in Academia: Stress, Anger and Energy" during the Modern Language Association Convention in Houston, December 27-30, 1980. I wrote the second paper largely as a response to criticisms I received on the first version. I wish to thank in particular J.S., Carol Meyer, Jonathan Goldberg, and Joe DeRoche for their patient assistance in this drawn-out endeavor.

[1]An interesting coda to this incident occurred on the plane back from Houston when I showed this paper to one of Joe's colleagues. After lengthy discussion, I still could not convince him that Joe's fears were grounded in reality. "Everyone knows about Joe and loves him," he insisted. The fact that no one said specifically to Joe, "We know; it's okay," bore no weight with him, though it meant everything to Joe. I am not sure what one does with such well-meaning obtuseness.

Black Lesbians in Academia: Visible Invisibility

Doris Davenport

By way of introduction, it seems to me that i have LIVED in academia all my life: from age five to the present (age thirty-two) i have always been in school, either studying, teaching, or dropping out and in. At the present stage, i am in a Ph.D. program (University of Southern California, English). It also seems to me that i have been a feminist all my life, and recently, a very political or politicized lesbian. I am proud of studying literature; i am equally proud of being a lesbian. But what that means is this:

i am the only Black student (that i know of) in my graduate English department. Before me, there was one other het Black woman, whom i knew slightly. In September 1979, when i first went to USC, i discovered (from a white womon student) that this Black-het had told certain people at the school that i was a feminist-dyke "going around trying to convert people." That Black sister meant to do me a lot of damage. Instead, she did me a favor. When i got to USC, i did not have to come out, so much as let a few folks know that physical seduction was the only part she had wrong. The white folks were a little confused as to how to approach me: i fit neither their stereotypes of a "Black nationalist" nor of a dyke. (i could *see* them thinking, about the latter, "but she doesn't 'look' like one.") It meant that i was either benignly ignored, or guardedly spoken to. i laughed and carried on.

At the same time, i got "stuck," by default, teaching the only Black literature class offered at USC. The only Black professor had quit, and with my being *Black*, i was offered the class as part of my teaching assistantship duties. i gladly accepted, since Black literature is one of my major fields. However, no one checked on my ability to teach the class. Again, stereotyped, and benignly neglected. i taught my class (well) and carried on.

Then, the following semester (January 1980), i took a class which ostensibly covered "American literature since World War II." There were no Blacks and/or wimmin on that syllabus. When i asked the professor (a middle-aged white boy) about this oversight, he said i could do a report on Leroi Jones or someone like that, or i could drop the class, that he would not alter the syllabus for me. i promptly told him no, to both alternatives, and called him on his stereotyping, and furthermore, told him that he addressed only what he could *see*: sex and color. i said, add to that, that i am a lesbian, so you can go ahead and insult *that* part of me too. (He was new, and apparently had not heard the "coming out story.") He had the grace to semiapologize privately, but our "discussion" was in front of the entire class.

Each semester, in my Black literature class, i have a beginning enrollment of at least 32 people, mainly Black. Each semester, a few either drop the class or get mighty nasty because of my feminism and my "strict" requirements. My feminism means i point out both feminism and chauvinism in the literature and in classroom responses, especially of the males. The requirements mean that students have to do original thinking—very painful, for lots of folk. i am, to them, simply another authority figure—the enemy—and the fact that we are all Black, all students, and all in "hostile" territory does not seem to make that much sense to them. If my color means anything to them at all, it's simply that my course must be an easy A.

Almost all Black students in predominantly white schools get a grade called "automatic B" (either for Black, or because you're Black you can't do no <u>B</u>etter). Sometimes, you get "automatic A," (<u>A</u>ctually, it means the prof is guilt/racist tripping), but either way, the work you produce is not judged on its own.

It is this fragmentation, in life and academia, that i want to address. It works like this: lesbian studies (and lesbians) belong in wimmin studies. Black literature is cross-listed under ethnic studies. English departments usually fall under the general heading of esoteric studies, to most people. So what happens to a hybrid like me? i fit into all the above categories, and then some. i have never tried to camouflage the fact that i am a lesbian. In fact, some folk say i flaunt it. (i wear a ♀♀ necklace and ring, and have the same symbol sewn in white on my brown book bag, so it will stand out more.) Oddly enough, that is hardly ever addressed directly, even by other lesbians. For the others, the most visible and the most accessible route of attack is via my color: i get what most Black students do, with a little added shit, due to being feminist-lesbian.

The added shit means that if i say *good* morning, they will challenge it. Maybe it is because i am also articulate, outspoken (or, speaking period), and un-grad-school-mediocre (although i sometimes do get bored to death by the ego trips of the white boy professors). So for them, here's this live and moving target that is not only Black, but Black-and-articulate, Black and i-don't-take-no-shit, Black and lesbian-feminist. All that at once, is a confusing target. But they try. And i, constantly, fight back, or at least, try to fight against the alienation and isolation, in any way i can. Sometimes, i send my mind back to Paine College, especially in the spring. Frequently, i read Hurston or Toni Morrison or my own prose. Often, i get drunk and go to sleep, reminding myself that i *do* have a vision of another reality....

Plus, i recently realized that i have been operating off an unconscious incentive (unconscious, but strongly and deeply ingrained). That is, the "legacy" of Black educators, a legacy of love, discipline, high standards, and commitment which i got from attending an all-Black high school and undergraduate school. That is, the fact that all the significant teachers in my life (excluding one white womon) have been Black. On the other hand, i want to carry on or instigate a "new" tradition: that of being a Black, brilliant, lesbian, educator—open and proud.

i am in this field because i passionately love literature, although i know there is a great deal of unnecessary, humiliating absurdity involved in academia, period. Yet, i know too that i am a lesbian, feminist, poet, writer, critic, teacher, and overall goddess-given seer. Therefore, i refuse to let any of this deter me—this time. In short, i fight the fragmentation as best i can, and as often as i get wiped out i regenerate myself, but it ain't easy, and it is *so* alone.

i wouldn't mind if "the enemy" would stick to one issue at a time, or would fight "fair" and up front. But we all know they don't work that way. For example, last fall (October 1980), the new white chairwoman of the department informed me that the school policies prevent T.A.'s from teaching literature courses. Moreover, she doesn't think we are *prepared* (that is, we are too dumb) to teach them. So in the fall (September 1981), i will not be teaching my Black literature course, if it's up to her—in spite of the fact that i have been teaching it for the last two years. i sense, in other words, around me an aura of intense hostility-fear-awe, at almost all times. i hear people relating to an image—a projection of their diseased imaginations and other stereotypic neuroses. i find myself fighting a constant battle on at least ten levels at once, just to complete course requirements!—even while i continue to write my womon poetry and do readings. All of which is ignored in academia: i recently self-published a book of poetry and announced the Great Event in the department newsletter. To date, no one has acknowledged the book. It seems to me that the main objective is to undermine me (us) in as many ways as possible, and most of the time, i don't even think it is intentional. They can't help themselves. But none of this helps my state of mind, either. What would help me is this:

That those of us who are Black lesbians in academia would at least start a survival and support network—newsletter, once-a-month-chain letter, union, whatever, so we won't feel so alone and isolated. In other words, establish some sort of system for our mutual survival and *celebration.* A system to prevent our being individually devastated and individually negated. After all, we know that being lesbian, at this point, is not a phase we are going to "grow out of." Nor, if you are as persistent as i am, are we going to give up on what we see as our professional goals. NOR should we look for that much support from anyone else but ourselves. We have to find a way to minimize the devastating bullshit, and maximize our potential—on all levels. (It might also help if more of our sisters came out of the closet.)

i guess we are a threat to the "system" (since Black wimmin are perceived as a threat to everyone, period), but not really, and not yet. i just want to stay here, and i want my sisters to stay here, long enough to make some radical, and positive, changes. Changes in the way Black lesbians are viewed and treated in academia, and the rest of the un-real world. Changes in the way we are presented and perceived. Changes from this death-oriented world, to a more Goddess-oriented, life-loving world.

"Out" at the University: Myth and Reality

Toni A. H. McNaron

For the first eleven years I taught at the University of Minnesota, I stayed in the closet I'd fled to within the first month of recognizing my lesbianism.[1] During those years, I was awarded tenure quite early (the end of my third year); I won both a collegiate and an all-University award for outstanding teaching; I almost got a book on Shakespeare's last plays published; I was active in my regional professional organization. During those years, I experienced increasing pain at the dislike my immediate superiors [sic] had for me, no matter what I did. I learned quickly that it was not helpful to talk of my devotion to teaching or about my hard-working, enthusiastic students. So I tried a variety of ways to win approval.

One year I spent over one thousand dollars throwing cocktail parties and feeding people elegant dinners; the next I was hardly ever seen at social functions. One year I served on numerous departmental committees; the next I refused all nominations. One year I went to every department meeting and spoke vigorously to the issues; the next I sat silent at those few meetings I attended. One year I frequented the faculty coffee lounge daily; the next I stayed inside my own office except to go to class or check my mail. Nothing worked. I was confused, angry, hurt, and exhausted.

During those same years, I was in one primary relationship for seven years, only to rush through five others in the next four years. All of them were essentially clandestine, full of the false excitement and real fear attendant upon such liaisons. I was significantly overweight and increasingly alcoholic; lonely and detached from my feelings and body at first, but eventually from my mind and spirit as well.

For a year or so, while I was in a state of transition, I taught courses and administered a new Women's Studies Program. Newly sober and out within the local lesbian community,[2] I remained hidden at my job. I was honest with students in my office if they needed me to be, and I told friends at school. But I held back from telling my chair-man or from coming out in classes or from sharing my work if the focus was lesbian. Being the coordinator of women's studies did not help me resolve this split, since, like all such programs, we were trying hard to appease male heterosexist administrators all too ready to believe that "women's studies is a lesbian plot."

Finally, in the summer of 1975, I had to face the hypocrisy and ill health of my position: I was teaching "Introduction to Women's Studies" and decided to make the history of the lesbian/straight split one of the issues to read about and discuss. Knowing I couldn't say "lesbians...they," I thought to invite a panel of younger community lesbians to talk directly from their lives. Then when I said "lesbian" in my lecture, I would use "we," letting students hear me or not, as they chose. Four friends agreed to participate, two others came to lend general support, and the students were assigned the relevant chapter in *Sappho Was a Right-On Woman*, dealing with the infamous scene in which Betty Friedan called lesbians a "lavender menace,"[3] and the Furies walked out of the New York chapter of NOW. That morning, driving to campus, I realized that I couldn't go through with the protective charade; so I came out that day, and no one left the room or the class. I didn't touch ground for several days; but by the beginning of that fall quarter, I had slunk back into my musty closet. My pretext was the Women's Studies Program, whose faculty was not eager for me to be declarative or assertive about my identity. Since the clearest negative cultural message I had internalized was that homosexuals are not fit to teach the young (or the old, I presume), I cooperated by silencing myself again.

In my third and final year as coordinator, I made a serious effort toward my own integration: I proposed a senior seminar on "The Woman as Other and the Lesbian as the Other Woman." At the curriculum committee meeting called to discuss courses, I heard the chair (a good lesbian friend in her own closet because untenured) object to my course, claiming that "students might be uncomfortable with that word in a course title." It was my friend who was uncomfortable, and I again colluded in our joint self-denial and betrayal because of my own shaky place, believing that our history is important, yet still holding to societal myths that we should at least have the decency to live quietly behind drawn curtains or in darkened bars. The pain of that meeting remains in me, long after the anger has gone.

I took a year's leave of absence without pay to decide if I could ever work at the University of Minnesota (or any other university) and be healthy. Two women stand out as crucial to my decision to return: Florence Howe pointed out that by leaving, I greatly diminished the tiny pool of radical lesbian-feminists with tenure in America and that it is not easy to work as a lesbian-feminist (or indeed as any feminist) in a patriarchal place; Adrienne Rich gave me an afternoon of her self and a small piece of raw amethyst (given in turn to her by Audre Lorde), symbol of clarity. I went back to the university, deciding that I must tell my chair that I intended to unify my private and public lives by teaching and writing from my lesbian-feminist perspective.

Since then, the fall of 1977, being out at the university has brought many benefits to me as a scholar and teacher and as a human being. I have successfully proposed and taught an upper-level course on American lesbian writers; I have written and published three pieces dealing with lesbian poetry and culture; I have served as a valuable resource person for my nonlesbian friends who want to include lesbian material in their courses; I have been a model for any woman wanting one. With the formation of the National Women's Studies Association, I served as one of the four original lesbian caucus members and was the lesbian representative to the Midwest regional association. I have participated in two sessions on teaching lesbian literature at MMLA and am about to be part of an exciting effort to introduce lesbian content into high-school curricula in Minneapolis.

During the past three years, I have lost a lot of weight and gained a measure of serenity as a recovering alcoholic. I have been able to see the men in my department as responding to me from their damaged psyches and having little to offer me that I value. I have begun to write more often and forcefully since I can speak in my whole voice. I have formed close bonds with two radical feminists in my department, finding that my openness about my private life is an invitation to them to share more about themselves.

A surprising aspect of my being open in the department and the profession has been the absence of increased hostility. In my myths and fantasies, I stayed closeted because "they" would get me if I told them in words what they already knew. This fear is real for untenured lesbians, since the record of tenure's being granted to lesbian-feminists on American campuses is grim. Of course, such women are given "logical" reasons for termination, but in a homophobic society, it is not simply paranoia to assume that such reasons cover the real one. Yet I was tenured after only three years and remained closeted for another nine. This process reminds me of Rosalind's staying in male dress (in *As you Like It*) long after questions of safety have passed; she keeps her boots and breeches because she gets something for her extended disguise. Well, so did I, though nothing as enjoyable as her rewards. But I got to stay scared, only partially in touch with my power, ashamed at some deep psychological level, cooperating in what society most wanted me to be—a victim. As late as 1978, as I was walking to my opening lecture on lesbian writers, my fantasy reasserted itself. I felt the cold knot of terror in my stomach and imagined two plainclothesmen at my classroom door who would step from the shadows to arrest me for presuming to instruct the young in essentially "dirty" material. They were not there; and I wrote a poem about that fantasy.

I have finally disarmed the enemy in the most powerful way—I have taken away the words they could use against me by naming myself precisely and with pride. I expect to become ever more at ease with my voice as a literary critic. In fact, I have plans to teach a graduate seminar examining similarities and differences between feminist and lesbian-feminist perspectives on literature. My energy to write criticism is at an all-time high since declaring myself intellectually has put me in touch with my truest material.

Perhaps the most exciting gain for me as a radical feminist who is then also a radical lesbian is that I now live the political axiom I insisted upon for years. My lesbianism truly is no longer a matter of "sexual preference" (a term of diminution coined by liberals in their continuing efforts to accept various so-called life-styles). Rather, my every idea/perception/opinion is colored by my woman-identified slant. I feel genuinely integrated for the first time in my life—my critical interpretations of literature are beautifully mingled with my best comprehension of sensuality and sexuality. I value my special eye as I read any work, by women or men, from the Renaissance or the Here and Now. I am a lesbian in my study and classroom as well as in my bedroom or kitchen, and no one can uncover me in any room whatever, because I no longer hide.

Notes

[1] I first acted on my feelings for women while in my initial months as a new teacher at an Episcopal girls' school in Vicksburg, Mississippi. I was twenty-one and the year was 1958. My employer, now the head of the Episcopal Church in America, threatened to fire me for "corrupting the youth." I denied my reality, kept my job, and made love with a wonderful young woman in a furnace room which had no window or light in it. Needless to say, "in the closet" has never been a metaphor for me.

[2] I will always be grateful to the women of that community for their patience and unqualified support of me as I inched my way out of a very scared place.

[3] I noticed with genuine humor recently that I had gone off to my favorite grocery store in my bright purple T-shirt with its bold white lettering: LAVENDER MENACE. At the checkout stand, the young woman working that shift said, in apparent innocence, "I like your shirt."

I Lead Two Lives: Confessions of a Closet Baptist

Mab Segrest

I lead a double life. By day, I'm a relatively mild-mannered English teacher at a Southern Baptist college. By night—and on Tuesdays and Thursdays and weekends—I am a lesbian writer and editor, a collective member of *Feminary*, a lesbian-feminist journal for the South. My employees do not know about my other life. When they find out, I assume I will be fired, maybe prayed to death. For the past four years, my life has moved rapidly in opposite directions.

When I started teaching English at my present school five years ago, I knew I was a lesbian. I was living with Peg, my first woman lover. But I wasn't "out" politically. I had not yet discovered the lesbian culture and lesbian community that is now such an important part of my life. The first time I had let myself realize I was in love with Peg, I had sat under a willow tree by the lake at the Girl Scout camp where we both worked and said aloud to myself in the New York darkness: "I am a lesbian." I had to see how it sounded; and after I'd said that, gradually, I felt I could say anything. When, three years ago, Peg left to live with a man, I knew my life had changed. I read lesbian books and journals with great excitement. I joined the all-lesbian collective of *Feminary*, then a local feminist journal, and helped turn it into a journal for Southern lesbians. I started writing. I did all this while working for the Baptists, feeling myself making decisions that were somehow as frightening as they were inevitable. Early issues of *Feminary* record the process. First there is a poem by "Mabel." Then an article by "Mab." Then the whole leap: "Mab Segrest." My whole name, and not much of a chance to say, "that was the *other* Mab Segrest." I knew if I could not write my name, I couldn't write anything. I also knew: if I can't be myself and teach, I won't teach.

Since my junior year in college, over a decade ago, I have wanted to be a teacher. For a long time—before Peg and I both made the brave, reckless leap that a woman makes when she loves another woman for the first time—teaching was the most important thing in my life. I have always liked school. It is fall as I write this, and September brings back memories of new plain cotton dresses, clean notebooks, pencils sharpened to fine points, and especially a stack of new books full of things I didn't yet know. And I always—always!—loved to read. During my childhood—which if it was full of small-town life and summers with my brother in the woods near the lake was also full of the deep loneliness of being queer—I spent many hours with books on the front porch swing or in my father's chair by the gas heater. I have always pondered things in long conversations with myself, walking home from school, my hands slightly waving as I held forth to some invisible audience. Now in my classes I love the challenge of trying to explain a body of material clearly and in ways that catch students' interest, in spite of themselves; of looking out over a sea of consciousness, watching eyes focus and unfocus, words register or float out the back window, every period the necessity to generate interest, every hour a hundred tiny failures and successes. Teaching is the work I love best. I can bring much of myself to it, and much of it into myself. But as a lesbian teacher in a society that hates homosexuals—especially homosexual teachers—I have learned a caution toward my students and my school that saddens me. The things my life has taught me best, I cannot teach directly. I do not believe that I am the only one who suffers.

The first time homosexuality came up in my classroom it was a shock to my system. It was in freshman composition, and I was letting a class choose debate topics. They picked gay rights, then nobody wanted to argue the gay side. Finally, three of my more vociferous students volunteered. I went home that day shaken. I dreamed that night I was in class, my back to my students, writing on the board (I always feel most vulnerable then), and students were taunting me from the desks—"lesbian! queer!" The day of the debate, I took a seat in the back row, afraid that if I stood up front IT would show, I would give myself away: develop a tic, tremble, stutter, throw up, then faint dead away. I kept quiet as my three progay students held off the Bible with the Bill of Rights, to everyone's amazement, including my own. (I certainly knew it could be done; I just hadn't expected them to do it. No one else in the class had figured any legitimate arguments were possible.) Then the antigay side rallied and hit on a winning tactic: they implied that if the opponents *really* believed their own arguments, they were pretty "funny." I called an end to the debate, and the progay side quickly explained how they didn't mean anything they had said. Then one of my female students wanted to discuss how Christians should love people even when they were sick and sinful. I said the discussion was *over* and dismissed the class. The only time I had spoken the entire debate was in response to a male student behind me, who had reacted defensively to a mention of homosexuality in the army with, "Yes, and where *my father* works, they castrate people like that." I turned with quiet fury—"Are you advocating it?" All in all, I survived the day, but without much self-respect.

The next year, on a theme, a freshwoman explained to me how you could tell gay people "by the bandanas they wear in their pockets and around their necks." She concluded, "I think homosexuals are a menace to society. *What do you think?*" A pregnant question, indeed. I pondered for a while, then wrote back in the margin. "I think society is a menace to homosexuals." I resisted wearing a red bandana the day I handed back the papers.

Sometimes, friends ask me why I stay. I often ask myself. I'm still not sure. A few years ago, Anita Bryant was appointed a vice-president of the Southern Baptist Convention. A Southern Baptist school is not the most comfortable place for a gay teacher to be—sitting on the buckle of the Bible Belt. I stay partly because teaching jobs are hard to come by, especially in this vicinity, where I'm working on *Feminary.* I have begun to apply for other jobs, but so far without success. But I

wonder how different it would be in other places, where bigotry might be more
subtle, dangers more carefully concealed. Mostly I stay because I like my students.
They remind me, many of them, of myself at their age: making new and scary breaks
from home and its values, at first not straying very far and needing to be told,
"There's a bigger world. Go for it." Teaching them is like being a missionary, an
analogy many of them would understand.

Two years ago, I came out for the first time to a student. I had resolved that if
any gay student ever asked me to identify myself, I would. So when Hank came up
to my desk after Christmas vacation, sporting one new earring and wanting to talk
about bars in Washington, I knew it was coming.

"Where do *you* go to dance?" he asked. (At the time, there was one gay disco in
the vicinity.)

"Oh," I evaded, "you probably wouldn't know it. What about you?"

"Oh, you wouldn't know it either." Then, quickly, "It's between Chapel Hill
and Durham."

Me: "I think I do. It start with a *C*?"

Him: "Yes. *You* go there?" His eyes lit up.

Me: "Yep."

Him, politely, giving me an out: "You probably just went one time and got
disgusted??"

Me: "Nope."

By this time, the class was filling with students, milling around my desk and
the blackboard behind us. I suggested to Hank that we finish the conversation after
class. We did—in the middle of campus on a bench, where we could see anyone
coming for at least half a mile. I felt a sudden sympathy for the CIA. He asked me if
he could tell his friends. I took a deep breath and said yes. But they never came to
see me. I still don't know how far word had spread; every now and then I have the
feeling I exchange meaningful glances with certain students. I would like for gay
students to know I am there if they need me—or maybe just to know I am
there—but I do not take the initiative to spread the word around. I have made the
decision to be "out" in what I write and "in" where I teach, not wanting to risk a job
I enjoy or financial security; but it is not a decision I always feel good about. I see
the unease of most college students over sexuality—whether they express it in
swaggering and hollow laughter over "queer" jokes or in timidity or in the worried
looks of married students from back rows—and I know that it is part of a larger
dis-ease with sexuality and the definitions of "men" and "women" in this society. I
see how they—and most of us—have been taught to fear *all* of our feelings. And I
understand all too well, when I realize I am afraid to write—to even know—what I
think and feel for fear of losing my job, how money buys conformity, how subtly we
are terrorized into staying in line.

The closest I ever came to saying what I wanted to was in an American
literature class last year. Gay rights came up again—I think I may have even steered
the discussion in that direction. And a student finally said it to me "But what about
teachers? We can't have homosexuals teaching students!" I resisted leaping up on
the podium and flashing the big *L* emblazoned on a leotard beneath my blouse.
Instead, I took a deep breath and began slowly. "Well, in my opinion, you don't
learn sexual preference in the classroom. I mean, that's not what we are doing here.
IF you had a gay or lesbian teacher, he or she would not teach you about sexual

preference." I paused to catch my breath. They were all listening. "What he or she would say, *if you had* a gay teacher, is this..." (by now I was lightly beating on the podium) "... don't let them make you afraid to be who you are. To know who you are. She would tell you, don't let them get you. Don't let them make you afraid." I stopped abruptly, and in the silence turned to think of something to write on the board.

And if they ever *do* have a lesbian teacher, that is exactly what she will say.

Harassment in Rural America

Sue Sturtz

As a counselor and women's center director at a small state university in rural Minnesota, I didn't anticipate any trouble when two women students approached me, requesting a lesbian support group. It was early in March 1978, a month before the St. Paul gay rights referendum.[1] Two years previously, I had coordinated a "gay support group" with no harassment. It had been advertised, however, by word of mouth, had evolved into an all-men's group, and had dissolved after two months when all but one of the men left town, a common occurrence among gay men and lesbians in our rural area. The university tended to be very supportive of "personal development" groups, especially those generated by student interest.

Because of the rising antigay national opinion (Anita Bryant's campaign was in full force) and the press coverage that the St. Paul referendum was getting, even in our isolated area, I decided to carefully follow university procedures for publicizing events (women's center activities were open to university students and the general public). I composed a brief newspaper advertisement to be placed in the Announcements section of both the university and local town newspapers. The ad announced simply, "Lesbian support group. For more information, call [Women's Center phone number], and ask for Support Group information." I and the other women's center staff surmised that this topic might be controversial. Using a blind ad would allow us to screen calls and give meeting information only to legitimate inquirers (we'd previously had some negative community reaction to an abortion forum). From the ad, readers knew only that it was a university telephone, because of the recognizable prefix. Staff members were told how to deal with callers.

I had the group and the ad approved by both the vice-presidents for Academic Affairs and Student Affairs. Although this was not common practice for every group held on campus, I felt that because of the possibly controversial nature of the subject matter, these administrators should be notified. Unfortunately, the reaction of the townspeople proved me correct.

The student newspaper ad ran about three days before the town ad and provoked little reaction; there were only two calls, and both seemed legitimate. Then the town ad ran, and the harassment began. The women's center was deluged with calls, many of them obscene and threatening, including a number from men imitating women in attempts to get the meeting information. The president of the university received abusive calls from local residents and alumni, threatening to withhold contributions or to dissuade students from attending the school. (The university was in a period of decreasing enrollment, and the legislature had warned of closing unless enrollment stabilized.) After consulting the two vice-presidents, who had been fully informed and who had approved the group and advertisements, the president backed the women's center's efforts and expressed this support to callers.

The next issue was whether to proceed with the first meeting of the support group. There was fear that some of the threatening callers might discover the meeting site, despite the screening of calls, and might harass any lesbians who attended (the campus had had several recent violent episodes, involving bomb threats and firearms). We decided to go ahead, providing additional security police for the building and stationing crisis intervention staff close by, in case of trouble. At least ten legitimate calls had been received, but on the night of the meeting, only the two women who had initially requested the group attended. And there were no opposing harassers.

The group never officially formed, but within the next month, ten gay men and lesbians "came out" to me in my counseling office. Most had been encouraged to do so by seeing the ad, a sign that someone on campus recognized their existence. But they were not yet able or willing to face the harassment for being "public" that membership in a support group would involve. Their understandable fears proved to me that the need for some kind of campus support for lesbians and gay men was very real.

Notes

[1]St. Paul voters rescinded a gay rights ordinance—Ed.

In The Classroom

Do these kids know I'm a lesbian? Should they know? Should I tell them, or lie, or pretend I'm not gay, be invisible? For many lesbian teachers the lack of any support structure often leads to very real feelings of confusion, fear, and isolation. What is a lesbian teacher to do?...

Up until recently school systems have generally ignored the existence of lesbians on both sides of the school desk. This refusal to acknowledge the presence of a portion of the school population (which can be calculated at a substantial 10 percent) has to affect education in general and lesbian students in particular.

Meryl C. Friedman
"Lesbian as Teacher, Teacher as Lesbian"
Our Right to Love, Ginny Vida, editor

Sexual Energy in the Classroom

Jane Gurko

Sexual energy in the classroom[1]—one of those taboo subjects we all experience but rarely talk about in public, especially we who are in women studies. It's one thing to trash male professors who exercise their droit du seigneur, blithely trading A's for ass without the faintest shiver of guilt over their abuse of power. But how do women teachers, in particular lesbian teachers, explain to a suspicious public the crushes, ego boosts, propositions, and temptations generated by a women's studies classroom? So we *are* in there recruiting after all, are we? (Are we?) What do we mean by "sexual energy" anyway, and what codes of ethics or behavior do we painfully fashion for ourselves as we negotiate our flimsy feminist life rafts through these dangerous patriarchal waters?

The phrase itself, "sexual energy in the classroom," suggests many possible situations: student's crush on teacher, teacher's crush on student, mutual student-teacher attraction, students' sexual interest in each other, individuals' excitement about themselves as they discover something new about their sexual identity, general excitement or interest in the subject of sexuality as it somehow relates to course content. All of these situations create problems and choices, especially for the teacher, about how to act or react: should she discuss her sexuality (whatever it is) openly? Should she encourage friendship with this student? Should she go to bed with that one?

I go back over my own experience for answers: Me, age 26 (pre-coming out), getting stoned one evening with a handsome male student of mine who often drives me to school from the East Bay. He tells me he has an open marriage, finds me fascinating, etcetera. I groggily but immediately button up my shirt, knowing vaguely that walking into class and facing him the next day will be impossible if I don't.

Me, age 30, "out" at home but not at work, listening to a student pour out her fear of men, love of women, wondering how I can tell her that lesbianism is fine without endangering my tenure.

Me, age 33, in a deep, intense friend-mentorship with one of my brightest but neediest students, suddenly confronted with the fact that my lover and I have used her cruelly (if unconsciously) as an ego boost for ourselves, leaving her always as the third wheel. (We promised intimacy, sexual and otherwise, that we couldn't or wouldn't deliver.)

Me, age 35-6-7-8, "out" all over the place (tenured now), listening to many attractive women confess admiration, desire, love for me, while I wonder how to refuse and affirm at the same time (the most difficult and touching question to answer: "How can I *be* you?").

My thirteen years teaching experience, nine of them including women's studies, have brought me to a deep caution about exploiting students' intimate feelings toward me or indulging my own toward them. Yet I am conscious of wanting to be personally attractive in the classroom, not so much in looks or dress as in my energy and tone. I realize that I've worked hard at this personal attractiveness, knowing that it's a crucial part of my teaching skill. This is especially true in women's studies courses, where I can be genuine and un-gamey, a woman among women. Is this exploitation? Cheap thrills? Abuse of power? I don't think so.

Certainly I have had my share of dreams and fantasies of being the lover-hero, inner scripts which are fed by my ego-gratifying professorial position. Certainly I have been flattered and aroused by the adulation of students, especially women students. Certainly I gear up for an intense personal exchange when I enter the classroom. What then makes me a literature teacher rather than a sexual guru? Perhaps the distinction is not so absolute. Because I do think the classroom is a sexual arena, but not in the conventional, physical sense. The real sexuality of the classroom lies in the intellectual interchange itself—orgasms for the mind.

If we define sexuality as "the anticipation of orgasm" then virtually all life activity, if it is fully experienced,[2] is "sexual," since it is our psychobiolgical nature to build up to—climax—and unwind from whatever we do. This is true for eating, working, lovemaking, and learning of every kind. We have all experienced intense feelings of anticipation and buildup as we study a new idea or concept, then a climax or orgasm (or multiple orgasms) as the various pieces fall into place and we achieve illumination, then the denouement of seeing ramifications and applications or of having lesser understandings as we "come down" from out stint of research. Sexual energy is thus inherent in every classroom in its intellectual form. It *ought* to be there; without it, nothing is happening. As a teacher, then, I do "make love" to and with my students. If I bring my best intellectual energy to bear on the subject at hand and try to stimulate their best energy in response, am I not teaching my students to "come"?

And if intellectual excitement and climax are not only permissible but expected in the classroom, why draw an arbitrary line between that form of sexuality and the more usual, physical one? Do we not wish to heal patriarchy's vicious mind-body split, or at least not reinforce it? In an ideal society no such arbitrary distinction need be made. In an ideal learning situation there are no grades or hierarchical judgments, even though there may be one person with more experience of the subject, i.e., a "teacher." In the *most* ideal learning situation, for me, there are only two participants, and intellectual excitement can lead very naturally to sexual excitement, and the two kinds of sharing become intertwined. I have my best conversations and illuminations in bed (does everybody?).

However, the classrooms in which we teach are not ideal. They are pointedly hierarchical, the teacher is invested with the authority and obligation to grade her students on their work and is invested with many other kinds of institutional power as well: to write recommendations, to advise and consent on programs, to sign graduation forms, to Give Answers. The intellectual lovemaking process is marred by this power differential, followers of Socrates notwithstanding. Many teachers, especially feminist ones, try to lessen the pain of this difference by "free" grading schemes, student decisions on syllabi and class process, and scrupulousness in avoiding abuse of their power. But no amount of tinkering or make-believe changes the reality: teachers have power over students. I think well-intentioned feminist teachers who try to alleviate the power imbalance in the classroom by denying its presence or importance, or by pretending to give it up, do their students a disservice. Many students are misled into thinking the teacher more accessible than in truth she can be and are rightfully resentful when the teacher withdraws her personal attentions or finally "pulls rank" in some way, tarnishing the intimacy that may have developed.

It behooves us to admit and accept our institutional power and try to use it as decently as we can. As long as the classroom contract is open and understood by all ("*I* give the grades, and they will be based on thus and so"), intellectual excitement and gratification is still possible to a large degree. As a feminist teacher in a patriarchal institution I have accepted the fact that my prostitution is an honorable one, since most women are too poor and resource-less to gain on their own all the skills and knowledge they need. Some must still come to academia for certain skills, and better they should find me there than someone less feminist or less concerned. So I will give the grades and hope for some shared learning, some mutual climaxes, despite that.

But to enter a physically sexual relationship with a person who is at the time one's student—this is not in the contract. I think it should absolutely not be done, regardless of the age, gender, or state of mind of the participants. I speak from my own experience here, and while the relationship which ensued turned out to be of long duration (eight years) and profound importance to me, it was fraught with power problems from the start; had I to do it over again unquestionably I would wait until we were no longer in our student-teacher roles.

The problem lies in the fact that any noncoercive power imbalance tends to trigger romantic fantasies on both sides of an unequal relationship, regardless of the sexes involved. It's almost automatic in the classroom: the teacher becomes an object of hero worship, and conversely, as "hero," indulges in ego-inflating fantasies of power over her "worshipper." I believe that human sexual excitement depends largely on each lover having a fantasy of power over the other. But ideally, in my value system, lovers play out their power fantasies in a mutual and role-shifting way, avoiding any overall inequalities or dependencies. In fantasy, power-over and power-under are in fact often interchangeable, since each side by definition depends on the other. In our mutual fantasizing we are equal—and equally responsible for our dreams and expectations.

But in a classroom liaison, the teacher in *fact* has more power—it's no fantasy. The lovers cannot play with it, shift it around, manipulate it for their mutual growth.[3] There's no way the two people involved can realistically keep their student-teacher and lover-lover relationships separate, if they are going on simultaneously. The teacher will wonder, "Can I grade her classwork with as much neutrality and impersonality as I try to grade the other students? Will she accept my grades neutrally?" The student will wonder, "Is she trying to be teacher in bed? Does she accept me as her peer? Am I being graded now?" (One friend of mine facetiously remarked, "I never worry about it. I'm only attracted to A students." "Yes," I replied, "but *you* still get to fill out the report card.")

Romantic fantasies which are triggered by real power imbalances are disasters if they are acted out. Even if the attraction between student and teacher is a serious one and their relationship has potential, both must be responsible for not pushing the other into it. The teacher at the very least is morally obligated not to pursue the attraction, since she is the one less likely to be hurt by the power difference. Moreover, if she is not attracted to the student who has seriously propositioned her, I think she is obligated to (1) affirm the student's feelings; (2) tell the student that such a liaison would be inappropriate as long as they share a classroom; and (3) admit that aside from their student-teacher roles she doesn't feel ready for such a relationship at this time.

The main reason, then, to avoid physical intimacy between student and teacher is that it's virtually impossible to maintain simultaneously two differently negotiated power relations without one affecting the other. If, in some hypothetical utopia, physical sharing were as much a part of the classroom contract as intellectual sharing, then this power differential wouldn't be an obstacle, since it would be understood to exist in bed as well as at the blackboard. I doubt, however, that bed would seem so attractive if grades and student evaluations were attendant upon our individual performances there.

On the other side of the coin, a teacher-student relationship which exists outside an institution—i.e., a nonhierarchical exhange of money and services, as in a private tutoring situation—need not be bound at all by distinctions between the intellectual and the physical. If I'm paying a person to teach me a subject (anything at all, from botany to auto mechanics) and we become attracted to each other, I see no reason not to become physical as well as intellectual sharers. If, as so often happens, the original subject disappears, then it couldn't have been that important to either one of us. If we agree that money payment is no longer appropriate, that's fine too, as long as some equal exchange of skills or talents takes place.

Inside the institution, however, even an open contract about physical intimacy wouldn't make such a liaison acceptable, because there is a second reason to abstain: numbers. Whether or not physical relations are part of the classroom contract, as long as the student-teacher ratio is more than one to one, the teacher cannot be expected to divide her energy in this way. Her ability to be an equal facilitator for *all* the students in the class will be weakened if she is giving so much intimate out-of-class energy to one or more selected few.

Everything I've said so far applies to all classrooms, regardless of subject matter, or the gender of teacher or students. Some specific distinctions between male and female (especially lesbian) teachers need to be made, however. First, lesbian teachers, particularly in women's studies courses, must go beyond the power principles I've outlined here to the simple political expediency of keeping our behavior clean. We have a responsibility to the women's studies program we serve to protect them from charges of "recruitment" and "seduction." It's painful to have to pander in any way to the prejudices of the dominant culture. But mere survival of these programs depends on such compromises, and we owe it to our students and colleagues to save personal indulgences for safer settings.

Second, the caveat about institutional power imbalance goes at least double for male teachers of female students, since even outside of their academic roles the woman is at a disadvantage.

Third is the most important difference between male and female teachers, and certainly between "regular" and women's studies classrooms. The real goal, after all, of women studies is teaching women to take themselves seriously as women, to study and analyze their cultural history, personal experience, and position in the world; in short, teaching women to love women, both others and themselves. In such a setting, especially if the teacher is an open lesbian in an all-female group, the classroom will vibrate with sexual energy among the students themselves. Thinking, talking, working together on the subject of women's growth and freedom is, in Audre Lorde's terms, the ultimate erotic experience. No male teacher could catalyze an atmosphere quite like it. Many women students will find themselves attracted to each other in the best sense of the word. And though physical intimacy is not a necessary ingredient of this exciting ferment, it may grow out of or be added to it later.

Similarly, the students may find themselves more powerfully attracted to the lesbian teacher than to the usual male authority figure, since the lesbian teacher's energy and involvement in their mutually stimulating material is quite different. The teacher becomes a model not simply of authority, but of freedom, risk-taking (if she is open about her orientation), and (to some) radically new ideas. The lesbian teacher in turn will be more stimulated by her women studies students than by her mixed classes, because both the material and the atmosphere free her from most of the gender-based sex games demanded in the ordinary classroom.

Both the special attractiveness of the lesbian teacher and her special sense of comfort have their pitfalls, however. On the one hand, even if she exercises her authority with scrupulous objectivity and care, misleading no one with false promises, flattery or flirtation, the love-feeling she will inspire in some of her students may still affect the class adversely. Deprived of mothering as all women have been in patriarchy,[4] the temptation to see the lesbian authority figure as Mother is overwhelming. And in the first flush of the semester's excitement, she is the Good Mother. But as soon as it becomes clear that Mom is going to criticize, give grades, and—crucially—*not* step in and take care of one for life, inevitably anger and resentment arise. The righteous rage of life-long, centuries-long deprivation eclipses the teacher's true face, and the betrayed student sees only the Devouring Mother. Many lesbian teachers find themselves confronted midsemester by harsh and totally unexpected criticism, ranging from vituperation to full-scale mutiny. The intensity of some students' bitterness seems incomprehensible; everything had been going along so well. The experienced lesbian teacher knows how to foresee this upheaval, to recognize the storm warnings of excessive enthusiasm or personal regard early in the semester. It is not always avoidable, but at least the disruptive effects on the class can be lessened if the teacher properly understands the psychology involved and can articulate clearly her sense of what is going on both to the individual(s) and to the whole group.

On the other hand, the lesbian's special feeling of comfort in the women's studies classroom often leads her to be more personally expansive and nurturing than is wise. For myself I tend to play down specifically "maternal" behaviors or tonalities—overly solicitous inquiries about students' personal lives, bringing of food to class gatherings, too much hugging or physical touching. In other feminist settings such behavior may be genuine and appropriate, even necessary. In the classroom I think it triggers deep expectations which simply cannot be met, a kind of love which ought not to be promised. In dealing with such powerful needs, however, the teacher must always affirm even her most troublesome students' pain. We are all in this boat together, and meeting hostility with its likeness will surely sink us.

There are other particular sexual dynamics set off by a lesbian teacher in a women's studies classroom, but the Mother-trap is the most dramatic that I have encountered. I know it happens to heterosexual women teachers as well, but not, I think, with quite the same intensity. As Nancy Chodorow, Adrienne Rich, and others have pointed out,[5] the mother-daughter relationship is profoundly lesbian (and sexual) at its core, and an openly lesbian woman will trigger those feelings at a more profound or perhaps violent level than the straight woman.

In a larger sense, the dynamic created by *any* minority person in an authority position in a majority institution is explosive, because power in the classroom must be realigned and redefined quite drastically. Minority students suddenly have permission to feel in the "majority" or accepted role. Majority students are forced to reexamine their unconscious assumptions about being right, about owning the world, and about what kind of validation they can expect from this teacher. The teacher must make some extremely difficult choices between her responsibility to the institution which pays her and her responsibility to her own identity and honest exposure of it (and all the political perspectives and opinions which come with it) to her students. When the minority-majority axis concerns sexuality—i.e., lesbian versus heterosexual—the class is surcharged with sexual energy of all kinds from the start. If the energy remains at an intellectual level, if the teacher does not promise impossible nurturance or attention, if she affirms both her own and her students' sexual feelings without acting them out physically, and if she is open and honest about her grading responsibilities, then the class should be a fine and proper lovemaking experience—one of the only ones possible inside these patriarchal walls.[6]

Notes

[1]Throughout this essay I refer to college-level classrooms only.

[2]See Audre Lorde, "The Erotic as Power," *Chrysalis* 9 (Fall 1979): 29: "...the erotic is not only a question of what we do. It is a question of how acutely and fully we can feel in the doing." (Reprint available from the Lesbian-Feminist Study Clearinghouse—see Resources.)

[3]I make a distinction here between the direct and immediate power imbalance in the teacher-student situation, and the indirect power imbalance created by class differences of two lovers. The latter power imbalance is very real and laced with inescapable problems. But I think they are resolvable, at least between the two individuals involved, since the more privileged lover always has the choice to share or renounce most of her privilege. This is not true for the teacher if she is to remain a teacher.

[4]Phyllis Chesler, *Women & Madness* (Garden City: Doubleday, 1972), pp. 18–19.

[5]Nancy Chodorow, "Family Structure and Feminine Personality," *Woman, Culture & Society*, ed. Michelle Z. Rosaldo and Louise Lamphere (Stanford: Stanford University Press,

1974), p. 53; Adrienne Rich, "Sibling Mysteries," *The Dream of A Common Language* (New York: W.W. Norton & Co., 1978), p. 52; and Adrienne Rich, "Compulsory Heterosexuality and Lesbian Existence," *Signs* 5(4) (Summer 1980): 637.

[6] I am indebted in the writing of this essay to many women for suggestion of issues; but in particular to Sally Gearhart, Helene Wenzel, and Marcia Keller for dialoguing with me about these ideas.

"Kissing/Against the Light": A Look at Lesbian Poetry

Elly Bulkin

Of those hours,
Who will speak these days,
if not I,
if not you?
     —Muriel Rukeyser,
     "The Speed of Darkness"

I.

It was easy, a few years ago, to think that lesbian poetry didn't exist. It had, of course, always been there—dusty in rare book libraries, lost in love poems with changed or ambiguous pronouns, absent from the published writing of otherwise acceptable women poets.[1] Yet until fairly recently, we didn't know all this. Those of us who are lesbians seemed to have come from nowhere, from a great blankness with only a few shadowy figures to suggest a history.

We could find Sappho's poetry, all right, but only when preceded by the (male) assurances that "Neither the gossip of scandalmongers nor the scrupulous research of scholars should cause us to forget that [her reputation as a lesbian] is nothing but speculation."[2] We could surmise about Emily Dickinson's life, but until the fifties we were confronted only with a selected number of her published poems and letters.[3] We could stubbornly claim Gertrude Stein and Amy Lowell and H.D. as lesbians—but they hardly constituted a lesbian literary tradition out of which to write or a history from which lesbians, especially lesbians of color or poor or working class lesbians, could draw strength.

The early women's movement in the late sixties and early seventies pulled together, uncovered, and touted a large group of respectable poetic foremothers. But not for lesbians. When commercial publishers decided several years ago that there was money in women's poetry anthologies, two appeared, but without more than token lesbian visibility. The 1973 publication of *No More Masks!* and *Rising*

Tides was tremendously important, but it did almost nothing to establish lesbians as significant contributors to women's literature. The problem stemmed not from the lack of lesbian poets in each book, but from the impossibility of identifying them unless they were represented by poems about subjects connected directly and explicitly to lesbian oppression and/or sexuality.

I remember trying to read between the lines of the biographical statements in *No More Masks!* and *Rising Tides* to figure out whether the author of a poem that moved me was a lesbian.[4] What, after all, did it mean when a woman was described as living with her young daughter? Who was the "you" addressed in very personal terms in a poem—a woman or a man? Where was I in these books? Was there a "we" in them?

The editors were of little help. In her long introduction to *No More Masks!* Florence Howe recognized the existence of lesbian poetry—at least *recent* lesbian poetry—but seemed to regard lesbianism as just one more theme women can write about; its political significance—and history—seemed lost. And *Rising Tides* managed to get through 400 pages (and five identifiably lesbian poets) without mentioning the word once (though we do have lesbian Judy Grahn's ironic description of herself as "insane, evil, and devious").[5]

Yet, however weakly, these early anthologies provided impetus toward the discovery of lesbian poetry for many women who lived away from urban and university centers and women's bookstores and who were unaware of and/or without access to women's press publications, readings, and periodicals. I did find in *No More Masks!* a poem by Wendy Wieber, "One, The Other, And," that I read over and over, having no other poems about the awakening that I myself was then experiencing; it begins:

> That sound like the scratch
> scratch of an old recording
> the static and scratch of an
> old recording that tight
> scratch was the sound of her
> hands in her head and that
> contracted scratch was the
> scar of her mouth and her
> eyes

and ends:

> They hadn't known
> for so much frost
> for bone cold fingers
> of the stunning hand
> and stings of the
> ice bee
>
> they hadn't known
> but gathered themselves

unto one another
gathered their selves

into such a wholeness
they took
the blue knife
and slit the belly of night
spinning the sun into life.... [6]

Experienced and written about by women all over the country, the expansive coming-out process Wieber describes resulted in a flowering of visible lesbian poetry. Included in such subsequent commercial-press anthologies as *We Become New* (1974), its own strength underscored its pivotal role in contemporary women's poetry.[7] A result was the type of critical consciousness about heterosexist assumptions displayed by Louise Bernikow in editing *The World Split Open* (1974). In her selection of women poets writing about loving women way back in the early 1600's, Bernikow begins to fill the contour of a lesbian literary tradition and explains why the men who have written literary history have chosen to ignore its existence:

> Such men not only see themselves as "the world," they also see themselves as "love." Women who do not love men, and women who do not have sex with men, in the eyes of men, have loveless and sexless lives. Yet, for all obfuscation about it, the truth seems to be that most of these women poets have loved women, sometimes along with loving men. Women have found in other women exactly the same companionship, encouragement, and understanding that they did not find in men. Whether all the woman-to-woman relationships that exist in the lives of these poets were explicitly sexual or not is difficult to know, for taboo was always in the way and evidence that might have told the true nature of those relationships is missing. Yet what matters most is not who did what to whom in what bed, but the direction of emotional attention. Mostly, then, these women turned to women—and understanding that might be the beginning and end of a nonpatriarchal biography.[8]

This is new-found history. So, all except the youngest lesbian poets—or those who started very recently to read and write poetry—have had their work shaped by the simple fact of their having begun to write without knowledge of such history and with little or no hope of support from a women's and/or lesbian writing community. The differences between them are explicable, to a considerable extent, by the absence or the state of the women's movement when they began to write seriously.

The work of lesbian poets who began to write long before the existence of the women's movement must be understood within that context. Poets like May Sarton and May Swenson have long worked in a world of traditional (white bourgeois male) academic values relating to every facet of poetry—its style, its structure, its subject, its audience.

We can sense Sarton's relief (and pain) when in her sixties—and only *after* her parents' deaths—she felt able to come out publicly through the appearance of her 1965 novel, *Mrs. Stevens Hears the Mermaids Singing.*[9]

Finding Swenson's poem, "To Confirm a Thing," in a 1975 lesbian anthology, *Amazon Poetry*, we can read it, more than twenty years after it was written, with particular clarity:

> We are Children incorrigible and perverse
> who hold our obstinate seats
> on heaven's carousel
> refusing our earth's assignment[10]

If readers initially had some difficulty understanding these lines, their response is comprehensible given the poem's date of publication, 1954, two years before the first issue of *The Ladder*, the pioneering lesbian magazine. Even *The Ladder* reflects for at least a decade society's negative view of lesbianism (or what was long described in its pages as "deviance").[11] The weakness of the poetry it published before the late sixties seems to have resulted not only from the relative absence of other lesbian poetry but from the understandable reluctance of lesbian poets to appear in an identifiably lesbian periodical, especially during the assorted witch-hunts of the fifties.[12]

Given this context, the obliqueness of Muriel Rukeyser's coming out as a lesbian in her poetry is thoroughly understandable. Though I try to be alert to nuances that can reveal a poet's sexual and affectional preference, I had read through Rukeyser's work without thinking of her possible lesbianism until *after* I had heard that she had agreed to participate in the lesbian poetry reading at the 1978 Modern Language Association convention; when illness forced her withdrawal, she expressed to Judith McDaniel her hope that she would be included the following year, a desire that went unfulfilled because of her chronic ill health (and death in 1980 at the age of sixty-seven). Sending me back to her work, the discovery allowed me to understand for the first time that the opening poems in *The Speed of Darkness* (1971) celebrate coming out.[13] Only my continued ignorance of Rukeyser's lesbianism could support another reading of them.

Using the persona of Orpheus, Rukeyser speaks first in "The Poem as Mask" of having been "split open, unable to speak, in exile from/myself"; and the poem ends: "Now, for the first time, the god lifts his hand,/the fragments join in me with their own music." A short lyric is followed by "The Transgress":

> . . . in the revelation
> thundering on tabu after the broken
>
> imperative, while the grotesque ancestors fade
> with you breathing beside me through our dream:
>
> bed of forbidden things finally known—

And the book's fourth poem, "The Conjugation of the Paramecium," describes how "when the paramecium/desires/renewal/strength another joy" it "lies down beside/another/paramecium," *like with like*, in a loving exchange that, we have been told in the poem's opening lines, "has nothing/to do with/propagating."

These few poems exemplify the potential for erroneous (or, at best, incomplete) reading of a writer's work if we are not aware of her lesbianism. "The Poem as Mask" has been—and can be—read as a positive statement of a woman's going beyond "masks" and "myth" to experience herself as an integrated whole. We can either perceive it in this general way—or apply what we know about Rukeyser's life (and about the following poems) and read it as a poem that thematically is very much like Wendy Wieber's "One, The Other, And." We have the further option of deciding whether to consider the "tabu" in "The Transgress" as a complete mystery or "The Conjugation of the Paramecium" as a purely playful extended metaphor without connection to the poet's lesbianism. We need, I think, to look at these poems within the historical framework of lesbian oppression and invisibility. How else to explain the obliqueness and obfuscation in work by a poet of characteristic clarity?

II.

The flowering of lesbian poetry that began slowly in the late sixties and had reached full bloom by the mid-seventies was rooted in the civil rights and antiwar movements, which supported challenging the various racist, imperialistic values of contemporary American society. Many of the lesbians who published their work in the growing number of feminist periodicals and who began the Women's Press Collective and Diana Press viewed themselves as radicals, as well as lesbians and feminists. Before we could find their poems bound in books, we could find them scattered through a newspaper like *off our backs*, whose 1971 headlines capture the general political climate into which this lesbian poetry was born—*Indochina Lives; Angela Davis Needs Defense Funds; Women March on the Pentagon; Underground in America.*

Many lesbian writers found themselves pushed even more firmly out of the American mainstream by the antiwar, radical left politics of the times. Martha Shelley wrote for *Rat*, a radical newspaper in New York City; Judy Greenspan organized in Madison, Wisconsin against the Vietnam War. Others came from a poor or working-class background that seemed ignored or denigrated by a predominantly white, middle-class women's movement; Rita Mae Brown helped establish *The Furies*, a monthly publication (1972–1973) concerned with issues of class, sexism, and racism. Still others, like Willyce Kim and Pat Parker, suffered additional oppression as lesbians of color.

These lesbian poets were outsiders in American society. They felt no stake in its traditions, in its establishments, in its social/political/aesthetic values. Instead they sought to create a tradition that was anti-literary, anti-intellectual, anti-hierarchical. The tone was captured by Judy Grahn, whose "The Common Woman" poems (first published in 1970 in *off our backs*) celebrate the waitress, the mother, the lesbian, the prostitute, the childhood friend:

> For all the world we didn't know we held in common
> all along,
> the common woman is as common as the best of bread
> and will rise
> and will become strong—I swear it to you

I swear it to you on my own head.
I swear it to you on my common
woman's
head.[14]

Grahn's direct, everyday language with a rhetorical drive draws on oral traditions of poetry—biblical, Black, beat, protesting—and seems meant to be read aloud at women's meetings. This oral quality, the sense that the poem should be heard with others, not read by oneself, is in the ending, too, of Judy Greenspan's "To Lesbians Everywhere":

and someday
there will be a great rumbling
and we will join with all people
charging forth like the wind
they will never know what hit them.[15]

The focus in these and other poems is on the poem as bridge, not as obstacle. The work of these early lesbian writers seems to be deliberately, perhaps even defiantly, "antipoetic." When they were gathered into books in the early seventies, the poems of these writers stood for a brief while as a separate, identifiable body of lesbian poetry.

Yet, even as these books were being printed, newer poems, appearing with increasing regularity in women's magazines and newspapers, were being written by an ever-widening group of women who defined themselves as lesbians. The reasons for this sudden increase in the number of women poets who so defined themselves are complex, involving changes within individual women, the women's movement, and women's poetry. These interactions—personal, political, poetic—are basic, but different for each woman.

Contemporary lesbian poetry comes from many sources. The earlier lesbian poets—Judy Grahn, Pat Parker, Fran Winant—continue to write. Long-established poets like May Sarton and May Swenson have allowed themselves to be identified publicly as lesbians. Lesbian poets like Audre Lorde (published by Diane di Prima's Poets Press in the late sixties and by a small black male press in the early seventies) and Susan Sherman (published by a small white male press in the early seventies) have become more direct in their work and more publicly perceived as *lesbian* activists. Women who had already published heterosexually identified poetry with large commercial presses and reaped establishment rewards for it—Marilyn Hacker, Adrienne Rich—write from a lesbian-feminist perspective. A whole range of lesbian poets (most of whom had written earlier heterosexual poetry) put out exciting self-published and women's press books.

III.

The dramatic increase in the number of lesbian poets has also helped provide the impetus for uncovering an historical tradition of lesbian poetry. Much of the work that has been done on the best-known lesbian poets—Sappho, Emily Dickinson, H.D., Amy Lowell, Gertrude Stein—has been done by lesbians since the early seventies, contemporaneous with the growth of this poetry. Ongoing current work by Judith McDaniel on white, economically privileged poets who wrote at the beginning of the century—Edna St. Vincent Millay, Sara Teasdale, Elinor Wylie, and others—reveals the tremendous extent to which they fueled each others' poetry and lives; while not necessarily lesbian in the narrowest sense, the community and the poetry they created certainly rests solidly on the "lesbian continuum" of woman-identified experience discussed by Rich in "Compulsory Heterosexuality and Lesbian Existence."[16] Unequivocally lesbian is the life of Angelina Weld Grimké, the Black descendant of slaves and slave-owners, whose unpublished love poetry, diary entries, and letters were unearthed by Gloria T. Hull in her research on women poets of the Harlem Renaissance.[17]

Uncovering a poetic tradition representative of lesbians of color and poor and working-class lesbians of all races involves, as Barbara Noda has written, reexamining "the words 'lesbian,' 'historical,' and even 'poet.'" A beginning problem is definitional, as Paula Gunn Allen makes clear in her exploration of her own American Indian culture:

> It is not known if those
> who warred and hunted on the plains
> chanted and hexed in the hills
> divined and healed in the mountains
> gazed and walked beneath the seas
> were Lesbians
> It is never known
> if any woman was a lesbian[18]

The search is further compounded when the goal is finding not just a lesbian, but a lesbian *poet*, especially among those groups—Latinas, Appalachian women, and others—whose historical poverty leaves them without a tradition of "literacy" (or "literacy" in English), and without a way to get their written or oral poetry reproduced and distributed. We face a particular obstacle in attempting to uncover historical material by/about American Indian lesbians: the obligation to respect the beliefs of those tribes which maintain that the very act of writing down myths and stories is an act of disempowerment.[19]

The near impossibility of doing certain kinds of historical research is illustrated by Noda's response to my question about the feasibility of locating an Asian-American lesbian poetry tradition:

> Perhaps I could ask my 87-year-old grandmother who is one of the still remaining Issei women *if* she remembers any "strange" women who did not marry and associated mainly with other women. *If* by chance she could relate to the question and did remember such a woman, I would then have to trace the whereabouts of the woman. *If* the woman was still alive or not, *if* the woman left any available writings, I would then have a glimmer of a source that is historical rather than contemporary of an Asian-American lesbian. With the Goddess' blessing she would have been a poet and truthfully such a woman would not be considered an Asian-American. Because if she was an Issei like my grandmother, then she had been born in Japan and emigrated to the United States to become the first generation of women to live here.[20]

While the exact situation Noda describes is specific to Japanese-Americans, a comparatively recent immigrant group, it also outlines general problems of finding lesbians—let alone lesbian poets.

Even where a lesbian poet is alive and quite ready to tell us that she has always been a lesbian, we need to look carefully at a concept of the "historical" that probably makes us more likely to place within a "lesbian historical tradition" someone like H.D., who was born in 1886 and died in 1961, than someone like Elsa Gidlow who was born in 1898, was writing lesbian love poetry at sixteen, and today continues to write. Gidlow, of course, lacked H.D.'s economic benefits—Bryn Mawr, travel to London, acceptance into the "cultured" world of Ezra Pound and the "Imagists." Instead, Gidlow reminds us to look for part of our tradition in the work and life of a lesbian who was the first born to a large, poor, white family; went without "the grammar school-high school-college education" she "craved"; spent "a lifetime of working fulltime to support... [herself] (and others at times)" and write both love poetry and "bitter social protest poetry."[21] Gidlow movingly depicts her attempts to combine writing and paid work "during decades when there was no unemployment insurance, if we (and those close to us) were out of work, no food stamps, no medicare, no social security or welfare for parents or others who might become dependent."[22] Despite the "crushing" burden of her economic situation, significantly compounded by her oppression as woman and as lesbian, Gidlow continued to write—and to fill in one chunk of an historical tradition of lesbian poetry.

No less valuable in beginning to put together that mosaic is Angelina Weld Grimké, whose unpublished work provides solid documentation of the forces that buried her own life and poetry—and certainly those of other lesbians of color who might have written poetry. As Gloria T. Hull writes:

> The question—to repeat it—is: What did it mean to be a Black Lesbian/poet in America at the beginning of the twentieth century? First, it meant that you wrote (or half wrote)—in isolation—a lot which you did not show and knew you could not publish. It meant that when you did write to be printed, you did so in shackles—chained between the real experience you wanted to say and the conventions that would not give you voice. It meant that you fashioned a few race and nature poems, transliterated lyrics, and double-tongued verses which—sometimes (racism being what it is)—got published. It meant, finally, that you stopped writing altogether, dying, no doubt, with your real gifts stifled within—and leaving behind (in a precious few cases) the little that manages to survive of your true self in fugitive pieces.[23]

While Grimké wrote in forms that were generally compatible with the white male literary definition of poetry, some other Black women (lacking Grimké's economic advantages and formal education) did not. Blues lyrics have proved a rich source of lesbian expression. Bessie Jackson, for instance, did a song called "B.D. Blues" (Bull Dagger Blues) during her career (1923–1935), while Bessie Smith sang several songs with explicitly lesbian lyrics.[24] Along with the songs of working-class white women, song lyrics by Black women and other women of color need to be explored seriously *as poetry* in order to find expressions of lesbian experiences, sometimes by women who might not meet a 1980's definition of "lesbian," most often by women whose own lives we can learn little or nothing about.[25] Where necessary, women's song lyrics—and other poems or poetic fragments—will have to be translated so that the words of lesbians whose sole or primary language was Spanish or Navajo or any of the multitude of immigrant tongues will not remain lost to us.

While we have survived as lesbians for centuries "without access to any knowledge of a tradition, a continuity, a social underpinning,"[26] that mode of survival is finally ending. The work has already begun that gives historical shape to our lives and our literature. Hopefully it will continue in directions that encompass the diversity of past and present lesbian poetry and lesbian existence.

IV.

Teaching women's poetry at all is, I think, nearly always a struggle: an effort to overcome most students' resistance to reading poetry by encouraging them to open to the personal immediacy, the urgency, the language and rhythm of contemporary women's poetry. Teaching lesbian poetry is even more difficult: nonlesbian teachers and students bring to it a multilayered set of assumptions that must be dealt with before the poetry itself can be explored.

An unknown to most of us, lesbian poetry, like lesbianism, is understandably threatening. When we think about teaching lesbian poetry, what most of us feel is fear. We hesitate to write about it in detail (if at all) for the same reasons that we hesitate to emphasize it—or even discuss it—in class and out. The fear of losing our jobs, of being denied tenure. The fear that, regardless of our sexual and affectional preference, we will be dismissed by our students as "just a lesbian." The concern that students who feel hostile or skeptical or even friendly toward feminism and the women's movement will be irretrievably "lost" if "too much" attention were directed toward the issue of lesbianism. The doubts about our colleagues' reactions to what we teach and how we teach it. The threat that the validity of a hard-earned women's course, women's studies program, or women's center will be undercut, and funding jeopardized, if it becomes perceived as a "dyke effort."[27]

The continued presence of this oppression is reflected in many ways. For all that has been written about teaching women's literature, detailed explorations of the impact on teachers and students of a discussion of lesbian literature (or anything else relating directly to lesbians) are conspicuously absent. From otherwise useful articles about classroom approaches and dynamics, we get little sense of ways to deal with lesbianism, let alone lesbian poetry. Each teacher does so, if at all, in a comparative vacuum, and hardly ever with space to dialogue with colleagues and/or friends about the issues that might be raised in the classroom.

Even for people who do acknowledge the existence of lesbian writers, the temptation to deny the significance of a writer's lesbianism is powerful in educational institutions that reflect society's general homophobia. About seven years ago, when I was teaching at an urban community college, I rather naively suggested a new course for the syllabus called "The Outsider in Twentieth-Century American Literature," which was to deal with the writings of lesbians and gay men and of people who were or had been in prison or mental hospitals. When it was brought up at the English department meeting (after enthusiastic approval by the appropriate committee), I was totally taken aback because everyone discussed it—with much laughter and side comments—as if I had suggested a course about homosexuality and literature.

Most of the faculty dismissed the course by saying, "Well, *that's* not so important. I don't see why that has any more influence on a writer than a thousand other things." No one was willing to consider the impact on one's writing of "having to live as a 'different' person in a heterosexist culture."[28] The course's chances for support disappeared under the weight of peer disparagement and discomfort. The feelings were so strong that a discussion of the academic "respectability"—or the true breadth—of the course content never took place.

My own failure at that point—and that of other lesbian and gay male faculty members—to speak out *as outsiders* aborted any further educating/radicalizing potential in the department meeting. Although not, of course, a classroom situation, the meeting reminds me of many classes in which I have since spoken as an open lesbian: the same personal discomfort; the same annoyance at having the issue raised at all; the same denial of the impact of lesbianism on literature; the same need of most women to go on record as being apart from lesbian women.

For any teacher who is not a lesbian, these responses need to be explored before she can effectively teach material dealing with lesbianism. The reactions of nonlesbian teachers and students to a poet's lesbianism stand, most often, is a significant barrier to her work. For the teacher, overcoming this barrier is especially important because of her general function as role model in the classroom. If she feels uncomfortable with the subject matter, but insists that she has "no difficulty at all" with lesbianism, she will teach the inappropriateness of discussing (and perhaps even recognizing) such discomfort. If she begins a class on lesbian poetry by "just happening" to mention her married status, she communicates her fear of being suspected a lesbian and discourages her students from asking "too many" questions or seeming "too interested."

If, on the other hand, she acknowledges the limitations of her own understanding of lesbianism and makes available information she has learned from lesbians or from a number of current books by lesbians, she will support her students' willingness to fill the gaps in their own knowledge. If she admits her own fears, her own stereotypes, her own myths, and places them within the framework of a society that has taught homophobia to each of us, and taught us well, she will help make the barrier to the poetry less formidable. She will also affirm the importance of taking risks in order to better understand the experiences and perceptions of women who differ significantly from herself and her nonlesbian students. At the 1977 Modern Language Association panel on lesbians and literature, Audre Lorde said:

> And where the words of women are crying to be heard, we must each of us recognize our responsibility to seek those words out, to read them and share them and examine them in their pertinence to our lives. That we not hide behind the mockeries of separation that have been imposed upon us and which so often we accept as our own: for instance, "I can't possibly teach black women's writings—their experience is so different from mine," yet how many years have you spent teaching Plato and Shakespeare and Proust? Or another: "She's a white woman and what could she possibly have to say to me?" Or

"She's a lesbian, what would my husband say, or my chairman?" Or again, "This woman writes of her sons and I have no children." And all the other ways in which we rob ourselves and each other.[29]

Although I do think that a nonlesbian teacher should deal with lesbian poetry in any case, to raise the relevant personal and political issues and to explore them most adequately require facilitation by a lesbian teacher, a lesbian student, a lesbian guest speaker, by someone who has herself experienced the freedom and oppression of being a lesbian and who can share that openly.[30]

My own perspective on teaching lesbian material parallels in some ways that of the identifiably lesbian teacher: when I speak in a classroom about lesbian poetry, I do so as a lesbian. But, since I usually am a guest lecturer, I have the freedom to teach one or two sessions of a class without the regular lesbian teacher's very real concerns about both her economic and professional survival and her ongoing relationships with students, colleagues, and administrators. When teaching lesbian poetry, I begin with two fundamental assumptions: the poet's lesbianism is an essential, not an incidental, fact about her life and her work; and a discussion of lesbianism must focus not only on our political ideas (what we think), but on our feelings (how we act, what we say, how we live our expressed politics).

V.

Students in one women's studies class were adamant about the "universality" of the selections in *Amazon Poetry*. Why, they wanted to know, had Joan Larkin and I called it "an anthology of *lesbian* poetry" (my italics)? Skeptical about my answers, they held to their sense of ready identification with the poets in the book; the fact of the poets' lesbianism was not, they insisted, sufficiently important for us to have stressed it. Other questions followed, more personal ones. I responded to their questions about coming out, being a lesbian mother, my parents' reactions to my lesbianism, lesbian sexuality, the relationship between lesbianism and feminism. I shared my feelings about the energy and time it took me even to be in the class, to answer all of those questions; I recalled times when my anger at the need to deal with people's homophobia and general ignorance about lesbianism had been too strong for me to be able to do so.

Although I have almost never been the only lesbian in such a class, I run the risk (unless other lesbians are vocal) of having my own perceptions and experiences applied to lesbians as a group. I emphasized that I was speaking as an individual. A white, middle class, able-bodied, comparatively young woman, I stressed my obvious inability to speak for the many lesbians who are American Indian, Asian American, Black, Latin, poor or working class, disabled, older.

After I began a second meeting of the same class with a twenty-minute reading from *Amazon Poetry*, we moved to a deeper level of dialogue. Most of the students had managed to "forget" Audre Lorde's "Love Poem"; others had felt too uncomfortable at its explicitness to initiate a discussion about it:

And I knew when I entered her I was
high wind in her forests hollow
fingers whispering sound
honey flowed
from the split cups
impaled on a lance of tongues
on the tips of her breast on her navel
and my breath
howling into her entrances
through lungs of pain.[31]

My reading seemed to give students "permission" to relate to and share their fears and confusion. Our point of departure was the visual image of two women loving each other physically. We spoke of the Western tradition of love poetry with its nearly total preoccupation—when sexually explicit—with intercourse. One woman said that because she was just starting to explore her own sexuality, references to anything sexual embarrassed her. Another said that because she couldn't identify with either woman in the poem, she had great difficulty relating to it.

Finally we began to discuss what makes lesbianism so threatening. A woman remembered a disparaging, upsetting comment made the day before by a male friend who has seen her with *Amazon Poetry* in the college library. A second commented that she found it hard to overcome her resistance to thinking about lesbianism, her feeling that I shouldn't be "bothering" her about it.

We spoke of the homophobia in the denial of our own and others' lesbianism. We looked at Susan Sherman's "Lilith of the Wildwood, of the Fair Places":

women   women surround me
images of women   their faces
I   who for years   pretended them away
pretended away their names   their faces
myself   what I am   pretended it away[32]

I spoke of the form of denial in Sherman's early love poetry: her use of the ambiguous pronoun "you" and the absence of specifically female sexual imagery; instead, in the early and late sixties, she described her subject subtly, through gentle images of grass, of rain, of "how the earth opens its body Almost/as an act of grace."[33] Reviewing *With Anger/With Love* several years ago, I had been pleased to conclude accurately from such images that Sherman was a lesbian poet (although I printed the review only after having had this confirmed); I had been appropriately embarrassed in 1973 (after I had come out as a lesbian) to find out that I had assumed mistakenly that the "you" in a love poem by Lorraine Sutton was a man.[34]

We discussed other forms of denial. I had needed to be *told*, for example, in 1971 by a friend of eleven years' standing that she and the woman she lived with were lovers, that they did *not* use their second bedroom for anything but guests. I connected my own past liberalism on sexual/affectional matters ("Anything people want to do is okay with me as long as it doesn't hurt anyone.") with the ready

acceptance of lesbianism that had been verbalized during the first class meeting by
women who were now admitting to much more complex feelings. By now, the
limitations of such "liberalism" seemed clear. I connected it to a tendency to see
selectively, to homogenize, to focus on women's shared experiences to the
exclusion of those profoundly influenced by sexual and affectional preference, as
well as by other significant differences among us.

I stressed that the experiences of lesbian and nonlesbian women *are* different.
Blurring the distinctions only denies the realities of many women's lives. Understanding that is a way into ourselves and into the poetry. I read aloud the final
section of Olga Broumas' "Sleeping Beauty":

> City-center, mid-
> traffic, I
> wake to your public kiss. Your name
> is Judith, your kiss a sign
>
> to the shocked pedestrians, gathered
> beneath the light that means
> stop
> in our culture
> where red is a warning, and men
> threaten each other with final violence: *I will drink*
> *your blood.*   Your kiss
> is for them
>
> a sign of betrayal, your red
> lips suspect, unspeakable
> liberties as
> we cross the street   kissing
> against the light, singing, *This*
> *is the woman I woke from sleep, the woman that woke*
> *me sleeping.*[35]

I wondered aloud whether someone who was not aware of the extent to which
lesbian and nonlesbian women lead different lives can appreciate fully the impact of
these lines. It is the daily oppression, not the pink triangle and the Nazi concentration
camps (in which up to a quarter million lesbians and gay men were executed):
simply two women who cannot, without shock, disgust, possible physical violence
from passersby, show affection on a city street.[36] "I am a pervert," Judy Grahn writes,
"therefore I have learned/to keep my hands to myself in public."[37]

I linked my own experiences, my own anger with that of the poets. I do not
want my own reality to be distorted by someone's insistence that my life is "just
like" that of a heterosexual woman. We ended the class with Adrienne Rich's
words:

> Two friends of mine, both artists, wrote me about reading the
> *Twenty-One Love Poems* with their male lovers, assuring me how
> "universal" the poems were. I found myself angered, and when I asked

myself why, I realized that it was anger at having my work essentially assimilated and stripped of its meaning, "integrated" into heterosexual romance. That kind of "acceptance" of the book seems to me a refusal of its deepest implications. The longing to simplify, to defuse feminism by invoking "androgyny" or "humanism," to assimilate lesbian experience by saying that "relationship" is really all the same, love is always difficult—I see that as a denial, a kind of resistance, a refusal to read and hear what I've actually written, to acknowledge what I am.[38]

VI.

As teachers, we make choices which, consciously or not, reflect such denial. I wonder, for example, how many women's studies teachers are using as texts Rich's *Diving into the Wreck* (1973), *Poems: Selected and New, 1950-1974* (1975), or the Norton Critical Education, *Adrienne Rich's Poetry* (1975). Do they choose to teach poems from these earlier books to the exclusion of the more recent, explicitly lesbian poetry in *The Dream of a Common Language* (1978)? How prepared are they to explore this change with students who probably believe, among other myths, that they can always identify a lesbian, that women "discover" their lesbianism at an early age, that their own heterosexual lifestyles are comfortably fixed? How do they feel about the poetry of this fifty-one-year-old woman who raised three sons, this lesbian who writes, "I choose to walk here. And to draw this circle"?[39] As teachers, they can choose to ignore a poem like Rich's "For Judith, Taking Leave," written in 1962, but not published until *Poems: Selected and New* 1950-1974:

> ...that two women
> in love to the nerves' limit
> with two men—
> shared out in pieces
> to men, children, memories
> so different and so draining—
> should think it possible
> now for the first time
> perhaps, to love each other
> neither as fellow-victims
> nor as a temporary
> shadow of something better...
>
> that two women can meet
> no longer as cramped sharers
> of a bitter mutual secret
> but as two eyes in one brow
> receiving at one moment
> the rainbow of the world.[40]

Speaking in a 1976 interview about her decision to withhold this poem from publication for so long, Rich said:

When I wrote that, I didn't think of it as a lesbian poem. This is what I
have to keep reminding myself—that at that time I did not recognize, I did
not name the intensity of those feelings as I would name them today, *we*
did not name them. When I first chose not to publish that poem, I
thought, this is just a very personal poem, an occasional poem, it doesn't
carry the same weight or interest as other poems I would publish. But my
dismissing of it was akin to my dismissing of the relationship, although in
some ways I did not dismiss it—it was very much with me for a long
time.[41]

Looking at Rich's poetry today with the knowledge of her lesbianism and then
"dismissing" that knowledge as "less than essential" to the teaching of her poetry,
without sufficient "weight or interest," perhaps too risky for students, colleagues,
administrators, is to censor a vital part of contemporary women's poetry:

> *Homesick for myself for her*—as, after the heatwave
> breaks, the clear tones of the world
> manifest: cloud, bough, wall, insect, the very soul of light
> *homesick* as the fluted vault of desire
> articulates itself: *I am the lover and the loved,*
> *home and wanderer, she who splits*
> *firewood and she who knocks, a stranger*
> *in the storm,* two women, eye to eye
> measuring each other's spirit, each other's
>   limitless desire,
>   a whole new poetry beginning here.[42]

Although a teacher can choose to teach Rich's poetry without totally upsetting the academic concept of what constitutes "good" poetry, the decision to teach
a poet like Judy Grahn is immediately more complicated. Working-class, female,
and lesbian, Grahn has never had a stake in the established literary tradition and its
social/political/aesthetic values. She seems, at times, to mock them intentianally:
she calls one book *Edward the Dyke and Other Poems,* even though the title work
is clearly in prose and the word "dyke" can hardly help the book slip unobtrusively
onto a college reading list.

First published in what now seems another era—one offering comparatively
little lesbian poetry—her poems have helped to establish a tradition of women's/
lesbian poetry that is personal, accessible, nonhierarchical. One rhythmic and
ironic eight-line poem makes us look again at everyday language:

> I am the wall at the lip of the water
> I am the rock that refused to be battered
> I am the dyke in the matter, the other
> I am the wall with a womanly swagger
> I am the dragon, the dangerous dagger
> I am the bulldyke, the bulldagger
>
> and I have been many a wicked grandmother
> and I shall be many a wicked daughter.[43]

Most often, she seems to hide the "craft" of her poems, giving the impression that she wrote them quickly—without careful attention to structure and language and rhythm.

In "A Woman Is Talking to Death," a deceptively "nonpoetic" opening, the narrative of a motorcyclist killed instantaneously on the bridge, leads into a tightly woven series of events, prose interrogations, lyric passages, and recurrent phrases that create a painfully wonderful poem that has become something of a touchstone of lesbian-feminist writing. "That's a fact," Grahn keeps observing as she builds image after image of women ignored, derided, abused. The central "fact" of the poem is finally the poet's own lesbianism. In a society that perceives lesbians as committing "indecent acts" and that leers at women who kiss each other, who call each other "lovers," who admit to "wanting" another woman, Grahn forces a rethinking of both language and the assumptions behind it. In "a mock interroga-tion," the fourth section of this nine-part poem, Grahn writes:

> I confess to kissing the top of a 55 year old woman's head in the snow in boston, who was hurt more deeply than I have ever been hurt, and I wanted her as very few people have wanted me—I wanted her and me to own and control the city we lived in, to staff the hospital I knew would mistreat her, to patrol the streets controlling the men who would murder or disfigure or disrupt us, not accidentally with machines, but on purpose, because we are not allowed out on the street alone—
>
> Have you ever committed any indecent acts with women?
>
> Yes, many. I am guilty of allowing suicidal women to die before my eyes or in my ears or under my hands because I thought I could do nothing. I am guilty of leaving a prostitute who held a knife to my friend's throat to keep us from leaving, because we would not sleep with her, we thought she was old and fat and ugly; I am guilty of not loving her who needed me; I regret all the women I have not slept with or comforted, who pulled themselves away from me for lack of something I had not the courage to fight for, for us, our life, our planet, our city, our meat and potatoes, our love. These are indecent acts, lacking courage, lacking a certain fire behind the eyes, which is the symbol, the raised fist, the sharing of resources, the resistance that tells death he will starve for lack of the fat of us, our extra. Yes I have committed acts of indecency with women and most of them were acts of omission. I regret them bitterly.[44]

In classes where I have read aloud these lines, students have spoken of being moved by them, of reacting emotionally to the lesbian oppression Grahn des-cribes. For students who do not themselves share that oppression, poetry that can transcend that gap in experience is, I think, especially important to teach. For students in women's studies or other courses who associate feminism and lesbian-ism exclusively with white, economically privileged women and of poetry as the province of the well-to-do and formally educated, Grahn's writing destroys more than one erroneous assumption.

Still more issues get raised when a teacher decides to teach the work of lesbian poets who suffer additional oppression because they are Asian Ameri-can, Black, Latina, or Native American, as well as of more than one racial/ethnic heritage. If homophobia throws up one formidable barrier between lesbian poetry and the non-lesbian reader, racism adds one that is at least as high for the non-Third World reader—and teacher—of poetry by lesbians of color. Those of us who are white teachers of this poetry need, I think, to be prepared to approach directly the issue(s) of racism, even as we recognize the complexity and difficulty of doing so.[45]

While most of the non-lesbian students I have taught have had strong negative responses to the explicit lesbian sexuality in Lorde's "Love Poem," most of the white students have had equally strong responses to her poem, "Power," about the acquittal of a white police officer in the fatal shooting of a ten-year-old Black boy:

> Today that 37 year old white man with 13 years of police forcing
> was set free
> by 11 white men who said they were satisfied
> justice had been done
> and one black woman who said "They convinced me"
> meaning
> they had dragged her 4'10" black woman's frame
> over the hot coals of four centuries of white male approval
> until she let go the first real power she ever had
> and lined her own womb with cement
> to make a graveyard for our children.
>
> I have not been able to touch the destruction within me.
> But unless I learn to use the difference
> between poetry and rhetoric
> my power too will run corrupt as poisonous mold
> or lie limp and useless as an unconnected wire
> and one day I will take my teenaged plug
> and connect it to the nearest socket
> raping an 85 year old white woman who is somebody's mother
> and as I beat her senseless and set a torch to her bed
> a greek chorus will be singing in 3/4 time
> "Poor thing. She never hurt a soul. What beasts they are."[46]

Faced with white students who focused on the pain of the eighty-five-year old white woman to the near or total exclusion of the dead boy, the Black woman on the jury, or the poet herself, I have talked about the need both to empathize with someone else's pain and to distinguish between institutional violence and violence that is a ("corrupt") response to it. Faced with students who argue that "anyone" could have written this poem, I have stressed the importance of reading it as a statement by someone who *is* Black, and therefore identifies strongly with a boy shot by a policeman who "said in his own defense 'I didn't notice the size or nothing else/only the color'..." Faced with white students who have found it difficult enough to read Lorde as "just" a political Black poet, and by Black non-lesbian students who clearly have preferred to focus exclusively on her Black identity, I have stressed that she is a lesbian, a mother, a feminist, a teacher, a poet who has also written:

I have no sister no mother no children
left
only a tideless ocean of moonlit women
in all shades of loving
learning the dance of electrical tenderness
no father no mother would teach them.[47]

Such poetry underscores once again the importance of not simplifying, not homo-
genizing, of recognizing fully the significant differences among individual lesbian
poets, as well as the difference between poets who define themselves as lesbians
and poets who do not. Although I would not argue that having all of this information about a given poet is always essential to a reading of her poetry, I do think that
it often makes a crucial difference in how we choose to read and then teach a poet's
work.

To teach such poems we need to model the kind of openness and directness
in exploring lesbianism in the classroom that we would like our students to adopt. I
recognize the difficulties of doing this—for women who define themselves as
lesbians and for women who do not. Still, I do not believe that we can effect
positive, radical changes in our students (and in ourselves) without pushing
beyond feminist analysis and thought to an approach that combines these with the
personal exploration which can lead to basic change.

VII.

Even as I put forth such an approach to teaching lesbian poetry, I am fully
aware of the growing number of external obstacles to it. This past summer a
University of Texas teacher "lost her teaching job because she invited speakers
from Austin Lesbian/Gay Political Caucus and Austin Lambda to speak to her class
on ' "The Politics of American Culture'."[48] Oklahoma has already passed a law that
closely paraphrases California's defeated Briggs initiative: "to fire or refuse to
hire ... any teacher, counselor, aide, or administrator (in the public school system)
... who advocates, solicits, encourages, or promotes private or public homosexual
activity ... that is likely to come to the attention of students or parents ...." The
Oklahoma law prohibits *anyone* who assumes its essential validity from discussing
lesbianism (or male homosexuality) in the classroom.[49] Although aimed specifically at public school teachers, such right-wing legislation seems designed to effect
repression and witch-hunts throughout the educational system. Along with the
lesbian and gay rights ordinances being consistently rejected or repealed across the
country, such legislation makes concrete institutionalized homophobia and
further compounds the difficulties both of teaching lesbian poetry and of being—
and being identified as—a lesbian.

The case for lesbian poetry can, of course, be allowed to rest on the academically acceptable belief in literary quality. Teaching it does, after all, expose students
to much of the "best" of contemporary women's writing. But teaching it as *lesbian*
poetry moves us to shakier, less traditionally academic ground. In its conscious
risk-taking, in its affirmation of our diversity, exploring lesbianism and lesbian
poetry as an integral part of women's lives and literature constitutes one facet of

what the National Women's Studies Association has characterized as women's studies "at its best": "a vision of a world free not only from sexism but also from racism, class bias, ageism, heterosexual bias—from all the ideologies and institutions that have consciously or unconsciously oppressed and exploited some for the advantage of others."[50] And such exploration adds one more, badly needed voice to the struggle to achieve some semblance of justice and compassion in this country.

Notes

[1] See Louise Bernikow's introduction to *The World Split Open 1552-1950* (New York: Vintage, 1974), especially her comments regarding Katherine Philips, "The English Sappho" (1631-1664); Aphra Behn (1640-1689); and Christina Rosetti (1830-1894). See also the entry on Margaret Fuller in Jonathan Katz, *Gay American History* (New York: Crowell, 1976), pp. 461-467; Josephine Donovan's "The Unpublished Love Poems of Sarah Orne Jewett." *Frontiers* (Fall, 1979), pp. 26-31; Willa Cather's *April Twilights* (1903) (Lincoln: University of Nebraska Press, 1976); and Lillian Faderman's *Surpassing the Love of Men* (New York: William Morrow, 1981).

[2] Dudley Fitts in his foreword to *Sappho: A New Translation* by Mary Barnard (Berkeley: University of California, 1958), pp. vii-viii. Fitts goes on to say: "We have heard a great deal about Sappho, and we know almost nothing." Has anyone who has read John Donne's heterosexual love poetry ever even suggested that only by going outside his poems to learn about the details of his life could we establish that he had been intimately involved with women? For a discussion of Sappho's reputation since her death in 558 B.C.; the burning of her poems in the Eastern Roman Empire (c. 380 A.D.) and Western Europe (eleventh century A.D.); and several distorting translations of her poems, see Dolores Klaich's "Sappho and the Lesbian Ghetto" in *Woman + Woman* (New York: Morrow, 1974), pp. 129-160.

[3] In "The Female World of Love and Ritual: Relations between Women in Nineteenth-Century America," Carroll Smith-Rosenberg writes: "The essential question is not whether these women had genital contact and can therefore be defined as heterosexual or homosexual. The twentieth-century tendency to view human love and sexuality within a dichotomized universe of deviance and normality, genitality and platonic love, is alien to the emotions and attitudes of the nineteenth century and fundamentally distorts the nature of these women's emotional interactions" (*Signs* 1, no. 1 (Autumn, 1975):8). I include Dickinson here because she wrote poetry that expresses profound emotional attachments to other women. For her and for other women who lived before this century, this seems to me to be the key issue, *not* whether her love for women was expressed sexually and regardless of the state of her relationships with men; I agree with Smith-Rosenberg that our definitions of lesbian and heterosexual, especially in the 1980s, have no applicability to an earlier period. For more discussion of Emily Dickinson, see Lillian Faderman's essay in this book. See also Frederick L. Morey, "Emily Dickinson's Elusive Lover," *Higginson Journal*, no. 18 (1978), pp. 28-34; Paula Bennett, "The Language of Love: Emily Dickinson's Homoerotic Poetry," *Gai Saber* 1 (Spring, 1977) and Jennifer Woodul, "Much Madness is Divinist Sense," *Furies* (February 1972).

[4] *Rising Tides*, ed. Laura Chester and Sharon Barba (New York: Washington Square Press, 1973); *No More Masks!*, ed. Florence Howe and Ellen Bass (Garden City, N.Y.: Doubleday Anchor, 1973).

[5] *Rising Tides*, p. 280

[6]Wieber, in *No More Masks!*, pp. 361–362; reprinted in *Lesbian Poetry*, ed. Elly Bulkin and Joan Larkin (Watertown, Mass.: Persephone Press, 1981).

[7]*We Become New*, ed. Lucille Iverson and Kathryn Ruby (New York: Bantam, 1975).

[8]*The World Split Open*, pp. 14–15.

[9]May Sarton, *A World of Light* (New York: Norton, 1976), p. 22.

[10]Swenson, "To Confirm a Thing," in *Amazon Poetry*, ed. Elly Bulkin and Joan Larkin (Brooklyn, New York: Out & Out Books, 1975), p. 81. "To Confirm a Thing" was originally published in Swenson's *Another Animal: Poems* (New York: Scribner's, 1954). See also "Poet to Tiger" and "Deciding" in *New & Selected Things Taking Place* (New York: Atlantic-Little, Brown, 1978).

[11]*The Ladder* was published by the Daughters of Bilitis from 1956 to 1970; it was published independently until 1972 when it ceased publication. A reprint of the complete *Ladder* was issued in 1975 by Arno Press (New York). *Lesbiana: Book Reviews from the Ladder*, ed. Barbara Grier, was published by Naiad Press (1976). *Lesbian Lives, Biographies of Women from the Ladder; The Lavender Herring: Lesbian Essays from the Ladder;* and *Lesbians Home Journal: Stories from the Ladder*, all edited by Barbara Grier and Coletta Reid, were published by Diana Press (1976). Editor of *The Ladder* from 1968 to 1972 and a frequent contributor for most of the life of the magazine, Barbara Grier wrote most frequently under the name of Gene Damon, as well as under a number of other pseudonyms.

[12]In *Gay American History*, Jonathan Katz documents "the simultaneous witch-hunting of 'perverts' and 'subversives'...taking place" from 1950–1955 (p. 91). A supporter of Senator Joseph McCarthy, Senator Kenneth Wherry, Republican floor leader, is quoted in a July 17, 1950, *New York Post* interview with Max Lerner: "'You can't hardly separate homosexuals from subversives,' the Senator told me. 'Mind you, I don't say every subversive is a homosexual. But a man of low morality is a menace in the government, whatever he is, and they are all tied up together'" (p. 95). In the same interview, he says: "You can stretch the security risk further if you want to...but right now I want to start with the homosexuals. When we get through with them, then we'll see what comes next" (p. 96).

[13]All quotes are from the Vintage edition. See also Judith McDaniel's "A Conversation with Muriel Rukeyser," *New Women's Times Feminist Review*, April 25–May 8, 1980, pp. 4–5, 18–19.

[14]*The Work of a Common Woman: The Collected Poetry of Judy Grahn, 1964–1977* (New York: St. Martin's Press, 1978), p. 73; Reprinted in *Lesbian Poetry*.

[15]*To Lesbians Everywhere* (New York: Violet Press, 1976), pp. 42–43.

[16]Unpublished material and discussions with Judith McDaniel. Rich, *Signs* 5:4 (Summer, 1980):648. Rich writes: "I mean the term *lesbian continuum* to include a range—through each woman's life and throughout history—of woman-identified experience; not simply the fact that a woman has had or consciously desired genital sexual experience with another woman. If we expand it to embrace many more forms of primary intensity between and among women, including the sharing of a rich inner life, the bonding against male tyranny, the giving and receiving of practical and political support; if we can also hear it in such associations as *marriage resistance* and the 'haggard' behavior identified by Mary Daly...we begin to grasp breadths of female history and psychology which have lain out of reach as a consequence of limited, mostly clinical, definitions of 'lesbianism'" (pp. 648–649).

[17]Hull, "'Under the Days': The Buried life of Angelina Weld Grimké," *Conditions: Five, The Black Women's Issue* (1979):17-25.

[18]Allen, "Beloved Women: The Lesbian in American Indian Culture," *Conditions: Seven* (1981): 65; reprinted in *Lesbian Poetry.*

[19]Conversation with Paula Gunn Allen; see also Allen, "Beloved Women," pp. 67-87. Jacqueline Higgins Rosebrook makes the same point regarding loss of power in "Look What You've Done to My Song," *Heresies,* 10 (1980): 84.

[20]Noda, letter to the author, October 4, 1978. See also Barbara Noda, Kitty Tsui, and Z Wong, "Coming Out: We Are Here in the Asian Community: A Dialogue with Three Asian Women," *Bridge* 7:1 (Spring, 1979):22-24.

[21]Gidlow, "Footprints in the Sands of the Sacred," *Frontiers* 4:3 (1979):48-49.

[22]Ibid., p. 50.

[23]Hull, p. 20. See also Audre Lorde, "Scratching the Surface: Some Notes on Barriers to Women and Loving," *Black Scholar* 9:7 (April 1978):31-35. Barbara Smith writes: "Black women are still in the position of having to 'imagine,' discover and verify Black lesbian literature because so little has been written from an avowedly lesbian perspective. The near non-existence of Black lesbian literature which other Black lesbians and I so deeply feel has everything to do with the politics of our lives, the total suppression of identity that all Black women, lesbian and not, must face" ("Toward a Black Feminist Criticism," *Conditions: Two* [Fall, 1977]:39).

[24]Bernikow includes blues lyrics and protest songs of working women in *The World Split Open,* although none of the songs she cites has lesbianism as a theme. "B.D. Blues" is available on *When Women Sang the Blues* and on *AC/DC Blues: Gay Jazz Reissues.* In Chris Albertson's discussion of Bessie Smith in *Gay American History,* he quotes "The Boy in the Boat": "When you see two women walking hand in hand,/Just look 'em over and try to understand..." (p. 76).

[25]Paul Lauter's "Working-Class Women's Literature—An Introduction to Study" contains a lengthy bibliography (*Radical Teacher* [December 1979]:16-26).

[26]Rich, "Compulsory Heterosexuality and Lesbian Existence," p. 649.

[27]Peg Cruikshank's experience reveals an important aspect of this problem: "I had been on campus less than a week when a woman professor said to me: 'Now, Peg, don't let those lesbians take over the women's center.' Curious, I went to the center to ask what it offered for lesbians. Nothing. 'We haven't been able to get any lesbians to come here,' said the person in charge. So much for lesbian takeover" ("Beware Young Ladies, They're Fooling You: Women's Studies at Minnewaska State," *Radical Teacher* 6 [December, 1977]:37). See also Bulkin's "Heterosexism and Women's Studies," *Radical Teacher* (December 1980); Cruikshank's "Lesbians in Academia," in *Our Right to Love,* ed. Ginny Vida, produced in cooperation with the women of the National Gay Task Force (Englewood Cliffs, N.J.: Prentice-Hall, 1978), pp. 164-166; and Judith McDaniel's "Is There Room for Me in the Closet or My Life as the Only Lesbian Professor," *Heresies* 7 (Spring 1979):36-39, reprinted in *The Lesbian Path,* 2d. ed. Margaret Cruikshank (San Francisco: Double Axe Books, 1981), pp. 196-202.

[28]Adrienne Rich in "An Interview with Adrienne Rich: Part I" by Elly Bulkin, *Conditions: One* (Spring 1977):58.

[29]"The Transformation of Silence into Language and Action," *Sinister Wisdom* 6 (Summer, 1978):14; reprinted in Lorde's *The Cancer Journals* (Argyle, N.Y.: Spinsters, Ink, 1980), p. 23.

[30]Teachers wanting a lesbian speaker but unaware of local groups that might be able to provide such a speaker can consult the "Lesbian National Resource List" in *Our Right to Love*, pp. 288-318, or contact the Lesbian Herstory Archives, P.O. Box 1258, New York, N.Y. 10116.

[31]Lorde, *The New York Head Shop and Museum* (Detroit: Broadside Press, 1974), p. 26; reprinted in *Lesbian Poetry*.

[32]Sherman, *With Anger/With Love*. (Amherst: Mulch Press, 1974), p. 8; reprinted in *Lesbian Poetry*.

[33]"Duration," in *With Anger/With Love*, p. 15.

[34]Bulkin, "Beyond the Word," *Majority Report*, August 8, 1974, p. 10; "Poetry," *Majority Report*, January 11, 1975, p. 9.

[35]Broumas, *Beginning with O* (New Haven: Yale University Press, 1977), p. 62; reprinted in *Lesbian Poetry*.

[36]Ira Glasser, "The Yellow Star and the Pink Triangle," *The New York Times*, September 10, 1977, Op Ed Page. Glasser's figure for the number of lesbians and gay men executed by the Nazis is for the period 1937-1945; they were required to wear pink triangles in the concentration camps.

[37]Grahn, "A Woman is Talking to Death," *The Work of a Common* Woman, p. 128; reprinted in *Lesbian Poetry*.

[38]Adrienne Rich in "An Interview with Adrienne Rich: Part II," *Conditions: Two* (Fall 1977):58.

[39]Rich, "Twenty-One Love Poems," *The Dream of a Common Language, Poems, 1974-1977* (New York: Norton, 1978), p. 36.

[40]Rich, *Poems: Selected and New, 1950-1974* (New York: Norton, 1975), p. 133; reprinted in *Lesbian Poetry*.

[41]"An Interview with Adrienne Rich: Part I," p. 64.

[42]Rich, "Transcendental Etude," *The Dream of a Common Language*, p. 76; reprinted in *Lesbian Poetry*.

[43]Grahn, *The Work of a Common Woman*, p. 98; reprinted in *Lesbian Poetry*.

[44]Grahn, *The Work of a Common Woman*, pp. 124-125; reprinted in *Lesbian Poetry*.

[45]Some of the basic issues involved are discussed in Margaret Strobel, "Fighting Two Colonialisms: Thoughts of a White Feminist Teaching about Third World Women," *Radical Teacher* 6 (December 1977):20-23; and Nancy Hoffman, "White Woman, Black Women: Inventing an Adequate Pedagogy," *Women's Studies Newsletter* 5 (Spring 1977):21-24. Hoffman writes: "There are two principles for white women who would teach about black women. First, do your research and class preparation more thoroughly than you would for teaching about your own female tradition or the majority white male Anglo-American one. You must be able to generalize about black women's culture when appropriate, and you will probably feel ill at ease when doing so. Second, be prepared to play dual and conflicting roles; only sometimes will your own anti-racism and your solidarity with other women protect you from representing the group oppressing black women" (p. 22). These comments are particularly relevant when the teacher of poetry by lesbians of color is both white *and* heterosexual. See also Bulkin, "Racism and Writing: Some Implications for White Lesbian Critics," *Sinister Wisdom* 13 (Spring 1980):3-22; Barbara Smith, "Racism and Women's Studies," *Frontiers* (Spring 1980):48-49. Adrienne Rich, "Disloyal to Civilization:

Feminism, Racism, Gynephobia," *On Lies, Secrets, and Silence* (New York: Norton, 1979), pp. 275–310; and *Top Ranking: A Collection of Essays on Racism and Classism in the Lesbian Community*, ed. Sara Bennett and Joan Gibbs (Brooklyn: February 3rd Press, 1980).

[46]Lorde, *The Black Unicorn* (New York: Norton, 1978), pp. 108–109; reprinted in *Lesbian Poetry.*

[47]"Scar," *The Black Unicorn*, p. 49.

[48]"No Gay Teaching," *off our backs* December 1980, p. 14.

[49]John Mehring, "The Briggs Initiative is Alive and Well—and Living in Oklahoma," *Gay Community News*, July 7, 1979, pp. 8–9; Jeanne Cordova, "Rights and Referendums," *Lesbian Tide* 8 (July/August, 1978):14.

[50]"Constitution of the National Women's Studies Association," *Women's Studies Newsletter* 5 (Spring, 1977):6.

Lesbian Literature:
A Third World Feminist
Perspective

Dialogue transcribed from a taped conversation, April 1981.

Cherríe Moraga and Barbara Smith

"A Baseline From Which to Build
a Political Understanding:
The Background and Goals of the Course."

Barbara Smith: I'd taught Black women's literature, interdisciplinary courses on Black women and talked about Lesbianism as an "out" lesbian in my "Introduction to Women's Studies" courses, but I really wanted to do a Lesbian lit. course. Lesbian literature had never been offered by the Women's Studies program at the University of Massachusetts in Boston, although the program is almost ten years old. There was a gay literature course that hadn't been offered for a while. It had been cotaught by a gay man and a Lesbian, but its orientation was quite a bit different from what I had in mind.

Cherríe Moraga: Well, Lesbian literature had been taught a number of times at San Francisco State through the English department. I had also taken some other women's studies courses which focused on Lesbianism. My major motivation for wanting to teach the class was that I thought it was a perfect place to intergrate a political perspective that basically centered on Lesbians of color, since my politics feel so Lesbian-identified. The other motivation came in response to taking other women's studies classes and Lesbian-related courses that were so completely white and middle-class. I wanted to teach a course that covered what I thought was missing from those classes. I thought I could bring in an integrated perspective.

B: I had no intention of teaching what I called on the first day of class "Rich White Women."

C: Indeed.

B: The Renée Viviens and Natalie Barney types and shit. No interest whatsoever, because they do get taught, and some of them even get taught in straight literature classes.

C: The other thing is too that in gay literature classes what is usually taught are books like *Rubyfruit Jungle* and whatever stuff is as mass-market as can be. Not necessarily feminist stuff. And then, in a Lesbian course taught by a white woman, you would get racist and classist selections by default.

B: One major goal was to familiarize the women who took the course with the writing of women of color. When you teach a Lesbian literature course on white writers, there will be segments of people in the class who know the material on some level. Whereas if you're teaching the work of women of color, you're basically dealing with a blank slate, people who don't know the writers at all, who haven't heard of them. The other goal was for them to get a grasp of how the issue of racism in the women's movement connected to them. I felt that it was impossible to talk about the literature of women of color without talking about the reality of racism also.

C: One of my goals was actually to teach a course on the theory of oppression through a feminist perspective. I really wanted to talk about how Lesbians function in a positive and visionary way for a feminist future, for progressive change, social change. But at the same time, I was really clear about wanting to talk about Lesbianism as oppression and to talk about homophobia. Regardless of their color, most of the women in the class had lesbian oppression in common, which gave them some sensitivity to making connections with racial oppression and class oppression. Some of the students didn't know they were oppressed. But as in teaching a class whose students are predominantly Third World and female, there would be a source of oppression to work from.

B: There'd be a baseline from which to build a political understanding.

"People Came Around": Our Students

B: Most of my class were white women and Lesbians. There were some white straight women and one Black straight woman, but no Lesbians of color who attended on a regular basis. I did everything possible to inform women of color about the class. I talked about this difficulty to the students from the beginning and I think at a certain point they thought I was saying that I didn't want *them* to be there, but I think that they began to understand what the significance was of having Third World women actually in attendance as we got into the subject matter. University of Massachusetts in Boston is an urban university that basically serves working-class and lower-middle-class students. The composition of the class did not reflect the racial composition of the campus. There are still, despite cutbacks, significant numbers of women of color. Not just Afro-American women, but Latinas, people from the Caribbean, Asian women, all kinds of people go there. But what began to be obvious is that the risks involved for a woman of color to take a course called "Lesbian Literature," whether she was a Lesbian or not were high, particularly if she *was* a Lesbian. As far as age was concerned, most of the people who took the course were in their early twenties.

C: Well, my class was also predominantly white. There were four women of color officially registered and fortunately often Third World women in the community would attend. The effect of the course? "People came around," as you would say. They had little or no exposure to the works of women of color, and they got some. In the first six weeks of the course, however, there was a great deal of tension in the room, particularly between the white women and Third World women. I experienced this tension as well. What came up was many of the white women in the room didn't know that they'd have to be dealing with racism when they came to a Lesbian lit. course.

B: Right, indeed.

C: What they told me, later, was that they had felt very intimidated by the subject matter; and that there was some unspoken resentment that this was a criterion for the course they had not anticipated. This tension didn't get resolved until enough time had passed where they indeed trusted that I wasn't just trying to make them feel bad. Instead they began to comprehend that the way I was defining "Lesbian Literature and Feminism" meant that they had to be antiracist.

B: Yep. Yep. Yep.

C: Because racism is an issue that makes white women feel so vulnerable, it early on set up a dynamic of some resistance between them and me and the women of color in the room.

B: Well, I must admit that despite what I consider to be the success of the course, I know that there were times that I felt alienated myself in the situation of virtually all-white women. I did feel like an anomaly at times. Sometimes some students were very sympathetic, like saying, "Isn't this hard for you to do? How can you do this? Don't you get tired of it?" I have found in all my teaching experience, I am constantly dealing with this contradiction of the powerfulness of being a teacher against the powerlessness of being Black. Most white university students have never had a Black teacher. That, in itself, is a mind trip. The teacher *is* in a position of power. I think it does a trip to white student's heads to have a Black person—a Black woman in particular—in that position over them when their general experience of Black persons in the society is in situations where Blacks are subordinate to them.

C: If not subordinate, then nonexistent.

B: Sometimes I really have the feeling in the classroom that the look in my white students' eyes is "What is she going to do next?!" Of just not knowing.... People have so many *negative* images of Black people. And teaching, particularly on a non-university level, has many *positive* connotations. A teacher is someone who *takes care.* In other words, their connotations of teacher are different from their connotations of Black.

C: Rightrightrightrightright.

B: Another thing is intellect. To have a Black person in a position of intellectual power over white people is UNKNOWN: You know? That's just a real mind trip on the children. (laughter) I mean how could the Black person know more than they do? AHHHHHHHHHH: (laughter) How could a Black person be teaching them *anything?* Just like I say in the introduction to *But Some of Us Are Brave: Black Women's Studies:* "How could somebody who looks like my maid or my fantasy of my maid teach me anything?"

C: Right. (laughter)

B: I'm supposed to know everything. I'm white.... (sigh, pause) Oh God save me.

C: My being a light-skinned Third World woman vs. being Black meant that in my class there was less of a specifically racial or color dynamic happening. But since my being Chicana formed my politics, which determined the makeup of the course, they felt at a disadvantage because they were being graded from my perspective. I think they wondered, "How can I learn something if I wasn't born into it?" when all along we, as working-class and Third World women, have been required to learn *and* teach outside of our own point of reference. But the existence of Third World students in the classroom made my existence much easier. It was a positive connection. However, I did notice, Barbara, what a difference it made to the Black women in the class when you came to visit and teach a section. Here was an unmistakable visible *out* Black Lesbian feminist. After your visit, in speaking to one Black woman in the class who was so moved by your appearance, I realized how rare it is to see someone like us teaching a class. I know the Latinas in the class felt that way about my teaching. The point is that I may be able to teach Black Lesbian literature well, but not like you. What I'm saying is that there's nothing like a passionate lived connection when you're teaching a subject.

B: Indeed. And also a cultural point of reference. When I was in your class I could use language and elicit responses that were useless in my class. There was no point in talking in Black language, about Black women's writing in a class that's basically white. I might have slipped occasionally, but, like Beverly Smith's old concept. they didn't "inspire the behavior."

"The Political Significance of Being a Dyke": The Design

B: We had arrived at wanting to teach these courses independently, but then when we found out what each other was doing, we talked about our course outlines together and actually developed courses that were fairly similar in topics, if not in reading lists.

C: I began the course trying to talk about the criteria on which Lesbian literature is examined. I used your definition of feminism. To paraphrase: *Feminism that is not about freeing all women, which means working class women, women of color, physically challenged women, etcetera, is not feminism but merely female self-aggrandizement.* We took some articles like Julia Penelope Stanley and Susan Wolfe's "Toward a Feminist Aesthetic" and an article by Bertha Harris, "Notes toward Defining the Nature of Lesbian Literature" and contrasted those against Elly Bulkin's article "Racism and Writing" and your article "Toward a Black Feminist Criticism." If Lesbian feminists are doing criticism then they are responsible for doing actively anticlassist, antiracist work, using anticlassist and antiracist criteria for examining those literatures.

B: We read the same articles and I guess had similar discussions. The students in my class—and this was pretty early in the semester—were quite critical of the white women writers, like Bertha Harris, June Arnold, et cetera who did not deal with issues of race and class, and it was good to have Elly Bulkin's article as a contrast.

C: Did you discuss Lesbian feminist aesthetics much?

B: No. We hardly talked about aesthetics at all, because to me aesthetics is talking about what makes something pretty as opposed to what makes something effective. We certainly talked about that—effectiveness.

C: When we discussed aesthetics we did so in relation to color and class. This led us to then examine the white middle-class bias of what is considered good art in the first place. What we did in terms of literary criticism grew from the perspective of trying to develop some kind of integrated (that is, not male and not white) defined sense of what is good work.

B: We also did a section in the course called "Forerunners, Prefeminist Lesbian Writing." I had an opportunity to show a slide show on Lesbian pulp fiction.[1] I wanted people to have an understanding that Lesbian literature existed pre-feminism. We had quite a debate over whether *The Black and White of It,* a recent book by Ann Allen Shockley, was feminist writing or not. I think that this was one of the first examples of how people's effort to be nonracist made it difficult for them actually to be critical of what we were discussing. In their eagerness not to be negative about a Black woman writer's work, they used different standards to approach it. In other words, because she was Black, they felt they couldn't say she wasn't explicitly feminist.

C: In my class we spent some time talking about Lesbianism outside of a feminist framework. Instead of using pre-feminist literature, however, we used some articles about specific sexual questions among Lesbians now. I felt that the majority of the women in the class came out as Lesbians through the feminist movement and had very little understanding of what it meant to be gay without the support of a woman-identified political movement. In some way, they had been sheltered from viscerally dealing with plain old queerdom. I felt that it was critical that a lot of them come to terms with that.

In contrast, I also included a section that was about Lesbian feminist visions of the future. This has been a heavy genre in Lesbian feminist writing. All the major books coming out around 1978 had a section that talked about a feminist vision in some way. Like the third section of *Gyn/Ecology,* which was supposed to be about Lesbian ecstasy. And then the last section of Susan Griffin's book *Women and Nature,* and the last section of Adrienne Rich's *The Dream of a Common Language.* And also Sally Gearhart's *The Wanderground* which is a feminist fantasy. These white writers were producing a body of literature that was talking about where we should go from here. My problem was that I could never get behind any of them (with the exception of Rich, who incidentally titled her final section "Not Somewhere Else, But Here," with the emphasis on the "Here"), and I didn't understand why. So in class we used *The Wanderground* as a way to seriously examine how that vision was in some way actually exclusive. It was not an all-encompassing vision, but was directed only to a particular group of women that could indeed feel liberated by the guidelines she had set forth. One of the best parts of the class was actually when Sally Gearhart came in and we could talk with her face to face. This then brought up the issue of a Lesbian feminist writer's commitment to speaking out of her reality but at the same time with a sense of inclusiveness.

Judy Grahn's work is a perfect example of doing just that. Judy is very clear about how her class has actually affected the kind of writing she does in terms of form and content. And also affected her politics. The pivotal point of the whole class was talking about the question of ethics by focusing on "A Woman is Talking to Death." That one long poem became the breakthrough for lots of women to really understand, not in an analytical way, or theoretical or abstract way, the political significance of being a dyke. Many white middle class feminists write ethical poetry but you can't get underneath it. It's not concrete. Judy's stuff in a very daily way helps you see how indeed she is up against all the forms of oppression and how they all collapse in on each other.

B: We talked about how the first moral dilemma that she poses is should she help out a Black man. Isn't it interesting that the poem actually begins with race? Besides accountability, violence, accidental violence, and the white-boy stupidity that got the motorcylce rider killed in the first place, race is up front. And when was the poem written? 1973? Before most people were even thinking about racial accountability as a feminist issue.

In my class we talked about the irony of the fact that the people who were really asking practical ethical questions were perverts—the people who were talking about having enough food for people to eat, trying to end race hatred, war, what-have-you. I think that's even different from so-called revolutionary male or nonfeminist women writers who might ask those very questions but whose perspective is ruined by homophobia. So we're talking about an ethical vision one could actually live with as opposed to an ethical vision that stops short of Lesbians and gay men.

C: Along with that I think a recurring theme that comes up in Lesbian literature—which is to me the heart of why I would bother to teach the course—is some kind of personal conviction that something between women could be different than what it has been before. By focusing upon the works of Audre Lorde, Judy Grahn, and Adrienne Rich as they come together you can see this basic theme repeated. Somehow maybe it's possible that between women racism, hunger, et cetera could be overcome.

B: As Adrienne says, "The decision to feed the world/is the real decision. No revolution/has chosen it. For that choice requires/that women shall be free."[2]

C: And along the same lines, the theme that goes through "A Woman Is Talking to Death" over and over again, is that of touching. Because she touches women she's a pervert, and yet the reality is that the true perversion or the true indecent act is when she didn't touch women.

B: Indeed, indeed.

C: Judy Grahn says, "Yes I have committed acts of indecency with women and most of them were acts of omission. I regret them bitterly."[3] And I think that there's the same kind of ethical frame of reference in Audre Lorde's work. Take a poem like "Between Ourselves," in which she writes, "I do not believe/our wants/have made all our lies/holy."[4] She refuses to use race as an excuse for imposing other forms of oppression. But it's all rooted in very concrete stuff. That's the critical difference.

B: I think the point about white working-class women being almost the only white writers who are appropriate to include in this kind of course is significant. It's not that we have a lot of white working-class writers to call upon, but the problem with white middle-class writers or upper-class women writers is that they only experience their oppression from at most two perspectives, which can limit the inclusiveness of their vision in their writing.

"Our Ideas Precede Our Means": The Materials

C: Unfortunately, things being as they are, there is very little literature by women of color, period, that's published, but particularly Lesbians of color, and so what we were both forced to do was to find it, to exchange some information ourselves and at the same time to get it from other people and copy. We had to use handouts because we don't have bound books. One of the things I wanted to say about that is that some of the strongest pieces of literature we had were on pieces of paper. One of the problems that is typically brought up about why women of color and/or Lesbians of color aren't really discussed in women's studies courses is that there isn't any available material and part of that is true. But it takes a real invested interest and commitment to find the stuff. Because it's actually there, but it's in feminist and Third World small-press form and published randomly in periodicals.

B: It's also much easier to find, at this point, collected writings of Black Lesbian writers because of publications like *Conditions: Five,* than writing of women of color who are not Afro-American.[5] It would have been much easier to teach a course using only Black Lesbians, but it would hardly have been comprehensive. Often white women in particular think only in terms of Black and white and think if they've added a few Black women to a course they've done what's expected of them. I think what we're describing is so typical of the position of Third World Lesbian feminists which is that our ideas precede our means.

C: Exactly, exactly.

B: The hardest to find book which dealt with racial issues was actually by a white woman writer: *The Changelings* by Jo Sinclair, written in the 1950s. We had only three copies of the book to pass among thirty people. Because of that process we ended up talking about the book last as opposed to where it actually appeared on the syllabus. And that was a really great book to end on since my class was almost entirely white. Although Jo Sinclair never publicly identified herself as a Lesbian, the book was written from a Lesbian and feminist perspective, and it talks about issues of race from the perspective of a Jewish woman. In other words, it brought together many of the themes of the course because it was talking about race, but from a white woman's perspective. It was Lesbian literature in that it focused upon a friendship between a Jewish girl and a Black girl. People really got into the book seriously, and most of them felt they had never read a book like that—and of course most people will never read it because it's out of print. Some feminist publisher should seriously consider reprinting Sinclair's work.

"They Taught White Men, So Why Can't They Teach Black Women": The Third World Lesbian and Women's Studies

B: What concerns me here about this dialogue is how much of an exception is it going to be to the body of the book *Lesbian Studies* as a whole? We're going to be talking about Third World Lesbian literature, and somebody else can be talking about the marvelousness of using Mary Daly's thing as a jumping-off point.

C: Could we speak to that issue? Because we're talking to each other, we're assuming a lot of stuff as givens which are givens to us. But maybe if you could articulate exactly why we're convinced that we're probably among the few people in the country who are teaching any women's studies courses from this perspective....

B: Okay. Number one, there are virtually no women of color who are out as Lesbians who are in a position to teach courses in universities. This is one of the ironies of our existence. There are Third World Lesbians, but very few have the wherewithal to be able to teach a class at a university. There are also Third World Lesbians who do teach at universities who are not out or who are not feminists. So in other words the pool of people who can teach these courses is virtually nonexistent. Very similar to how there are very few people involved in Third World women's studies from a feminist perspective, period. Like what I have found is that the people who have the politics don't have the jobs, or the credentials. The people who have the credentials and the jobs don't have the politics.

C: So you mean also white women who could be teaching stuff about Third World women...

B: Aren't at universities, either? Probably, probably.

C: In women's studies there aren't the Third World women. But what about the white women who are already teaching there?

B: The white women who are teaching there—they definitely don't have the perspective in the main because if they did women's studies would have a whole different look than it does. I don't think it's trashing to say that white women have been extremely limited by their whiteness and their class backgrounds, because every text, every piece of tangible evidence that you pick up indicates that. In other words it's not just an impression, it's a reality. You can document it. All you have to do is go into your women's studies section at your university and see what's being taught.

C: I think that on our various campuses, there has been at least some effort to begin. There are some white women teaching who do some Third World women's studies and are trying to do some substantial integration in the curriculum. But it's very slow.

B: Another thing is that there's little Lesbian literature taught anyway. Of all the women's studies courses taught, it might be the one taught least, because of the issues and risks involved. This brings up the issue of so-called professional security and whether you're intending on making it in the university system. I think it's also significant that the two people who taught *these* Lesbian lit. courses had *no* interest whatsoever in having careers in the university.

C: Indeed. So we didn't have as much to lose.

B: Yeah, in other words we could be Third World Lesbians, teaching Third World literature, teaching Lesbian literature. And the thing is we didn't expect a future.

C: Right.

B: Another thing I was going to say is that what really makes me angry about straight white women's studies teachers in general is like how they can never see where women of color and Lesbians would logically fit into their subject matter. Women in my classes would come back and talk about other women's studies courses they were taking simultaneously, and they would complain bitterly about the narrowness of a women's studies course that the very semester before they might have taken on face value. And I think they only had this consciousness by having been involved in my course at the same time.

C: Right, exactly.

B: But the thing is, it really makes me mad that I can look at a course outline and say, "Well, Third World women should go here, Lesbianism should go there, blah, blah, blah," and yet women's studies teachers are so totally incapable of doing this. Why?

C: I think basically the mentality of most programs is we will teach white middle-class, heterosexual women for all our courses *except* in the Lesbian literature course where we will teach white lesbians and in the Third World women's course where we will teach straight Third World women. And that's it. (laughter)

B: Perfect.

C: I mean then everything's covered in the curriculum.

B: Perfect, perfect.

C: So if you happen to be a Third World Lesbian, forget it. Because there's not going to be one course that you could totally relate to. Your Lesbianism gets dealt with in an all-white atmosphere and your color gets dealt with in a straight context. Then they want to know why there are no Third World women or Third World Lesbians taking women's studies.

B: Right, indeed.

C: And certainly you're not going to hear anything about Lesbianism in any other department.

B: Right, unless it's abnormal psychology.

C: And what you find in ethnic studies programs is probably not going to be very much about women.

B: Another factor is that we are active as feminists. That's another thing that would bring us to this commitment about what to do in a classroom. I don't see teaching as political work, but certainly my political consciousness affects what I think is important to teach. Which brings up the point, how translatable is this? Do we really believe white women can teach these classes? Because my feeling is, they can.

C: Oh yeah, sure.

B: It's not about them teaching it as we would teach it, but teaching it as opposed to all that alien crap that they are teaching.

C: Well, to repeat a point that has been made over and over again. If white women could teach white-boyism for so many years, why couldn't they teach Third World women's stuff? After all, they aren't white men, anymore than they are Third World women. They could particularly teach Third World women's literature because literature opens you up into the mind of another person. They taught white men, so why can't they teach Black women?

B: Hey? Well, you see, because white people are *normal.* The norm. (laughter) But in reality the reason that one thing appears easy and the other hard is that confronting the experience of women of color calls white women's lives into question in a way that the writing of white boys just doesn't. They can remain aloof.

Because they're not having to examine their relative power in relationship to poor and Third World people, nor their own role as collaborators with the very people who oppress them.

C: See, I believe that the design of our Lesbian lit. courses could be applied to virtually any women's studies course.

B: Oh, of course, absolutely.

C: Hopefully, our own students have a hit now, to go into other courses and check out if the only writers being discussed are Susan Griffin, Adrienne Rich, Mary Daly, you know...

B: Honor Moore.

C: Honor Moore. Olga Broumas, and the only issues being examined are "transformation of language."

B: "Silences in language."

C: Yeah. "Changing silence into language".... It's not that for women and particularly Lesbian, writers that this is not an important critical approach, but it's only *one* theme. It's only *one* way to look at our writings. It's only *one* mode of expressing our conflicts as Lesbian writers. Compare, for instance, how often the word "language" comes up for one writer and how often the word "seeing" or "hunger" or "touch" comes up for another. What might these two writers have in common, what is the difference between them in terms of color, class, et cetera. The point is that if you do teach a course that involves a Third World woman's perspective, a lot of the assumptions that you are making in the course are going to be turned around. I think this is terrifying to teachers because to bring in another body of information would mess up their whole system.

B: Sure. Absolutely. Without question.

C: Like, for instance, I know a woman who is nearly completing a thesis on a certain aspect of Lesbian literature. I asked her why it was she had not included the work of Third World women, she being politically a very conscious woman. She told me that for her at this point to try to include Third World women would mean including a whole set of other issues that would alter her thesis entirely. What I began to think of then was, "Well, how valid, then, are her conclusions?" If, for instance, you're making the point that such and such is a common thread in Lesbian literature and Lesbian experience but are excluding a whole mass of people, how true are your points, ultimately?

B: Virtually, not at all, You see, this is the fallacy of white knowledge.

C: Here we go. What Lesbian feminists need to be responsible for is producing a body of literature that makes people have to get up and move. Why use the word "feminist" if you're talking about a body of literature that rationalizes people's complacency? Their internal psychological dilemmas may be very interesting, but if they prevent the reader from ever having to deal with the woman down the street...

B: With race, class, and color...

C: What's happened in Lesbian literature too often is romanticizing relationships between women. We only have to look very close at home and can go off in our little enclaves and never have to be accountable to a larger struggle.

B: The criterion for women's studies courses is that they should reflect the experiences of *all* women.

C:AAALLLLI.

B: Given the practicality, that's not always physically possible. But that's the goal. And that does not mean tokenism.

C: But if a course is designed to reflect differences and commonalities between women, then to mid-way introduce an issue that was overlooked—for instance, aging women or physically challenged women—should not throw the intent of the entire course off, but instead enhance its goals, whether the course be "Women and Psychology," "Women's Spirituality," what-have-you. We have to teach courses with the desire to be challenged by our students. We're all ethnocentric. There's always something more to know.

[See Appendix for course syllabi.]

Notes

[1]This slide show by Maida Tilchen and others has never been distributed. See Resources.

[2]Adrienne Rich, "Hunger," *The Dream of A Common Language* (New York: Norton, 1978), p. 13.

[3]Judy Grahn, "A Woman Is Talking to Death," *Collected Poems* (New York: St. Martin's Press, 1978), p. 125.

[4]Audre Lorde, "Between Ourselves," *The Black Unicorn*, (New York: Norton, 1978), p. 113. "Between Ourselves" was originally published in 1976 by Eidolon Editions, Point Reyes, California.

[5]With the completion of collections like the Latina Anthology *Comapaneras,* edited by La Colectiva Latinoamericana (in progress) and *This Bridge Called My Back,* edited by Cherrí Moraga and Gloria Anzaldúa (Watertown, Massachusetts: Persephone Press, 1981), works by Lesbians of color from many racial/cutural backgrounds are becoming increasingly available in print.

Homophobia in the Classroom

Nancy Manahan

I teach English and women's studies at a small community college. One evening after my "Philosophy of Women's Roles" class, a student took me aside.

"I just thought you ought to know that some of the people in the class are very upset. They say that if you bring up the gay lifestyle one more time, they are going to the administration and complain. And they're telling other people not to take your class unless they want to learn about gay lifestyles."

I felt afraid, hurt, and angry. It seemed to me I almost never brought up lesbian or gay issues. I had been silent about my own lesbianism. I had shut my mouth so many times when I'd wanted to speak. If the students who were upset only knew how much they *might* have heard about "the gay lifestyle," perhaps they would have had something to complain about.

But, as Evelyn Beck says in her article on Jewish lesbian literature in *Lesbian Studies*, any mention of a taboo topic is so charged that it expands to fill a much larger space than it actually occupies. I had already experienced this phenomenon with race, class, and sex issues I raised in standard composition and literature classes. Studying a story by James Baldwin, a passage by Maya Angelou and a poem by Nikki Giovanni in an otherwise white literature anthology was perceived by my white students as "reading about Blacks all the time."

Closer to my present situation was another incident. Two years earlier, when I was teaching a college literature class to advanced placement students in a local Catholic high school, two parents had written letters to the college board of trustees protesting my assigning *Rubyfruit Jungle* by Rita Mae Brown. They labeled the book "immoral; trash," "garbage," "filth," and "far from being classified as a novel." They called me a "crackpot." I had merely included the book among forty others on a suggested reading list to supplement the establishment literature text I was using that quarter. I listed literature by Blacks, Native Americans, Asian Americans, and Mexican Americans as well as works by working-class, gay, and lesbian writers. I asked students to pick one book and report on it to the class. Several young women chose *Rubyfruit Jungle*.

I think I came close to losing my job at that school. I will never know how close since I was an outsider to most of the process. Administrators wrote memos about me. They discussed me by phone. Copies of the parents' letters and offending pages from *Rubyfruit Jungle* were sent to the dean, who showed them to me and suggested I write a letter to the parents, explaining the assignment and apologizing for whatever was unsuitable in the material. After angry and fearful soul-searching, I did so—not because I was contrite, but because I wanted to keep my job. No parent replied to my letter.

Finally the board of trustees dealt with the problem in a closed-door session. I was not invited to present my side of the story.

Throughout the whole process, my powerlessness frightened me. When I learned that the board of trustees had decided to take no action on the matter, I felt reprieved. I resolved to be more careful in the future.

I was careful, but two years had passed, and in my present class I decided again to take some risks. After all, I was not teaching Catholic high-school students but mature adults on a college campus. Besides, the course itself—"Philosophy of Women's Roles"—allowed looking at lesbianism as a possible role for women.

The texts for the course had, as their basic assumption, heterosexual reality. Class discussions focused on readings from these texts and on the lives of the fifteen heterosexual women and three heterosexual men in the class. Given that context, I felt justified in including lesbian roles in three ways.

Early in the quarter, I assigned "The Abdication" by Ruth Wolff (in *The New Woman's Theatre*, edited by Honor Moore). The play is about an actual woman who loved women: Queen Christina of Sweden. While barely mentioning Christina's relationships with women, the playwright explores in depth Christina's passion for and rejection by three men in her life. During our discussion of the play, I passed around four or five biographies to illustrate that in several areas of Christina's life, affectional preference being one, the playwright had used artistic license rather than conforming to available data. One of the accounts was from *Lesbian Lives: Biographies from the Ladder* (edited by Barbara Grier and Coletta Reid). The other six plays we read from that anthology contained no hint of lesbianism.

Later I showed a documentary film about Gertrude Stein, *When This You See, Remember Me*. Although the film does not use the term lesbian or indentify Alice B. Toklas as Gertrude's lover, it is not difficult to deduce those facts from the pictures and script. Three other films I showed had no overt or covert lesbian or gay content.

The same evening I showed that film, I invited a guest speaker, Ruth Baetz, to discuss what she had learned about women's roles in the process of interviewing dozens of women for her book, *Lesbian Crossroads*. In the half hour she was with us, Ruth was a model guest speaker: personable, informed, open to questions and comments. Ruth identified herself as a lesbian that evening.

I never did come out to that class; I didn't feel safe enough. In fact, I was so intimidated by my student's warning that I never again even spoke the words "lesbian" or "gay."

There was one lesbian student in the class. Dana and I came out to each other early in the quarter. I offered support should she decide to come out to the class.

Every time Dana sat silent during a discussion of women's roles, fears, or relationships, I was tense, imagining her desire to speak in conflict with her inability to take the risk. Watching her across the room intensified the same struggle in myself. When Dana did open her mouth, I also tensed, for no matter how safe her comment turned out to be, I feared each time she would take the plunge. I, who had promised to be supportive.

Finally, at the last class, without warning, Dana came out as part of her final project. She did a guided fantasy on what homophobic oppression feels like by reversing the roles and asking us to imagine that women who loved men had to hide their affection because society viewed different-sex relationships as sick and perverted. The central section read:

> You cannot touch the man you love in public; you don't dare. If you do, you're seen with suspicion and fear by "normal" people as having made overt sexual gestures. Something as simple as a touch, holding hands, having your arms around each other, a friendly kiss — all these create shock waves around you.
>
> People and their body language are saying to you, "OK, you love this person, this man, but do you have to let everyone know? Why flaunt it?" Having someone know who you love is not my idea of flaunting anything. Anyone who has been in love knows how it feels. Sometimes you want to shout it from the rooftops with your joy. How unfair it is to have all this additional pressure in an already pressure-filled world.

The guided fantasy was effective, and Dana got a warm response from every student in the room. I felt proud of her, but confused and irritated by her classmates' response. These were the very people, nodding and smiling and congratulating Dana for her bravery, who had criticized me for mine.

Why?

As I thought about this question, several answers occurred to me.

1. The play, film, and guest speaker opened people's minds so that by the time Dana spoke, the other students were ready to hear her.

2. It was harder to accept threatening ideas from an authority figure than from a peer. I was pushing information down their throats; Dana was simply doing her final project.

3. I was functioning on an intellectual level and not speaking to my students' feelings. Dana's guided fantasy helped them relax, and it engaged them on a feeling level.

4. While these answers may be true, especially the third one, I have come to believe that the most important reason for the student's feeling hostile toward me while feeling warm toward Dana was the difference between Dana's internalized homophobia and mine.

Dana had shared herself as a lesbian. It was obvious that she was taking a big risk, that she was trying to communicate something crucial to her, and that their response made a difference. In my fear, I kept my students at a distance. I didn't trust them, wasn't honest with them, didn't risk being *me* with them.

My decision not to take that risk may have been wise given that particular class and my own feelings at the time. And I believe it reinforced whatever homophobia my students and I felt. At a nonverbal level, I communicated my fear of being found out, of being rejected, of being fired. My fears were confirmed when, as soon as I took even small risks, trouble threatened. My students' homophobia was confirmed whenever I referred to lesbianism with tension in my voice; when I listened to our guest speaker, my face an impassive mask; when I was silent about my own life. How could they trust anyone who was that afraid, that defended, that dishonest?

Last quarter, in my "Literature by Women" class, I realized I had to do it differently. Two conditions made it easier to be honest: there were no men in the class and nearly one fourth of the students were lesbians.

At the third class meeting, I came out in the process of doing an assignment I had given my students: to share a book that had been important to them. I chose *The Well of Loneliness*. I told about discovering the book in 1970, furtively checking it out of the library, sitting up all night devouring every page, and then slipping it back into the library the next morning, hoping nobody would notice I'd ever had it. I shared my struggle with all the negative images of lesbians in that book, how damaged I was by them, how glad I am that there exists today so much literature that portrays us in truer ways.

Once I started speaking, it wasn't so hard to share the book and my story. My students asked a few questions about the book and its trial. Some wrote in their journals how much they admired my courage, others how much it meant to them that I was willing to be open.

Later in the quarter, we read Jane Rule's *Desert of the Heart*. The night we discussed it I felt centered, passionate, in touch with myself and with my students. It was an exciting session.

I never heard of anyone threatening to complain about me or warning other students not to take my class. In fact, it was the best class I had ever taught. I do not think that is coincidental.

This quarter, I am again teaching "Literature by Women." One of my students beat me to *The Well of Loneliness*. But I have generally been out, saying "we" when referring to lesbians, using "she" when referring to my partner/lover. It is still hard for me. I am just learning to be less guarded, to not automatically avoid opportunities to be open. It is possible that many students have missed my "we's" and "she's."

I spent this morning preparing a presentation on Emily Dickinson for class this evening. I will discuss her love poems, many of which are woman-identified. I am afraid, for it means confronting homophobia — in the poems, in the biographers and critics, in my students, and especially in myself. I am also eager. I am learning to do that confronting more effectively. And I like knowing that tonight my students will not leave class enlightened about the poet while remaining in the dark about the teacher. They will know that I too am a lesbian.

Teaching the Psychology of Women: A Lesbian-Feminist Perspective

Coralyn Fontaine

The subject of this article is how a lesbian-feminist teaches the psychology of women, or, at least, how *this* lesbian-feminist teaches the psychology of women. The question might be asked, "Is there an identifiable lesbian-feminist perspective on the psychology of women and on women's studies in general?" I believe that there is, and it is envisioned in a variety of creative and emerging ways by lesbian-feminist teachers and students, arising from our individual and collective experiences and political work. I see this perspective, or perspectives, as evolving over the past decade as part of the thinking within women's studies, within woman-identified lesbian culture, and within feminist theory and activism.

I believe that a lesbian-feminist perspective can be applied to the teaching or study of any discipline or any interdisciplinary topic in women's studies, from the social sciences to the biological sciences to literature.[1] The perspective can be utilized whether or not the "content" under study is "about" lesbians, and whether or not the teacher herself is "out" to the class as a lesbian. Conceivably, a nonlesbian-feminist teacher could apply a lesbian-feminist teaching perspective.[2] However, from my observations of other teachers and from my own life experience of having moved from being a heterosexually identified feminist teacher to a lesbian-feminist several years ago, I think that, in practice, this seems to be an unlikely occurrence and quite difficult to accomplish. Actually living as a woman-identified lesbian has helped me to "see" the world, as well as my "subject," in profoundly different ways, and I think it is that very personal world view which we as teachers ultimately communicate to our students. Still, both lesbian-feminist and nonlesbian-feminist teachers of women's studies may be able to identify potentially valuable insights and teaching approaches through considering the lesbian-feminist perspective and teaching suggestions described in this article.

My view of lesbian-feminist theoretical perspective involves three major concepts: (1) patriarchy, (2) heterosexism, and (3) woman-identification. For me, each of these *concepts* is embedded in a basic *premise*: (1) that *patriarchy*, which is also racist and classist, has, through its oppression of women and fear/hatred of women and of female values, created a pervasive "male point of view" on reality[3] (e.g., on knowledge, values, images, sexuality, language,[4]) and this point of view is political and necessary to the maintenance of male power; (2) that institutional-ized *heterosexuality* with its resulting heterosexist ideology[5] is the pivotal political/cultural mechanism employed by patriarchy to bind women and woman-energy (reproductive, spiritual, sexual, political, et cetera) to male-identification; and (3) that *woman-identification* on intellectual, emotional, political, and sexual levels is a necessary basis for any feminist strategy aimed at ending patriarchal oppression of women.

This theoretical perspective as it is described above is a simplified synthesis of what I perceive as an evolving analysis created by a living lesbian-feminist culture. Its roots are in the "cultural" or "radical" feminism of the late sixties and early seventies. Early emphasis on the "personal as political" spawned the exploration of premise one, the nature and effects of patriarchy.[6] From this early analysis and concurrent political activity emerged the realization of the central role of "sexual-ity," that is, institutionalized heterosexuality, in the oppression of women, an analysis described in the classic article "Woman-Identified Woman" by Radicales-bians.[7] The perspective continued to be extended and developed through the seventies and has been articulated in a variety of ways in the writings of Adrienne Rich, Ti-Grace Atkinson, Marilyn Frye, Audre Lorde, Mary Daly, Charlotte Bunch, and Monique Wittig, among many others.[8]

The three concepts of patriarchy, heterosexism, and woman-identification outlined above define the feminist perspective from which I teach; it informs and guides my teaching of the psychology of women and of other women's studies courses. I do not necessarily *teach* the perspective, and at least in my introductory level courses (i.e., "Psychology of Women" and "Introduction to Women's Stud-ies") I "moderate" the perspective somewhat in initial stages of the course. In those initial stages I focus most strongly on premise one. An appreciation of premises two and three, the role of heterosexism and the need for woman-identification, can only be gained by women in light of perception of the realities of patriarchy.

Many students,[9] especially those relatively new to a feminist consciousness, may be unable to move during the course beyond premise one in their conscious-ness except in limited ways. Their relation to the concepts of heterosexism and woman-identification by the end of the course may be limited to a new apprecia-tion for "lesbian/gay rights" or to lessened fear and distrust of other women. Lesbian students may be able to move more quickly than nonlesbian students towards premise three of woman-identification, but I doubt that this is consistently true, judging by the range of political viewpoints which I have experienced among nonfeminist lesbian women in courses. The intellectual/emotional movement by students from a minimal feminist consciousness to the development of a lesbian-feminist consciousness of all three premises in one course is, I think, a rarity for all but a few women. That process of deeper radicalization and awareness took me and many other lesbian-feminists the better part of a decade, including years of personal struggle and, on my part, what I can only call "blindness." The role of the lesbian-feminist women's studies teachers is, I believe, to make contact with each student at her present level of consciousness and by doing so enable her to move through her own consciousness-raising process at her own pace. On the other hand, lesbian-feminist teachers also have the rather unique ability and the respon-sibility to create through our courses some visions of and conditions for a deeper level of consciousness that includes full appreciation of the roles of heterosexism and woman-identification, an understanding which may not be actualized by students until much later.

For purposes of illustration in this paper, the "Psychology of Women" course is taken as the example of a women's studies course to which a lesbian-feminist perspective is applied. However, it is also the basis from which I teach "Introduction to Women's Studies," "Human Sexuality," "Women and Power," and "Perspectives on Lesbian Women."[10] In none but the latter course have I been "out" to the class as a whole because of the unstable nature of my teaching position.

Within the context of the psychology of women course, I will describe some of the teaching methodologies and approaches which I have found useful in conveying a lesbian-feminist perspective. While each of the three elements—patriarchy, heterosexism, and woman-identification—is obviously very much intertwined both conceptually and in actual teaching, I will describe methodologies regarding each in turn. The reader should be able to see potential applications to her own discipline or area of teaching or study.

Patriarchy

In teaching from a lesbian-feminist perspective, the most fundamental conceptual framework for me involves a continuing analysis of patriarchal perspectives on reality and experience. For the first week or two of the course we focus on the concept of and manifestations of patriarchal power over societal institutions. The result of this patriarchal power structure over the past several thousand years has been the imposition of a pervasive and unacknowledged male point of view on reality, with maleness as normative, primary, representative, and valued. Much of the first two weeks of the course is devoted to bringing this male point of view and patriarchal ideology into awareness by critically examining such issues as language, stereotypes, historical and philosophical treatment of women, religious and other cultural myths and images for patriarchal bias, often with the aid of "reversals," i.e., generating with the class images, language use, et cetera, that might occur in a matriarchy as comparisons.

From this beginning analysis of the pervasive effects of patriarchy on our general perceptions of reality, the next step is to critically evaluate the discipline of psychology as being itself a manifestation of patriarchal ideology. For example, the idea of a "vaginal orgasm" would not have been proposed in a matriarchy. "Why not?" you may ask students. Why is there a consistent overuse of male subjects from which to generalize to a psychology of "humans"? Why are characteristics or behaviors which are found through "sex-difference research" to be (supposedly) associated with males (e.g., "field independence," aggressiveness, mathematical skills) consistently interpreted as being more valuable or important than those associated with females? These kinds of questions help to show how patriarchy and psychology project the male and maleness as normative, representative, primary, and valuable, and, simultaneously devalue the female and define her as "other" through a variety of misogynist images and viewpoints.

For purposes of illustration, let us take one example, the "myth of the Black matriarchy," to explore in more detail how a lesbian-feminist teaching perspective might analyze patriarchal ideologies within psychology and social science. In dealing with the much discussed and controversial Moynihan proposition of a "Black matriarchy"[11] it is important to show students how to critically examine not only the *content* of the question or assertion, *i.e.*, whether statistics on "female-headed households" do or do not in fact support the existence of such an entity as a "Black matriarchy," but also to examine the unspoken ideologies underlying the very framing of the question.

The framing of the proposition that a Black matriarchal family structure is the "cause" of the oppression of Black people illustrates how mutually reinforcing sexist, racist, and classist ideologies masquerade as "objective social science." Moynihan's widely publicized "scientific work" shamelessly blamed the working-class Black woman for the oppressed condition of Black people through her "emasculation" of the Black man. This "blaming the victim," i.e., Black people and poor people, rather than the racist, capitalist, patriarchal oppressors neatly dovetails with that other patriarchal penchant for the blaming of women, particularly mothers, for the ills of society. It is thus significant to point out to students that poor and Black *women*, and specifically *mothers*, were singled out as sources of blame for their own and Black men's downfall.

That this is not an isolated case but rather part of a pervasive pattern of patriarchal ideology reflecting hatred and blaming of women can be illustrated by comparison of this social scientific "explanation" with patriarchal religion's blaming of the woman/mother, Eve, for the downfall of "mankind," psychoanalytic blaming of the "over-protective mother," mother-blame in theories of schizophrenia, blaming of the rape victim, the battered wife, the prostitute, the "frigid" woman, and so on.

Of the several available texts and anthologies in the psychology of women area, only two take an approach which rigorously examines patriarchal culture and perspectives. They are Jean Baker Miller's *Toward a New Psychology of Women* and Sue Cox's anthology, *Female Psychology: The Emerging Self.* Sheila Ruth's interdisciplinary introductory women's studies text, *Issues in Feminism: An Introduction to Women's Studies*, also does a fairly good job of identifying patriarchal perspectives. Unfortunately, none of these books analyzes or draws interconnections with race and class issues. Also, none of these books really deals adequately with the other two elements of lesbian-feminist perspective—heterosexism and woman-identification.

Heterosexism

In teaching from a lesbian-feminist perspective, I believe that one of the most important tasks is to remove lesbianism from its position as an issue of "sexuality" or of "sexual preference," a position where patriarchal society and its social science/psychology have placed it. This "sexualization" of lesbianism conveniently both trivializes and depoliticizes woman-bonding. It obscures the social and political implications for patriarchy of the primary bonding of women to *each other* and to an authentic self rather than to the *oppressor class* of males, as enforced by institutionalized heterosexuality. Significantly, the sexualization of lesbianism simultaneously hides the political nature of heterosexuality—to expose one is to expose the other. The political nature of enforced heterosexuality means that the mechanism by which the male class oppresses and controls the female class is through ownership of the means of reproduction, accomplished by institutionalizing heterosexuality. The enforced sexual/reproductive bonding of each woman to a member of the oppressor class rather than to her own people serves to divide and conquer women as a class. The coercive separation of women from each other to bond with the oppressor also serves to enforce male-identification and to preclude woman-identification. When the revolutionary acts of primary bonding to women and woman-identification are reduced by patriarchy to an issue of mere genital preference or even to sexual attraction, it is no wonder that many women, lesbian and heterosexual, perceive the relationship of lesbianism to feminism as constituting some sort of "gay rights" or "sexual preference" issue.

The sexualization of lesbianism within women's studies is reflected in and encouraged by textbook structuring. For example, what little information is included in psychology of women textbooks on lesbianism or lesbian women is typically located in the chapter or section on sexuality.[12] Rarely in texts is lesbianism discussed again in any other context but sexuality and sexual activities. Lesbianism as an option for women is not mentioned in such chapters as "adult roles" or "adult lifestyles."[13] It is also notably absent in sections on feminist political theory, female stereotypes, research critiques, motherhood, aging, et cetera.

Heterosexism-by-sexualization combines with heterosexism-by-omission in virtually all current texts, with most texts devoting approximately two to three pages out of hundreds to lesbianism.[14] The total effect serves to encourage the view in students (both lesbian and nonlesbian) that lesbianism is a trivial, nonpolitical "bedroom issue" of minor importance to women and to feminism, relative to such issues as "sex roles," "marriage," and "sex differences," which receive substantial and recurring textual treatment.

Adding yet another dimension to the problem is, of course, the more familiar, outright heterosexism of the (minimal) information that is typically presented. For example, "causes of homosexuality" (but not heterosexuality) are often discussed, and lesbians are generally portrayed as "other."[15] Given the inadequacies and heterosexist biases in most psychology of women (and other women's studies) texts and materials, it falls to the women's studies teacher to counteract the pervasive effects on student thinking of sexualization, trivialization, omission, and distorted content in terms of lesbianism.

In an attempt to counteract the pressure toward sexualization of lesbianism, I try to bring lesbian content and lesbian issues into the class discussion as often as possible during the term in a variety of contexts: stereotypes, adult "lifestyles," feminism, adolescent development, pay discrimination, et cetera. A panel of lesbian-feminist guest speakers, including, if possible "out" lesbians from the class, also helps to change the lesbian issue from a "sexual" one to a "woman/people" one, and from an issue of "them out there" to "us in here, lesbian and nonlesbian, woman and woman." Such rather straightforward classroom methodologies are, nevertheless, powerful in validating the lesbian students and in raising the consciousness of nonlesbian students.

Another teaching technique useful in combating the sexualization and "otherness" of lesbianism is to have the class generate the stereotype of a "single woman."[16] Typical adjectives generated include: old maid, unattractive, promiscuous, immature, aggressive, independent, frigid. I then ask what characteristics would have to be added or subtracted from the list in order to describe the stereotype of a "lesbian woman." They typically identify few characteristics that differ in the two (male-defined) stereotypes, illustrating that the "crime" of both the lesbian and single woman is that of daring to live without bonding to a man in patriarchy, regardless of her "sexual preference."

Another class exercise useful in extending lesbianism beyond the purely "sexual" connotations is to have each student list five advantages to making one's life with a woman partner-lover and five advantages to making one's life with a man. We then put this information on the board. The exercise can be a real eye-opener to many heterosexually identified women who by the middle of the course sometimes have difficulty thinking of *any* advantages beyond "social approval" and "economic security" to life with a man. On the other hand, they readily describe a variety of advantages to life with a woman partner-lover, such as "emotional understanding," "equality of power," "sexual satisfaction and orgasm," "sharing and closeness," and "sensitivity to needs." Lesbian students often find this exercise very validating and supportive. Last semester, I put this question on the midterm, both to show the seriousness of the issue and to make sure that everyone in the class, including those who may have avoided the exercise or "tuned-out" for the discussion, actually confronted directly her own attitudes and life choices on this issue.

In addition to confronting heterosexist sexualization of lesbianism, heterosexist language and assumptions also need to be confronted in the women's studies course and reconceptualized into woman-defined modes.[17] For example, in patriarchal language, the terms "married" and "single" relate women only to men; "sexually active" in most contexts (e.g., birth control, "premarital" sex) typically refers to "*heterosexually* active"; "female friendship" excludes sexuality-/love; "family" connotes heterosexual couple and children. For the teacher or the textbook author to say "about 10 percent of women are lesbian," indicates that the rest of "us" need no label of (sexual) identity. Heterosexuality is thus portrayed as normative and "natural" and lesbian as "other" and requiring causal explanations. In fact, the simple statement, "*people* hold negative stereotypes about lesbians," portrays "people" as heterosexual (normative) and lesbian as "other." Clearly, as Mary Daly has said, "we have inherited a contaminated language."[18]

While it seems to be a relatively straightforward solution for the women's studies teacher to simply make an effort to use non-heterosexist language in class, it surprises me how difficult this can sometimes actually be in practice. When I am not actively thinking about language and assumptions, I often find myself slipping into heterosexist patterns. It is illuminating to monitor one's own language for a typical week of teaching to observe how powerful and "unconscious" are the patriarchal models of thinking within our own heads, reinforced, if anything, by our "academic training." Nevertheless, I do try to confront heterosexist language and assumptions in class as much as possible. When a student asks about the research on "relationships," I ask her if she means "heterosexual relationships," and if so, to say this. I try to interject the adjective "heterosexual" where it is assumed but not acknowledged (*"heterosexually* married," *"heterosexual* attraction research").

I also often use a "same-sex relationship" or "a female couple" or a "lesbian mother" as examples when illustrating any point or topic in class. For example, if we are discussing adolescent "interpersonal attraction," which in the text is described only in terms of male-female attraction, I may use the example, without preamble, that "Marita and Joan are attracted to each other and would like to live together after finishing school but have conflicts because of different class backgrounds," and ask the class how the two teenagers might try to resolve these conflicts within their relationship. Or, if the topic is wage discrimination against women I may ask the class to compute median combined salaries for female-female couples, male-female couples, and male-male couples, rather than giving the data only for male-female couples as the text and other sources typically do.

It is clear that challenging heterosexism is a necessary and difficult task in women's studies. Heterosexism is expressed through sexualization of lesbianism, omission and trivialization, language and assumptions, and definitions of lesbian-as-other, as well as in the more familiar outright sexist and homophobic content of texts.

Woman-Identification

To me, an essential complement to the focus on *patriarchy* and on *heterosexism* is a course emphasis on *woman-identification*. I see woman-identification as the development of woman-defined realities and visions that confront rather than ignore racism and classism among us, and including a primary identification and bonding with women. Part of a lesbian-feminist teaching perspective is to actively explore with students the alternative of developing for themselves woman-defined perceptions of the world, an alternative to the patriarchal perspectives which they generally have begun to question because of the women's studies course. Thus, I have begun to set for myself a direct, articulated course goal of creating conditions for woman-identification on intellectual and emotional levels rather than seeing woman-identification as an indirect, hoped-for by-product of the process of exposing and confronting patriarchy and heterosexism. I have thus begun to develop and use increasing numbers of experiential as well as "intellectual" teaching methodologies designed to explore and foster woman-identified perceptions and woman-bonding through the course.

There are several teaching techniques which I have found to be supportive of woman-identification processes, and I am sure that other women's studies teachers can think of many more that will work for their situations. One technique is for each student (and myself) to do an oral history of her mother (or other significant woman in her life) through a structured interview. We then share the information and the experience of doing the interview with the class. Not only is the sharing of the histories a means of woman-bonding among women in the class and a validation of woman-defined realities, but the experience of sharing on this level tends to produce a powerful sense of reconnecting with the woman-energy of our mothers as women and sisters. For several women in my class, lines of communication with their mothers opened or reopened in very personally significant ways. Such a project could be included in a variety of women's studies courses, including literature, sociology, and history.

Other powerful experiential work which encourages woman-identification processes is a group sharing of "matrilineages."[19] Each woman (and myself) writes on the board her matrilineal line as far back as she knows it, for example: "I am Coralyn, daughter of Adeline, daughter of Mary Wilhemena, daughter of a woman from Germany." On another section of the board each woman writes her responses to: "What I would like to tell my mother" and "What I would like to hear from my mother." After everyone reads each other's responses, we join hands in a circle, and each woman in turn recites her matrilineage as she had written it on the board, going around the circle a second time to give each woman the opportunity to repeat her matrilineage while adding a brief description of one of the women in her past. Very deep emotional levels of consciousness are often touched by this seemingly simple experiential process which continue to be shared and discussed afterward during the class session. Many women have never before had the opportunity to validate and experience their female connections and roots.

Another experiential process which I use very early in the course, both to expose patriarchal ideology in our culture's description of reality in the "creation story" and to begin woman-identified thinking, is to ask students in class to write a short "creation story" as it might exist in a "bible" in a matriarchal culture. In this context students typically imagine a female "god" who creates the world and the first person/woman in her image, with a man as some kind of derivative of woman.[20] We then discuss the feelings of power, wholeness, pride encountered in experiencing such images of ourselves (and as well as mental and emotional blockages we felt) and how different our self concepts might be if we saw such images of ourselves in "churches" and "bibles" as males do now. The experience of daring to imagine a female-centered reality is often an important first step for women in the course, and many will refer back to it in their journals or in course evaluations.

The use of experiential journals as part of the course requirements also seems helpful in supporting woman-identification processes. As in many women's studies courses, these journals supplant the traditional term paper and allow much greater depth of emotional, personal, and intellectual exploration. As women begin to share their anger, their frustration, and questioning and get validating feedback from me and from my own life on their entries, a lot of movement tends to occur. In many ways I think the journals are the most valuable aspect of the entire course and complement the processes going on in class.

Psychological Stages

Setting woman-identification as one of the course goals and consciously attempting to create conditions for its occurrence throughout a women's studies course has implications for the psychological/emotional stages that students may be able to move through during the course as they confront patriarchy and its impact on women. From my observations there often seem to be four identifiable psychological stages that women in the course experience, though not at the same pace or in the same manner. These identifiable stages are: discovery, denial (for some women), anger, and woman-identification. Interestingly, and not accidentally, these psychological stages tend to parallel the sequential historical stages of consciousness within the radical feminist movement of the past twelve to fifteen years. The psychological experience of students during a women's studies course becomes, a microcosm of the historical process of the emerging theoretical/political consciousness of the modern feminist movement. Students' early psychological experience in the course, like feminism of the late 1960s, is characterized by a sense of repeated "discoveries" of patriarchal oppression and biases in one area of life after another. Much of this "discovery" stage is expressed in journals as well as in class.

A psychological experience often following or interspersed with students' discoveries of patriarchal oppression of women is the experience of denial of the new awareness, a denial which was experienced by many of us emerging feminists of the late 1960s as familiar realities began to be questioned. The discovery and denial stages tend to be followed by a powerful sense of anger and rage which tends to reflect the very angry stage of the radical feminist movement in the early 1970s. The anger stage in radical feminist movement has been followed in the mid- to late-1970s by focus on the creation of woman-identified political theories, culture, images, communites, scholarship, music. The anger and early experiences of discovery have not, of course, disappeared from feminist consciousness. But the focus on the healing processes of self-affirmation through woman-identification while continuing the struggle is a natural and crucial developmental stage of feminism.

In the microcosm of the women's studies course, discovery on a deeply personal level of the painful truths about patriarchy's treatment of women usually occurs in the first several weeks of the course. This stage of discovery (or deepening of discovery for students who are already "feminist") of the realities of oppression and the questioning of some very familiar assumptions about the world (e.g., patriarchal male "god," pervasive male bias within the holy lands of "objective" science, psychology, or history) for some students triggers a reaction of anxiety expressed as denial. Statements in students' journals and in class to the effect that "men are oppressed, too," as well as vigorous defenses of misogynist religious doctrines, often reflect, I think, a defense against the anxiety of their losing a familiar if oppressive reality description. These discovery and denial stages that students experience are typically followed by an intense and very personally felt anger, a sense of outrage at the now-visible oppression. This stage of anger seems to be experienced quite strongly by the middle of the course and peaks towards the end of the course.

Therefore, without a deliberate teaching focus on woman-identification processes throughout the course, many women's studies courses may unintentionally leave students at this stage of anger at the conclusion of the semester. Male-identified realities have been profoundly shaken but not replaced with positive woman-defined concepts and support systems. Having raised students' consciousness of oppression and then leaving them with their anger at the end of the course can produce feelings of despair,[21] frustration, and/or cynicism rather than the positive woman-energy we would like them to experience through feminism. The lesbian-feminist teacher, in particular, who has herself experienced through woman-identification and incredible "coming home" to one's sisters and mothers, to the primacy of women and woman-defined realities, has the rather unique potential and responsibility to bring the fourth stage of woman-identification to life for students through her teaching. It is this experience of woman-identification that is one of the most valuable aspects of a lesbian-feminist teaching perspective, and I think it needs to be recognized as such and cultivated to the greatest extent possible in women's studies courses.

Conclusion

In conclusion, a lesbian-feminist teaching perspective based on the concepts of patriarchy, heterosexism, and woman-identification can, in my view, bring some powerful insights to the psychology of women and to other women's studies courses. The perspective, an evolving product of lesbian-feminist experience and culture, is in a process of perpetual creation and recreation through the lives and thinking of women-identified women. Without the articulation and application of such a perspective, women's studies can too easily remain locked within the boundaries of patriarchal thought, a situation which we as women, teachers, and students, must struggle against continuously.

Notes

[1]Barbara Smith, "Toward a Black Feminist Criticism," *Conditions: Two*, 1977. Reprints also available from the Lesbian-Feminist Study Clearinghouse, Women's Studies Program, 1012 CL, University of Pittsburgh, Pittsburgh PA 15260.

[2]For a view which suggests that a nonlesbian can take a lesbian-feminist political perspective, see Charlotte Bunch, "Lesbian-Feminist Theory," *Our Right To Love*, ed. Ginny Vida (Englewood Cliffs: Prentice-Hall, 1978).

[3]This concept is discussed clearly in the introduction to *Female Psychology: The Emerging Self*, ed. Sue Cox, (Chicago: SRA, Inc., 1976). This is a good anthology for a course on the psychology of women.

[4]Julia Penelope (Stanley), "Prescribed Passivity: The Language of Sexism." (Paper delivered at the Southeastern Conference on Linguistics, Nashville, Tennessee, March 1975).

[5]Bunch, "Lesbian-Feminist Theory," pp. 80–81.

[6]For a sampling of this early work see: Robin Morgan, ed., *Sisterhood Is Powerful* (New York: Random House, 1970); and Vivian Gornick and Barbara Moran, *Woman In Sexist Society* (New York: Basic Books, 1971).

[7]Radicalesbians (Rita Mae Brown, Cynthia Funk, Lois Hart, March Hoffman, Suzanne and Barbara XX), "The Woman-Identified Woman," *Radical Feminism*, ed. Anne Koedt, Ellen Levine, and Anita Rapone (New York: Quadrangle, 1973).

[8]See Mary Daly, *Gyn/Ecology* (Boston: Beacon Press, 1978); Adrienne Rich, *Of Woman Born* (New York: W.W. Norton, 1976); Ti-Grace Atkinson, *Amazon Odyssey* (New York: Links, 1974); Marilyn Frye, "Some Reflections on Women and Power," *Sinister Wisdom*,

Summer 1978; Audre Lorde, "Uses of the Erotic: The Erotic as Power," (1978), Lesbian-Feminist Study Clearinghouse; Charlotte Bunch, "Lesbian Feminist Theory," *Our Right to Love*; Monique Wittig and Sande Zeig, *Lesbian Peoples* (New York: Avon, 1979).

[9]When I speak of students, I am referring to women students; I regard male students somewhat in the category of "observers."

[10]The course syllabus for the interdisciplinary course, "Perspectives on Lesbian Women," is available, along with other lesbian course syllabi, from the Lesbian-Feminist Study Clearinghouse, address above.

[11]Discussed in Joyce A. Ladner, *Tomorrow's Tomorrow: The Black Woman* (New York: Doubleday, 1971), pp. 36-39; and Toni Cade, ed., *The Black Woman* (New York: New American Library, 1970), specifically, Jean Carey Bond and Patricia Peery, "Is the Black Male Castrated?" pp. 113-117.

[12]See, for example: Carole Tavris and Carole Offir, *The Longest War: Sex Differences in Perspective* (New York: Harcourt Brace Jovanovich, 1977), chapter 3, pp. 70-72, 85; Irene Frieze, Jacqueline Parsons, Paula Johnson, Diane Ruble, Gail Zellman, *Women and Sex Roles: A Social Psychological Perspective* (New York: W.W. Norton, 1978), chapter 11, pp. 231-33; Juanita Williams, *Psychology of Women: Behavior in A Biosocial Context* (New York: W.W. Norton, 1977), chapter 7 pp. 233-235; Elaine Donelson and Jeanne Gullahorn, *Women: A Psychological Perspective* (New York: Wiley, 1977), chapter 12, p. 202, and chapter 14 p. 245.

[13]The possible exception, depending on how you read between the lines, is Donelson and Gullahorn, *Women and Sex Roles*, p. 245.

[14]The number of pages devoted to lesbianism in current psychology of women texts can be deduced from note 11. Jean Baker Miller's *Toward A New Psychology of Women* (Boston: Beacon Press, 1976), while providing an excellent critique of patriarchal values, does not even mention lesbians.

[15]Unfortunately the one text which devotes a chapter (or any more than a few pages) to lesbians, Janet Hyde and B.G. Rosenberg's *Half the Human Experience: The Psychology of Women* (Lexington, Massachusetts: D.C. Health, 1976), is the *most* thoroughly heterosexist in content of all the available texts.

[16]Maureen McHugh and Suzanne Rose developed this exercise in their psychology of women courses at the University of Pittsburgh.

[17]See, for example: Julia Penelope (Stanley), "The Articulation of Bias: Hoof in Mouth Disease" (Paper delivered at the annual convention of the National Council of Teachers, San Francisco, 1979); Daly, *Gyn/Ecology*, pp. 368-371.

[18]Daly, *Gyn/Ecology*, p. 368.

[19]I first participated in this experiential process following the play *Daughters*, presented at the 1979 Conference of the National Women's Studies Association, Lawrence, Kansas.

[20]A version of this "creation story in a matriarchy," which I wrote a few years ago for a study guide for the psychology of women course, is available from me with a stamped, self-addressed envelope (Dept. of Psychology, University of Pittsburgh, Pittsburgh PA 15260).

[21]Feelings of despair as part of students' reactions to a women's studies course are discussed by Cherie in the Spring 1980 *Newsletter* of the National Women's Studies Association.

Teaching about Jewish Lesbians in Literature: From **Zeitl and Rickel** to The Tree of Begats

Evelyn Torton Beck

The patriarchy is especially good at fragmenting the loyalties of those of us who are members of more than one minority group. If we wish, in spite of the push to make us choose sides, to keep all components of our identities intact, we must be prepared to struggle, both within the minority groups to which we belong and against the dominant culture.

A consciousness of being Jewish has no doubt been with me since childhood, when, under Hitler, I experienced anti-Semitism firsthand. Thereafter, growing up in the United States (where anti-Semitism was less visible but far from dead), I was involved in a variety of Jewish activities, mostly of a cultural-political rather than a religious nature. As an adult, I integrated this continuing interest in Judaism into my professional life by offering a course in "Yiddish Literature in Translation" and by including major Yiddish writers in the world literature curriculum.

Being a conscious member of one minority group can make one more sensitive to the oppression of other groups. I had no sooner altered the curriculum to include these men when I began to notice the absence of women writers. Since it was the early seventies, the rise of the second wave of feminism, this omission was being noticed by others as well; collectively, we began the long, slow, and exciting process of uncovering, teaching, and researching women writers. In the process, we began to notice the absence of many other minorities. Nonetheless, it was years before I was satisfied that the material in most of my classes was reasonably representative of previously excluded groups. The sole and glaring exception was the Yiddish literature class, whose texts remained solidly male. Because it was difficult to obtain translations of the few women who had written in Yiddish, I found that the only satisfying way to integrate women into the course was to shift the focus from Yiddish writers to Jewish women.

I knew from the start that I wanted the material in this course to be as integrated as my other classes, but I was also aware that it would be a less easy process. Jewish-identified students have not always been overly eager to explore their own prejudices. Yet, for several years I had experienced oppression as a lesbian and as a result had become dedicated to making the invisible visible.

Parallels came to mind. Never in all my years as a Jew had I ever dreamed of denying my people's history or my own past experience. Increasingly, as I rid myself of internalized negative prejudices about lesbians and began to see myself through my own eyes, I wanted to break through the denial that silence imposes, at least in the content of the course. So I learned to say the word lesbian out loud, without blushing or stammering or feeling as if I were leaping over a precipice; to hear it as a positive term, not only in the privacy of my home or among my lesbian friends, but out there, in the face of the patriarchy and its explicit determination to oppress and perhaps eradicate us.

This determination had the strange result of reawakening in me the memory of an older oppression. When I was in lesbian circles I often became anxious about anti-Semitism. I began to notice a new set of omissions. When lesbian and gay liberation groups spoke of needing the support of the churches, I noted that they didn't include the synagogues; when we talked of ministers, we never mentioned the rabbis. This idea wasn't new with me; there had been discussions about anti-Semitism in the movement press. In big cities Jewish lesbians had formed their own groups. I did not know what to do with this reawakened Jewish consciousness; it brought back my younger years when I had been actively involved with the Jewish struggle for survival. But now I was no longer a Zionist or even a strong supporter of Israel; nor was I an Orthodox Jew or even a believing one. I was simply a cultural Jew, a "Jewish atheist." Yet, I wanted to be visible and accepted *as a Jew* among lesbians, much as I wanted to be visible and accepted *as a lesbian* among Jews.

In the struggle to be heard, it is enormously helpful to have some visible support. While the National Women's Studies Association explicitly recommends the inclusion of lesbian/feminist material (as well as that of other minority groups) into women's studies curricula, the same kind of support is not forthcoming from the National Jewish Studies Association, which, at this time, is just beginning to recognize the contributions of Jewish women, but not yet the existence of Jewish lesbians. Where, then, does this leave the Jewish lesbian/feminist who is dedicated to being heard in Jewish as well as feminist contexts? Why insist on refining the oppressions and placing ourselves in triple jeopardy? And what happens in the classroom when we do?

With these questions still unanswered, I proceeded to plan the course on the Jewish Woman which was offered for the first time in the Spring of 1978 at the large state university in which I work. We began with a history of the Yiddish language, since Yiddish is inextricably linked with women. It is a language that is both beloved and denigrated—not accidently also known as *mame loshn* ("mother tongue")—and characteristically associated with exaggerated emotion, earthiness, lack of rigor, and impurity, particularly in contrast to Hebrew, the holy tongue, associated with men's concerns—prayer and study. With this in mind, we read accounts of Jewish communities in Eastern Europe and other books that provide an historical context for the Jewish woman.[1]

The scope of the course was broad, ranging from the seventeenth century to the present, and including Europe, Canada, and the United States. Texts included works by the "fathers" of modern Yiddish literature, Mendele Mocher Sforim, Sholom Aleichem, and I. L. Peretz, as well as *Memoirs* by Glückel of Hameln (1690; published 1932; reissued New York: Schocken, 1977) and Bela Chagall (*Burning*

Lights, 1946 reissued New York: Schocken, 1963). We read fiction by Anzia Yezierska (*Bread Givers,* 1925, reissued New York: Persea 1975), Tillie Olsen (*Tell Me A Riddle,* New York: Dell, 1960), and Susan Fromberg Schaeffer (*Anya,* New York: Avon 1975); writings by Holocaust survivors, and contemporary essays and poems.

In the syllabus I also included Martha Shelley's poem, *The Tree of Begats,* the first poem I had ever come across that dealt explicitly with the experience of being a Jewish lesbian.[2] As further points of reference, I included recent personal essays by other Jewish feminists including a few lesbians,[3] and with some hesitation I also assigned two short stories by the notoriously misogynistic but extremely popular contemporary writer, Isaac Bashevis Singer.[4] While these stories are no exception in Singer's oeuvre, they do deal with women's relationships to women: *Zeitl and Rickel* is an explicitly lesbian love story that ends with the death of both partners; *Yentl the Yeshiva Boy* tells the story of a young girl who poses as a man in order to be allowed to study and in this disguise ends up marrying a woman.

The majority of students who take "Yiddish Literature in Translation" are Jewish students with a strong Jewish identity, although non-Jewish students also sign up for the class. Most of the students have little feminist consciousness, and in the past close to half have been men. This semester, because of the topic and perhaps also due to the feminist questions I posed in the class flyer, about forty-five of the students were women and five were men. The format for this kind of class at our university calls for two lectures a week which are supplemented by smaller sections led by a discussion leader. It was my function to provide the lectures. I was extremely fortunate to have had the assistance of so excellent a discussion leader as Biddy Martin (an advanced graduate student in the German Department at the University of Wisconsin/Madison) who had had experience in teaching introductory women's studies. Her support and sensitivity contributed greatly to the success of the class, and I am indebted to her for many of the observations in this paper.

On the very first day of class I drew parallels between anti-Semitism, racism, sexism, and the oppression of homosexuals. At this time I also introduced the idea of overlapping or multiple oppression and mentioned lesbians as part of the diversity of Jewish women. Moreover, I also pointed to the historical parallels between Hitler's persecution of the Jews and his treatment of homosexuals. Homosexuals were also exterminated in large numbers, a fact that has received little publicity. By showing that Jews are not unique in being persecuted and by placing the oppression of both Jews and homosexuals in the same concrete historical context, students began to see that oppression is never arbitrary, but is always related to power relationships and control within a society.

For most students, the idea that women have been oppressed in the society at large was not new, and they accepted it to varying degrees. But the idea that women are also oppressed within Judaism, not only by the attitudes of individual Jewish men, but by the very institutions of Judaism and the Jewish law itself, proved to be difficult for most to contemplate. It was even harder for students to believe that Jewish lesbians feel oppressed when they are not accepted into the Jewish community (unless they remain closeted of course). Most of the students had never knowingly met a lesbian, and most were so uptight about the idea that they did not even know how to express their discomfort directly. Instead, their negative attitudes came out obliquely: they objected to the "blatancy" displayed by Jewish lesbians who, like Martha Shelley and the essay writers, "made an issue" of their oppression; they failed to see the irony of their own position as Jews who were "making much of their Judaism" in a Christian world.

Yet the students liked Martha Shelley's poem a great deal and appreciated the feminist impulse behind it. They could especially understand Shelley's feelings of being cheated of full personhood as a Jewish woman: "These clean shaven rabbis merely pretend to reform/saying in English, 'Thank God for a healthy child'/and in the ancient tongue '...for giving us a healthy son.'" It was somewhat harder for them to empathize with Shelley as a Jewish lesbian who was insisting on her right to be who she really was, struggling to keep all parts of her identity, "I am each day less the wandering lesbian/my father dares not own." This was an oppression they had never experienced and could not understand. While most responded with absolute and unthinking anger about anti-Semitism and the Holocaust, Shelley's bitterness, particularly her refusal to bear children ("My womb, like my fist/is clenched against the world") seemed excessive. They had great difficulty seeing the ideological assumptions behind their gut feeling that some kinds of oppression produced "justified" anger, while the oppression of those they saw as "other" did not merit the same response and was therefore necessarily exaggerated and "unjustified." They were also very upset at the parallels made by one of the essay writers between Zionism (Jewish separatism) and lesbian separatism, both of which serve similar needs for autonomy. Ironically, it was the more traditional Jews who could see the parallels better than the assimilated ones (or non-Jews), even though Orthodox Judaism forbids male homosexuality and ignores lesbianism altogether.

Another way that the students' unacknowledged prejudices came to the surface was in their insistent misreading of the two Singer texts. First, they read right over Singer's explicit statement in *Yentl the Yeshiva Boy* that the two consummated their marriage. Singer is quite explicit: Yentl, disguised as a man, marries a woman who is so naïve she never notices anything unusual in their lovemaking. Moreover, he even explains that Yentl found a way to deflower the bride so that the sheets were bloody the next morning as they were supposed to be. Yet, the students were so uncomfortable with the idea of two women making love, they preferred to ignore this evidence. Second, they objected to *Zeitl and Rickel* because Singer portrayed the relationship between the two women as "perverse." It was not that they themselves approved of lesbianism. They insisted, however, (against the clear evidence of the text) that Zeitl and Rickel were not *really* lesbians; the town had misinterpreted their relationship; they were, to use the old cliché, "just good friends."[5]

Friendship between two women was something they could all understand; it was something they had themselves experienced and which they valued. As a result, they worried about definitions: how could you tell for sure where friendship left off and lesbianism began? This is indeed a significant and valid question when raised in a feminist context that challenges the insistent patriarchal emphasis on lesbians as purely sexual beings. Here, however, it was clear that the students were raising these questions in order to protect themselves and their understanding of the world. They wanted badly to assume that whatever lesbianism was, it was totally different from anything they had ever known or could ever experience themselves.

Because they believed it to be something essentially evil, they wanted to reassure themselves that what they had experienced had nothing to do with lesbianism. This need to protect themselves created a great distance between the students and the lesbians in the text.

Although in lecture I gave every signal I could think of (including wearing a labyris to class), I never came out on the podium. Some students picked up on the cues (particularly those who were lesbians themselves); others guessed, but some never realized that a lesbian had been lecturing to them all semester. (In private conversations I always came out if the students seemed to want to know.) I believe that this semi-"out," semicloseted stance hurt the class. I believe it would have been less easy for students to distance themselves from the lesbian material if I had been explicitly out. Yet, it is hard to know how those taboo words about one's private self will affect a class. I have found it easier to be "out" in small classes where one can talk "person to person." I am still not sure what I will do in the next large lecture class. One feels very naked standing up there alone.[6]

Singer's stories were assigned in the first few weeks of the semester, in the context of the "fathers" view of Jewish women. In the midsemester evaluations, the students' response to the lesbian material was fairly typical of heterosexuals who are confronted with lesbianism for the first time: they felt we had placed "too much emphasis" on lesbianism, although it was only one topic among at least a dozen topics we discussed. It has been my experience that any mention of lesbianism, no matter how brief, in a heterosexual environment seems to expand until it takes up all the space. Students are so unused to this most taboo topic, that once they hear about "it" all else seems to recede into the background. This is a good indication of just how important it is for us to continue to integrate lesbian material into our classrooms. Only in this way is it possible to defuse the subject and destroy the myths.

The major focus of the course had been on what it meant to be a Jewish woman, historically and in the present. Within this focus, a number of questions arose. There was a continuum ranging from "Can a woman lead her own life and still be part of institutionalized Judaism?" to "Can a woman be a lesbian and maintain a Jewish identity?" For the religious students the answers to both were negative, though there was some possiblity of stretching Jewish institutions to accommodate the feminist challenge. For the religious, lesbianism didn't fit in at all. For other students the question remained: to what extent was it worth fighting to save these institutions? The cultural Jews felt it was more possible to be a Jew and a lesbian, but the heterosexual imperative in Judaism is so strong, many were not hopeful that attitudes would really change within the Jewish community. For a culture that relies on the family for its survival, the idea of lesbianism still poses a serious threat, especially since the idea of lesbian motherhood is unthinkable to most people in the Jewish community.

Nonetheless, in spite of the initial resistance, something positive did happen to the students' attitudes toward lesbianism in the course of the semester. Because the topic was integrated into the course material and not relegated to special sessions, students found it less easy to dismiss it as unimportant. And in the course of time, the idea became less strange, and they were decidedly more comfortable discussing the topic. By the end of the semester, it seemed entirely appropriate to bring in and discuss a newspaper clipping about Anita Bryant's statement that the United States needed to get rid of all Jews and homosexuals. The topic had become part of an ongoing discussion and had filtered into the students' consciousness. Those who did not speak to the issue in lecture or discussion section said that they continued to think about it outside of class. When, in one of the small discussion groups one student raised the question "Could it be that the only reason the professor brought in lesbian material is because she is a lesbian?" a number of students came to my "defense." What difference did it make why the topic was brought in? It was important that it be there, and besides, what was wrong with bringing a subject into class if it meant something personally? This was a big shift in attitude from the beginning of the semester, when almost all the students had believed that to challenge the patriarchy was to be "biased" (only the status quo was capable of objectivity); to bring in anything personal was to be unacademic; to bring in any political dimension was to be unliterary. Some students never got beyond this, and a few said they resented having their opinions shaken, but on the whole, the course was a huge success. Most said, in the final evaluations, that the course had really opened their minds; ultimately, the lesbian material was accepted as part of my commitment to teaching literature in a feminist manner, using a feminist approach.

Notes

[1]Mark Zborowski and Elizabeth Herzog, *Life is with People* (New York: Schocken, 1962); Charlotte Baum, Paula Hyman, and Sonja Mickel, *The Jewish Woman in America* (New York: New American Library, 1977); Leslie Hazelton, *The Israeli Woman* (New York: Simon & Schuster, 1979). For further references see Aviva Cantor, *The Bibliography on the Jewish Woman* (Fresh Meadows, New York: Biblio Press, 1979). Unfortunately, none of these texts give any attention to Jewish lesbians.

[2] This poem appears in the following places: Martha Shelley, *Crossing the DMZ* (Oakland: Women's Press Collective, 1974), pp. 51-52; *Ms.* 3 July 1974:84; Elly Bulkin and Joan Larkin, eds., *Amazon Poetry* (Brooklyn, New York: Out and Out Books, 1975), reissued as *Lesbian Poetry* (Watertown, Massachusetts: Persephone Press, 1981). I would now also include the poetry of Irena Kelpfisz, *Periods of Stress* (Brooklyn, New York: Out and Out Books, 1975).

[3]These are: "The Ways We Are," *Lilith: The Jewish Women's Quarterly* 1, no. 2 (1974): 4-14; Janet Meyers, "Diaspora Takes A Queer Turn: A Jewish Lesbian Considers Her Past" *Dyke* 5 (Fall 1977): 12-14. The entire issue of *Dyke* 5 is devoted to ethnic lesbians and contains some other relevant essays. A recent collection, *Chutzpah: A Jewish Liberation Anthology* (San Francisco: New Glide Publications, 1977) also includes material concerning Jewish lesbians and gay men. Significantly, several of the women writing in the Jewish publications use pseudonyms in telling their stories. My anthology of writings by and about Jewish Lesbians (published by Persephone) will greatly facilitate the integration of material on the subject into any curriculum.

[4]These are: I.B. Singer, "Zeitl and Rickel," *The Seance and Other Stories* (New York: Farrar, Straus & Giroux 1968) and I.B. Singer, "Yentl the Yeshiva Boy," *Short Friday and*

Other Stories (New York: Fawcett, 1978). For a more detailed analysis of Singer's attitude toward women, see my article, "I.B. Singer's Misogyny," *Lilith* 6 (1979): 34–36.

[5]While this was true for the majority of the students, it is important to mention that some of the students with a generally more progressive political perspective had a more positive attitude and read the texts accurately.

[6]For further thoughts on being "out" in the classroom, see my unpublished paper, "Self-Disclosure and the Commitment to Social Change" (paper delivered at the Forum on Feminist Pedagogy, Modern Language Association, Houston, Texas, 1980).

A Journey into Otherness: Teaching <u>The Well of Loneliness</u>

Toni A. H. McNaron

Teaching *The Well of Loneliness* brought me face to face with a question underlying our entire profession—why read? My answer comes from a core that I trust: to salvage as much sense of potential and decency as I can, given the details of my personal life and of the culture around me; to affirm not merely that I exist and am possible but that I am capable and worth any struggle to survive and flourish.

The Well of Loneliness was a text I chose for a women's studies seminar* on "Women as Other and the Lesbian as the Other Woman."[1] My hypothesis was that Simone de Beauvoir's argument that men vest women with their best and worst fantasies and dreams could be extended: that heterosexual women similarly vest lesbians with the status of "The Other." The course was made up of twelve white women, all contemplating a women's studies major. For me, this was the first time I assigned curricular materials by and about lesbians, though I had spoken the summer before on lesbianism as an issue within the women's movement. In that earlier setting, I had for the first time in fourteen years of university teaching told students directly that I am a lesbian. I include these autobiographical details because they suggest the importance of the ovular to me emotionally and because they hint at a certain defensiveness and adamancy which was likely to creep into my teaching all during the quarter. This course was also the first time the University of Minnesota women's studies (then in her third year) had devoted any substantial portion of time to the subject of lesbianism, though several courses had included brief treatments or readings, and certainly research by students had been encouraged. So I was tense and excited about the effects of the course on lesbian and nonlesbian students alike.

---

*Since the etymology of "seminar" is semen, and since I believe it is crucial for feminists to rid our language of anti-female words, I will hereafter refer to the Senior Seminar as ovular. I am indebted to teachers at Goddard-Cambridge and the Los Angeles Women's Building for encouraging me to use this word organic to me and other women rather than a term relating intimately to men.

During the first four weeks of the quarter, we read and analyzed de Beauvoir's *The Second Sex.* We then applied her basic thesis to the several disciplines most represented in the class: history, psychology, literature, biology, and psychobiology. We read articles about the methodologies within each field and looked at how each treated women. We discovered that women have been blanked out by the very systems for conducting research and study within a given field. What this work gave us was a particular awareness of the depth of patriarchal values within formal academic settings. In fact, it became clear that to trivialize or omit women at this point is actually no more than to follow the prescribed outlines of one's discipline. We came to feel the pervasive Otherness of women not merely as students and faculty within academies but as legitimate material about which to do serious research and teaching.

The effect of these opening weeks was to depress and anger us. The sheer weight and longevity of neglect were at times overwhelming. As each of us articulated her own experience within the discipline(s) in which she spent her time and energy, the pattern emerged sharply: we had been asked to focus on male values and subjects; we had been increasingly taught by male persons; we had been asked to become invisible or to feel strange for not being male. In a word, we had all been assigned the status of Other.

From this relatively safe context of Them-Against-Us, we proceeded into the course's more hypothetical realm. We set out to see if and how women duplicate this destructive system among ourselves. Acknowledging several possible structures for exploring the question, for example, black and white women, poor and well-off women, old and young women, we turned our attention to the frame chosen for this course—lesbian and nonlesbian women. We posed the question as follows: Do heterosexual women apply de Beauvoir's thesis to lesbians, thereby projecting onto them the worst (and, more recently within feminist circles, best) aspects of being a woman?

The Well of Loneliness was the first text we read. Though several students had heard about the novel, no one had read it. As for me, it had been at least ten years since I had. I reread it fairly quickly, looking for ways in which it might illustrate our emerging thesis. Try as I did, however, I could not brush away the ghosts who kept breaking in on my orderly process. Finally, I abandoned my scheme and simply let the book work on me again. As had been true on each reading, Stephen Gordon's relationship with her horse, Raftery, moved me repeatedly to tears. As had been true on each reading, the scenes with Mary during their stint as ambulance drivers and in their early times together at home played into all my deepest lesbian romantic fantasies. As had been true on each reading, I identified with Stephen's struggle to believe in herself and her work in spite of social expectations of her as an "invert" and despite her own feelings of fear and repugnance at underground scenes of the homosexual world. As was not true on former readings, I grew progressively more uncomfortable with the heavy role-stereotyping between Stephen and Mary, at Hall's seemingly unexamined racism and classism. As certainly had not been true on former readings, I sensed that the book was not written for a lesbian audience but rather for a homophobic heterosexist culture in an attempt to have readers view homosexuals as being "just like" everyone else. This conservative, even reactionary, stance caused me to pull back and begin to rethink Hall's contribution to that body of material we are coming to name lesbian culture. I also saw the novel as overwritten and ludicrously gothic, while being little more than a vehicle for a sociological tract about the decency of homosexuals.

I approached our initial discussion of the book, then, with a range of emotional and critical/political responses. I was eager to see how the students would react. Beginning on a low key, I asked for first reactions. What I got was a volley of negative, impatient, angry, and hostile statements. No one had liked anything about the book. The nonlesbians objected to it as non- or even antifeminist, while the lesbians hotly rejected it as heterosexual in its notions of relationships and negative in its presentation of lesbians. My initial response was defensiveness: I felt personally attacked and argued with their subjective responses, trying to show them that they were "wrong," "ahistorical," or in some way not being "logical." Our discussion ended with everyone's feeling pummeled and with all the students aligning on one side, leaving me on the other.

My journal entries for the next few days are illuminating as indications of how complicated it can be for us to teach a subject which is not merely *about* ourselves, but *is* ourselves. Those entries reflect a process of making myself into an other—of casting myself as the "authority" on intellectual and literary grounds while in reality I asserted power on a level of age and longevity of being a lesbian. I pulled rank, simply, and did that on blatantly autobiographical planes. I was essentially subjective and, fooling myself momentarily, I turned my subjective reality into the objective case. I fell into the very trap and lie of male scholarship which we had spent the first four weeks decrying and analyzing so painstakingly and well.

Fortunately, we began our work on *The Well of Loneliness* on a Thursday and returned to it Tuesday, thereby giving ourselves four days in which to cool off from our fracas. I was not the only one who wrote in her journal about what had happened and how she felt about it. The day had shaken virtually every ovular member. We came back together with shyness, wariness, and wounds whose thin scabs were still forming. I asked for a sharing of how we felt about the previous class and everyone did that honestly and powerfully. Several of us read directly from our journals rather than trusting ourselves to say what it had felt like in the first afterglow. We never returned to the text that day; rather we worked hard on what had gone on within each of us and among us as a group. We recognized the process of other-making, as we called it, that most of us had gone through. Eventually we could laugh together as we realized that virtually every one had walked out of the room feeling that she was the outsider, the other. Though logically impossible, everyone felt that all the other students had ganged up against her to force her to reject her own tentative perceptions of the book. We found *The Well of Loneliness* with its basic theme of being a lesbian in a homophobic society causing each one of us to harden her position and to push her reading forward over any other reading. We each seemed to have more passionate investment in the outcome of our sharing than on other topics. We wanted to convince rather than to explore.

Lesbianism was the only topic that affected us in this way, and as we worked toward our core responses we discussed a truth which rocked us all: We had dramatically demonstrated the fundamental validity of the ovular's thesis. We had each participated in making the lesbian into our own special other or in making ourselves as lesbians into everyone else's other. We had oppressed and divided ourselves, fighting it out as if we had some genuine argument among ourselves. By our own behavior, we had answered the first question we had raised as we worked on *The Second Sex*. De Beauvoir asserts that women are the largest class ever to be oppressed, that our oppression has lasted longer than any in history, and that we have individually and collectively assented to that oppression. In the face of her challenge, we had framed one potent question: Why? Our analysis on that first day showed us clearly that we had created that historical process in microcosm. Furthermore, it had shown us *how* we had done that. From our realization, we were able to move in on the question of *why* from an experiential rather than a theoretical base. Our resulting work, in class for the remainder of the quarter and in our journals which were widely circulated among us, was radical and important.

Each of us began discussing Hall with an unarticulated but highly structured system for handling the world around her. The *Well of Loneliness* called aspects of every one of our survivial systems into question such that each of us came to class with something vital to lose if the rest of the group refused to see the novel her way. The heterosexual students had been forced to see heterosexuality through the caricatured lens of butch-femme relationships and were anxious to dismiss this book in order to retain their shaky sense that it is all right to be a feminist and continue having a primary relationship with a man. The lesbian students had been forced to see lesbianism and homosexuality as it has traditionally been conceived and practiced—without the support of a women's movement and an increasingly visible culture of other lesbians. They were anxious to deny the validity of this book, since it called up myths about a life choice they were struggling to affirm amidst the loudly heterosexist backdrop of college, their families, and the larger society. What I had to lose turned around being the teacher as well as being a lesbian. Here I was, finally willing to teach a lesbian novel and to relate it to me personally. This book was an emblem for my choice of how to live and a mirror of my oldest values. Furthermore, I was willing to do all that not in some street agency or women's space but in the middle of a patriarchal institution. I felt isolated and vulnerable on one hand and mildly heroic on the other. I turned to the class to validate me as a human being and as a selector of reading material.

No single novel or any other text can serve such a matrix of needs, especially when none of the needs has been articulated and when many of them are only half-understood or perceived by those of us who are trying to talk with each other. So we exploded blindly and passionately. By not understanding that survival systems designed to help us move in a patriarchal and dangerous world could turn on us in an all-female environment, we simply used a behavior model classic in oppressed groups. We attacked each other, dividing and wounding ourselves, while leaving the patriarchy, with its powerful sexist and heterosexist assumptions, untouched and even strengthened.

We decided to devote an extra class meeting to *The Well of Loneliness*, wanting to return to the book itself after our painful and productive self-criticism. That discussion extended past our designated class period and was one of the most exciting of the entire quarter. We talked frankly of our feelings about "butch" and "femme" pairings among women, pondering whether they had gone underground in feminist groups in which they have become unfashionable. We talked about Hall's audience, why she might have cast her book the way she did, and whether the book had any effect on the general public. We talked of the lingering power of

Krafft-Ebing's thesis, especially for those lesbians who discovered our sexuality before 1960. (This was especially healing for me, since it gave me a chance to tell these younger women what *The Well of Loneliness* had meant to me when I first read it in the late fifties as I tried to believe that I was capable of being a decent creative person and not the drunken factory worker who had entered my head instantly upon my discovering that I loved women.) We talked about ways in which the gothic style allows women writers to escape some of the linear, social restrictions within the form of the novel. By choosing the gothic, they can free themselves to envision alternative modes for living and feeling as females.

Finally, we talked about two topics which continue to interest me about Hall's novel and about lesbian writing in general. We spoke movingly about the silence erected around Stephen by all the adults in her life, even gentle Puddle. We saw that silence as an attempt by those adults to meet their own needs, forgetting that the young Stephen might have had need for information about what was going on inside her. And we touched on Stephen's relationship with her mother, naming her mother's primal attraction to her daughter and seeing that by utterly denying that attraction, she denied any contact with Stephen. We acknowledged that her terror communicated itself as a basic unlovableness to her child. Cast aside by a frightened mother, Stephen naturally turned to her father for support. That support, feeble and erratic as it was, was predicated on his selfish desire for a son. We were able to credit Hall with revealing that potent and all-too-familiar pattern of the female child who comes to feel at a very early age that she is not quite acceptable to either parent, not quite "enough." This risky work on silence and incest created a space in the class in which we each could identify with Stephen's earliest sense of inadequacy and strangeness. So a text which had begun by splitting us into thirteen distinct fragments became one in which each of us could see herself, whatever decisions we made about sexual expression. At the same time, we continued to understand our different responses to the book—responses which depended on those decisions.

I believe the movement from harmful fragmentation to healing and radical identification turned on our analysis of that initial blow-up. We were willing to suspend content and descend into the more frightening and liberating fears of process and feeling. I also believe that it was no accident that it was a novel focusing on lesbian reality which precipitated that journey. This subject about which we have remained so silent, even within the women's studies context, touches every woman's psyche at its roots. To bring those unspeakable, formerly even unnameable responses up and out into the open, especially within a classroom setting, is to put us in touch with our own self-repressions (sexual and creative repressions at the very least). Just as important, our process work showed us our ability to oppress other women who are "unlike" us by some patriarchally defined standard. For this reason alone, quite apart from the historical and aesthetic value to be had from teaching lesbian material, I believe it behooves us to begin more and more to include such writing and discussions in our academic teaching and research. For me, personally, *The Well of Loneliness* remains a lifeline from my past and a splendid starting point for addressing those feelings of fundamental otherness which each of us lodges somewhere within ourselves and which we will continue to project out onto other women unless we acknowledge their presence and power in our own lives.

Learning Through Teaching: A Lesbianism Course in 1972

Madeline Davis

Since the early 1970s, numerous courses on lesbianism, lesbian literature, lesbian history, and other topics relating to lesbian life have been taught in colleges and universities across the country, sometimes under the auspices of women's studies programs. More often, a daring soul from English or psychology has braved the shock and outrage of administrators and has fought to offer a course in a more traditional department. Although these courses have differed significantly, the women who have conceived, researched, and taught them have shared similar experiences. We have had few models either for syllabus development or for teaching methods, and we have faced the special problems related to teaching and learning about our own lives in the context of an academic environment. This paper will explore these personal, political, and academic issues as they relate particularly to the development of the women's movement and the lesbian/gay movement in Buffalo, New York in the 1970s.

Early in 1971, a small group of women who had been active in the Mattachine Society of the Niagara Frontier, a mixed gay liberation organization, attempted to discover what the new radical feminist group, Buffalo Radicalesbians, was offering gay women that gay liberation was not. We attended an evening CR group of about a dozen women on the city's east side. I, for one, could not imagine a gay group functioning without men—after all, weren't we all brothers and sisters in the struggle? And what was this nonsense about working in a coalition with straight women? Weren't they as much our oppressors as straight men? At the meeting we were assailed by the clear voices of organized feminism, coupled with the fearsome undertones of socialist revolutionary politics. To clarify my own naïvete at the time, I must admit to having seriously questioned why Israel was not a Third World country! I suppose we all have to start somewhere.

The commitment of those early Radicalesbians brought us back to other meetings and finally to membership, with a daring consciousness of the power of women working together. In the fall of 1971, a reorganized group with the name Lesbians Uniting formed for consciousness raising, study, and political action. After months of meeting, one of the primary concerns that surfaced was the need of young women who were exploring their sexuality, both those at the university and those in the community, for a place in which to discuss lesbianism as a personal, political, and academic issue.

Margaret Small, a doctoral candidate in American studies, and I decided to explore the existing literature to see if there might be enough material to be the basis for a course at the newly formed Women's Studies College at SUNY Buffalo. Up to this time, I had never envisioned lesbianism as a subject for academic study. But primarily due to the influence of Margaret, a dedicated and charismatic socialist-feminist, I slowly and sometimes painfully came to understand the value of organized study as a part of our movement for change.

We read and weeded; we informally canvassed members of the university women's community and the lesbian community at large; and finally we identified our list of concerns: coming out; literature, especially novels and poetry; race; class; role-playing; sexuality; lesbian motherhood; political ideologies and the movement; repression; and the new forms of woman-identified culture. Surely this was a modest collection of issues for one semester of study! We felt some panic as we wondered what readings to assign—who had ever written anything on these topics?

Fortunately we discovered a gold mine of material in back issues of *The Ladder*, lesbian novels that had been lovingly stored away, and current political publications such as *Furies*. We were also fortunate that our course plans coincided with the publication of Del Martin and Phyllis Lyon's *Lesbian/Woman*, Sidney Abbott and Barbara Love's *Sappho Was a Right-On Woman*, and *Patience and Sarah* by Isabel Miller.

The political and personal effects of this six-month process of search and discovery in the annals of lesbian-feminist and socialist-feminist literature were more profound than I had anticipated. I had been a diligent worker for gay civil rights and continued to believe in the cause and to work in mixed organizations for some time to come, but more and more often I found myself siding with women against the sexist language, slights, and ignorance of the men in our group. More and more energy was devoted to explaining, to teaching, and to meeting with other organization women to develop strategies for raising the consciousness of men we had come to love but whose politics continually frustrated us.

Other areas of my life also began to change rapidly and radically. I had been a songwriter and singer in the gay community for many years. Suddenly I was writing women's music for lesbian-feminist audiences, and as coffee houses and benefit concerts continued, more women attended, generating inspiration for women's music. The movement world in which I loved and worked was evolving into a women's world.

Major changes come about as much through struggle as inspiration. A particular area of struggle in preparing the first lesbian course at SUNY Buffalo was one which became for me one of the greatest intellectual and emotional hurdles of my life. As a staunch and unbending individualist, I found the time and energy output of even a two-person collective interminable. I railed at tasks and consultations. Criticism/self-criticism was boring and time-wasting. I was resolutely against collective work; Margaret was resolutely committed to it. In retrospect, her tenacity was my good fortune. Over the years I have come to realize the quality of collective work, and although I still tend to pull against the system, I have a new understanding of the value of this kind of struggle.

Our course syllabus in many ways reflected the times and current interests of the lesbian-feminist community of the early 1970s. We were being pushed by an angry, threatened world into justifying our existence. "Why are you gay?" "Prove you're not sick." We needed solid arguments with which to fight back. Dispelling origin theories became a vital issue. Our fledgling movement was not yet strong enough to give us support for answering back "Why are you straight?" So those early days found us poring over theories, postulating that lesbianism might be the ultimate stand against women's oppression. We did learn, however, that trying to answer "why" was playing into the hands of those who felt they could "cure" us or future generations of lesbians. We learned well to question the questions.

We also explored variations in lifestyles within the community and began to build a sense of what lesbian culture was all about. Because we found little reading material on the Black lesbian experience, we contacted Third World women in the community who were willing to share with us their views on being Black, gay, and female in America.

A number of topics assigned were controversial, but none seemed to have the impact that role-playing had on our first class of twenty women. Many students had recently come out within the women's movement and had a firm intellectual foundation in feminist politics. At this point in our history, the lesbian-feminist movement was committed to the eradication of butch-femme roles, seeing them solely as imitative of heterosexist culture and therefore negative. An historical perspective on roles as important elements in developing strategies for resistance was not to surface until several years later. Roles were seen simply as the outward manifestation of the bad habit of male identification that could be eliminated if lesbians developed feminist consciousness.

Therefore, the battlelines were drawn between two factions: newer lesbians who were antirole and who had solid political analysis, versus older lesbians who felt that roles had somehow made life easier for them, but who had no organized way of discussing this issue. There were also a few straight women in the class who weren't quite sure why this issue aroused so much emotion. Certainly we were unable to resolve the question of roles, but the kinds of discussions that ensued did cause us to consider, for the first time, the relationship between an important tradition in lesbian social life and its implications for us as lesbian activists in a changing movement.

Although roles, in particular, were a source of controversy for our students, one of their greatest sources of excitement came in the reading and discussion of fifties and sixties novels. Authors like Ann Bannon and Claire Morgan brought to life the bar scenes, clothing styles, music, and speech patterns of a period they had thought of as both legendary and predominantly negative. These works also made clearer the place of roles and role-playing in lesbian life of the past. As students came to know characters like Beth and Laura and Beebo, the complexity of the times emerged and they developed a better understanding of the vitality and passion of earlier lesbian life, as well as the dangers and self-destructiveness. Most of all, they began to know more fully that lesbian history does not consist only of Sappho, Gertrude Stein, and the second wave of the women's movement but is larger and more varied in its scope than we imagined in 1972.

Another area of the course we all found particularly rewarding was the section on emerging lesbian culture. We discussed first theories of culture and feminism: What is women's art? Is there a special lesbian art? Music? Drama? Poetry? What about nonverbal media such as instrumental music? Are we to pay attention to circles and ovals in graphic art? Why? What difference does all this make and to whom? The debates were unresolved. Rather, the questions we raised became for many of us the beginnings of a heightened awareness of similarities and differences in the expressions of lesbian women through many kinds of art forms.

Finally I must reflect on what researching and teaching this kind of course did to my own further educational activities in the following years. Teaching one's own life is very different from teaching an academically oriented course in which one finds a tradition of analysis and commentary. There are, certainly, similarities in subject matter, organization, et cetera, but much more profound is the terrible need to push for understanding and to impart more than a personal view; to be open to hearing even opinions which threaten one's life and values without becoming either defensive or devastated. We wanted the class to know that we were talking, not about some foreign culture, but about ourselves, our days and nights, our prior and current agonies, and our hopes for a better future. We, ourselves, were the soldiers; we, ourselves, were the victims of a real, ongoing war.

It is hard to speak of your life and the lives of those you love in terms of topics, concepts, theories, issues, and then go home and live them. It is hard, but because it is your life, it comes uniquely alive and its impact is especially forceful. For this reason, the course seemed to me to be particularly successful. It was joyful and painful, and we all loved it.

[See Appendix for course syllabus—Ed.]

"But What About Men?..."[1]
Clare Bright

Scene 1: A class discussion of lesbianism. The speaker talks about loving women, being woman-identified, developing a woman's culture. When it's time for questions, someone asks "Why do you hate men?"

Scene 2: A meeting of women philosophers. Two interesting papers are given. As discussion begins, the first question is about neither paper. A woman says "Some of us were wondering at lunch whether it's acceptable to have sex with men."

Scene 3: A conference session of mothers and daughters. After a brief discussion of the topic, it's pointed out that we shouldn't neglect literature on fathers and/or sons.

Scene 4: A workshop on feminist education. Someone interjects the idea that a man who is not in the political mainstream faces problems similar to those of feminist teachers in the classroom.

These are all actual situations which took place recently, but examples could be multiplied endlessly. The format is familiar: discussion of some aspect of women's concerns proceeds until interrupted by someone (male or female) asking, "But what about men?" The implication of this recurring question is that it is acceptable to focus on women for a while, but we are remiss if we do not then bring in men as well. Why, in a women's studies context, is there vague uneasiness about leaving out males as objects of discourse?

One could speculate about psychological or emotional causes of this continuing attention to men; suggestions might allude to aspects of female socialization related to our needs and priorities, on woman's traditional reluctance to put herself first. However, while this dimension is certainly of interest, I will leave it to the social scientists to explore. Instead I would like to examine the arguments generally given to legitimate raising the question "But what about men?"

In brief, the usual claims are: 1) that men are also oppressed by the system under which we live; 2) that at least some men are not oppressive; 3) that men are half the human race and it is unrealistic to ignore them.

All these points have, I believe, been sufficiently challenged by feminist authors. Radical feminist literature delineates in detail the privilege that all men enjoy under the present system and the ways in which this privilege is gained at women's expense. My thesis is, however, that even if all the above claims are taken to be true, it would still be inappropriate to attend to questions about men in a women's studies context.

Women studies and feminist scholarship came to exist out of a recognition that education is not a neutral, objective enterprise; rather it mirrors society as a whole in ignoring, distorting, and devaluing women. As feminists we regard this as morally and philosophically untenable (to say nothing of the material harm experienced daily by the female sex as a result of such a mentality). We see women's studies ideally as providing an academic base for contesting the pervasive ideology which defines women as secondary and lesser beings.

The task involved in developing such a base in enormous. Those who have spent time generating a feminist perspective on human knowledge are aware of how much remains to be done. Each layer of lies and distortions peeled away reveals another needing to be questioned. Each discovery of new knowledge about women points the way to further exploration. This is the richness, the astonishing breadth and depth of feminist scholarship.

Perhaps at some point we will have retilled the epistemological soil sufficiently that nothing is left of the androcentric perspective. But the completion of this all-encompassing pursuit is nowhere in sight and in fact cannot even be conceptualized at this point. To the extent that we can vaguely imagine our final goal, we may envision a new beginning for the human race and a future society whose structure will provide open-ended possibilities for all beings. Hierarchical divisions which now polarize us by sex, class, race, lifestyle, and so forth may one day be devoid of power implications.

But that time is not now. Patriarchy has had a several millenia head start on any more humane world view. Dismembering it will require all our energies for the foreseeable future. The thesis of masculist scholarship is firmly established; the feminist antithesis is barely beginning to take form. Before there can be a transformation to a new plane of thought for humanity, a new synthesis of female and male, women must complete an investigation of their own metaphysical realm. Then and only then can we realistically talk about a comprehensive philosophical system in which men are an integral part. To concern ourselves with males at this point is to sabotage the essential work of women's studies.

This is not to suggest that developing a woman-oriented world view would have implications for or be relevant to women only. Precisely because of the far-reaching nature of the task, everything and everyone would be affected by this conceptual revolution. My claim is not that our topic of study should be women and women only, but rather all topics should be approached with a paradigm that has women at its center. I suspect that those who feel men must be given equal intellectual time are still operating with the paradigm that sees women primarily in relation to men.

Perhaps some may object that to undertake research which focuses on women to the exclusion of men is to commit the same moral error as that of patriarchal scholarship; radical feminologists have been accused of "reverse discrimination." To make such a charge ignores the relevance of power. For the powerless to exclude those who do not share their oppression is a necessary stage in building a power base, whereas those in power exclude the oppressed in order to retain resources and privileges. As Chris Pierce and Sara Ketchum have pointed out, "There is a moral difference between organizing to keep the presently powerless from power and organizing the powerless as such."[2]

When there is a feminist body of knowledge which rivals traditional scholarship in breadth, depth, efficacy, and legitimacy, the concept of reverse discrimination might have some credibility. Until that point, the development of a separate feminist epistemological base is simply a crucial step toward any eventual genuinely humanistic enterprise.

It seems relevant to note that some of the most exciting and creative theorizing is being done by lesbian-feminists, women who pursue topics centered on women. I think of Adrienne Rich, Mary Daly, Julia Penelope (Stanley), Charlotte Bunch, Marilyn Frye—women who frankly assume a woman-identified perspective as their starting point. They provide us with some evidence of the progress that is possible when one is ready to move beyond the traditional structure of priorities and take autonomous women as the appropriate universe of discourse. Lesbian-feminist scholars are serving as the vanguard in developing a feminist paradigm.

But to take one last objection, what are men to do while women are creating a feminist world view? While I do not believe men can be feminists, they can be sympathetic to and supportive of the work of women's studies. They can do this by educating themselves and other men to the necessity of leaving behind the androcentric conceptual framework. And they can support us first and foremost by realizing why for now and for the indefinite future our educational enterprise must be for and about women.

Notes

[1]Gratitude for helpful conversations goes to Marilyn Frye, Jacqueline Zita, Claudia Gorman, and Carolyn Shrewsbury.

[2]Sara Ann Ketchum and Christine Pierce, "Separatism and Sexual Relationships," in *Philosophy and Women*, eds. Sharon Bishop and Marjorie Weinzweig (Belmont, California: Wadsworth Publishing Co., 1979), 164–165.

New Research/New Perspectives

[We] could leave to our cultural posterity a way to organize our chaotic, often painful experience into some body of data (hard and very soft) which would let lesbians fifty or five years from now build new layers from an already-articulated base. Such a system would offer lesbians and the (homophobic) society at large much-needed information about our history, our artifacts, and our day-to-day lives. For most of us, no such information existed, and we had the grim alternative of reading false, even destructive things about ourselves in standard textbooks, or of remaining ignorant. Presently, much is being published by individual lesbians and by clusters of lesbians. What is missing is a systematic analysis of us as a culture, and that is where we hope our work can be helpful.

Toni A.H. McNaron
"Finding and Studying Lesbian Culture"
The Radical Teacher

Eventually, we may not only be asking different questions but also making significant changes in the nature of research itself.

Barbara E. Sang
"Lesbian Research: A Critical Evaluation"
Our Right to Love, Ginny Vida, editor

Black Lesbians Before 1970: A Bibliographical Essay

JR Roberts

In the spring of 1981, Naiad Press published my *Black Lesbians: An Annotated Bibliography*. Besides this comprehensive survey of more than three hundred annotated entries, there are several discussions of selected Black lesbian materials by Ann Allen Shockley in "The Black Lesbian in American Literature: A Critical Overview" (*Conditions: Five*, Autumn 1979, pp. 133-142) and by Linda Brown in "Dark Horse: A View of Writing and Publishing by Dark Lesbians" (*Sinister Wisdom* 13, Spring 1980, pp. 45-50). Five years ago, the idea of such bibliographical surveys, while not inconceivable, was at least premature. In the interim, the continuing development and articulation of Black lesbian/feminist sensibilities and a renewed lesbian historical consciousness have contributed to the creation and recognition of a large body of works known as "Black lesbian materials."

This bibliographical essay will focus on the identification and description of selected works by and/or about Black lesbians before 1970. These particular materials have been the least visible and the least accessible and are due some attention. A further goal is to provide self-help information to sources so that the reader may continue to locate, identify, and make more materials accessible.

Black Lesbian Voices/Black Lesbian Lives

The most important and authentic sources of information on Black lesbians are, of course, those documents in which Black lesbians speak for themselves in their own words. These include oral histories, diaries, interviews, and first-person written narratives.

Since there are few known published personal narratives written by Black lesbians in the so-called "preliberation" period, the creation and collection of numerous oral histories of older Black lesbians is most crucial in creating a collective history of the twentieth-century Black lesbian life. As these women grow older, their stories are in danger of being lost for all time due to death, loss of memory, or loss of speech. The potential of the oral history method is evident in an article concerning a New York City community event entitled "The Black Lesbian Griots." In her article, "The Black Lesbian: Times Past—Times Present" (*Woman-News* 6, no. 2, May 1980, p. 8), Luvenia Pinson describes four Black lesbians, two of them in their late seventies, sharing stories of their lives. They covered such topics as Black lesbian marriages, clothing and dress styles, street life, and surviving police violence and harassment. Several tapes of the event exist but are presently inaccessible.

There are several pioneering oral history projects such as *The Mabel Hampton Collection* (Lesbian Herstory Archives). *The Collection* consists of photographs and seven taped interviews of a seventy-seven-year-old Black lesbian talking about her life. The Buffalo Women's Oral History Project has interviewed several Black lesbians for a history of the pre-1970s lesbian community in Buffalo, New York. This later oral history is not yet accessible but does indicate the kind of work being done.

Published interviews and first person narratives are sources that can be found in Black, women's, lesbian, and gay literature. Few of these appear before 1970. In the mid-sixties, Ernestine Eckstein (pseudonym) gave an interview to *The Ladder*, an early lesbian periodical. Accompanying the interview by Kay Tobin and Barbara Gittings is a front cover photo of Ernestine (*The Ladder* 10; no. 9, June 1966, pp. 4–11). The former vice-president of the New York Daughters of Bilitis and early activist in the Homosexual Rights Pickets talks about her personal experiences and compares the politics and strategies of the homophile and Black movements. In a more recent interview appearing in a lesbian periodical, Mabel Hampton, born in 1901, recalls her Southern childhood and her migration North (*Feminary* 10, no. 2, 1979, pp. 6–16).

A rare personal account written by a Black lesbian-turned heterosexual appears in a national Black magazine in the early fifties (Bentley, Gladys. "I Am a Woman Again." *Ebony* 7, August 1952, pp. 92–98). "A colorful character of Harlem" in the 1920s and 1930s, Gladys Bentley was a prolific songwriter, male impersonator, and popular piano player. A contemporary biographical sketch indicated that she was "queer and sported a girl friend" and could be seen almost daily marching down Seventh Avenue in her men's clothing (Federal Writers' Project. *Negroes of New York, 1936–1941*. Original typescript in the Schomburg Collection, New York Public Library. Microtext: Kraus-Thompson Organization Unlimited, Microfilm Division, Milwood, N.Y. Microfilm Reel 7274-001—7274-005. This collection was also published as *The Negro in New York: An Informal Social History*. Edited by Roi Ottley and W.J. Weatherby [New York Public Library and Oceana, 1967]). By 1952, after "hormone treatments," Gladys Bentley had renounced her former lesbian lifestyle for a heterosexual marriage. Her *Ebony* article is a rather veiled and negative account of her past identity and how she was able to overcome it. She also mentions a nearly finished manuscript of a no-holds-barred autobiography. So far, publishing records do not indicate that the book was ever published. Photographs accompanying the article also show a scrapbook apparently kept by Gladys during her career. The discovery and preservation of these documents would be, to say the least, of great importance.

Audre Lorde's recent autobiographical writing, "I've Been Standing on this Street Corner a Hell of a Long Time!" (In *Our Right to Love: A Lesbian Resource*

Book, edited by Ginny Vida, pp. 222–225. Englewood Cliffs, New Jersey: Prentice-Hall, 1978), focuses on being young, black, and lesbian during the 1950s. Lorde's fictional piece "Tar Beach" also set in the 1950s, complements her reminiscences (*Conditions: Five*, Autumn 1979, pp. 34–47). She also explores her childhood and relationships with her mother and two older sisters in "My Mother's Mortar" (*Sinister Wisdom* 8, Winter 1979, pp. 54–61) and in "Of Sisters and Secrets" (*The Lesbian Path*, edited by Margaret Cruikshank, pp. 186–195. 2d ed. San Francisco: Double Axe Books, 1981).

While editing the diary of Black writer and editor Alice Dunbar-Nelson (1875–1935), a Black feminist researcher discovered passages indicating that Dunbar-Nelson had lesbian relationships (Dunbar-Nelson, Alice Ruth Moore. *The Diary of Alice Dunbar-Nelson*, edited by Gloria T. Hull. New York: Burt Franklin Publisher, forthcoming). In a recent essay, "Researching Alice Dunbar-Nelson: A Personal and Literary Perspective" (*Feminist Studies* 6, no. 2, Summer 1980, 314–320), editor Hull describes the "engaged process" of researching and writing about Dunbar-Nelson. In a brief reference to Dunbar-Nelson's lesbian relationships, she stresses the importance of letting Dunbar-Nelson stand as she is without distortion or lies. The existence and discovery of this diary furthers the hope that other diaries kept by Black women may also be sources for Black lesbian history.

Other sources of pre-seventies information on Black lesbian life are interviews, biographies, and autobiographies written by individuals not known to be Black and/or lesbian. A recent interview with a white lesbian revealed her involvement with a Black lesbian community in New York City during the sixties (Bulkin, Elly. "An Old Dyke's Tale: An Interview with Doris Lunden." *Conditions: Six*, Summer 1980, pp. 26–44). While gathering material for his biography of Bessie Smith, Chris Albertson interviewed her niece Ruby Smith, who disclosed information concerning Bessie's lesbian relationships as well as reminiscences of Black urban homosexual subculture during the 1920s–1930s. Tapes and transcriptions of these interviews are on file at the Library of Congress in Washington, D.C. Excerpts appear on *AC/DC Blues: Gay Jazz Reissues* (Stash Records, ST-106, Mattituck, N.Y., 1977) and in Albertson's biography *Bessie* (New York: Stein & Day, 1972).

Two autobiographies by Black women contain some information on black lesbianism during the 1930s and 1940s. In *Lady Sings the Blues* (Garden City, New Jersey: Doubleday, 1956), Billie Holiday recalls lesbianism among prison inmates and also offers observations on how race and class affects lesbian identities. In her series of autobiographies, *I Know Why the Caged Bird Sings* (New York: Random House, 1970) and *Gather Together in My Name* (New York: Random House, 1974), Maya Angelou reveals early girlhood confusions and fears about being lesbian and includes a story about two Black lesbians who lived together and worked as prostitutes during the 1940s. These autobiographies also illustrate two Black women's attitudes toward lesbianism.

Besides the Gladys Bentley article mentioned previously, *Ebony* has also published several biographical accounts of Black lesbians or Black women who led what might be termed "variant" lifestyles. Actor Gary Cooper, also an historian of the West, contributed an article, "Stagecoach Mary" (*Ebony* 32, October 1977, pp. 96–98; 100; 102). Mary Fields (1832(?)–1914), born a slave and later a pioneer of the West, contributed an article, "Stagecoach Mary" (*Ebony* 32, October 1977, pp. The second woman in the United State to drive a stagecoach route, she also maintained an intimate and lifelong relationship with Mother Amadeus Dunne, a white nun. Much of Mary's life was spent working with a community of nuns in Montana. Another account related the dramatic and frank story of a Black lesbian "passing woman," Annie Lee Grant, who passed as "Jim McHarris" from the late 1930s until her discovery in 1954 in a small Mississippi town ("The Woman Who Lived as a Man for Fifteen Years." *Ebony* 10, November 1954, pp. 93–96).

Literature and Lyrics

Before 1970 Black lesbian writers did not write openly from their experience and get published. That they *did* write, however, is barely evidenced in the life and work of Angelina Weld Grimké (1880–1958), a poet and playwright of the Harlem Renaissance (Hull, Gloria T. " 'Under the Days': The Buried Life and Poetry of Angelina Weld Grimké." *Conditions: Five*, Autumn 1979, pp. 17–25). The papers of Angelina Weld Grimké at Howard University contain love poems and letters written to women (Moorland-Spingard Research Center, Howard University, Washington, D.C.). Gloria T. Hull's discovery of these documents while researching Black women writers of the Harlem Renaissance suggests the need to search methodically for other lesbian-related material in black women's manuscript collections.

Although published literary works appear to be nonexistent during this period, the blues lyric is one form in which lesbian images openly abound especially during the twenties and thirties when such women as Bessie Smith, Ma Rainey and Bessie Jackson sang them and possibly created them (*AC/DC Blues: Gay Jazz Reissues*). Some of these lyrics have also been recorded in written works (Charters, Samuel. *The Poetry of the Blues*. New York: Oak Publications, 1963; Katz, Jonathan. *Gay American History*. New York: Crowell, 1976; McKay, Claude. *Home to Harlem*. New York: Harper & Bros., 1928). Again, the abundance of these images indicates the need for a methodical search of blues lyrics, especially those attributed to the women blues singers. Identifying and collecting such lyrics would be an important contribution to the discovery of an earlier Black lesbian culture.

Works of fiction containing images of Black lesbians predate 1970. These, however, were written by authors not known to be Black lesbians, and usually the Black lesbian characters were "minor." Many of the literary stereotypes applied to Black women generally were also applied to Black lesbian characters. The first known "Black lesbian" character to appear in the American novel was Jane Rouser. She is portrayed as a maid in a late-nineteenth-century variant novel written by two white male authors (Gunter, Archibald, and Redmond, Fergus. *A Florida Enchantment*. New York: Home Publishing Co., 1892. Available on InterLibrary Loan in microtext format from Strozier Library, Florida State University, Florida 32306). Jane and her white mistress, heiress Lilly Travers, ingest the seeds of the African Sex-Change Tree and in time are transformed into "she-men"—outwardly women but acting in liberated ways prescribed only for the male sex. They both relate to other women, and Jane is depicted as a "headstrong, wild and harum-scarum" character who very actively goes "girl-hunting" in contrast to her white mistress' *seemingly* genteel and decorous courtship of women. The contrast is of interest from a racial, class, and sexual perspective.

A number of novels written in the twenties and thirties include minor Black lesbian-related content or characters often reflecting the Black homosexual urban subcultures of the period. Black writer Claude McKay's previously mentioned novel *Home to Harlem* is one such work. Others were written by white authors (Baker, Dorothy. *Young Man With A Horn*. Boston: Houghton-Mifflin, 1938; Dos Passos, John. *The Big Money*, 1936, later in the trilogy *U.S.A.* Boston: Houghton-Mifflin, 1960; Niles Blair. *Strange Brother*. New York: Liveright, 1931). White characters, both male and female, are often shown frequenting the Black clubs of Harlem which was a commonplace activity in actual life. Black and white women dance together and occasionally "cruise" one another. Sometimes the Black lesbian characters are portrayed as piano players or singers in these clubs.

In the fifties and sixties Black lesbian characters continue to be minor but are more substantial than the fleeting glimpses of the previous decades. Several pulp lesbian novels include Black characters (Bannon, A. *Women in the Shadows*. Greenwich, Connecticut: Fawcett, 1959; Martin, Della. *Twilight Girl*. New York: Softcover Library, 1961). Bannon's character Tris denies both her lesbianism and her Black heritage while Mavis, a somewhat more major character in the Martin novel, maintains her lesbian identity even after her father and husband ostracize her. Among white lesbians, she continues to remain strong in her Black awareness despite being placed in exploitative and token positions. The characters again are cast as maids and piano players.

Paule Marshall, a Black woman writer, was also creating minor lesbian characters and episodes in novels published during this period. A portion of *Brown Girl, Brownstones* (The Feminist Press, 1981) focuses on the close and intimate relationship between two adolescent girl friends, Beryl and Selina, as they "come of age" in Brooklyn. A later novel, *The Chosen Place, The Timeless People* (New York; Harcourt, Brace and World, 1969), is more explicit and also more negative. Merle Kinbona, the main character descended from slaves and colonists, confronts the prejudices and insensitivities of the white American scientists come to "redevelop" her island home in the West Indies. In the course of the novel, Merle, who was educated in England, reveals an earlier exploitative and destructive lesbian relationship with a wealthy Englishwoman.

Several short stories from this period also include Black lesbian characters or content. Emily Jones's "Chanson du Konallis" (*The Ladder* 2, no. 12, September 1958, pp. 8–10, 20–26) places white, wealthy, Southern-born Konalis Martin-Whiteside Heplin II in a Paris bistro where, in the presence of her husband, she seeks to seduce singer Mirine Tige, a Black American sharecropper's daughter. "Fitting" by Lin Yatta (*Evergreen Review* 66, May 1969, pp. 23–24) is the earliest identified piece of fiction published to date that explicitly portrays two Black lesbian lovers. Black lesbian survival in a violent, male-dominated urban society is the theme of this somber and moving short story.

Several critics of lesbian literature have suggested that the fiction of Ann Allen Shockley published since 1974 was probably written before 1970 (Shockley, Ann Allen. *Loving Her*. New York: Bobbs-Merrill, 1974; *The Black and White of It*. Tallahassee, Florida: Naiad Press, 1980). If this is so, it strengthens the theory that Black lesbians were writing lesbian content material but not finding publishers for it during the pre-seventies period. It would be crucial to ascertain if these materials do, in fact, exist, and to make attempts to collect them.

Scientific Studies

Over the last century a number of sociological/psychological studies have been conducted using white gay men and white lesbians as subjects. Very few, however, have focuses on Black lesbians or Black gay men. The first major study of "female sexual inversion" in the late nineteenth century cited briefly a report from a legal psychiatrist in the United States identifying a murder case caused by "perverted sexual jealousy" which involved a Black woman (Ellis, Havelock, and Symonds, John Addington. *Sexual Inversion*. London: Wilson and MacMillan, 1897; New York: Arno Press, 1975). In the midsixties, two popularized "studies" on lesbians briefly mentioned Black lesbians (Cory, Donald Webster. *The Lesbian in America*. New York: Citadel, 1964; Stearn, Jesse. *The Grapevine*. Garden City, New York: Doubleday, 1964).

During this same decade, several substantial research projects focused either in part or totally on Black lesbians. Two studies were conducted by students within academic institutions and, although unpublished, have fortunately been preserved and are accessible. In her paper, "A Study of a Public Lesbian Community" (Master's thesis, Washington University, 1965), Ethel Sawyer explores firsthand the community of a midsixties Black lesbian bar group in St. Louis, Missouri. Sawyer approaches lesbianism as a social rather than as a primarily sexual phenomenon and looks at lesbian behavior within the context of the social structures of the gay community. (The Sawyer paper is available on InterLibrary Loan from Washington University Library, St. Louis, Missouri 63130).

Sawyer's contemporary, Eleanor Hunter, was a student at the University of California when she conducted field work among Black lesbians in Northern California in the late 1960s. She also consulted with members of the Daughters of Bilitis and the Kinsey researchers who were gathering data for their study of homosexuality (discussed later). Hunter's paper, "Double Indemnity: The Negro Lesbian in the 'Straight' White World" (Sociology Paper, University of California at Davis, 1969), focuses on the social and political conditions of Black lesbian life in the Black Community, in the white lesbian community, and in the white-dominated society, analyzing how each may influence lifestyle choices. Sawyer and Hunter each exhibit a keen understanding and in-depth knowledge of both Black life and gay life. Hunter was also aware of Sawyer's earlier unpublished works on Black lesbians and lesbians and class.

Several other studies partly focusing on Black lesbians came out of the white-dominated scientific profession (Bass-Hass, Rita, "The Lesbian Dyad." *Journal of Sex Research* 4, no. 2, May 1968: 108–126; Bell, Alan P., and Weinberg, Martin S. *Homosexualities: A Study of Diversity Among Men and Women*. New York: Simon and Schuster, 1978). The Bass-Hass study included 75 "nonwhite" lesbians (later identified by other researchers as "Black") born between 1918 and 1949. The Black lesbian data, gathered by a Black woman researcher, was compared with data gathered from 125 white lesbians. Differences between the two groups center on age when lesbian relationships started, previous heterosexual experience, and expectations and stability of lifestyle. The results suggest the need for further investigation of how Black culture influences Black lesbian lives.

Although not published until a decade later, the data for the federally funded Bell and Weinberg study was gathered in the late 1960s under the auspices of the

Kinsey Institute. Seventy Black lesbians were interviewed in a sampling of 1,500 interviewees. In their later analysis, the researchers do not consider the possible impact of Black culture and white racism on the differences they found among their informants. The raw data, on file at the Institute for Sex Research, is open to "qualified" researchers.

These unprecedented studies on Black lesbians no doubt resulted from the general interest in Blacks and lesbians which the Black and homophile movements were generating during the sixties.

This essay reflects what I believe is the "tip of the iceberg." I am certain there are more early materials waiting to be uncovered and created. The potential is challenging, and the methods are varied and within reach: creating oral histories with older Black lesbians, searching through Black women's manuscript collections for lesbian-related materials, collecting, preserving, and publishing unpublished materials written by Black lesbians prior to 1970, methodically searching for lesbian related articles in Black periodicals, writing or recording on tape one's own life story, collecting early photos and snapshots. These "raw materials" are fundamental to the development of Black lesbian studies with relationship to Black women's studies and lesbian/gay studies. Making these materials visible and available should be a challenge to all who are committed to a women's studies that represents the rich diversity of women.

Reference and Research Aids

Manuscript Collections: *Bibliographic Guide to Black Studies; Black Academic Libraries and Research Collections: An Historical Survey; Directory of Special Libraries and Information Centers; National Union Catalog of Manuscript Collections; Women's History Sources: A Guide to Archives and Manuscript Collections in the United States.* (See indexes for "negroes," "Black," and "Afro-Americans." Subject terms may vary from source to source and over time.)

Periodical Literature: *Index to Periodical Articles by and about Blacks,* 1973–1977 (and its predecessors: *Index to Periodical Articles by and about Negroes,* 1960–1972; *Index to Selected Periodicals,* 1950–1959; *Guide to Negro Periodical Literature,* 1941–1943; *Index to Black Periodicals* (newspapers); *Black Information Index: The Black List; Directory of Black Literary Magazines.*) (Subject terms vary.)

Projects/Organizations/Collections: Buffalo Oral History Project, 255 Parkside Ave., Buffalo, NY 14214; Institute for Sex Research, 416 Morrison Hall, Indiana University, Bloomington, IN 47405; Lesbian Herstory Archives, P.O. Box 1258, New York, NY 10116. (Most of the lesbian, women's, and gay materials mentioned in this essay are on file at the Lesbian Herstory Archives. Please write to them for more information about sources, photocopies, and contacts for further research.)

See Resources section for information on Buffalo Women's Oral History Project and Lesbian Herstory Archives in New York City—ED.

Resources for Lesbian History

Estelle Freedman

Lesbian history has become the focus of research by scholars in women's studies and by community-based history projects throughout the country.[1] These researchers approach the subject from a variety of perspectives, including the lives of individual lesbians;[2] the social networks and institutions of urban lesbian subcultures;[3] and the emergence of lesbian political consciousness and organizations.[4] By choosing one of these subjects, focusing on a particular historical period, and identifying available sources, students can engage in similar research. As a guide to their studies, research based on six types of historical sources are discussed below. These sources are personal papers; literature; newspapers; legal records; oral history; and photographs.

Intimate friendships between women are well documented in personal papers, such as letters and diaries, left in manuscript collections of families or organizations. Carroll Smith-Rosenberg and other historians have written about these relationships in the eighteenth and nineteenth centuries.[5] The definition of "lesbian" in these studies varies from primary commitment to another woman to evidence of sexual relations. In general, though, the term "lesbian" will not be found until well into the twentieth century, even in relationships where clues to lesbian relationships are strong.

An excellent example of the use of personal papers for studying women's intimate relationships appears in the work of Judith Schwarz.[6] Manuscript collections like those on which her studies are based can be located through imaginative use of library reference tools. A guide to these sources is provided by Nancy Sahli in her article "Sexuality in 19th and 20th Century America."[7] In addition to the library, the family attic or local flea market should not be overlooked as repositories of women's personal papers. One historian actually chanced upon a collection of love letters between a lifelong female couple when their belongings were thrown in the garbage on a New York City street!

Literature, both fiction and poetry, also provides clues primarily for educated and middle-class women's history. Lillian Faderman's rereading of Emily Dickinson's love poems, for instance, challenged the traditional heterosexist interpretation of them and inspired Faderman to write a broader study of women's relationships, one based largely on literary sources.[8] Gloria Hull's essay on the black poet Angelina Weld Grimké draws on poetry, diaries, and letters to disclose the woman-loving at the heart of Grimké's writing.[9] In the special lesbian history issue of *Frontiers: A Journal of Women's Studies,* Josephine Donovan has documented the passionate female relationships of Sarah Orne Jewett through Jewett's unpublished love poems.[10]

For the twentieth century, a self-consciously lesbian literature details a variety of lesbian possibilities, from the literary salons of Paris to the bars of Greenwich Village.[11] The "pulp novels" published between the late 1940s and mid-1960s, for instance, provide a gold mine for studying social attitudes and means of communication among lesbians.[12] Modern literature by lesbian authors such as Elsa Gidlow, Jane Rule, or Gale Wilhelm explore the meanings of women's relationships in this century.

One of the historian's traditional sources, the newspaper, has proven useful for studying lesbians of varied class backgrounds. Given the lack of serious attention to lesbianism in the contemporary press, this source may seem suspect. But in the past, a combination of journalistic sensationalism and lack of censorship allowed numerous stories to appear in American newspapers. The best examples are stories about "passing women" in the years between 1860 and 1940.[13] Dozens of newspaper accounts describe and sometimes quote women who lived as men, "made love" to other women, and sometimes legally married them. While the press accounts must be read with caution, they do contain useful information on relationships and on conflicts with the law. Finding these stories is a challenge, unless one's local newspaper has an index or a subject file in which to look for "passing women," "masquerade," or "cross-dressing."

An even more problematic newspaper source is the obituary, past or present. Historians know, for example, that the generation of women who were active in early twentieth century politics, education, social welfare, and government service often had "Boston marriages," or lifelong companionships with each other. Unfortunately, the survivors in these relationships are rarely listed in obituaries. Still, some clues to significant female friendships can be found in them.

Like the passing woman described in newspaper stories, other lesbians are known to us today because they came into conflict with the law. A fourth type of source, the records of "deviant" women, can expand our knowledge of lesbian history beyond the educated middle classes, for many of the women who appear in court and prison records are from immigrant, working class, and Third World cultures. While the records of court proceedings are less important for lesbian than for gay male history—where prosecution was more frequent—prison records can reveal an unexplored subculture within lesbian history. For example, an article attached to the record of an inmate in a woman's prison in the 1870s told that "Captain Jack"—alias Fred Fiske, alias Arthur Holmes—was in fact a twenty-seven-year-old married woman who wore men's clothes, had "a hard, masculine face and a strong frame," and had repeatedly "made love to blue-eyed misses and been passionately loved by them." More important than such isolated cases are the networks of lesbians in twentieth-century prisons. Investigations began to reveal such groups after about 1915. Further research into women's prison experiences is needed to explore both repression of and resistance by lesbians in prison.[14]

A fifth source, oral history, can help in this task and in many other approaches to lesbian history. Through oral history interviews with women who lived as lesbians in previous generations, researchers are finding a variety of subcultures:

rural and urban; black and white; private and public. They are beginning to piece together the patterns of lesbian community life, as shown by the pioneering work of the Buffalo Women's Oral History Project. For a guide to the methodology of women's oral history, see the special issue of *Frontiers* (Summer, 1977).

In addition to investigating these written and oral sources, researchers have begun to appreciate visual sources as clues to the lesbian past. From the family album to the girls' school yearbook, and to the works of lesbian photographers, we are learning to "reread" pictures much as we reread women's literature. Removing the homophobic lens exposes the nuances of women's relationships in old photographs. A good example is an album found at a flea market in California: its cover is engraved "No Man's Land." Inside are snapshots of two female couples in the years before World War I in which the women cross-dressed, romped in the fields and in bed, and smiled lovingly at each other.

Both historical and contemporary works by lesbian photographers and artists have been examined by Joan Biren and Tee Corinne in their individual slide talks.[15] Members of the Lesbian Herstory Archives in New York have been carefully preserving the photographic record of the contemporary lesbian movement at the same time that they search for images from the past. The work of the New York, Washington, San Francisco, and other local archival projects will thus be invaluable for further research on lesbian history.

Researching lesbian history presents enormous challenges of defining lesbian relationships, decoding closeted sources, and transcending layers of censorship. Nevertheless, the discovery of new sources and the intellectual task of interpreting their meaning for women's and lesbian history has distinct rewards. The researcher not only helps expand the base for further historical studies; she is likely as well to expand her own historical and personal consciousness and gain new appreciation of the lesbians who came before

Notes

[1]Community-based lesbian and gay history projects currently exist in San Francisco, Chicago, New York, Washington, D.C.. Boston, and Buffalo, New York; other cities have archival projects. For information, see "1981 Survey of Archival and Local History Projects," *Lesbian/Gay History Researchers Network Newsletter* 4 (March 1981): 18–21. (Available from LH/DC, c/o Washington Area Women's Center, 1519 P Street, N.W., Washington DC 20005.)

[2]For example, Gayle Rubin's introduction to Renée Vivien, *A Woman Appeared to Me* (Tallahassee, Florida: Naiad Press, 1979), pp. iii–xxi; Judith Schwarz, "Researching Lesbian History," *Sinister Wisdom* 5 (Winter 1978): 55–59.

[3]The Buffalo Women's Oral History Project has pioneered this approach. See: "Buffalo Lesbian Bars, 1930–1960" (paper presented to the Berkshire Conference on Women's History, Vassar College, June 1981), by Madeline Davis, Liz Kennedy, and Avra Michelson.

[4]The Circle of Lesbian Indexers, for example, is preparing an index to cover one hundred lesbian periodicals published in the U.S. since 1947. This index will be important for tracing political consciousness, organizing and strategies.

[5]Carroll Smith-Rosenberg, "The Female World of Love and Ritual: Relations Between Women in Nineteenth Century America," *Signs* 1 (Autumn 1975): 1–29; Nancy Sahli,

"Smashing: Women's Relationships Before the Fall," *Chrysalis* 8 (Summer 1979): 17-27; Lillian Faderman, *Surpassing the Love of Men* (New York: Morrow, 1981); Blanche Cook, "Female Support Networks and Political Activism: Lillian Wald, Crystal Eastman, Emma Goldman," *Chrysalis* 3 (1977): 43-61.

[6]Judith Schwarz, "Yellow Clover: Katherine Lee Bates and Katherine Coman," *Frontiers* 4 (Spring 1979): 59-67; "Mary Ellicott Arnold, Mabel Reed and the Karoks," (paper presented at the Berkshire Conference on the History of Women, Vassar College, June 1981); and her forthcoming book, *Close Friends and Devoted Companions.*

[7]Sahli, "Sexuality in 19th and 20th Century America," *Radical History Review* 20 (Spring/Summer 1979): 89-96.

[8]"Emily Dickinson's Letters to Sue Gilbert," *Massachusetts Review* (September 1977): 197-225; Faderman, *Surpassing the Love of Men.*

[9]"Under the Days: The Buried Life and Poetry of Angelina Weld Grimké," *Conditions: Five* (Fall 1979): 17-25.

[10]"The Unpublished Love Poems of Sara Orne Jewett," *Frontiers* 4 (Fall 1979): 26-31.

[11]Rubin, introduction to Vivien, *A Women Appeared to Me*; Blanche Wiesen Cook, "Women Alone Stir My Imagination: Lesbianism and the Cultural Tradition," *Signs* 4 (Summer 1979): 718-739; Susan Sniader Lanser, "Speaking in Tongues: *Ladies Almanak* and the Language of Celebration," *Frontiers* 4 (Fall 1979): 39-46.

[12]Gene Damon (Barbara Grier), "The Lesbian Paperback," *Tangents* 1 (June/July 1966): 4-7, 13-15; Jeannette Foster, *Sex Variant Women in Literature* (Baltimore: Diana Press, 1976).

[13]See Jonathan Katz, *Gay American History* (New York: Crowell, 1976), for documents on passing women. Other sources are Allan Berube, "Jeanne Bonnet," unpublished paper, San Francisco, and "Lesbian Masquerade," a slideshow by the San Francisco Lesbian History Project, which discusses the phenomenon of passing and tells stories of three passing women in San Francisco.

[14]Estelle B. Freedman, *Their Sisters' Keepers: Women's Prison Reform in America, 1830-1930* (Ann Arbor: University of Michigan Press, 1981), pp. 86, 139-140; Karlene Faith and Robin Ruth Linden, "Sex is Always the Headliner," *Sinister Wisdom* 16 (1981): 2-10. On information from U.S. military investigations of lesbian activity in the armed forces, see Allan Berube, "Marching to a Different Drummer," a slide talk on lesbians and gay men during World War II, excerpted in *The Advocate,* 328 (25 September 1981).

[15]"Lesbian Images in Photography: 1850-1980," slide talk presented by JEB (Joan E. Biren); "Lesbian Images in the Fine Arts," slide talk presented by Tee Corinne.

Additional References

Vern Bullough and Bonnie Bullough, "Lesbianism in the 1920s and 1930s: A Newfound Study," *Signs: Journal of Women in Culture and Society* 2 (Summer 1977): 895-904.

Lisa Duggan, "Lesbianism and American History: A Brief Source Review," *Frontiers* 4 (Fall 1979): 80-85.

Lillian Faderman and Brigitte Eriksson, eds. and trans., *Lesbian-Feminism in Turn-of-the-Century Germany* (Naiad Press, 1980).

Elsa Gidlow, "Memoirs," *Feminist Studies* 6 (Spring 1980), 106-127.

JR Roberts. "In America They Call Us Dykes: Notes on the Etymology and Usage of 'Dyke'," *Sinister Wisdom* 9 (Spring 1979): 3-11.

Leila J. Rupp, " 'Imagine My Surprise': Women's Relationships in Historical Perspective," *Frontiers* 5 (Fall 1980): 61-70.

[Several sources mentioned in this article and notes are described in the Resources section: lesbian history projects in Buffalo, New York City, San Francisco and Boston; the Circle of Lesbian Indexers; slide talks by JEB (Joan E. Biren), Tee Corinne, and Allan Berube; and the slide talk "Lesbian Masquerade"—ED.]

Who Hid Lesbian History?

Lillian Faderman

Before the rise of the lesbian-feminist movement in the early 1970s, twentieth-century women writers with great ambition were generally intimidated into silence about the lesbian experiences in their lives. In their literature, they gave male personae the voice of their most autobiographical characters, and they were thus permitted to love other women; or they disguised their homoerotic subject matter in code which is sometimes all but unreadable, or when they wrote of love most feelingly and even laid down rules for loving well as Margaret Anderson did, they left out gender altogether. We cannot blame them for not providing us with a clear picture of what it was like for a woman to love other women in their day. If they had they would have borne the brunt of anti-lesbian prejudice which followed society's enlightenment by late-nineteenth-century and early-twentieth-century sexologists about love between women,[1] and they knew that if they wished to be taken seriously they had to hide their arrested development and neuropathic natures. But we might expect that before the twentieth century, before love between women was counted among the diseases, women would have had little reason to disguise their emotional attachments; therefore, they should have left a record of their love of other women. And they did. However, it is impossible to discover that record by reading what most of their twentieth-century biographers have had to say about their lives.

While pre-twentieth century women would not have thought that their intensest feelings toward other women needed to be hidden, their twentieth-century biographers, who were brought up in a post-Krafft-Ebing, Havelock Ellis, Sigmund Freud world, did think that, and they often altered their subjects' papers. Other twentieth-century biographers have refused to accept that their subjects "suffered from homosexuality," and have discounted the most intense expressions of love between their subjects and other women. And where it was impossible to ignore the fact that their subjects were despondent over some love relationship, many twentieth-century biographers frantically searched for some hidden man who must have been the object of their subject's affection, even though a beloved woman was in plain view. These techniques of bowdlerization, avoidance of the obvious, and *cherchez l'homme* appear in countless pre-1970s biographies about women of whom there is reason to suspect lesbian attachments.

In our heterocentric society, the latter technique is the most frequent. What can it mean when a woman expresses great affection for another woman? It means that she is trying to get a man through that woman. What can it mean when a woman grieves for years over the marriage or death of a woman friend? It means that she is really unhappy because she had hoped to procure her friend's husband for herself, or she is unhappy because there must have been another man somewhere in the background who coincidentally jilted her at the same time—only all concrete evidence has been lost to posterity. So why did Lady Mary Montagu write to Anne Wortley in 1709 letters which reveal a romantic passion? e.g.,

> My dear, dear, adieu! I am entirely your's, and wish nothing more than it may be some time or other in my power to convince you that there is nobody dearer (to me) than yourself...[2]

> I cannot bear to be accused of coldness by one whom I shall love all my life....You will think I forget you, who are never out of my thoughts.... I esteem you as I ought in esteeming you above the world.[3]

> ...your friendship is the only happiness of my life; and whenever I lose it, I have nothing to do but to take one of my garters and search for a convenient beam.[4]

> Nobody ever was so entirely, so faithfully yours.... I put in your lovers, for I don't allow it possible for a man to be so sincere as I am.[5]

Lady Mary's 1920s biographer admits that Mary's letters to Anne carry "heart-burnings and reproaches and apologies" which might make us, the readers, "fancy ourselves in Lesbos,"[6] but, she assures us, Lady Mary knew that Anne's brother, Edward, would read what she wrote to Anne, "and she tried to shine in these letters for him."[7] Thus, Mary was not writing of her love for Anne; she was only showing Edward how smart, noble, and sensitive she was, so that he might be interested in her.

Why did Anna Seward, the eighteenth-century poet, grieve for thirty years over the marriage of Honora Sneyd? Why in a sonnet of 1773 does she accuse Honora of killing "more than life,—e'en all that makes life dear"?[8] Why in another does she beg for merciful sleep which would "charm to rest the thoughts of whence, or how/Vanish'd that priz'd Affection"?[9] Why in still another peom does she weep because the "plighted love" of the woman she called "my life's adorner"[10] has now "changed to cold disdain"?[11] Well, speculates her 1930s biographer, it was probably because Anna Seward wished to marry the recently widowed Robert Edgeworth (whom Honora ensnared) herself. After all, "She was thirty years old—better suited to him in age and experience than Honora. Was she jealous of the easy success of [Honora]? Would she have snatched away, if she could have done so, the mature yet youthful bridegroom, so providentially released from his years of bondage?"[12]

But surely such distortions could not be made by a biographer of Mary Wollstonecraft. Even her husband, William Godwin, admitted in his memoirs of her that Mary's love for Fanny Blood had been "so fervent, as for years to have constituted the ruling passion of her mind."[13] But what was regarded as a fact of life by an eighteenth-century husband, boggles the mind of a twentieth-century scholar. For example, how was one biographer of the early 1950s to deal with the information that in 1785 Mary underwent a terrible depression and that she complained in a letter to Fanny Blood's brother, George, "My harassed mind will in time wear out my body. . . . I have lost all relish for life—and my almost broken heart is only cheered by the prospect of death. . . . I almost hate the Green [her last home with Fanny] for it seems that grave of all my comforts."?[14] The biographer states himself that at the Green Fanny's health worsened and she could no longer teach, and for that reason Mary urged her to marry a man who would take her to a warm climate where she might recover. Then he asks, quoting the above letter to George Blood, "What had happened [to cause her great depression]? Surely her father's difficulties could not have suddenly plunged her into such a despondent state; nor could loneliness for Fanny or George."[15] His explanation is that Mary must have been madly in love with the Reverend Joshua Waterhouse and had been spurned by him. The biographer admits that there is no evidence he can offer to prove his hypothesis, and even that "On the surface Waterhouse seems like the last man in the world who would have attracted Mary Wollstonecraft." But he was the only man around at the time so "apparently he did."[16] "Something drastic," the biographer points out, must have happened "to provoke such despair," and the loss of a much-loved woman friend cannot be seen as "drastic" by a heterocentric scholar.

When there is no proof that a subject was involved in a heterosexual relationship, such biographers have been happy enough to accept circumstantial evidence rather than acknowledge the power of a same-sex attachment. Characteristically, the same Wollstonecraft scholar quotes a letter to George Blood which Mary wrote six months after Fanny's death ("My poor heart still throbs with selfish anguish. It is formed for friendship and confidence — yet how often it is wounded.") and then points out that the next sixteen lines have been obliterated by a later hand and suggests that they must have referred to her affair with Waterhouse. "Surely the censor did not go to such pains to conceal Mary's lamentations on the death of her friends," he asserts. It must have been Mary's love of a man the censor was trying to hide.[17] However, considering Godwin's complete honesty regarding Mary's affairs with Fuseli, Imlay, and himself, it is doubtful that a considerate censor would wish to spare her the embarrassment of one more youthful affair. What is more likely is that the letter was censored by someone from our century, aware of the twentieth-century stigma regarding "lesbianism," who wished to spare Mary that more serious accusation.

Despite that biographer's flimsy proof of the Waterhouse affair, subsequent Wollstonecraft biographers, uncomfortable with the evidence of her attachment to Fanny, have been happy to accept Waterhouse as fact. The myth is even propagated in a 1970s biography of Wollstonecraft by a woman. After discussing Mary's attachment to Fanny and pointedly distinguishing it from "lesbianism," she introduces Mary's "affair" with Waterhouse with the statement, "In spite of these emotions and professions [to Fanny], a certain secret disloyalty to Fanny did take place. It is rather a relief to discover it" [sic].[18]

The cherchez l'homme technique has been used most frequently by biographers of Emily Dickinson who have filled up tomes looking for the poet's elusive lover and have come up with no fewer than ten candidates, generally with the vaguest bits of "evidence." Concrete evidence that the ruling passion of Dickinson's life may well have been Sue Gilbert was eradicated from Dickinson's published letters and has become available only within the last couple of decades through Thomas Johnson's complete edition of her correspondence.[19] The earlier publications of a sizable number of Dickinson's letters was the work of her niece, Martha Dickinson Bianchi, the author of *The Life and Letters of Emily Dickinson* (1924) and *Emily Dickinson Face to Face* (1932). Bianchi, a post-Freudian, felt compelled to hide what her aunt expressed without self-consciousness. Therefore, Bianchi reproduced a February 16, 1852 (Johnson date) letter to Sue thus:

> Sometimes I shut my eyes and shut my heart towards you and try hard to forget you, but you'll never go away. Susie, forgive me, forget all that I say.[20]

What she did not produce of that letter tells a much more potent story:

> … Sometimes I shut my eyes, and shut my heart towards you, and try hard to forget you because you grieve me so, but you'll never go away, Oh, you never will — say, Susie, promise me again, and I will smile faintly — and take up my little cross of sad—*sad* separation. How vain it seems to *write*, when one knows how to feel — how much more near and dear to sit beside you, talk with you, hear the tones of your voice; so hard to "deny thyself, and take up thy cross, and follow me"! — give me strength, Susie, write me of hope and love, and of hearts that *endured*, and great was their reward of "Our Father who art in Heaven." I don't know how I shall bear it, when the gentle spring comes; if she should come and see me and talk to me of you, Oh it would surely kill me! While the frost clings to the windows, and the World is stern and drear; this absence is easier; the Earth mourns too, for all her little birds; but when they all come back again, and she sings and is so merry — pray, what will become of me? Susie, forgive me, forget all that I say….

Similarly, in the letter of June 11, 1852 (Johnson date) Bianchi tells us that Emily wrote to Sue:

> Susie, forgive me Darling, for every word I say, my heart is full of you, yet when I seek to say to you something not for the world, words fail me. I try to bring you nearer, I chase the weeks away till they are quite departed — three weeks — they can't last always, for surely they must go with their little brothers and sisters to their long home in the West![21]

But by checking the complete letter in the Johnson edition we find that what Emily wrote to Sue in that letter of June 11, when Sue was about to return to Amherst from her semester-long stint as a schoolteacher, was much more in the nature of a love letter than we could have guessed from the Bianchi version:

> Susie, forgive me Darling, for every word I say — my heart is full of you, none other than you in my thoughts, yet when I seek to say to you something not for the world, words fail me. If you were here — and Oh that you were, my Susie, we need not talk at all, our eyes would whisper for us, and your hand fast in mine, we would not ask for language — I try to bring you nearer, I chase the

weeks away till they are quite departed, and fancy you have come, and I am on my way through the green lane to meet you, and my heart goes scampering so, that I have much ado to bring it back again, and learn it to be patient, till that dear Susie comes. Three weeks —they can't last always, for surely they must go with their little brothers and sisters to their long home in the West!

Sue Gilbert was later to marry Austin Dickinson, Emily's brother, and Martha Dickinson Bianchi was the daughter of Sue and Austin. As anxious as she was to prove that Sue played a great part in making Emily a poet and to show that they were the closest of friends, she was even more anxious to prove that Emily and Sue were *only* friends. Thus, she includes in *Face to Face* an affectionate note that Emily sent Sue on June 27, 1852 (Johnson date):

Susie, will you indeed come home next Saturday? Shall I indeed behold you, not "darkly, but face to face" or am I *fancying* so and dreaming blessed dreams from which the day will wake me? I hope for you so much and feel so eager for you — feel I cannot wait. Sometimes I must have Saturday before tomorrow comes.[22]

But what Emily really said in that note, as Johnson shows, places their relationship in quite a different light:

Susie, will you indeed come home next Saturday, and be my own again, and kiss me as you used to? Shall I indeed behold you, not "darkly, but face to face" or am I *fancying* so, and dreaming blessed dreams from which the day will wake me? I hope for you so much, and feel so eager for you, feel I *cannot* wait, feel that *now* I must have you — that the expectation once more to see your face again, makes me feel hot and feverish, and my heart beats so fast — I go to sleep at night, and the first thing I know, I am sitting there wide awake, and clasping my hands tightly, and thinking of next Saturday, and "never a bit" of you.
Sometimes I must have Saturday before tomorrow comes.

Where biographers have been too scrupulous to bowdlerize they have nevertheless managed to distort lesbian history by avoiding the obvious. Sometimes this has been done to "save" the reputations of their subjects (e.g., Emma Stebbins, Alice B. Toklas, and Edith Lewis were the "companions," respectively, of Charlotte Cushman, Gertrude Stein, and Willa Cather), although illicit heterosexual affairs are seldom treated with such discretion by even the most sensitive biographers. Sometimes this has been done out of willful ignorance. For example, while Amy Lowell so obviously made her "companion," Ada Russell, the subject of her most erotic love poetry that even a casual acquaintance could observe it, and Lowell herself admitted "How could so exact a portrait remain unrecognized?"[23] It did remain unrecognized by those who saw Lowell only as an overweight unmarried woman whose "sources of inspiration are literary and secondary rather than primarily the expression of emotional experience,"[24] and whose characters thus never breathe, except for those "few frustrated persons such as the childless old women in 'The Doll,'" who share Lowell's "limited personal experiences."[25]

Although many biographers of the 1970s have been much more perceptive and honest with regard to their subjects' lesbian loves (e.g., Jean Gould's *Amy: The*

World of Amy Lowell and the Imagist Movement, New York: Dodd, Mead, 1975; and
Virginia Spencer Carr's *The Lonely Hunter: A Biography of Carson McCullers,*
Garden City, New York: Doubleday, 1975) we cannot assume that lesbian history
will never again be hidden by scholars who live in this heterocentric world. One
otherwise careful, contemporary feminist critic totally ignores Margaret Anderson's
successive passionate relationships with Jane Heap, Georgette LeBlanc, and
Dorothy Caruso, and explains that ambitious women of Anderson's day were
forced into loveless existences. But even where lesbian relationships are admitted
in biographies of the 1970s, their importance is often discounted. A recent author
of an Edna St. Vincent Millay biography squeezes Millay's lesbian relationships into
a chapter entitled "Millay's Childhood and Youth" and organizes each of the
subsequent chapters around a male with whom Millay had some contact, all of
them ostensibly her lovers. Six who had relatively short contact with her are treated
together in a chapter entitled "Millay's Other Men," although the author admits in
that chapter that three of "Millay's other men" were homosexual.

This essay no doubt reads like a long complaint. It is. But it is also a warning
and a hope. It is as difficult for heterocentric biographers to deal with love between
women in their subjects' lives as it is for ethnocentric white scholars to deal with
Third World subject matter, and their products are generally not to be trusted. If we
wish to know about the lives of women it is vital to get back to their diaries, letters
(praying that they have not already been expurgated by some well-meaning
heterosexist hand), and any original source material that is available. It is also vital
to produce biographies divested of the heterocentric perspective. Women's lives
need to be reinterpreted, and we need to do it ourselves.

Notes

[1] See my article, "the Morbidification of Love Between Women by 19th Century
Sexologists," *Journal of Homosexuality* 4 (Fall 1978):73-90.

[2] *The Complete Letters of Lady Mary Wortley Montagu,* ed. Robert Halsband (Oxford:
Clarendon Press, 1965), I: 4.

[3] Ibid., I: 5.

[4] Ibid., I: 12.

[5] Ibid.

[6] Iris Barry, *Portrait of Lady Mary Wortley Montagu* (Indianapolis: Bobbs-Merrill,
1928), p. 61.

[7] Ibid., p. 54.

[8] Walter Scott, ed., *The Poetical Works of Anna Seward with Extracts from her Literary
Correspondence* (Edinburgh: John Ballantyne and Co., 1810) III: 135.

[9] Ibid., III: 134.

[10] Ibid., I: 76-77.

[11] Ibid., III: 133.

[12] Margaret Ashmun, *The Singing Swan: An Account of Anna Seward and her Acquaintance with Dr. Johnson, Boswell, and Others of their Time* (New Haven: Yale University Press, 1931), pp. 28-29.

[13]William Godwin, *Memoirs of Mary Wollstonecraft*, ed. W. Clark Durant (1798; reprinted London: Constable and Co., 1927), p. 18.

[14]Quoted in Ralph M. Wardle, *Mary Wollstonecraft: A Critical Biography* (Lawrence: University of Kansas Press, 1951), pp. 40–41.

[15]Ibid., p. 41.

[16]Ibid., p. 37.

[17]Ibid., pp. 41–42.

[18]Claire Tomalin, *The Life and Death of Mary Wollstonecraft* (London: Harcourt Brace Jovanovich, 1974), p. 18.

[19]Thomas Johnson and Theodora Ward, eds., *The Letters of Emily Dickinson*, (Cambridge: Harvard University Press, 1958).

[20]Martha Dickinson Bianchi, *Emily Dickinson Face to Face* (Boston: Houghton Mifflin, 1932), p. 184.

[21]Ibid., p. 216.

[22]Ibid., p. 218. I discuss these letters at greater length in "Emily Dickinson's Letters to Sue Gilbert," *Massachusetts Review* 18 (Summer 1977).

[23]Letter John Livingston Lowes, February 13, 1918 in S. Foster Damon, *Amy Lowell: A Chronicle, With Extracts from her Correspondence* (Boston: Houghton Mifflin Co., 1935), p. 441.

[24]Hervey Allen, "Amy Lowell as a Poet," *Saturday Review of Literature* 3 (February 5, 1927):558. See also Horace Gregory, *Amy Lowell: Portrait of the Poet in Her Time* (New York: Thomas Nelson and Sons, 1958), p. 212; and Walter Lippmann, "Miss Lowell and Things," *New Republic* 6 (March 18, 1916):178–179.

[25]Allen, "Amy Lowell as a Poet," p. 568.

Lesbian Biography, Biography of Lesbians

Frances Doughty

Lesbian biography can mean biography of lesbians or biography by lesbians. We need both.

Biography of Lesbians

On the most basic level, we need biographies of lesbians simply to give us back our history, our foremothers, and our role models. We also need biographies that examine women's lives as political statements. Lesbian-feminist political analysis in biographies allows a woman to be seen not just as an individual but also as an example of the interaction of the categories *female* and *lesbian* (if she is a lesbian) with her individual personality and social setting. In this context, I would define lesbian-feminism as taking woman as the reference point for constructing both a politics that includes all women and an analysis that integrates all forms of oppression, especially sexual, in its explanation of how societal forces oppress women.

Definitions

What *is* a lesbian in historical terms? One fundamental irony of this question is that our culture has defined lesbianism as male-identified, whereas in fact it is our woman-centeredness that permits lesbians to express the full range of possible ways of being a woman. We live as lesbians in a culture where woman's very being is defined as conditional to the male. Whatever maleness is defined as, woman is seen as its opposite or complement; she is the not-male. We ourselves are not free of the effects of having the definition of our most essential selves subject to others' whims. The tenuousness of definition by not-being is one of the most basic and insidious forms of our oppression. Part (if not all) of the transgression of lesbians is that we refuse this conditionality and insist on our own firm ground of being. But what most observers see first when they look at us is the category *woman* so we share the acculturation that affects all women. In the existential sense of the word, we women do not exist. Lesbians also share the "mythical monster" status, so that, although lesbianism is admitted to exist somewhere as a theoretical possibility outside the realm of the speaker's immediate experience, cognitive dissonance sets in if the label *lesbian* is applied to any specific individual. Therefore no subject of a biography is actually allowed to be labeled a lesbian.

Besides these basic philosophical/psychological difficulties in the definitions of women and lesbians in this culture, a third difficulty is the professional historians' emphasis on a sexual/genital definition of lesbianism, which follows the generally narrow (male) definition of *all* sexuality as genital. Even the expression "genital contact," used as a criterion of "real" lesbianism, imposes male heterosexual imagery on lesbian sexuality.

But, despite our use of new, nonsexual labels, such as *woman-centered-woman*, in rebellion against the male definition of lesbianism as nothing but genital sexuality, sexuality between women *is* important. It is important because it means that those women have taken the risk of breaking cultural definitions, of being passionate. To be passionate requires connectedness—that firm sense of oneself that is denied most women. What is called female sexual passion by the culture is permitted only tentatively and in relation to men. Real passion manifests itself across the whole spectrum of emotionality, not just sexually, but it does make of sexuality as profound a force as any other overwhelming and deeply rooted emotion. Just because the culture has debased it to a genital itch, the sexual force of caring passionately for women and its power to break through myths, definitions, and taboos must not be lost sight of in redefining lesbianism.

The real issue, however, is the mythical quality of the lesbian, which allows the almost unprovable issue of specific sexual practices to be used as an escape hatch by historians who cannot bear to see any specific individuals made into monsters by the label lesbian. For how many heterosexual subjects is there specific evidence of what they actually did in bed? Why are there different standards of evidence in establishing heterosexuality as opposed to homosexuality?

Sexuality is not *the* single criterion (if there *is* any single criterion) that defines lesbianism, though it is one of its most powerful elements. In response to this pressure demanding a strictly sexual definition, a new definition of lesbianism as a woman-centered way of life was developed; another definition is a way of life that values women for themselves.

Cultural Differences

Over and above the perhaps simplistic assumption that all the varieties of our experience can be described by one definition, there is another problem in trying to develop a universal definition of lesbianism. The word carries our whole culture with it, not just in its denotation (however we define it), but in all its connotations, both negative and positive. I do not believe that we can—or should even attempt to—cleanse it of all those encrustations for use in other cultural contexts. I would prefer that we first understand and describe woman-loving in terms of the culture in which it occurs, as best we can within our own cultural limits, and only then look for labels. We must look at the specifics of how gender roles are defined and enforced, and how the enforcement varies for each cultural setting. A close study of the popular nineteenth-century word *spinster* and how its use as a pejorative resembles the current use of *lesbian* would be an important contribution to lesbian-feminist theory and history. Analysis of the use of scare-words such as *spinster* in a specific cultural context is an example of the issues lesbian biographers face, especially when we are dealing with subjects from cultural settings different from our own. We need to be aware of the political implications of our own personal histories, so as not to mistakenly inflate the specifics of our experiences into universal truths.

Lesbian Historiography

Biography of lesbians is entangled right now in a defensive position, simply trying to prove that it is legitimate to call individuals lesbians. This position is forced on us from the outside, and we must deal with it, but it obscures our own issues. If lesbianism were not viewed negatively, how often would we have to prove its existence? Lesbianism is not a visible physical attribute, so, unlike the history of other oppressed groups such as blacks and women, lesbian history is in the peculiar historical position of having to prove the very existence of its subject matter.

What are the unbiased rules of historical evidence appropriate to establishing lesbianism? Certainly not the homophobic and heterosexist criteria now generally in use. It is up to us as lesbians to establish our own historiography and promulgate it until the old standards are replaced. At least for women of backgrounds similar to our own, we as lesbians have "instincts" about identifying other lesbians, and these instincts can be articulated in terms of evidence.

What are the almost subliminal signs that we read as lesbian? First, the general context of a life spent mainly in the company of other women, sometimes joined with overt feminist statements or negative statements about male culture. Participation in lesbian culture—a sign many nonlesbians miss because they do not know the culture. An intimate women companion or companions who may have shared housing and daily life. Friendship networks with women and a conscious valuing of friendship between women; friendship patterns in which two women cease being a couple but remain close friends; friendship networks made up of former lovers and their current and/or former lovers and friends, as well as long-standing and powerful friendships between women who may not have been lovers. A tone in writing to or about women that is markedly more intimate/affectionate/passionate than that used in general. Also, self-defined work that is a central theme of the subject's life, or an unusual occupation. Interest in and struggles on behalf of other oppressed or deviant groups. Also, friendships with gay men, and an ironic or ambivalent relationship with male homosexuals resulting from our forced community.

Lesbian historians may absorb these details almost unconsciously, but nonlesbians almost always miss them or discount them as insufficient evidence. Furthermore, since there is no single criterion for establishing lesbianism, perhaps we should talk about patterns of evidence. For ourselves as lesbian-feminist biographers, we need to establish the limits of the validity of the above set of signs in terms of distinctions of class, race, age, date, and geographical location. We also need to establish rules of evidence for cultural settings other than those with which we are familiar.

Coding

As another aspect of establishing our own historiography, we need to continue to expand and to discuss the concept of coding, already accepted in connection with Gertrude Stein's poetry, for instance, in the broader terms of lesbian survival techniques. The biographer must be able to read the signs and must know the lesbian context in which those signs must be read. This coding occurs both verbally (in conversations, letters, journals) and nonverbally (in choices of books, pictures, clothing styles, body language, friends, entertainment, places to socialize). Instead of asking for approval of our perceptions by nonlesbians, we should point out that we are far better equipped to read these codes than nonlesbian biographers and historians. Our standards, not theirs, should prevail.

Public Selves, Private Selves

Another question of lesbian-feminist analysis for the biographer is how the subject presents herself—to herself (in diaries and journals), to intimates and acquaintances (in letters), and to the world (in her work and in autobiography). Our culture has a tradition of dividing the private and the public self. The public self embodies male values, especially those of achievement. The product or the persona is carefully separated from the person. Some women maintain this tradition; some do not. What happens when women do or do not obliterate this distinction in their presentations of themselves?

Women usually attain historically valued status through their relation to males. Women's achievements in any sphere tend to disappear from the historical record; women's achievements that take place in spheres valued only by women have no public selves because our achievements become part of the public record only if we are connected with males. In another sense, because we are not allowed to escape our role requirements as females, who are by definition private persons, women in history often appear only as extensions of our private selves—as mothers, as sex objects, as emotional creatures. We are not seen as having both careers *and* private lives.

Lesbians have used both of these models, the private and the public, in their presentations of self. Janet Flanner, author of "Letters from Paris" for the *New Yorker* and one of the American lesbians living in Paris from the 1920s into the 1970s, consistently and rigorously separated her public and private presentations of self, even signing her columns with the pseudonym Genêt. For twenty years the lover of Solita Solano, who was a novelist, editor, and poet, Flanner presented to the public only her persona as a journalist. There are reminiscences in her work, but never unmaskings. She covered all the great events of her day, accepting as a journalist the mainstream culture's definition of great events and great men, with whom she associated, especially as a war correspondent during World War II. Thus, she survives in history as a personage in her own right, the Genêt of the *New Yorker's* "Letters from Paris," friend of Hemingway, wartime journalist, caretaker of those in trouble (including Alice B. Toklas after Stein's death).

The need to attach women in history to famous men is especially apparent in biographies, and even autobiographies, of lesbians where in book after book, there is what I have come to call the "obligatory great men" chapter in which the single woman is legitimated by detailing her connections with Great Men. Again, the basic idea is that women are *in-valid* unless connected to, and validated by, men. This pattern is too striking to be passed over.

Flanner's acquaintance and contemporary, Margaret Anderson, on the other hand, made her life her work. Before moving to Paris in 1923, she had shared responsibility for the *Little Review* with Jane Heap, her lover and coeditor for eight years. Her own instincts governed her decisions on what to publish, and the magazine included people ranging from Emma Goldman, the anarchist, to Mary Garden, the singer. The *Little Review,* however, entered history because of its early publication of James Joyce and Ezra Pound, both on their way to being Great Men. Because of the male-connected definition of the public self, nurturing Great Men in the *Little Review* is what history records as Margaret Anderson's only mainstream achievement. Yet her own self-definition is as someone whose work was the creation of her own life, that is, whose private self was also her public self. She devoted the last two volumes of her three-volume *Autobiography* to her life after the *Little Review.* But, since they showed no conventional public self or achievements that met male standards, her work in creating and recording her own life, successful by her own standards, has disappeared from the historical record.

The contrast between the two women is particularly apparent in how they present their lesbianism. Anderson names her three great loves: Jane Heap, Georgette Leblanc, and Dorothy Caruso; near the end of her life, she attempts to publish an overtly lesbian love story, apparently written almost forty-five years earlier. Flanner says nothing. And this is where the distinction between the public and private self overlaps with coding as a means of disguise. Especially for a male-identified lesbian, such a distinction may be a genuinely held belief (the popular image of the selfless scientist, for example), but it also allows her to obliterate the fact of being a lesbian from the public record. These motivations are intertwined and probably often unconscious for the subject, but the biographer of a lesbian should not simply accept the public-private separation at face value. The presentation of only the public self seems to be linked with male identification and with silence about being a lesbian. Lesbians who present the private self seem to be attempting to be valued for themselves, including their lesbianism, but their self-definition often seems to be ignored.

Biography by Lesbians

Biography, if done with love, is a vicarious relationship: we should know what in us is attracted to our subjects and what role they are playing in our own emotional and political lives. In order to write lesbian-feminist biographies, the researcher needs to be explicit about her own politics. For instance, the need for recognition not accorded females in our culture leads me to write about "extraordinary" women such as Maragaret Anderson. But there is also a contradiction between my identification with her rather elitist life and my own identification as a lesbian-feminist that is important to recognize and to understand.

Access

The biographer who is an open lesbian may have practical problems with access to materials, particularly interviews, especially if she is not affiliated with a recognized and "respectable" institution such as a university. Access may also be difficult if all her previous work is overtly lesbian (or even feminist); above all, difficulties arise when she has no institutional affiliation and needs to present her previous work to establish her credentials. Ease of access to archival materials varies, depending on the institution. For some (Library of Congress Manuscript Division), no credentials are required. For others (the Kinsey Institute), access is difficult, requiring letters of introduction. In others, access is impossible because papers are closed to the public or even deliberately suppressed by the archives to "protect sensitive materials." Researchers should also be aware of the copyright laws allowing brief quotations from personal papers in scholarly articles but requiring permission for the formal publication of entire letters and journals. If possible, it is often easier to use short quotations than to have to get permissions, especially if the material concerns lesbianism and/or the researcher is an open lesbian. Permission may be denied, and such censorship is not uncommon when the subject was a lesbian.

Problems of access may also occur if there is an "approved" biographer who has exclusive use of the subject's papers, particularly if the estate is trying to keep the subject's lesbianism invisible. Furthermore, some people may refuse to be interviewed by anyone other than the official biographer.

The most difficult problem, however, is probably that of how to approach interviews, especially the question of whether or not to be open about one's lesbianism. There are excellent guides to doing interviews and oral histories but there is no single answer to the particular problem. If one is not open, eliciting information may be difficult; if one is open, the interview may become suddenly constrained. Sensitivity, tact, persistence, and ingenuity are required to obtain information on a subject's lesbianism.

Lesbian biography, then, means understanding the tools of the biographer's trade; it means understanding the specific cultural context of the biographer as well as of the subject; it means understanding how woman-loving manifests itself differently in different cultural settings, and it means finding appropriate terminology for those different manifestations; it means understanding the signs and codes of lesbianism that cannot be open; it means developing and establishing a lesbian-feminist historiography; and it means understanding individual lives as responses to the oppression of women and of lesbians and especially as resistance to that oppression. We as lesbian biographers can nourish other women by bringing alive our lost sisters and by speaking as truly as we can of the circumstances of their lives from the perspectives of our own.

One Out of Thirty: Lesbianism in Women's Studies Textbooks

Bonnie Zimmerman

Tillie Olsen, in her classic article, "One Out of Twelve: Writers Who Are Women in Our Time," noted that in gauges of literary achievement such as courses and anthologies, one woman writer appears for every twelve men. For open lesbian writers in women's studies texts, the figure is close to one out of thirty, forty, or fifty.[1] In the books that structure introductory women's studies courses, lesbians are at best tokens, and at worst, invisible. I surveyed twenty paperbacks used in these courses and found that lesbianism is represented by at most one article or a handful of pages.[2] Editors and authors seem to be too uncomfortable with or oblivious to the experience, politics, culture, and oppression of lesbians to seriously include our perspectives in their texts.

In the early 1970s, many publishing houses latched onto the mass market for women's liberation literature by signing activists to edit collections of articles culled primarily from feminist publications. These paperbacks are equally popular with lay readers and with introductory course instructors. Partly because of the movement experience of the editors, these books—*Liberation Now!, Woman in a Sexist Society, Women's Liberation: Blueprint for the Future, Sisterhood is Powerful,* and *Voices from Women's Liberation*—each contains at least one article (1 to 4 percent of its total page content) on lesbianism. Only *The Black Woman* avoids lesbianism, possibly because of the strong stigma against homosexuality in the Black liberation movement at the time, although women like Anita Cornwell had been writing for *The Ladder* for years. Although one article cannot present the information and variety of perspectives one might desire for an introductory student, the editors, as political activists, chose their material responsibly. The articles are all by early spokeswomen for lesbian literation: the Radicalesbians Collective, Barbara Grier, Sidney Abbott, and Barbara Love, and Martha Shelley (whose work is included in three of these collections as well as one other anthology). Most of these articles provide a general overview of lesbianism: a little bit of life experience, a little bit of oppression, a little bit of politics. These articles reflect the highly political consciousness of their time, thus proving to be very challenging and possibly disturbing to novice women's studies students. It would be very easy for instructors to skip these articles and, therefore, skip lesbianism entirely in their courses.

In addition to books designed equally for classrooms and living rooms, publishers began to produce special textbooks for the growing women's studies market. Of those that appeared in the early 1970s, only *Up Against the Wall, Mother* includes any material on lesbianism. The rest—*Female Liberation, The Women, Yes!,* and *Roles Women Play: Readings Toward Women's Liberation*—are silent about the lesbian members of the female population. Either their publishers and editors deliberately decided to omit any controversial material, or they simply never thought that lesbianism might be a significant issue of women's liberation. Both explanations point to the heterosexism of the early women's movement. Ignorance, however, can be no excuse for texts that were developed after 1972 or 1973. Lesbianism had become such a significant issue within women's liberation that a text or course could ignore it only out of fear or prejudice. Two such anthologies widely used in introductory courses are *Beyond Intellectual Sexism* (but not heterosexism) and *Women: A Feminist Perspective.* The latter is an irritating example of entrenched heterosexism in the women's studies establishment. Edited by Jo Freeman, well known as a feminist activist, theoretician, and educator, *Women: A Feminist Perspective* included no article on lesbianism when it first was issued in 1975 and continued its silence in the 1979 second edition. This is particularly damaging since the anthology is probably the most widely used text in a variety of introductory women's studies courses. The most recent addition to textbooks that offers an instant "Introduction of Women's Studies" course is *Issues in Feminism*, which may prove to be as popular as Freeman's book. This collection offers Charlotte Bunch's "Learning From Lesbian Separatism" as its only lesbian article. While this excellent piece argues a strong political perspective on lesbianism (thus demonstrating courage on the editor's part since academic feminists usually avoid separatist analyses), it unfortunately is not balanced by other political positions nor by general consciousness raising material.

Most women's studies texts have problems integrating lesbian material into their structures because lesbianism is ghettoized: a lesbian perspective is not presented on the variety of social, cultural, and political issues explored by women's studies. Editors are then faced with the politically volatile question of where to place their token lesbian article (a parallel situation often occurs with the one or two articles included on women of color). Most feminist editors avoid identifying lesbianism as a purely sexual issue, choosing instead to include lesbianism in a section on sex roles and socialization, or political activism. Lesbianism, however, is seldom integrated throughout the entire text. The only anthology that attempts to avoid this ghettoization is *Feminist Frameworks,* another popular textbook. Since its orientation is philosophical rather than sociological, it presents feminist issues within different theoretical frameworks. Topics such as the family and sexuality are explored by writers representing conservatism, liberalism, traditional Marxism, radical feminism, and socialist feminism. Radical feminist theory is often argued by lesbian-feminists: Charlotte Bunch on "The Roots of Oppression," Rita Mae Brown on "Family," and Coletta Reid on "Sexuality." Although this approach has the virtue of integrating lesbian feminism into the totality of the text, problems do exist. All these articles articulate the political perspective of the Furies, an early 1970s lesbian separatist collective, and as a result, lesbianism is identified with separatist politics to the exclusion of all other perspectives (such as socialist or liberal lesbian feminism.)

In addition to anthologies, women's studies courses use a number of histories of the women's liberation movement and overviews of its main issues. Of these texts, only *The American Woman: Who Will She Be?* concludes that she certainly won't be a lesbian. The rest—*The Women's Movement, Rebirth of Feminism, What Women Want: The Ideas of the Movement,* and *Women Today*—devote from three to nine pages to lesbianism and the women's movement. The content of their discussion is usually limited to the 1969–70 controversy over the "lavender herring" issue in NOW, the 1971 *Time* magazine attack on Kate Millett's "bisexuality," and the general phenomenon of lesbian-baiting in the media. *Women Today* includes a moderately offensive review of sociological and psychological literature on lesbianism (included in the section, "Women Who Are Not Married"!). One of these historical overviews, *A Group Called Women,* does provide an accurate and enlightening view of the role of lesbian-feminism in the women's liberation movement. Otherwise, even the more recent texts are silent on the history and ideology of lesbianism after 1971. We learn nothing about the "gay-straight" split in the women's movement, separatism, the development of lesbian organizations and journals, lesbian conferences and political actions, or lesbian culture, to name a few areas of concern.

What do we learn from all this? Heterosexism is alive and well in the women's studies textbook market. Introductory, interdisciplinary texts either exclude material on lesbianism or include one token article (and a quick survey would demonstrate a similar situation with women's studies texts in the traditional disciplines). What material is included is ghettoized under one catch-all topic heading; when specific issues such as family, work, culture, history, and sexuality are discussed, women once again are conceptualized as straight, and usually white. The articles, while excellent, are necessarily unable to present the range of lesbian experience. Bibliographies are extremely limited. Thus, the heterosexual biases and fears of women's studies students are not challenged by their textbooks. Lesbians remain the unapproachable, feared Other. The nature of existing women's studies introductory texts once again suggests that, to many heterosexual feminists, there are feminists and then there are lesbians; there are women and then there are lesbians. It does not seem that editors and publishers have learned many lessons from the past decade of lesbian activism.

Final Note: For those women's studies instructors who are interested in supplementing their text with material about lesbians, here are some suggestions. First, of course, is the book you are now holding: *Lesbian Studies.* In addition, *Our Right to Love* (Englewood Cliffs: Prentice Hall, 1978), edited by Ginny Vida, is an excellent collection of articles on a wide variety of topics. *Sinister Wisdom* and *Conditions* are two lesbian journals that can provide articles, poetry, and fiction appropriate for the classroom. Diana Press has reissued selections from *The Ladder,* edited by Barbara Grier and Colletta Reid, in three volumes: *Lesbian Lives* (biographies), *The Lesbian Home Journal* (short stories), and *The Lavender Herring* (essays). A fourth volume of reviews from *The Ladder, Lesbiana* by Barbara Grier, is available from Naiad Press. Persephone Press has reprinted *Amazon Poetry* under the title *Lesbian Poetry: An Anthology,* edited by Joan Larkin and Elly Bulkin. Political writing from

The Furies has been collected in Diana Press's *Lesbianism and The Women's Movement*, which, unfortunately, is out of print. *The Coming Out Stories*, edited by Julia Penelope (Stanley) and Susan J. Wolfe, and *The Lesbian Path*, edited by Margaret Cruikshank, provide moving personal stories that might overcome students' ignorance of lesbians' lives. All of these texts might provide short readings for women's studies classrooms.

Books Surveyed in "One Out of Thirty"

Adams, Elsie, and Mary Louise Briscoe. *Up Against the Wall, Mother*. Beverly Hills, Ca.: Glencoe Press, 1971.

Babcox, Deborah, and Madeline Belkin, *Liberation Now!* New York: Dell, 1971.

Baker, Mary Anne, et al. *Women Today: A Multidisciplinary Approach to Women's Studies*. Belmont, Ca. Wadsworth 1980.

Cade, Toni. *The Black Woman*. New York: Mentor, 1970.

Cassell, Joan. *A Group Called Women*. New York: McKay, 1977.

Deckard, Barbara. *The Women's Movement*. New York: Harper and Row, 1975, 1979.

Freeman, Jo. *Women: A Feminist Perspective*. Palo Alto: Mayfield, 1975, 1979.

Garskoff, Michele Hoffnung. *Roles Women Play: Readings Toward Women's Liberations*. Monterey: Brooks/Cole, 1971.

Gornick, Vivian, and Barbara K. Moran. *Woman in Sexist Society*. New York: Mentor, 1971.

Hecht, Marie B., et al. *The Women, Yes!* New York: Holt, Rinehart & Winston, 1973.

Hole, Judith, and Ellen Levine, *Rebirth of Feminism*. New York: Quadrangle, 1971.

Jaggar, Alison M., and Paula Rothenberg Struhl, *Feminist Frameworks*. New York: McGraw Hill, 1978.

McBee, Mary Louise, and Kathryn A. Blake, *The American Woman: Who Will She Be?* Beverly Hills, Ca., Glencoe Press, 1974.

Morgan, Robin, *Sisterhood is Powerful*. New York: Vintage, 1970.

Roberts, Joan L. *Beyond Intellectual Sexism*. New York: McKay, 1976.

Ruth, Sheila. *Issues In Feminism*. Boston: Houghton Mifflin, 1980.

Salper, Roberta. *Female Liberation:* New York: Knopf, 1972.

Stambler, Sookie. *Women's Liberation. Blueprint for the Future*. New York: Ace, 1970.

Tanner, Leslie B. *Voices From Women's Liberation*. New York: Signet, 1970.

Yates, Gail Graham *What Women Want: The Ideas of the Movement*. Cambridge: Harvard, 1975.

Notes

[1]Tillie Olsen, of course, was writing about writers who are women, not literature about women or feminism. Here, I am considering articles about lesbianism, not articles by lesbian writers (an indentification which is neither easily made nor particularly relevant). I use the statistic "one out of thirty" merely to point out the inadequate representation of lesbianism in women's studies textbooks. I am indebted to Florence Howe for this clarification.

[2]The books surveyed in this article include several that are widely used in women's studies courses, as well as others—not so popular—that demonstrate publishers' and editors' attitudes toward lesbianism. I collected them from my own library and those of other members of my department. I would be interested in dialogue about these and other current texts, as well as about revising old texts and writing new ones.

Lesbian Images In Women's Literature Anthologies

Kathy Hickok

Teachers and students of women's literature generally rely for their study materials upon whatever anthologies of women's writing are available to them at the time. Even though courses such as "Women Writers" or "The Image of Women in Literature" have grown remarkably during the last decade, the variety of anthologies published to meet their needs has not been particularly impressive. A few successful general literature anthologies are in wide use around the country. In addition, there are numerous small paperback collections of drama, fiction, or poetry by and/or about women. And recently, the trend has been toward collections with a somewhat more specific focus: mothers and daughters, women's literature in translation, black women poets, et cetera. Women's literature teachers commonly adopt either a general literature anthology or some combination of genre anthologies with supplements as needed (e.g, individual novels, collections by a single poet, et cetera.) Unfortunately, the available anthologies differ markedly in their inclusion of selections by and about women of different class backgrounds, ethnic groups, and sexual identities.

Furthermore, one is unlikely to be familiar with all of the contents of every available book, even when it is possible (as it often is not) to find out in advance of ordering a book just what selections it includes. Both lesbian and nonlesbian teachers of women's literature courses, if they are trying to choose books which will not only present lesbian writers and themes, but present them clearly and positively, can have a difficult time making decisions which will reflect that goal. Many of the books currently available are marred by heterosexism and homophobia. This annotated bibliography aims both to document that problem and to become part of its solution, by analyzing more than thirty-five general literature and genre anthologies as to the presence or absence of lesbian writers and themes, and the attitude toward them in each book. Anthologies that present lesbian materials and writers in a comparatively full and sensitive way are marked with an asterisk.

In the process of accomplishing this task, I have found myself naming names, so to speak. The lesbian writers, or women who have written on lesbian themes, whose names I cite are either self-named, or dead, or both; or the lesbian orientation of their work is clear from the title or content. A helpful guide for students and teachers who may not already know which authors and books are lesbian in outlook is *The Lesbian in Literature,* 3d revised edition, edited by Barbara Grier et al. (Tallahassee, Florida: The Naiad Press, 1981), which is complete through 1979, indexed and cross-referenced, and contains about seven thousand entries. The second edition of *The Lesbian in Literature,* published in Reno by *The Ladder,* can still be found in many women's bookstores. The editor is Gene Damon (Barbara Grier).

General Anthologies Of Literature

Berg, Stephen, and S. J. Marks, eds. *About Women: An Anthology of Contemporary Fiction, Poetry and Essays.* Greenwich, Connecticut: Fawcett, 1973. Avail. paper $1.75.

Berg and Marks are two (apparently heterosexual) men. *About Women* is an early anthology of fiction, poetry, and essays from the women's movement in the early seventies—focused chiefly upon the male/female conflicts arising therefrom. It includes both women's and men's writing and was an attempt to open dialogue, to explain women's anger and distress, and to enable men and women to better understand one another. Joyce Carol Oates, Lillian Hellman, Joan Didion, and various other well-known women writers appear in the book alongside Eldridge Cleaver, Erik Erikson, and Bruno Bettelheim. In "Growing Up Female," Bettelheim attributes "an alarming rise in both female and male homosexuality" to women's frustration with patriarchal men. "But unlike most male homosexuals, such women can often switch their affections to the other sex if they can find a man who really wants and needs to 'look outward with them'... in the same direction. (This, of course, does not hold true for a hard core of female homosexuals)" (p. 76). Bettelheim hopes that after a rewardingly close relationship with another woman "which need not, and preferably should not, be of a gross sexual nature" a young women will be able to "move on to a successful heterosexual relation" (p. 77). Even aside from its homophobia, this book wouldn't be very useful in a women's studies classroom because of its heavy male orientation.

Efros, Susan, ed. *This Is Women's Work: An Anthology of Prose and Poetry.* San Francisco: Panjandrum Press, 1974. Avail. paper $3.95.

Susan Griffin's "The Song of the Woman with Her Parts Coming Out" and "This Is a Story About Two Women Who Love Each Other" seem to be the only lesbian content in this book. The contributors are mostly little known writers. Their work is good, but the anthology is not inclusive.

Fannin, Alice; Rebecca Lukens, and Catherine Hoyser Mann., eds. *Woman: An Affirmation.* Lexington, Massachusetts: D.C. Heath, 1979. Avail. paper $8.95. Free instructor's manual on request.

Most "Images of Women" books are divided into sections roughly correspond-
ing with a) traditional female family roles, with a nod to the single woman, and/or
b) stereotypes of literary representations of women. In either schema, the antithesis
of "Wife/Mother" is usually "Woman Alone": the spinster, the aging widow, or,
occasionally, the independent woman. "Women Together" as a category seems not
to exist; and certainly a "Lesbian" category does not occur. According to its preface,
Woman: An Affirmation is "an attempt to present affirmative images of women in
literature, those that show women in their wholeness." The editors note that
women through the years have received a message which has been a self-fulfilling
prophecy: "You are incomplete without a man, and you must choose either
aggressive bitchery or pathetic nothingness" (p. vii). To avoid perpetuating this
attitude, the editors have structured their book in a way which is roughly chrono-
logical, but not role-oriented. Section titles are drawn from works collected in the
book: "Ain't I A Woman," "An Unfinished Woman," "The Way It Is," "This Gathering Up of Life," "The Soul Selects Her Own Society," and "Stepping Westward."
Unfortunately, the book contains no lesbian material whatsoever. A few lesbian
authors are included, but they are not identified as such. Nor are there any lesbian
references in the suggestions for further reading. It seems ironic that a book which
tries to counter the role orientation and negative emphases in most women's
anthologies, and which shows careful attention to women of color, overlooks the
lesbian alternative entirely.

Ferguson, Mary Anne. ed. *Images of Women in Literature.* Boston:
Houghton-Mifflin, 1973. 1st edition. Superseded by subsequent editions.

The structure of this book typified the emphasis criticized by the editors of
Woman: An Affirmation. Section titles included "The Submissive Wife and the
Feminine Mystique"; "The Mother: Angel or 'Mom'?"; "The Dominating Wife: The
Bitch"; "The Seductress-Goddess"; "Man's Prey: The Sex Object", "The Old Maid";
and "The Liberated Woman: What Price Freedom?" In the introduction, which
remained unchanged in the second edition (except that "Lesbian" was for some
reason no longer capitalized), Ferguson defined lesbians in an essentially sexual
way and then, seemingly, attempted to disassociate the women's movement from
charges of lesbianism in its ranks:

> Women's achievement of sexual freedom has aroused the greatest hostility
> toward the Women's Movement. The tendency of myth toward universalizing
> has made the most prominent image of the liberated woman that of the
> Lesbian: fear of any change has made the most extreme danger into a horrifying
> bogyman. Although recent studies have shown that only 3 percent of women
> are practicing Lesbians and not more than 10 percent exhibit a tendency toward
> homosexuality, any aggressive woman is viewed not only as bitchy but as a
> "butch," the masculine partner in a Lesbian union. Yet the facts of female
> sexuality are that neither partner need be "masculine"; since women experi-
> ence orgasm much more from sensual stimulation and clitoral excitation than
> from vaginal penetration, life-long Lesbian unions need no masculine over-
> tone. These unions also are more likely to be permanent and happier than male
> homosexual relationships. (pp. 27-28)

Ferguson went on to cite D. H. Lawrence's *The Fox* as a negative image of lesbians, but she asserted that Radclyffe Hall's *The Well of Loneliness* "shows Lesbian desires from the female view" (p. 28). Since *The Well of Loneliness* was the only lesbian book cited anywhere in *Images of Women*, it seems likely that students looking for an introduction to the subject would decide to read it. Unfortunately, Hall's book is a very discouraging first look at lesbian life, for either gay or nongay readers.

The only lesbian selection anthologized in the book was "Alraune," a chapter from *The House of Incest* by Anais Nin. The headnote does not address Nin's sexual orientation, and Ferguson's introduction to this piece suggests that lesbian love is incestuous, is love of one's sister, and is therefore likely to be destructive, unproductive, et cetera. "Alraune" was surely a strange choice to represent lesbian lives, even in 1973.

Feguson, Mary Anne, ed. *Images of Women in Literature*. 2d ed. Boston: Houghton Mifflin, 1977. Avail. paper $8.50 until publisher's stock has been exhausted.

Ferguson's book continued to be a popular choice for use in women's studies classrooms. On the second edition, "The Old Maid" section was renamed "Women Alone"—"to reflect the fact that now there are more women than ever living without men, many voluntarily and happily" (p. 1). Nevertheless, this edition of the book contained no lesbian selections at all. The bibliography cites *The Lesbian in Literature* and May Sarton's (nonlesbian) novel *Crucial Conversations* in addition to *The Well of Loneliness*. Nothing in the book indicates that any of the authors— May Swenson, Susan Griffin, and Adrienne Rich among them—are lesbians. Rich's theme in "Night Pieces for a Child" is "the anguish of her role conflict as wife and mother as well as writer" (p. 125). Of Griffin, Ferguson wrote, "A divorcée and single parent, she lives in San Francisco with other women" (p. 435).

*Ferguson, Mary Anne, ed. *Images of Women in Literature*. 3rd ed. Boston: Houghton Mifflin, 1981. Avail. paper $10.50.

Ferguson's third edition of *Images of Women in Literature* is only somewhat improved. Although the offensive passage cited above has been deleted, no commentary at all about lesbian themes has replaced it. The "Liberated Woman" section has been renamed "Woman Becoming," and the first six sections of the book now come under the heading of "Traditional Images of Women in Literature." Added selections include "Unlearning to Not Speak" by Marge Piercy, "Middle Children" by Jane Rule, "Joy in Provençe" by May Sarton, and "Artemis" by Olga Broumas. Rich's biography notes that in addition to wife/mother/writer role conflicts, "More recently she has written of lesbian experience" (p. 496); "Diving into the Wreck" replaces "Night Pieces for a Child." Jane Rule's story is placed in the thematic context of female bonding. Ferguson comments, "Rule in 'Middle Children' calmly suggests that lesbianism is a normal and rational outcome of the psychological situation of the middle child" (p. 411).

Ferguson's changing anthology is an interesting case. According to the editor herself, she has not had as much say with the publisher as she would have liked, and she has not been unaware of the book's failings on the issue of lesbian images in literature. Although feminist editors of textbooks and collections can certainly be held accountable to the women's community for the content of their books, it seems clear that so long as the final word rests with policy makers in mainstream publishing houses, many of us will continue to be disappointed with the materials available for study.

Goulianos, Joan, ed. *By A Woman Writ: Literature from Six Centuries by and About Women.* New York: Bobbs Merrill, 1973. Avail. paper (Penguin) $2.95.

Goulianos's book contains nothing whatsoever about lesbians. Mary Woll-stonecraft is included, but *Mary: A Fiction* and Wollstonecraft's love letters to Fanny Blood are not mentioned; Goulianos has chosen to present her letters to Gilbert Imlay instead.

Hall, James; Nancy J. Jones, and Janet R. Sutherland, eds. *Women: Portraits.* New York: McGraw Hill, 1976. Avail. paper $5.60.

Women: Portraits is part of a series called Patterns in Literary Art. The book seems to be aimed at secondary school students, so it is not surprising to find no lesbian material within its covers. (Note also that one of the editors is a man.) Selections by lesbian authors include "What My Child Learns of the Sea" by Audre Lorde, "Now I Become Myself" by May Sarton, "The Sink" by Susan Griffin, and "Jane Eyre: The Temptations of a Motherless Woman" by Adrienne Rich. None of these writers is indentified as lesbian, nor are lesbian themes addressed in any way. However, given the intended audience for the book, it is encouraging that these writers do at least appear, so that students can get to know them. Perhaps, if they ever learn that these women are gay, the students' established respect for them will continue and carry over to other lesbians as well.

Hamalian, Linda, and Hamalian, Leo, eds. *Solo: Women on Woman Alone.* New York: Delacorte Press, 1977. Avail. paper (Dell) $1.95.

Although most special-theme anthologies were not considered for this listing, *Solo* seemed worth investigating because of its title. However, although a few lesbian writers are represented in the book, evidently the editors really mean "alone" by their title, and not "manless," as the word so often designates in this context. No lesbian content is apparent in the book.

Kirschner, Linda, and Marcia Folsom, eds. *By Women.* Boston: Houghton Mifflin, 1976. Avail. paper $9.32. Instructor's resource book $3.80.

Section titles in *By Women* are "Short Stories," "Search for Self," "Drama," "In a Role," "Poetry," and "Breaking Free." The introduction to "Breaking Free" notes,

"In the final section of this book are gathered works of literature which explore the problems and the rewards of different ways of breaking free" (pp. 365–66). Yet the lesbian alternative is not included. The only lesbian acknowledged in *By Women* is Sappho, and she is not represented by any lesbian poems. In fact, the lesbianism of Sappho is seen as conjectural, open to controversy and opinion; and the word "lesbian" is never actually mentioned. Selections by Sappho include one poem to her daughter, two fragments addressed, evidently, to men, and two on the themes of friendship and song. Biographical notes on the authors in the book include references to their marriages, divorces, children, and sexual liaisons with men. Any lesbian experience or orientation is ignored. Writers treated in this way include Colette, H.D. (Hilda Doolittle), Amy Lowell, Charlotte Mew, Adrienne Rich, May Sarton, and several others. To exclude this information must have been a conscious decision. The inevitable question arises: How and why does this occur? Do living lesbians not wish to be so identified? But then, what is the value or point of obscuring the lives of deceased ones?

Murray, Michele, ed. *A House of Good Proportion: Images of Women in Literature*. New York: Simon & Schuster, 1973. Avail. paper (Touchstone Books) $4.95.

The chief virtue of Murray's anthology is the excellent and responsible bibliography, which contains numerous and representative references to classics of lesbian literature. The organization of the book is based on the social stages of women's lives. Section titles include: "The Little Girl," "The Young Girl," "The Virgin," "Women in Love," "Independent Women," "The Wife," "The Mother," "Scenes from Family Life," "Women Lost," "The Old Maid," "The Old Woman," and "The Unattainable Other."

Four selections in *A House of Good Proportion* touch on lesbian themes in some way; nevertheless, the overall impact is not good. The best of these is Sarah Orne Jewett's "Martha's Lady," in which a servant girl is ennobled and inspired by her love for an upper-class woman, who, however, doesn't become aware of Martha's devotion until some forty years have gone by. Martha's love for her lady is romantic, but not sexual. Students reading the story remain unpersuaded that Martha has not merely wasted her life. An excerpt from *The Bostonians* by Henry James depicts Olive Chancellor's attraction to Verena Tarrant as vampirish and implies that Verena does well to escape. In introducing the excerpt from Dorothy Bussy's *Olivia*, Murray observes that the schoolgirl Olivia's love for her teacher Mademoiselle Julie, "is an affair of the heart, not the flesh, for Julie, already tied to the jealous and hysterical Cara, then to the devoted Signorina Baietto, shrinks from corrupting [sic] the child sent into her care." Murray adds, "This concentrated moral tale breathes the essence of youthful sensuality turned aside from its natural expression and forced to flower in the overheated atmosphere of a gynaeceum" (pp. 61–62).

The fourth selection, and excerpt from *Nightwood*, by Djuna Barnes, is placed in the "Women Lost" section of the book. Murray's notes call attention to the "decadence and sensuality of the subject" and to the destructive nature of the relationship between Nora Flood and Robin Vote (the "lost women" in the case) (p. 271). Like *The Well of Loneliness*, *Nightwood* is an important early piece of lesbian fiction, but it does not serve well as an introduction to lesbian lives or literature. Not one of the four selections included in the anthology is unambiguously positive in its treatment of lesbian relationships.

Pearson, Carol, and Katherine Pope, eds. *Who Am I This Time?: Female Portraits in British and American Literature.* New York: McGraw Hill, 1976. Avail. paper $8.95

This book includes literature from two countries and five centuries, much of it by men or male-oriented women. Chapter headings include "The Heroine (The Virgin, The Mistress, The Helpmate)" and "The Hero (The Sage, The Artist, The Warrior)." Of these, "only the warrior openly refuses to be seen as a supporting character in a man's drama and attempts to change her world through direct action" (p. 10). She is "a revolutionary who moves beyond her culture's female role definitions and refuses to be dependent on a man; she therefore ventures alone onto the road of trials, obstacles and temptations. . . . She risks destruction at the hands of a patriarchal society which sees her 'unfeminine action' as psychologically unhealthy and in need of remedy or as socially and theologically evil and deserving of punishment" (p. 243). A clearer statement of the character and problems of a lesbian woman could scarcely be formulated. Yet, unless we choose to claim Joan of Arc, the lesbian warrior is not represented.

This kind of disappointing failure to draw obvious conclusions and make obvious connections occurs elsewhere in the book, notably in a discussion of Robin Morgan's "Lesbian Poem." The editors observe that "the prospect of female friendship and cooperation replacing competition is threatening to the patriarchal system" and that "the women's movement, therefore, is often interpreted as a threat to men." In Morgan's poem, they suggest, "the assertion of lesbianism works . . . to free women from patriarchy" by "dispel[ling] the power of the stereotype which has served to enforce socially acceptable, docile female behavior" (p. 245). They might have gone on to point out that lesbian choices can be inherently positive and/or "threatening to the patriarachal system."

The bibliography is also disappointing. The only relevant references are to Mary McCarthy's *The Group*, Henry James's *The Bostonians*, D.H. Lawrence's *The Rainbow*, and, of course, Radcylffe Hall's *The Well of Loneliness*.

Warren, Barbara, ed. *The Feminine Image in Literature.* Hayden Humanities Series. Rochelle Park, New Jersey: Hayden Book Co., 1973. Avail. paper $5.94.

Like *Women: Portraits, The Feminine Image in Literature* seems to be intended for high school students. It asserts humanistic, androgynous premises, and it contains no overt homophobia. Section headings are: "The Phantom Lady and the Marble/Plastic Doll"; "The Virgin Shrouded in Snow: The Nun Syndrome"; "The Masked World: Martyrs, Mannequins, and Monsters"; and "The Androgynous Mind: The Marriage of Self and Soul." Selections include S.T. Coleridge's "Christabel," which is sometimes interpreted as lesbian; however, the study questions that follow the poem usurp this possible reading. The book also contains three fragments from Sappho, but with no mention of sexuality. Suggested supplementary readings include D.H. Lawrence's *The Rainbow*. Otherwise, no lesbian materials appear in the book.

Drama

*France, Rachel, ed. *A Century of Plays by American Women*. New York: Richards Rosen Press, 1979. Avail. cloth $12.50.

A Century of Plays is a very up-to-date anthology of one-act plays, including feminist experimental plays of various sorts from the sixties and seventies—e.g., Megan Terry's and Martha Boesing's works. In *The Mothers*, the lesbian orientation of the author, Havelock Ellis's wife, is made quite clear. Her marriage, however, is described as "tortured," due to her "view of absolute sexual freedom" (and her husband's impotence) (p. 42). The biography of Djuna Barnes accompanying *Three from the Earth* is a bit less clear; it merely refers to the prior expurgation of her works for supposedly being sexually too avant-garde. Gertrude Stein's *The Mother of Us All* (about Susan B. Anthony) is included. In the notes, France mentions the "unhappy triangular love affair with two other women" (while Stein was in medical school) which led to *Q.E.D.* She also cites the *Autobiography of Alice B. Toklas*, but without clarifying Stein and Toklas's relationship. One other play, Marjean Perry's *A Trap Is a Small Place*, while not explicitly lesbian, explores an "interesting if normally taboo subject—that of one woman's love for another" (p. 152). All in all, both the selection and annotation of the plays in this anthology seem to have been handled with some measure of sensitivity to lesbian lives and themes.

Kriegel, Harriet, ed. *Women in Drama: An Anthology*. New York: New American Library, 1975. Avail. paper $2.50.

This is a disappointing book; only two of the eight plays are by women (Susan Glaspell's *Trifles* and Megan Terry's *Approaching Simone*), and neither treats a lesbian theme.

Moore, Honor, ed. *The New Women's Theatre: Ten Plays by Contemporary American Women*. New York: Random House, 1977. Avial. paper (Vintage) $5.95.

The New Women's Theatre contains a thorough historical introduction to women and drama. Many of the authors mentioned are lesbian, though Moore does not identify them as such. Playwrights' biographies likewise do not identify anyone as lesbian; generally those notes consist of authors' remarks about their work. The collection does include Ruth Wolff's *The Abdication*, about the unconventional seventeenth-century queen of Sweden, Christina, whose "sins," confessed during the course of the play, include wearing men's clothes and a passionate attraction and love for a dear woman friend from childhood. Christina addresses her confessor: "Love so rare! Must we deny it when we've found it? Is it to be called hideous just because the object is the same sex? Don't you love the Pope?" (p. 379). However, the focus of the play—the growing respect and attraction between Christina and the priest—overrides these few references to Christina's lesbianism.

Sullivan, Victoria, and James Hatch, eds. *Plays By and About Women.* New York: Random House, 1973. Avail. paper (Vintage) $3.95.

According to the introduction, "Although the plays here are *about* women, the anthology is not strictly feminist in viewpoint.... Lillian Hellman's *The Children's Hour* treats lesbianism as a legitimately scandalous accusation" (p. viii). (The editors go on to assert that the accusation in the play is untrue; however, it is possible to disagree with that interpretation of the play.) The anthology also includes Maureen Duffy's *Rites*, in which a group of women hostile to men pounce upon and kill a "male" intruder into the ladies' "loo." The "male" is then revealed to be a woman who looks and dresses in a masculine way. A lesbian? Probably. Says one, as they prepare to dispose of the body, "She couldn't have been happy." Replies another, "Why not, she was alive?" (p. 376).

Fiction

Baker, Denys Val, ed. *Twelve Short Stories by Famous Women Writers.* New York: St. Martin's Press, 1978; reissued 1979 as *Women Writing.* Avail. cloth $8.95.

This book would not be particularly useful for teaching, since it has no apparent philosophy or thesis, and no apparatus. Nor are the "famous" women writers even very well known, for the most part. Information on contributors makes no reference to lesbian lives. Olivia Manning's "A Romantic Hero" is about a gay man and is told with great sympathy. However, I could find no lesbian material at all in the book. Other authors included are Mary Lavin, E. Taylor, Fay Weldon, Doris Lessing, Daphne du Maurier, Edna O'Brien, Penelope Mortimer, Muriel Spark, Ruth Fainlight, Susan Hill and A.L. Barker. All are British.

Cahill, Susan, ed. *Women and Fiction: Short Stories By and About Women.* New York: New American Library, 1975. Avail. paper (Mentor) $2.50.

Three stories in this anthology—"Cousin Lewis" by Jean Stubbs, "The Secret Woman" by Colette, and "Miss Furr and Miss Skeene" by Gertrude Stein—are concerned, as Cahill states, with "the mystery of sexual definition" (p. xviii). Nevertheless, none of them has a lesbian theme, although Stubbs's story concerns a wife and mother who is also a transvestite. Colette's interest in the world of women is mentioned, and *The Pure and the Impure* is described as treating homosexual relationships "with friendly but uncommitted impartiality" (pp. 36–37). The introductory material on Stein doesn't make her orientation explicit, but rather describes Alice B. Toklas as "Miss Stein's companion and secretary until her death" (p. 42). "Miss Furr and Miss Skeene" is a whimsical tale about a relationship between two women who were "quite regularly gay" (p. 44). Given the sexual allusiveness of the diction and the repetition of the word "gay," it seems likely that most readers would get the point.

Cahill, Susan, ed. *Women and Fiction 2: Short Stories By and About Women.* New York: New American Library, 1978. Avail. paper (Mentor) $2.50.

Women and Fiction 2 contains two stories with more or less subtle lesbian overtones: "Girls Together" by Olivia Manning, and "Camp Cataract" by Jane Bowles. In neither case is the lesbian orientation of the characters the central issue of plot or theme.

*Dean, Nancy, and Myra Stark, eds. *In the Looking-Glass: Twenty-One Modern Short Stories by Women.* New York: Putnam, 1977. Avail. cloth $8.95.

In the Looking-Glass is divided into sections entitled "The Girl," "The Woman," and "The Older Woman." An excellent collection of stories, it includes selections by Viriginia Woolf, Sandy Boucher, Marge Piercy, and Jane Rule, among others. Biographical notes identify both Boucher and Rule as lesbians—at least, their publications with "Lesbian" in the title are referenced. According to the introduction, *In the Looking-Glass* "presents stories written out of what can best be described as a feminist consciousness" (p. xiii). The editors mention *The Ladder* as a pioneering "little magazine ... established to publish women's writing" (p. xix), and note that "small presses are permitting women to publish stories about lesbianism, a subject usually rejected by establishment presses" (p. xx). In regard to Jane Rule's "In the Basement of the House," it is acknowledged that where the heroine lives (in the basement) "is a metaphor for her membership in a submerged population" (p. xx).

*Grahn, Judy, ed. *True to Life Adventure Stories.* Vol. I. Oakland: Diana Press, 1978. Avail. paper $5.00.

This is an extraordinary collection of stories, each "based on information which is close to, or is, the original source of the story" (pp. 7–8). These stories are not upper-class art, not "high" art; rather, they are by little-known authors addressing working-class themes in working-class diction and grammar. Several openly lesbian stories are included—"The Light" by Linnea A. Due, "Susie Q" by Red Arobateau, "Glass" by Judy Grahn, "The Three Bears" by Ruth Babcock, and "Masks and Warrior" by Nancy Green—and like all the other stories in the collection, they ring very, very true. There are also stories on other themes by Sharon Isabell and Pat Parker. (Volume 2 was published by Crossing Press, Trumansburg, NY in 1981.)

Rotter, Pat, ed. *Bitches and Sad Ladies: An Anthology of Fiction By and About Women.* New York: Harper's Magazine Press, 1975. Avail. cloth $10.95.

The title refers to the collection's organizing principle: the themes of anger and pathos. The introduction does not acknowledge a healing alternative to these emotions. No lesbian references appear in any of the biographical notes, nor does any story except Andrea Dworkin's "Bertha Scheider's Existential Edge" address a lesbian theme. In that story, the narrator, a battered woman who has finally given up on men, tells about her amorous relationships with women, from age thirteen on. "To tell the truth," she says, "I gave up women after some very bittersweet love affairs which got fucked up because I was still fucking men and was still very fucked up by men . . . finally I figured that since I couldn't do anyone any good I might at least stop doing monumental harm" (p. 281). She concludes with a vision of herself and her mother "alone somewhere kissing and hugging and sucking like God intended" (p. 282).

Schneiderman, Beth K., ed. *By and About Women: An Anthology of Short Fiction.* New York: Harcourt Brace Jovanovich, 1973. Avail. paper $6.50.

This book seems designed as a college text, but its preface declares, "Unlike many of the 'women's books' currently in print, this anthology is not meant to be a feminist tract. Its purpose is neither to convince nor to convert. . . . The purpose of this book, then, is to show the reader what it means to be a woman . . . " (p. vii). The four sections of the book are "Promise and Disappointment," "Expectation and Defeat," "Success and Failure," and "Triumph and Death." The third section promises to "deal with the alternatives to marriage as a source of fulfillment for a woman" (p. viii), but none of the contents of that section are lesbian stories. Further, there are no identifications of authors as lesbian in their brief biographies, and there are no lesbian references in the book's bibliography.

Schulman, L.M., ed. *A Woman's Place.* New York: MacMillan, 1974. Avail. cloth $7.95.

The man who edited this collection also edited *Winners and Losers: An Anthology of Great Sports Fiction.* He acknowledges that "No man can truly conceive of the special agonies" of a woman's existence, yet he is certain that the stories he has chosen are "painfully exact" (p. vii). Only Katherine Mansfield's "Bliss" touches even remotely on a lesbian theme. Considering the book's doleful vision of womanhood and its comparatively high price for ten stories readily available elsewhere, it cannot be recommended.

Soloman, Barbara H., ed. *The Experience of the American Woman.* New York: New American Library, 1978. Avail. paper (Mentor) $2.50

This collection contains 30 stories, approximately one-third of them written by men. Despite the editor's specific, announced intention to "reveal the widely differing lives women have led" (p. 1), not even the section entitled "Women Among Women" contains any stories with lesbian themes. Other sections are "Female-Male Encounters," "Insights and Identities," "Women and Madness," "Courtships," "Married Women," and "Women with Children." To judge from this anthology, lesbian experience has not entered into "the experience of the American woman."

Swansea, Charleen, and Barbara Campbell, eds. *Love Stories by New Women.* New York: Avon Books, 1979; Charlotte, North Carolina: Red Clay Books, 1978. Avail. paper (Avon) $2.75, (Red Clay) $5.95.

Red Clay Books, a women's publishing house in North Carolina, requested stories dealing with love—both heterosexual and homosexual—in a new way; they received over 300 responses. *Love Stories by New Women* collects 18 of those, all of which are worth reading as a corrective to traditional love stories for women readers, even though most of the stories are heterosexual.

Washington, Mary Helen, ed. *Midnight Birds: Stories by Contemporary Black Women Writers.* New York: Doubleday, 1980. Avail. paper (Anchor) $3.50.

Washington's introduction, "In Pursuit of Our Own History," notes that of the fifteen stories in the book, all five of the love stories are heterosexual (p. xix). No lesbian themes or writers seem to be included in the book.

Poetry

*Bernikow, Louise, ed. *The World Split Open: Four Centuries of Women Poets in England and America, 1552-1950.* New York: Random House, 1974. Avail. paper (Vintage) $3.95.

In the preface to this book, Muriel Rukeyser states the issue clearly:

> Have you ever known the double joy and despair of women as daughters and poets? Or the joy and until recently the despair of women homosexuals; or wives or mothers? These may be extremes of what we see here, but they may not be. These cries, these formalities, these bursts of song, this formal music, seen in a brief sampling of four hundred years, will let you make your own decision. (p. xiii)

The title of *The World Split Open* comes from Rukeyser's poem "Käthe Kollewitz": "What would happen if one woman told the truth about her life?/The world would split open." A stance of courage and frankness informs this anthology from beginning to end.

Bernikow's introduction to the poetry is absolutely exemplary in its analysis of the politics of literary reputation and critical standing in the patriarchal establishment. For example, when preparing her "complete" works, William Michael Rossetti, brother of Christina Rossetti, excluded all of her Sappho poems. "Male approval," Bernikow comments, "the condition of a poet's survival, is withheld when a woman shapes her poetry from the very material that contradicts and threatens male reality.... Homosexual love between women may meet indulgence but certainly not understanding.... When women move into the area of political consciousness, particularly feminism, but in fact any political consciousness, we move out of place" (p. 7).

Lesbian writers and themes are not only included in this anthology, but sensitively handled and, generally, clearly identified. Among them are Katharine Philips (known in her day as "the English Sappho"), Aphra Behn, Angelina Weld Grimké, Amy Lowell, Charlotte Mew, and Gertrude Stein. In each case, poetry has been chosen which has excellent literary qualities and is personally revelatory. Bernikow admonishes the literary biographer: "She or he would do well to entertain the possibility that poets who are women mean 'she' (when they write 'she') in poems of passion" (p. 15). In 1975 Gene Damon considered *The World Split Open* to be "by far the best anthology of pertinent poetry to date" (*The Lesbian in Literature*, p. 14).

Chester, Laura, and Sharon Barba, eds. *Rising Tides: Twentieth Century American Women Poets.* New York: Washington Square Press, 1973. Avail. paper (Kangaroo Pocket Books) $1.95.

Rising Tides is somewhat inconsistent in its presentation of lesbian lives and themes. At least a dozen lesbian poets are represented—among them Gertrude Stein, H.D., Amy Lowell, May Sarton, Adrienne Rich, May Swenson, Judy Grahn, Lynn Strongin and Susan Griffin—yet most are not identified as lesbians. Anne Sexton's "Rapunzel" presents a bizarre image of "a woman who loves a woman" (p. 174) as a possessive and domineering older woman. On the other hand, among Judy Grahn's "Common Woman" poems is "Carol, in the park" who "has taken a woman lover" and who is "as common as a thunderstorm" (pp. 283–84). Biographies of Stein and Lowell do not mention their lesbianism; however, Stein's picture is quite masculine-looking, and Lowell's "Madonna of the Evening Flowers" is a first-person love song addressed to a woman. And Lynn Strongin's classic poem "Sayre (Woman Professor)" depicts a lesbian professor who triumphs over her masculine colleagues' envy and oppression. With sufficient background or guidance, student readers could glean quite a lot from *Rising Tides;* without one or the other, they might possibly miss what these lesbian authors have to offer on the subject.

Cosman, Carol; Joan O'Keefe; and Kathleen Weaver; eds. *The Penguin Book of Women Poets.* New York: Viking Press, 1979. Avail. paper (Penguin) $4.95.

This anthology has been indicted in a paper (read at NCTE, November 1979) by Bonnie Zimmerman for being particularly heterosexist in its assumptions and its annotations. To cite just a few examples, concerning Sappho the editors write, "Much legendary gossip without historical basis surrounds the story of Sappho's life. It can be fairly stated that she was a poet of high reputation and that young girls of birth and education came to the island of Lesbos where they studied under her tutelage and perhaps took part in a form of service dedicated to the goddess Aphrodite" (p. 41). The implication is that it is entirely legitimate to dismiss Sappho's erotic poems to women by relegating her lesbianism to the status of "gossip." Aphra Behn's relevant poetry is included, but Behn is labeled a "disreputable" woman (p. 135). Lowell, Stein, and H.D. are represented by poetry, but none of their erotic verse appears and their lesbianism is disregarded or denied. Then, surprisingly, the biography of Adrienne Rich states, "She is a lesbian and has three sons" (p. 351). Why identify Rich in this way, but not Sappho, or Stein, or H.D.? Since virtually none of the lesbian poets in the anthology are represented by poems with lesbian themes, the book would not be very useful to teachers trying to include lesbian literature in their course, nor to lesbian readers trying to discover their literary heritage.

Gill, Elaine, ed. *Mountain Moving Day: Poems by Women*. Trumansburg, NY: The Crossing Press, 1973. Avail. paper $3.95.

Mountain Moving Day is a sampler of contemporary poetry by seventeen American and Canadian women, including Alta, Marge Piercy, Fran Winant, and Susan Griffin. Only Alta's and Winant's poems touch upon lesbian themes.

*Howe, Florence, and Ellen Bass, eds. *No More Masks! An Anthology of Poems by Women*. Garden City, New York: Doubleday, 1973. Avail. paper $4.50

Though not quite as straightforward as *The World Split Open, No More Masks* at least does not shrink from presenting and discussing lesbian literature. More than fifteen lesbian poets are represented, including Audre Lorde, Pauli Murray, Lynn Strongin, Judy Grahn, Susan Griffin, and Rita Mae Brown. (Only Grahn is specifically identified as a lesbian in the biographical sketches.) In Part 3, Howe and Bass state that "a few" of the contemporary poets included are lesbians, noting that "sexuality in the poems of younger poets is very distinctive. Partly it is the presence of lesbian themes and images" (p. 19). However, even Part 3 is not particularly daring in this regard. Rita Mae Brown's "Dancing the Short to the True Gospel *or* The Song Movement Sisters Don't Want Me to Sing" is an appropriate commentary on the problem on homophobia within the women's movement.

*Iverson, Lucille, and Kathryn Ruby, eds. *We Become New: Poems by Contemporary American Women*. New York: Bantam, 1975. Currently out of print.

In the Preface, Kathryn Ruby states, "Feminism means, among other things, liberation, a casting off of the old roles and a desire for new alternatives, for . . . new ways of relating to women—sisterhood, supportive behavior, lesbianism . . ." (p. xiii). Fran Winant, Judy Grahn, and Martha Shelley are specifically identified in their biographies as lesbians. Poems with lesbian themes include Winant's "Nora," Grahn's "A Woman is Talking to Death," Rochelle Owen's "Wistful Butch Poem," Rita

Mae Brown's "Dancing the Short to the True Gospel *or* The Song Movement Sisters Don't Want Me to Sing," Martha Shelley's "Note to a New Lesbian" and "The Transparent Closet," and more.

Kaplan, Cora, ed. *Salt and Bitter and Good: Three Centuries of English and American Women Poets.* New York: Paddington Press, 1975. Avail. paper $6.95.

Lesbian poets include Aphra Behn, Katharine Philips, Charlotte Mew, Amy Lowell, H.D., Vita Sackville-West, and others. Of twenty four poets, at least eight are definitely or possibly lesbians (a pretty fair ratio). Some of the notes on these writers are ambiguous, however. On Philips, for example, facts are related, but their significance goes unclarified. Of the poems to Lucasia: "Philips has hit on a theme [Kaplan doesn't say what] to which she could add feelings not yet exploited [sic] in the poetry of the period" (p. 42). Kaplan does not comment upon the lesbian content of Amy Lowell's infatuation with actress Eleanora Duse; instead, she sees Lowell's weight as an explanation for her not marrying and having a "normal" family life (p. 203). Revealingly, in Vita Sackville-West's case, she worries that Vita's "bold bisexuality" places her "in danger of being transformed historically into an androgynous messenger of sexual liberation and forgotten as a writer" (p. 257).

*Konek, Carol, and Dorothy Walters, eds. *I Hear My Sisters Saying.* New York: Crowell, 1976. Avail. paper $4.95.

Organized thematically into ten sections, this book is a remarkably comprehensive and well-chosen collection of modern and contemporary poetry with a feminist bent. As such, its approach to lesbian themes is easy and matter of fact. Examples include "Fire Island" by Rita Mae Brown, "Coming Out" by Jacqueline Lapidus, "Sailing in Crosslight" by Anita Skeen, "Invocation to Sappho" by Elsa Gidlow, "Sayre (Woman Professor)" by Lynn Strongin, and "Lesbian Poem: Dedicated to Those Who Turned Immediately from the Contents Page to This Poem" by Robin Morgan.

Newman, Felice, ed. *Cameos: 12 Small Press Women Poets.* Trumansburg, NY: Crossing Press, 1978. Avail. paper $4.95.

Most of the contributors to this volume are as yet little-known writers. Several are apparently lesbians, and lesbian content and sensibility inform some of the poems in the book. However, only Jan Clausen is clearly identified as a lesbian. The small presses referred to in the book's title are not, for the most part, lesbian or feminist.

Segnitz, Barbara, and Carol Rainey, eds. *Psyche: The Feminine Poetic Consciousness.* New York: Dial Press, 1973. Currently out of print.

A promising introduction calls for "reasons why and how women's lives are secret" to be a theme in the poetry chosen (p. 15) and acknowledges Sappho as the first woman poet. The " 'definition of one's own premises' " (from Adrienne Rich's poem on Emily Dickinson) is seen to be "the dominant idea unifying the poetry of women" (p. 17). Furthermore, "the qualities women perceive to be thwarted in their lives are only those which would allow them to be more fully themselves: honesty, spirit, creativity, transcendence, autonomous power, and most important, the freedom to know and realize their individuality and full potential" (p. 19). Despite all this, the book makes no mention whatsoever of lesbian sexuality, politics, or literature.

Stanford, Ann, ed. *The Women Poets in English*. New York: McGraw Hill, 1972. Currently out of print.

Gene Damon has called this collection, which was pioneering in its day, "a curiously unsatisfactory anthology with at least 20 known lesbians represented, but few of them by their lesbian verse" (*The Lesbian in Literature*, p. 82). Nor is there any lesbian information in the biographical sketches.

Recommendations

Teachers and students may want to supplement their readings in women's literature to include more lesbian selections than are available in their texts. Mary Barnard's excellent translations in *Sappho* (Berkeley: University of California Press, 1958) will allow students to form their own judgments about Sappho's erotic orientation as well as to appreciate her beautiful lyrics. A fine new collection of modern lesbian poetry by many different writers is *Lesbian Poetry*, edited by Joan Larkin and Elly Bulkin (Watertown, Massachusetts: Persephone Press, 1981). Jan Clausen's short stories, *Mother, Sister, Daughter, Lover* (Trumansburg, New York: Crossing Press, 1980), and Ann Allen Shockley's story collection, *The Black and White of It* (Tallahassee, Florida: Naiad Press, 1980), are also excellent. *Sinister Wisdom* and *Conditions* both contain poetry, fiction, reviews and essays (see Resources, under periodicals).

Those wishing to learn more about the lesbian imagination or lesbian images in literature should read Jeannette Foster's *Sex Variant Women in Literature* (New York: Vantage, 1956; reprinted Baltimore: Diana Press, 1975); Lillian Faderman's *Surpassing the Love of Men*, and the third edition of *The Lesbian in Literature* (Tallahassee, Florida: Naiad Press, 1981).

Lesbian writers and themes have much to offer the feminist classroom, especially when presented in an informed context. Despite the silence which has thus far surrounded the lesbian contribution to women's heritage, women's studies students are usually not only willing, but eager, to begin the process of "Unlearning to Not Speak" about lesbian literature and lives. It is up to women's studies teachers, lesbian and nonlesbian alike, to guide them.

Is Feminist Criticism Really Feminist?

Becky Birtha

While I have always loved books, I have had a longtime aversion to literary criticism. The critical analysis that my college English courses required me to read (the only way I would go near the stuff) convinced me that it was dry, dull, confusing double-talk, a product of some discriminatory intellectual club, and completely beyond me. It was only when I found myself in the position of starting to write some things that might be called criticism that I began to explore the subject again.

I found out that there is such a thing as feminist criticism, and that a tradition of feminist criticism has already been in formation. While it goes back at least as far as Virginia Woolf (who wrote book reviews and the classic work on women and writing, *A Room of One's Own*), the current wave of feminism has produced a surprising number of articles, essays, and reviews, including several whole books on critical essays.[1] Some of these have made it so far into the mainstream that I was able to find them at the Philadelphia public library.

Over the past few months, I have attempted to read some of these essays in what is called feminist criticism, with a little more success than I had with the male stuff. However, it is not easy and I often have to reread each paragraph and to keep a dictionary beside me. My idea in writing *this* essay is to bring out what some of the problems are.

Being Black, a feminist, and a lesbian places one squarely outside of the academic tradition. There has been no role for a Black lesbian in the world of literature. When I was asked, several months ago, to contribute to an anthology of lesbianism and women's studies, I wanted to very much but drew a complete blank. I knew I could hold my own on the lesbianism part. But I saw women's studies as something that exists only on college campuses, in scholarly, intellectual, academic environments, an isolated, esoteric world I've been away from since I was a student seven years ago.

Even when I *was* a women's studies student (and *not* a lesbian), I was never quite sure I fitted in. I had returned to school after a three-year dropout. Besides being overage, at twenty-three, I didn't live near the campus (the rents were too high) and didn't even consider myself a feminist. Luckily, I was still young enough or from a middle-class-enough background, to study something as impulsive as women's studies, which clearly did not lead to a career or provide credits which could be easily used toward a practical major.

In my first women's studies class (this was at the State University of New York at Buffalo in 1971) I felt very self-conscious about being the only woman who always wore a skirt to class. My most revealing moment in the course came when I found out that I was also the only woman in the class who was working for money within the system (thus the skirt), living alone, and completely self-supporting.

Among other things, my experience taught me that women's studies departments are headed by professors and Ph.D.s, women who *wrote* those books of essays that were so hard for me to read, and who, I could tell from their essays, hadn't had any trouble understanding those male critics, either. What could I have to say to women like that?

Like other Black feminist critics who have, thankfully, begun to break ground in this area,[2] I am realizing that the women in those academic positions *do* need to hear from us. They need to hear our feedback, to know when their words ring true for us, and to know when their words are not reaching us or are denying our reality. But they also need to listen to *our* ideas, to hear concerns and approaches, hypotheses, and conclusions which originate with us. It is time for Black lesbians to stop internalizing our own invalidation. A feminist culture without our voices will be as limited and limiting as the culture it is trying to be an alternative to.

In spring 1980, the current lesbian-feminist-oriented literary magazine, *Sinister Wisdom*, published an exciting issue on lesbian writing and publishing.[3] Many Black women volunteered or were asked to write articles on subjects such as the Third World Lesbian Writers Conference and "Writing and Publishing by Dark Lesbians." I certainly don't mean to criticize those black women for writing on subjects of special interest to black women (or the editors for asking them to), which is, of course, very appropriate. In the same issue, however, there is an article about "Lesbian Classics in the Year 2000." I found the article both enjoyable and informative and found its content, which gives considerable attention to the work of Black writers, to be of value. But I couldn't help noticing that it was a *non-Black* woman who was asked to write *that* article. And not just any non-Black woman, but one with an advanced degree, qualified to teach on a college level, and who mentioned, in her footnotes, her participation in the Modern Language Association.

I am concerned when I see us perpetuating the same standards that, as feminists, we should be dedicated to destroying. Too often, I see us still valuing those patriarchal credentials, as we try to evaluate and respond to our sisters' work. I do mean *us*, don't consider myself exempt. For example, I recently applied to a university graduate program in writing.

At the heart of the question is language. The thing which makes those essays and books of criticism so hard to read, that turns off all but the most determined academics, is the language they are written in. I have finally come to recognize elitist, overly intellectual language for what it is: a class privilege. A woman who chooses to make her language inaccessible to less educated women is exploiting her class position.

There is also sexism involved here, since the academic world, to whom the critics' language is readily accessible, is overwhelmingly male. To adopt its language and style is to accept patriarchal values. Not only is the use of this sophisticated language a privilege but also it clearly functions to oppress other women, keeping them outside the circle of understanding.

Raising these issues generates more questions for which I don't have answers yet. I'm still troubled by one that a friend raised last year[4]: What about the women who *can't* speak or write more simply? What if those big words and complex sentences are her natural language, the one she is most comfortable with?

Another friend wondered how far this "making language accessible" should be taken. Must everything one writes be readable by women with a fifth grade education? I am well aware, as I write this, that some women will consider the language of *this* essay too "uppity" also. I hope that, in time, other feminists will begin to suggest answers to questions like these.

My definition of "feminism" involves working against the oppression of *all* women, Black and non-Black, lesbian and straight, with little education or with a lot. It no longer has much to do with being equal to men or being able to compete with them successfully on their terms. I think we've outgrown that. At this point in our development it is essential for us to begin to incorporate some new ideas into our criteria for deciding what is "feminist" in literary criticism. Intellectualism does not equal intelligence. Complicated language is not necessarily needed to express complex ideas. A book which insists on using language that most women can't understand—language which oppresses women by class—*can't* be feminist. A book for example, on important women writers, that only discusses *white* women writers *can't*, by definition, be feminist.

Language isn't the only element we should look at in a discussion like this; it is only the most obvious. But I have begun to question some values commonly held by feminists on some other topics, too:

Universality. In terms of content, we've gained some ground on this one—a lot more subjects are now okay to write about. But aren't we still rejecting the validity of some things because they are not "universal"? Could a Black woman's ideas about "lesbian classics" be universal? Are they less valid if they are not? Whose experience defines universal?

Traditional versus Experimental. Does writing in a nonlinear, nonsequential fashion really make a work more feminine, or feminist? (I have encountered this view point more and more frequently in my reading.) Or is this belief just filtering down to us from the experimental trend going on in male fiction? If we do value a nonlinear style, can we achieve it through riddling the work with footnotes, or is this another hand-me-down? Why are we so opposed to a straightforward, narrative style, to realistic rather than abstract portrayals?

Documentation. Speaking of footnotes, another thing we seem to have inherited from the male academic tradition is the need to document our every idea and opinion with proof that other more famous critics (or more famous feminists) have already thought the same thing. (Again, I'm not exempt, as demonstrated by the notes to this essay.) Does this really increase the truth of what we say? Must we have this "proof" to trust the validity of what our sisters tell us?

Sentimentality. That unspeakable, filthy word! It is always associated with things that are too emotional, subjective, "female," things which appeal to one's feelings rather than one's intellect (as if there were no connection between the two.) Who told us sentiment was wrong? Why must we feel guilty if all we've been reading is love stories? If the personal can be political, then surely the romantic can be revolutionary.

Sex. Is it true, as another friend maintains, that a work of fiction must have sex in it in order to get published today, even by a feminist publisher? Who made that rule?

Women reading this will undoubtedly think of other values which might also be called into question. But the real question, growing from all of these thoughts and wonderings, is this: Are we still letting someone else define what literature is? The time has come for women who consider ourselves feminists to look closely at every attitude we have about literature and criticism and to ask: Is this really coming from us? At the same time, we must keep on asking: Is this attitude sexist? Classist? Racist? As we work toward a place where we can honestly answer those questions the way that we now wish we could, we also work toward a criticism that will be truly feminist.

Notes

¹Cheryl L. Brown and Karen Olson, eds., *Feminist Criticism: Essays on Theory, Poetry and Prose* (Metuchen, New Jersey: Scarecrow Press, 1978); Josephine Donovan, ed., *Feminist Literary Criticism: Explorations in Theory* (Lexington, Kentucky: University of Kentucky Press, 1975); and Arlyn Diamond and Lee R. Edwards, eds., *The Authority of Experience: Essays in Feminist Criticism* (Amherst, Massachusetts: University of Massachusetts Press, 1977). There are also two periodicals devoted almost exclusively to reviews: *The New Women's Times feminist Review*, available from 804 Meigs St., Rochester, NY 14620; and *Motheroot Journal*, available from 214 Dewey St., Pittsburgh, PA 15218.

²Some women who have written Black feminist criticism are Lorraine Bethel, Evelynn Hammonds, Gloria Hull, Audre Lorde, Ann Allen Shockley, Barbara Smith, and Renita Weems. For example, see Lorde's "An Open Letter to Mary Daly" in *Top Ranking: A Collection of Articles on Racism and Classism in the Lesbian Community*, February 3rd Press, 1980 (available from Joan Gibbs and Sara Bennett, 306 Lafayette Ave., Brooklyn, NY 11238); and Smith's "Toward A Black Feminist Criticism" in *Conditions: Two*, 1977 (now available as a reprint from the Lesbian Feminist Study Clearinghouse Women's Studies Program, 1012 Cathedral of Learning, University of Pittsburgh, Pittsburgh PA 15260), and in Gloria T. Hull, Barbara Smith, and Patricia Bell Scott, eds., *But Some of Us Are Brave: Black Women's Studies* (Old Westbury, New York: The Feminist Press, 1982), pp. 157-175.

³*Sinister Wisdom* 13, edited by Beth Hodges, is available from Box 660, Amherst, MA 01004. Especially interesting is Elly Bulkin's "Racism and Writing: Some Implications for White Lesbian Critics." Other articles include "Culture Making: Lesbian Classics in the Year 2000?" by Melanie Kaye; "To the Sisters of the Azalea Collective and Lesbians Rising...." by Anita Cornwell; "Dark Horse: A View of Writing and Publishing by Dark Lesbians" by Linda Brown. Also of interest is *Sinister Wisdom* 2—a special issue on the same subject.

⁴Friends who deserve credit for inspiring me with ideas on this subject are Claudia Scott, Laura Murphy, Ceil Kinney, Elizabeth Humphries, Meg Brigantine, Becky Davidson, and Jackie Spilman.

The Lesbian Periodicals Index

Clare Potter

For the Circle of Lesbian Indexers: JR Roberts, Ruth Pettis, Karen Browne, Judy L, Barbara Burg, and Catherine Risingflame Moirai.

Lesbian women in the United States have created a rich and a varied periodical literature since our first serial appeared in 1947. Called *Vice Versa*, it ceased publication after only nine issues, and no other periodical appeared until *The Ladder* in 1956, which began as the newsletter of the premier lesbian organization, the Daughters of Bilitis. *The Ladder* was the only lesbian periodical during most of the years of its existence (1956–1972). It is justifiably respected for its sheer staying power and acknowledged as an incomparable storehouse of information about lesbian women during the 1950s and 1960s. Its pages are filled with factual data and imaginative literature presented from a distinctly lesbian point of view. Any research on the history of lesbian women in that period must be founded on the record of lesbian life that *The Ladder* provides.

I think that the importance of *The Ladder* as a primary resource for lesbian history will also characterize the lesbian periodical literature that succeeded it. More than one hundred lesbian journals came into existence in the late 1960s and 1970s. This startling increase in periodical publishing resulted from the impact of the post-Stonewall gay movement and the second wave of feminism on the lesbian community. The energy released through the historical convergence of these forces profoundly changed lesbian existence; the phenomenal growth in periodical publishing was just one effect of that transformation.

Although the new lesbian periodicals appeared in every region of the United States, they usually originated in cities with relatively large lesbian communities. The publications varied in content, form, and frequency of appearance. Often organizational newsletters with community calendars and digests of national news of relevance to lesbian women, they might also be fundamentally concerned with lesbian-feminist theory or with the expression of literary ideas, publishing primarily short fiction and poems interspersed with graphic art. Many, unlike *The Ladder*, have been short-lived or single-issue publications.

But in each case they continue the tradition begun by *The Ladder*: they are primary documents of lesbian culture. They have served as open forums for discussion of ideas and issues of concern to the lesbian community. They have provided a means of expression for any lesbian woman to voice her views and opinions and have therefore provided unique access to individual community voices. This periodical literature of the 1960s and 1970s is a vital record of our emerging lesbian consciousness, and through it researchers will be able to discern the pattern and shape of the lesbian experience in America.

It was our conviction about the absolute centrality of lesbian periodical literature for any future writing of lesbian history that led the Circle of Lesbian Indexers to put our energies into a project to create an author/subject index to the contents of lesbian journals. As individual researchers ourselves, we are aware of the dire need that exists for indexes and bibliographies in lesbian studies. Without their facilitating role, the researcher of contemporary lesbian history has recourse only to references supplied by word of mouth, or to scanning footnotes and bibliographies in published books, or to the painstaking labor of individual searches in the periodical literature itself.

We are fortunate that the Lesbian Herstory Archives in New York City has worked assiduously to collect and preserve a large number of lesbian periodicals. Other public and private collections also exist. But at the present time, with the exception of some minimal indexing in, for example, the *Alternative Press Index* and in *Women's Studies Abstracts*, there simply is no access to the contents of lesbian journals. Although this lack of access also characterizes women's and gay movement periodicals in general, lesbian periodicals by comparison are always underrepresented in the limited indexing that is presently undertaken. Without access, the ideas, people, and events that are recorded in our journals are effectively lost, easily ignored and forgotten.

It is our hope that the Lesbian Periodicals Index will be a generative force for making possible the study and research of lesbian culture. We also hope that our efforts will encourage in the lesbian community an awareness and understanding of the responsibility we have to ourselves to preserve our records and personal papers. We further see our attempts to build a thesaurus of subject terms applicable to lesbian realities as a way to help us pose the kinds of questions we need to ask about our experience. The thesaurus is truly a conceptualizing medium with an organic relationship to the culture—its people and ideas—from which it is derived.

We welcome inquiries about our work and will search our files for interested researchers. We also need the continuing support of women to help us locate copies of periodicals not presently in our collection in order to expand the resource base of our indexing.

The appended lists of lesbian periodicals are divided into those that are currently in print and those that have ceased publishing. The list of ceased publications is arranged geographically. The annotated information supplied is as accurate as we were able to determine it. These lists were compiled and are continuously updated by Deborah Edel (of the Lesbian Herstory Archives), JR Roberts, and myself as a resource for women who want information about the lesbian community. If we have not included your periodical or if the information listed is incomplete or inaccurate, please let us know by writing:

Lesbian Herstory Archives
(L.H.E.F., Inc.)
Attn: Deborah Edel
P.O. Box 1258
New York NY 10116

Lesbian Periodicals Index
c/o Clare Potter
2260 Yale St.
Palo Alto, CA 94306

Lesbian Periodicals
That Are Currently in Print

Atlanta (earlier: ALFA *Newsletter*). No. 1, Sept. 1973–; monthly. Atlanta Lesbian Feminist Alliance, PO Box 5502, Atlanta, GA 30307.

Azalea: A Magazine for Third World Lesbians. Vol. 1:1, Winter 1977/78–. c/o Linda Brown, 314 East 91 St. Apt. 5E, New York, NY 10028 or 306 Lafayette Avenue, Brooklyn NY 11238.

BLN Newsletter. No. 1, Nov. 1978– Boulder Lesbian Network Newsletter, PO Box 4912, Boulder, CO 80306

Big Apple Dyke News. Vol. 1:1, March 1981–, monthly. B.A.D. News, 192 Spring St. #15, New York, NY 10012.

Changes. 1977?–. Published by and for the Greater Orlando Lesbian/Feminists. PO Box 1441, Winter Park, FL, 32790.

Coalition of Gay Sisters *Newsletter.* 1978–. PO Box 222, Columbia, MD 21045.

Common Lives/Lesbian Lives. Aug. 1981. PO Box 1553, Iowa City, IA 52244.

Conditions: A Magazine of Writing by Women with an Emphasis on Writing by Lesbians. Vol. 1:1, 1977–. PO Box 56, Van Brunt Station, Brooklyn, NY 11215.

Dinah (earlier: *DinahSoar News*). 1976?–. Lesbian Activist Bureau, PO Box 1485, Cincinnati, OH 45201.

DONT: Dykes Opposed to Nuclear Technology *Newsletter.* 1979?–. c/o Women's Center, 243 West 20th St., New York, NY 10011.

Feminary: Lesbian Feminist Journal for the South. Lesbian focus from Oct.

1978–. PO Box 954, Chapel Hill, NC 27514.

Focus: A Journal for Lesbians (earlier: *Maiden Voyage*). Vol. 1:1, Dec. 1969–, bimonthly. Boston Daughters of Bilitis, 1151 Massachusetts Ave., Cambridge, MA 02138.

Klondyke Kontact (earlier: *Lesbian Milepost, Cunni Linguist, Klondyke Cuntree*). Vol. 1:1, Nov. 1976–, bimonthly. PO Box 1173, Anchorage, AK 99510.

The Lavender Express: New Jersey's Lesbian Journal. Vol. 1:1, April 1978–, monthly. PO Box 218, Kearny, NJ 07032.

Lavender Prairie News. Vol. 1:1, Dec. 1976–, monthly. PO Box 2096, Station A, Champaign, IL 61820.

The Leaping Lesbian. Vol. 1:1, Jan. 1977–, bimonthly. PO Box 7715, Ann Arbor, MI 48107.

Lesbe'informed. 1974?–monthly. c/o Lesbian Resource Center, 2708 E. Lake St., Suite 229/230, Minneapolis, MN 55406.

Lesbian Center News. 1975–, monthly. Ambitious Amazons, PO Box 811, E. Lansing, MI 48823.

Lesbian Community Center *Newsletter.* Vol. 1:1, Sept. 1979–. c/o Lesbian Community Center, 3435 N. Sheffield, Chicago, IL 60657

Lesbian Community News. 1981?–. Lincoln Legion of Lesbians, PO Box 30137, Lincoln, NE 68503.

Lesbian Connection. Vol. 1:1, Nov. 1974–. Helen Diner Memorial Women's Center/

Ambitious Amazons, PO Box 811, E. Lansing, MI 48823.

Lesbian Feminist Flyer. 1976?–. PO Box 7216, Richmond, VA 23221.

Lesbian Feminist Organizing Committee *Newsletter.* No. 1, Sept. 1979–, monthly. 2104 Stevens Ave. South, Minneapolis, MN 55404.

Lesbian Feminists of Trenton *Newsletter.* c/o Carol Demech, 1307 Scenic Drive, West Trenton, NJ 08628.

Lesbian Herstory Archives *Newsletter.* No. 1, June 1975–. PO Box 1258, New York, NY 10116.

The Lesbian Insider/Insighter/Inciter. No. 1, 1980–. PO Box 7038, Powderhorn Station, Minneapolis, MN 55407.

Lesbian Lavender Morning. Vol. 1:1, June 5, 1980–. PO Box 729, Kalamazoo, MI 49005.

Lesbian Network News: LSBN Newsletter (Lesbians Sisters Building a Network). Vol. 1:1, Aug, 1979–, monthly. c/o Hershelf Bookstore, 2 Highland Ave., Highland Park, MI 48203.

The Lesbian News. Vol. 1:1, Aug. 1975–. Jinx Beers, 6507 Franrivers Ave., Canoga Park, CA 91307.

Lesbian Resource Center *Newsletter.* Pacific Women's Resources, 4253 Roosevelt Way, NE, Seattle, WA 98105.

Lesbian Voices. Vol. 1:1, Winter 1974–, quarterly. Jonnik Enterprises, PO Box 2066, San Jose, CA 95109.

Lesbians in Law *Newsletter.* L.I.L., c/o Rachel Ginsburg, 6616 Telegraph Ave. #305, Oakland, CA 94609.

Lesbians of Color *Newsletter.* Lesbians of Color, PO Box 5077, San Diego, CA 92105.

Lesbians Rising. 1976?–, biannual. Hunter College, 695 Park Ave., Room 245, New York, NY 10021.

Lunatic Fringe: A Newsletter for Separatist, Anarchist, and Radical Feminist Lesbians in Chicago. July 1980–, bimonthly. c/o

Sidney Spinster, 5201 S. Blackstone, 3W, Chicago, IL 60615.

Maine Lesbian Feminist Newsletter. 1979?–, monthly. PO Box 125, Belfast, ME 04915.

Matrices: A Lesbian Feminist Research Newsletter. Vol. 1:1/2, Fall/Winter 1977/78–. Julia Penelope (Stanley), University of Nebraska, Dept. of English, Lincoln, NE 68588.

Matrix: Olympia's Feminist/Lesbian Magazine (earlier: *Lesbian/Feminist Community Newsletter*). No. 1, 1979?–. PO Box 7221, Olympia WA 98507.

Mom's Apple Pie: Lesbian Mother's National Defense Fund. No. 1, Nov. 1974–, quarterly. 2446 Lorentz Place West, Seattle, WA 98109.

Monthly Cycle. Vol. 1:1, Aug. 1980–, monthly. c/o Spinsters Books, PO Box 1306, Lawrence, KS 66044.

Moonstorm: Lesbian Feminist Newsletter for Women. Vol. 1:1, Aug. 1973–, monthly. PO Box 4201, Tower Grove Station, St. Louis, MO 63118.

The New Dawn. Vol. 1:1, June 1980–. Box 907, Phoenix, AZ 85001.

New Hampshire Lambda *Newsletter.* No. 1, 1979?–. PO Box 1043, Concord, NH 03301.

A Newsletter. Vol. 1:1, 1978–. Box 120834, Nashville, TN 37212.

Notes from LARC: Newsletter of the Lesbian Alumnae of Radcliffe. Vol. 1:1, 1980–. C/o Peggy Anderson, RFD 3, Box 10, Putney, VT 05346.

The Other Side (Newsletter of the Organization, The Other Side). Vol. 1:1, 1974?–, monthly. PO Box 132, San Rafael, CA 94902.

Otherviews/Innerviews. No. 1, Dec. 1978–. C/o Aradia, Inc., PO Box 7516, Grand Rapids, MI 49410.

Out and About: Seattle Lesbian/Feminist Newsletter. Vol. 1:1, May 1976–, monthly. 4535 Thackeray NE, Seattle, WA 98105.

Part of the Process (earlier: *The Rhode Island Lesbian Times*). PO Box 6563. Providence, RI 02940.

Puce Mongoose (earlier: *D.O.B. News Journal, Lazette*). Vol. 1:1, Sept. 1971-. United Sisters, PO Box 41, Garwood, NJ 07027.

Sapphire Speaks. 1981-. C/o Leigh Mosley, 1752 U St., NW, Washington, D.C. 20009.

She: For Women in Touch with Women. No. 1, 1979?-. PO Box 2245, Carol City Branch, Opa-Locka, FL 33055.

Sinister Wisdom. No. 1, July 1976-, quarterly. PO Box 660, Amherst, MA 01004.

Sisterspace *Bulletin.* 1977-. 3500 Lancaster Ave., Philadelphia, PA 19104.

Sisters United: A Lesbian/Feminist Magazine. Vol. 1:1, Sept./Oct. 1979-, bimonthly. Woman Prints Enterprises, 118 West Sparks St., Galena, KS 66739.

Southern California Woman for Understanding *Newsletter* (earlier: SCW/WRF *News*—Southern California Women for the Whitman-Radclyffe Foundation). Vol. 1:1, 1976-, bimonthly. 205 South Beverly Dr., Suite 206, Beverley Hills, CA 90212.

Telewoman. 1978-, monthly. C/o Anne, PO Box 2306, Pleasant Hill, CA 94523.

Third World Women's Gay-Zette (a publication of the SalsaSoul Sisters). Vol. 1:1, Sept. 1976-. C/o Candice Boyce, ed., 41-11 Parsons Blvd., No. 616, Flushing, NY 11355.

Thursday's Child: San Diego Lesbian Organization Newsletter. Vol. 1:1, May 1978-, monthly. PO Box 5093, San Diego, CA 92105.

Ultimate Womon *Newsletter* (earlier: *Sapphic Condition*: title varies). n.d.-. C/o BFMS, 504 Cathedral Street, Baltimore, MD 21201.

The Wishing Well. No. 1, Jan. 1976-. PO Box 117, Novato, CA 94948.

Lesbian Periodicals
That Have Ceased Publishing

Mid-Atlantic Region

Pennsylvania

Daughters of Bilitis: Philadelphia *Newsletter*
1967-68
Philadelphia

Getting It Together
1971
Philadelphia

Lesbians Fight Back
1972
Philadelphia

Wicce
1973-75
Philadelphia

New Jersey

Albatross: Lesbian Feminist Satire Magazine

1974-79(?)
East Orange

The Jersey Lesbian
1976
New Brunswick

Sapphic Sisters *Newsletter*
1978
Union

New York

The Cosmic Lesbians
1975
New York City

Cowrie (earlier: *The Udder Side*)
1973-74
New York City

Daughters of Bilitis: New York *Newsletter* (later: *Lesbian Letter, Lesbian Newsletter, Coming Out Rage*)

1961–73(?)
New York City

Dyke: A Quarterly
1975–78
Preston Hollow

Dykes and Tykes *Newsletter*
1977–79(?)
New York City

Dykes Unite
1974
Geneseo

Echo of Sappho
1972
Brooklyn

Gay Revolution of Women (later: *Women in Sunlight,* Lesbian Resource Center *Newsletter*)
1973–74(?)
Rochester

Green Thursdays (published by Lesbian Feminist Coalition)
c. 1977
White Plains

Hera
n.d.
New York City

Hikin Dykes
n.d.
New York City

Lavender Grapevine
1977
Buffalo

Lesbian Activist of the Gay Activist Alliance
1973
New York City

The Lesbian Feminist
1973–79
New York City

Lesbian Life Space *Newsletter*
1973
New York City

Lesbian Mothers Unite
n.d.
Rochester

One-To-One
1973
New York City

Purple Rage
1971
New York City

Sisterhood Songs
1971
New York City

Tribad
1977–79
New York City

Midwestern Region

Illinois

Amazon Nation *Newsletter*
c. 1973
Chicago

Blazing Star (earlier: *Secret Storm*)
1974–75(?)
Chicago

Chicago Lesbian Liberation *Newsletter*
1973–74(?)
Chicago

Cries from Cassandra
1973
Chicago

Daughters of Bilitis: Chicago *Newsletter*
1963–66(?)
Chicago

Gay Women's House *Newsletter*
n.d.
Champaign

Killer Dyke
1971
Chicago

Lavender Woman
1971–76
Chicago

Lesbian Feminist Center *News*
1974–75(?)
Chicago

Only You
1974
Aurora

Original Lavender Woman
1974
Chicago

Indiana

Dyke Life
1976
Indianapolis

Lesbian Journal
n.d.
Bloomington

Iowa

Ain't I A Woman
1970–74(?)
Iowa City

Better Home and Dykes
n.d.
Iowa City

Kansas

Lavender Luminary
1976(?)
Lawrence

Michigan

The Daily Dyke
1974
Ann Arbor

Daughters of Bilitis: Detroit *Reach Out*
1971
Detroit

Lesbian Lipservice (earlier: *Lesbian Newsletter*)
1975
Ann Arbor

Purple Star
1971
Ann Arbor

Sappho's Sisters Rising
n.d.
Detroit

Spectre
1971
Ann Arbor

Minnesota

So's Your Old Lady
1973–79
Minneapolis

Missouri

Gay Women's *Newsletter*
1973
St. Louis

Lesbian Alliance *Newsletter*
1974–75(?)
St. Louis

Rising Up Swiftly
1975
Holts Summit

Ohio

Coming Out
1975(?)
Oberlin

Purple Cow: Lesbian/Feminist Newsletter
1974–76
Columbus

Wisconsin

We Got It
1975–76
Madison

New England Region

Maine

Uva Ursi: A Funky Down Home Lesbia Journaul Storees Pictuas Pomes How Ta Dos
1973–76(?)
Robbinston

Massachusetts

Lavender Visions
1971
Cambridge

Dyke Undoings
1980
Northampton

Northshore Lesbian Community
   Newsletter
1976–79
Salem

Rhode Island

The Lesbian Newsletter
1977
Providence

Vermont

Green Mountain Dykes
1980
Bennington

Pacific Coast Region

California

The Amazon Mime Grapevine
1979
Burbank

Amazon Quarterly
1972–75
Oakland (also: Somerville MA)

Bay Area Lesbians in Law Newsletter
1976(?)
San Francisco

Burn't Out Lesbian Newsletter
1973(?)
San Francisco

Circles Edge Newsletter
1975(?)
Frontera

Daughters of Bilitis: San Diego Doblings
1969
San Diego

Daughters of Bilitis: San Francisco Newsletter (later: Sisters)
1965–75
San Francisco

Dykes and Gorgons: Dyke-Feminist
   Newspaper
1973
Berkeley

The Keyhole: Lesbian Feminist Alliance
1976
Campbell

The Ladder (D.O.B. until 8-9/70)
1956–72
San Francisco (also: Reno, NV)

Lesbian Communication Collective
   News
c. 1979
Eureka

Lesbian Mother's Union Newsletter
1972
San Francisco

The Lesbian Tide
1971–80
Los Angeles

Lesbian Visions
1975(?)
Stanford

Mother (later: Proud Woman)
1971–72
Stanford

National Lesbian Feminist Organization
   News (earlier: It's About Time)
1978
Los Angeles

National Lesbian Information Service
   Newsletter
1972
San Francisco

Nova Narratio
1970–72(?)
Albany

Portcullis: A Feminist/Lesbian
   Publication
1972
Los Angeles

Rubyfruit Readher: A Lesbian
   Communique
1977(?)
Felton

Sapphа Speaks
1978(?)
San Jose

Sapphire
1973
San Francisco

Satin
1973–74(?)
San Jose

Sisters of Sappho of San Jose
   Newsletter
1974
San Jose

Tres Femmes
1972
San Diego

Uranian Mirror
1971–74(?)
Berkeley

Vice Versa
1947–48
Los Angeles

Oregon

Pearl Diver
1977–78
Portland

Washington

Gayly Forward: Come Out, Come Out
1972
Seattle

Lesbian Home Journal
1976
Seattle

Lesbians of Color Quarterly
1979
Seattle

The Woman's Woman: A Lesbian
   Newsletter
1975–76
Seattle

Rocky Mountain Region

Montana

   Amazon Spirit
   1978–79(?)
   Helena

Wyoming

   Twelfth Letter
   n.d.
   Cheyenne

Southern Region

Arkansas

   Amazon Farmers *Newsletter* (Ozark Wim-
      min on Land)
   c. 1977
   Fayetteville

District of Columbia

   Furies
   1972-73

Florida

   Dykes Central *News Bulletin*
   1976(?)
   Tampa

   Free and Proud
   1973
   Tallahassee

   Lesbian Lifeline
   1977(?)
   Daytona Beach

   Lesbiana Speaks
   1976–77
   Dade County

   Sisters
   1979
   Ft. Lauderdale/Hollywood

Georgia

   Womansword
   1977–78(?)
   Athens

Kentucky

Lesbian Feminist Union *News*
1975–78
Louisville

Womin Energy (earlier: *Women Energy*)
1978–79
Lexington

Louisiana

Daughters of Bilitis: New Orleans
Gay-La
1974–75(?)
New Orleans

Dyke Digest (earlier: Community for
the Development of Wimmin's
Resources)
1978-79
New Orleans

Maryland

Desperate Living
1969–77
Baltimore

Lesbian Community Center *Newsletter*
1976–80
Baltimore

Mississippi

Lesbian Front (earlier: *Unnamed Lesbian Newsletter*)
1975–77
Jackson

North Carolina

Lesbian Center *Journal*
1976–77(?)
Charlotte

Tennessee

East Tennessee Alliance of Lesbian
Activists *News*
1979
n.p.

Mother Jones Gazette
1973
Knoxville

Southwest Region

Texas

Austindyke
1979–80
Austin

Daughters of Bilitis: Dallas *Newsletter*
(earlier: *Monthly Dob'r*; later: *Women
for Action*)
1974–76(?)
Dallas

Goodbye To All That: A Lesbian Feminist
Publication
1975–78
Austin

Lone Star Lesbians
1977–78
Austin

Our Time Has Come
1978(?)
Austin

Point Blank Times
1975–78
Houston

Two Dykes and Others
1978(?)
Austin

Note on "Reading a Subject" In Periodical Indexes

Ida VSW Red

One way to make a quick assessment of material available for a research topic is to "read the subject" in periodical and literature indexes. Such "reading" involves identifying in the selected index the subject headings relevant to the chosen topic and tracing both the ways in which the subject headings change over time and the numbers and types of articles listed under each subject. Often, index changes reflect evolving social attitudes toward the subject as well as trends in popularity, focus, audience, and authorship of articles on the topic.

An hour spent examining the indexes can help prevent the "I had a great topic but couldn't find anything on it" blues and can also produce new ideas for research focus. Indexes, like dictionaries and library card catalogs, are slow to change their systems and evolve only under the pressure of significant change in publication or public opinion trends. A researcher planning to write, for example, about public attitudes toward lesbianism in the past ten years will find in a perusal of *The Readers' Guide to Periodical Literature* (RG) and *The New York Times Index* (NYT) for 1970–1980 an increasing interest in and changing attitudes toward the subject.

The level of popular interest in lesbianism can be measured by the number of articles, which peaked in 1976. *Readers' Guide* lists no articles under Lesbianism in the 1950s. In the 1960s there were no more than one a year. In the 1970s the number of articles increased five-fold and was supplemented by fifteen or more related articles under Homosexuality. The fact that *Ms.* was added in 1974/75 to the list of periodicals indexed accounts for part of the increase. The influence of a single publication on the attention given to the subject illustrates the importance of examining which periodicals are included in an index and being aware of the sources not covered. *The New York Times Index* indicates how much is lacking from RG by listing in 1973, for example, forty-four long sets of articles under Homosexuality while RG indexed only sixteen individual articles. Numbers are not everything, of course, and can be deceptive under a general heading like Homosexuality: of thirty-five citations in the 1976 NYT, only two had specific lesbian relevance.

Attitudinal change is reflected in the focus of articles, often obvious in the titles. Early 1960s judgmental titles focused on the immorality, illegality, sexual perversion, mental illness, and criminality of homosexuality. These aspects are still reflected in a few titles, but are far outnumbered by themes of political activism, pride of identity, religious affiliation and ordination, demythologizing, liberation, custody, and equal rights. Titles in *Ms.* give an "inside" view of subtopics such as coming out, separatism, peer group pressure, second-generation lesbians, and custody. Titles from news weeklies and general women's magazines reflect "outside" perspectives on concerns such as artificial insemination, lesbians in public life, attitudes of straight women toward lesbianism ("Who's Afraid of Lesbian Sex?" in *Vogue* and "If Lesbians Make You Nervous..." in *Mademoiselle*), and lesbian motherhood as a surprising phenomenon. Identification of source clarifies the focus of content.

Another indication of movement in the subject area is shifting authorship patterns. Articles in the 1960s were written about homosexuality or lesbianism by others; 1970s articles were almost without exception written by lesbians and gay men and/or about their public activism (seeking custody rights, state rights, employment rights, federal rights, religious rights, parade for rights, coalition for rights, et cetera).

An example of a subject heading reflecting changing attitudes is the NYT placement of Homosexuality under Sex Perversion in the 1950s, then under Sex, now alone. In the 1960s and 1970s Sex Perversion continued to carry See Also references to Homosexuality, but with fewer and fewer relevant articles. In the 1973/74 RG, Sexual Perversion gave way to Sexual Deviation, a somewhat less pejorative term. The NYT maintains its See Also references from Sexual Perversion to Homosexuality and to Sex Crimes, but the contents of articles listed do not justify the references. There is little mention of perversion in the articles under Homosexuality, and those under Sex Crimes refer almost exclusively to heterosexual rape rather than to homosexuality. Sex Crimes seem to be broadly defined by NYT indexers, who direct in the 1979 index, See Abortion and in 1980, See Also Basketball. The term Gay appears increasingly in headings, from one first use in 1970/71 to nine in the 1974 NYT. Gay has been associated from its first appearance with the Gay Liberation Movement.

Interestingly, cross references from Feminism to Woman–Equal Rights, and to Woman–Social and Moral Questions, have been used by RG since the 1920s. In the 1970s Feminists–See Women's Liberation Movement was added. Lesbianism, formerly under Sex, is now under Homosexuality in the NYT. Lesbian Feminist Liberation (the organization) has been a heading in the NYT since 1976; *Lesbian Tide* (the publication), since 1978; and Lesbian and Gay Rights, Coalition (organization), since 1979. That index reading provides mystery and humor along with history is indicated by some unexpected See Also's to the RC Church, Pope, and to North Star Food. RG gives Lesbianism an independent heading and in 1976/77 adds See Also Bisexuality. Note again that the periodicals indexed determine subject focus. RG sources such as *Ms., Time, Newsweek,* and *Mademoiselle* naturally give a different focus from that of feminist and progressive political publications, for example. The researcher needs to examine indexes to alternative sources (e.g., *Alternative Press Index, Access: The Index to Little Magazines,* and *Alternatives in Print*) in order to get a balanced view of a subject; the selected indexes in this instance give only the general interest or popular perspective.

Although periodical and literature indexes, as illustrated, are quick and valuable guides to the level of popular interest in and changing attitudes toward a subject, several cautions are in order. It is easy to jump to wrong conclusions or overgeneralize the trends observed in an index reading. Scientific or social science periodicals treat a subject differently from popular or special interest publications, such as those by and for feminists, gay men, or lesbians.

Additionally, the subject of an article is not always evident from the title. The NYT offers a brief abstract of contents, but RG, like most indexes, gives titles only. Some indexers are dependent on title only for placement of an article, so relevant material can easily be missing from a subject section. This problem is, of course, not encountered in indexes based on key words rather than an established subject structure (e.g., *Social Sciences Citation Index* and *Humanities Citation Index*). It is wise to follow all See Also's and use a variety of subject approaches to each topic searched. The final caution is a reminder of how hidden a subject like lesbianism may be. There are no Lesbian as Poet, Lesbians in Government, or Lesbians as Library Activists guides, like the condescending old Library of Congress subject headings for Women. Subjects, like lesbians themselves, are often in the closet and must be lured out with a variety of creative approaches. One is to track individuals known to be active in the area of the chosen subject, perhaps using tools like the *Personal Name Index to the New York Times Index, 1851–1974* or *A Gay News Chronology, 1969–May 1975*. (New York: Arno, 1975). Another is to read literature indexes with an eye for the evolution of subject headings. These initial steps can quickly establish the availability of material for research. Reading a subject index with care is a valuable research tool and can be a fascinating step in reclaiming lesbian herstory.

Older Lesbians

Matile Poor

There is a growing consciousness about older lesbians, not only among lesbians themselves but also among some gerontologists and service providers for aging women. Since 1975, and more significantly, since 1977, writing and research on the subject has become available, and in larger cities lesbians over forty have formed support and social groups. Because relatively few women over sixty-five identify themselves as lesbians, the term "older lesbian" has come to mean lesbians over fifty, and in many instances, over forty. In this article I will raise some general issues for older lesbians and will then discuss support groups, including a therapy/support group which I co-facilitate in San Francisco.

Since the early 1970s, the combination of the women's liberation movement and the gay rights movement has encouraged women to call themselves lesbians who would have found the label too dangerous earlier. In the last ten years, an increasing number of women in their twenties and thirties who had not lived though so many years in secrecy and hiding felt free enough to acknowledge their lesbianism. Even though there have always been women over forty who were "out of the closet," the growing number of younger lesbians has provided an atmosphere in which more and more women over forty have been able to come out. If this process continues, we can expect in the next five years an increase in the number of identifiable lesbians over sixty-five, many of whom will want to participate in lesbian and gay organizations and to have special services available for them if they live in large cities.

We do not know the number of lesbians over sixty-five. In 1977, there were 13.9 million women (and 9.5 million men) over sixty-five in the United States. If only 6 percent of these women are lesbians, that would mean some 834,000.

A majority of the older lesbians interviewed for a study by Marcy Adelman were integrated into mainstream culture and would not want to use services specially designated for lesbians and gay men. Probably this is true because no special services have been available for older lesbians; the women in the study may have felt that their only choice was to hide their identity and integrate into the larger culture. Because of this assimilation, older lesbians are hard to find, even for research purposes, and if this is true for white, middle-class lesbians, it is even more true of lesbians of color. In 1980, an informal group of lesbian and gay male gerontologists who worked in various city and county agencies in the San Francisco area tried to identify older lesbians who came for services and found it very difficult to identify many. Finding older men who were willing to identify as gay was much easier, perhaps because lesbians, having been oppressed not only as lesbians but as women, feel more fear about being open than gay men.

This unusual situation, where the elders of the lesbian community are for the most part hidden from us, means that women between forty and sixty are considered the "old" women in the community. And lesbians in their early fifties often feel they have no models for aging and that they are living on a kind of frontier. Younger lesbians do not know if lesbians over sixty-five have found creative and unusual living arrangements; what they do for recreation; whether lesbians of color over sixty-five have needs and concerns not shared by white lesbians their age; whether older lesbians would like more interaction with younger lesbians or what kind of support from a community of younger women would be helpful to them.

When I give workshops for social workers and others in the San Francisco area, I suggest that information about lesbian and gay activities be posted in every senior home and at the site of every day and recreational program for seniors. But even in a city noted for its atmosphere of openness, some service workers thought there would be objections to posting such information on bulletin boards, and some even suggested that asking that such information be made available would be a risk for lesbian and gay male workers.

We are beginning to learn, though, that there are older women who could benefit from knowing more about the lesbian community and from getting support from women like themselves. In research from her master's thesis, Mina Robinson interviewed some women who had their first same-sex experience when they were over sixty, and some members of the group I co-facilitate have identified themselves as lesbians only after age fifty. We do not know enough about these experiences. With the large and growing number of single women over sixty-five in the general population, perhaps an increasing number will identify as lesbians, if the political climate remains the same or improves, if community organizations welcome older lesbians, and if older lesbians become more visible to each other. Images of lesbians over sixty-five, including women of color, in the slide shows of the Lesbian Herstory Archives remind us that a whole part of our history has been hidden.

Older women who are coming out for the first time need all the supports that a younger woman needs. For these women, for example, it is as hard to tell children and grandchildren that they consider themselves lesbians as it is for younger women to tell their parents. And once an older woman has come out of the closet, she will want to have medical and social services where her special needs can be recognized and met.

At this time, such recognition would be hard to find in most day programs for seniors, in residential treatment centers, or in medical facilities. In a few cases where two male lovers have wanted to be placed in the same nursing home, it has been nearly impossible, even in California, to find homes to accept them. The stories about families of older lesbians and gay men who take over and ignore the wishes of lovers are heartbreaking to hear, as are stories of unclear wills which left longtime lovers without any inheritance. Many questions also arise concerning the term "spouse." Until now, only heterosexual spouses have been acknowledged in nursing homes and hospitals where the spouse has special visiting privileges, and the heterosexual spouse is also the person who is consulted when critical decisions have to be made or when emergencies arise. There is a great need for more consciousness raising and change in these areas. Sometimes excellent materials are available, but their distribution is too limited. This is the case with a wonderful cartoon story by Jan Dickson, which is a first of its kind. In the story, Concha and Clara find each other in a nursing home and fall in love. In the end, they are accepted by the staff and can live openly and happily as a couple and as "roommates" in the home. We are a long way from being able to expect this kind of recognition for older lesbians and gay men who are in nursing homes. In our own community, ideas for housing and nursing homes for lesbians are being discussed on both coasts, but so far no plan has been carried out.

Deborah Wolf's research comparing pre-retirement and post-retirement lesbians and gay men suggests that older lesbians can serve as models for heterosexual women. Wolf shows that older lesbians are more independent than their heterosexual counterparts because they have had to build supports for themselves before they reach retirement age. Her study is especially valuable because it allows us to see some relationship between middle age and old age, a new subject in lesbian research.

The slowly growing consciousness of older lesbians is reflected not only in research but also in recently published literature. We recognize the impact literary images can have from the influence of *The Well of Loneliness*. Far more positive are the images of older lesbians now in print: in autobiographical pieces, journals, interviews, novels, and photographs. (Also important for making older lesbians visible are the slide shows described in the Resources section of this book.) These recent descriptions of older lesbians not only provide us with new insights but also help us validate our lives and give us more courage to be open.

Sinister Wisdom was the first lesbian periodical to publish a special issue on aging (no. 10, Summer 1979). Its unusual consciousness of aging was due in part to one of the founding editors, Catherine Nicholson, herself an older lesbian, and to guest editor Susan Leigh Star, a gerontologist.

When I read Barbara MacDonald's story "Do You Remember Me?" in that issue of *Sinister Wisdom*, I realized that just as younger lesbians want to know more about their elders, older lesbians also want to hear from their contemporaries. Barbara wrote:

> Wherever we go, Cynthia and I, to the pubs, to the theater to see "Word Is Out," to hear Adrienne Rich or Olga Broumas, Mary Daly or Kate Millett, or to some meeting of the lesbian caucus of NOW, I am always the oldest woman.
> I keep wondering where everybody else is. Where are the friends I drank beer with in the Fifties? Where are the young women I slept with in the Thirties and Forties? Did they never grow old? Did they never reach sixty-five along with me? I look about me and feel there has been some kind of catastrophe from which only I have been spared. (*Sinister Wisdom* 10:11.)

After I read her story, I thought of the thousands of older lesbians who must feel as though they are living in a strange landscape where their peers have disappeared, and I realized that there is a great need for more older lesbians to write about themselves.

In 1980, A New York group called SAGE (Senior Action in a Gay Environment) published a collection of writing by ten of its members. Although these stories and pictures are wonderful to have, they are not specifically about lesbian or gay male life and thus are a little disappointing to someone searching for positive images of aging lesbians.

In her recent journals, *House By the Sea* and *Recovering*, May Sarton has written about her friend Judy who has become increasingly senile and who has been living in a nursing home for about seven years. These are the first writings by an older lesbian which describe the pain of seeing a dear friend who has declined to the point where she must live in a nursing home. The opening of *Recovering* describes a Christmas when May has brought Judy to her home:

> ...I need to commemorate with something better than tears my long companionship with Judy that began thirty-five years ago and ended on Christmas Day.
> Now I am more alone than ever before, for as long as Judy was here at least for the holidays, and even though only *partially* here, as long as I could recreate for a few days or hours a little of the old magic Christmases at 139 Oxford Street and then at 14 Wright Street in Cambridge, I still had family.

And further:

> It is often a small thing that shatters hope. For me it came when a male pheasant appeared close to the porch window—such a dazzling sight in all the gloom that I called out, "Come Judy, come quickly!" She didn't come, of course. I found her shuffling about in the library and by the time I had dragged her to the window, the pheasant was out of sight. At that moment I knew that Judy had gone beyond where being with me in this house means anything. (*Recovering*, pp. 9–11).

May Sarton is still in her sixties; others who are older have also spoken out about themselves. Mabel Hampton, a Black woman in her late seventies, told her story in an interview in *Sinister Wisdom 10*. In spite of hard times in her younger years, she said that she would choose to be a lesbian if she had to do it all over again. Not only her words but photographs of her by Joan E. Biren (JEB) give us images which help us envision ourselves. JEB has also photographed other older lesbians who appear in *Eye to Eye: Portraits of Lesbians*. Elsa Gidlow, now in her eighties, wrote "A View from the Seventy-Seventh Year," a positive view of lesbian aging, in 1976:

> I believe it may be easier for a lesbian to accept without pain the changes that come with the years and what society views as diminished sexual desirability, not having to be concerned with the approval of male concepts of attractiveness. Personally, I do not feel that, given lifelong care for health and general bodily fitness, one need lose attractiveness. *Women: A Journal of Liberation* (1976):35.

There are at least two novels with older lesbian characters. June Arnold's *Sister Gin* (1975) is about a middle-age couple, Su and Bettina, and their friend, Mamie

Carter, who is in her seventies. The novel describes lesbian life in a small town where the three friends are bound together by their secrets from the rest of the world. Mamie Carter is portrayed as witty, wise, engaging, and very sexual. She is alone and without chances for finding a partner in that town. She has a wild affair with Bettina, but also recognizes that Su and Bettina have a long-term relationship which will outlast the "fling."

In a more recent novel by Doris Grumbach, *Chamber Music*, the wife of a famous composer has her first lesbian relationship after her husband's death. I have wondered if this novel is having an impact on older women. We know very little about women who turn to other women after their husbands die. Now that positive lesbian images are more common than they were in the past, will more older women turn to same sex relationships? We can only speculate; we do not yet know the answers. We do know that some women, after many years of marriage and sexual frustration, experience a sexual awakening when they begin lesbian relationships, and in some cases have their first orgasms. A writer named Kady (formerly Kady van Deurs) discusses this subject briefly in her article "A Lesbian at Alderson Prison" *The Lesbian Insider* (April 1981): 19.

Without knowing very much about the lives of lesbians over sixty-five, lesbians between forty and sixty have begun to organize different kinds of groups which will help them build supports for themselves as they age. There is a sense among these women that they want to get to know each other and to prepare against the isolation many older women experience.

In some major cities, older lesbians have formed rap groups which meet regularly. In the Bay Area, there are four such groups which meet once a week: one in San Francisco, one in Berkeley, one near Palo Alto, and one in Marin. These groups do not require regular participation and can be enjoyed on a drop-in basis. The format of the meetings combines discussions with time to socialize. Topics for discussion include such issues as coming out, family relationships, intimate relationships, menopause, and sexuality. More and more women in their forties and fifties have participated in these groups in the past few years, but very few women over sixty have participated. This fact not only emphasizes the hidden and "closeted" nature of those over sixty, but also that the needs of those who are younger are different. Lesbians between forty and sixty want to grow older sharing with others like themselves. The ongoing, open rap groups which have been organized for several years seem established enough to have a future. These support organizations could serve as a model for other women, whether or not they are lesbians.

Older gay men in San Francisco have also organized a group which meets regularly. Women were invited to this group when it was formed, but none have ever joined. This raises a question: What kinds of organizations would attract both older lesbians and gay men? Cooperation between the two groups seems necessary in order to use all the resources we have within the lesbian and gay community and also to deal effectively with the state and local agencies which generally fund services to the elderly and who would not give money to women-only projects. On the other hand, some women choose not to share with men; they would not want, for example, a nursing home with men.

Since 1979, Operation Concern, the gay counseling center in San Francisco, has sponsored a closed therapy/support group for older lesbians. Dottie Fowler and I co-facilitate this group which meets each week for an hour and a half. This group can continue as long as the women want it. It differs from the open rap groups because the membership is limited, and participants must attend regularly.

Since the group is open-ended, it can meet the needs of both those who have urgent problems and those whose personal issues are not pressing but want the benefits of a support group. Therapy/support groups for older lesbians which have lasted for such a long time as ours are very unusual. Our group has allowed us to consider our experiences in depth and to begin to articulate the needs of older lesbians. Although the group has only about eight members at any one time, there have been about twenty women in the group during the two years it has been meeting. A core of four women have been in the group since it began. They seem to look upon the group as a source of support which they want to be permanent in their lives. Others have joined the group at a time of some particular crisis in their lives and leave after four to six months when they feel they no longer need the group.

The group is fairly diverse even though all the members are white. Usually the ages range from forty to sixty, but one woman in her late sixties belonged to the group for a short time. One member is Peruvian, and the rest are second- and third-generation Americans from European backgrounds. Economically, there is a great span. One woman lives on welfare, four live on $600–800 a month, and two live on more than $1,200. This diversity is broadened by the way in which the women have identified themselves during their lives. Half of the group has been married and has grown children. These women did not consider themselves lesbians until their children were mature (over age sixteen). Three of the women who have been in the group are grandmothers. The women who never married or had children are further divided into two groups: those who were homosexually active in their younger years, and those who were either heterosexual or for the most part celibate as young women.

The major issues discussed in the group are the same as those which would be important to all older women: aging, possible disability, loss of security, sexuality, loneliness and isolation, and building supports or networks. What is different is the way these women approach the issues. At base, how comfortable they are with their identities as lesbians and where they are in the "coming out" process, determines how they can work out problems. If, for example, a woman needs a place to live, she may want to share with other lesbians, or she may feel all right sharing with a sympathetic relative. It is important that the group be able to understand why, for example, she may not want to take a less expensive apartment with a relative who does not know she is a lesbian.

Some of the women in the group have begun to think of themselves as lesbians only after age fifty. They are often uncertain about their identities and how to come out to others. It is validating to these women to hear the experiences of others who have considered themselves lesbians for many years. What is realized in this ongoing group process is that as these women age, they have to decide over and over again how much of themselves they want to reveal to the outside world. Every new job interview or involvement with service providers or change in housing means deciding how much they want to reveal, or come out to others. The importance of the coming-out process and its relation to every part of our lives is difficult for heterosexuals to understand because there is no equivalent experience for them. Racial minorites are identifiable by physical appearance; homosexual men and women have to choose whether to be identified.

Some of the women in the group have felt more guarded as they age because they feel less secure in the job market and in finding adequate housing. One of our recurrent issues has been the difficulty these women have had in gaining recognition and acceptance of their lesbianism from the medical establishment, especially from male physicians. Sharing these problems in a group is helpful to those who need support to demand the recognition they deserve. What is clear to all members is that their identity as lesbians is continually changing and that coming out is a lifelong process. In the past we have not been so aware of the extent to which this process continues, even for those who have been lesbians all of their adult lives.

Some women in the group were in heterosexual marriages which lasted twenty years or more, but no one has been in a lesbian relationship of such duration. Most of the women are presently in relationships which seem to last no longer than five years. One woman who was in the group has not found another lover since her partner of ten years died. In general, most of the women have had monogamous, sequential lesbian relationships. The divorce rate among heterosexuals indicates that they, too, can reasonably expect to have several major partners in a lifetime; lesbians have already been experiencing the sequential relationships which heterosexual women are beginning to experience more frequently.

One of the women in our group lives in a communal house with her lover and several other women. Another member has tried to find compatible women to form a commune. Several women live with their lovers, and some live alone. One still lives with teenaged children. For all of these women, housing arrangements, like relationships, are impermanent. During the two years we have been meeting, almost every women in the group has gone through changes in relationships and housing. Consequently, the stability of the group has been very important.

An older lesbian experiences a kind of triple jeopardy—as a woman, as an older person, and as a lesbian. Therefore, older lesbians have as much need of support groups as younger lesbians, perhaps more. One of my dreams is that someday we will have support groups all over the country, so that older lesbians can attend whether they are at home or traveling.

Besides support groups, we need organizations which can offer outreach to older lesbians and gay men. In the San Francisco area, for example, there is no group comparable to SAGE (Senior Action in a Gay Environment) in New York. Temporarily sick or housebound people could be visited by younger members of the community. In some places it might be possible to add gay services to existing ones. Meals on Wheels, for example, could encourage lesbian and gay volunteers to visit the lesbian and gay users of their service. Similarly, lesbians in nursing homes could be visited by younger lesbians, but only, of course, if they could be open about their identities. Lesbians over sixty-five also ought to have access to special counseling services, health care, and housing.

In 1980 in San Francisco, a group of lesbian and gay gerontologists asked that a section on older lesbians and gay men be included in the county needs assessment. I think this was the first time this has happened anywhere in the country. Such documents are read by professionals in service fields; calling attention to older lesbians and gay men is a way to begin educating those who allocate funds. In the past, there was so little awareness of the aging population among us that it seemed as if the thousands of younger lesbians and gay men in the community were not expected to grow old. As the new awareness of older lesbians increases, perhaps there will be a time when we are as visible as younger members of the lesbian community.

I wish to thank Dottie Fowler for her help with part of this article.

Bibliography on Lesbians and Aging

Adelman, Marcy. *Adjustment to Aging and Style of Being Gay: A Study of Older Gay Men and Lesbians.* Unpublished Ph.D. thesis, Wright Institute, Berkeley, California, 1980.

Arnold, June. *Sister Gin.* Plainfield, Vermont; Daughters, 1975.

Baracks, Barbara, and Jarratt Keni, eds. *Sage Writings.* New York: An Artists and Elders Project Book, Teachers and Writers Collaborative Publications, 1980.

Copper, Baba. "On Being an Older Lesbian." *Generations: Journal of the Western Gerontological Society,* Summer 1980, pp. 39-40.

Country Women 11 (July 1974). (Issue on older women.)

Dickson, Jan. *Clara and Concha in a Nursing Home Romance.* Self-published, 1977.

Fenwick, R.D. "Perspectives on Aging." In *The Advocate Guide to Gay Health,* (chapter 6). New York: Dutton, 1978.

Gidlow, Elsa. "Memoirs," *Feminist Studies* 6, 1 (Spring 1980):107-127.

Gidlow, Elsa. "A View from the Seventy-Seventh Year," *Women: A Journal of Liberation* 4, 4, 1976.

Grumbach, Doris. *Chamber Music.* New York: Dutton, 1979.

JEB. *Eye to Eye: Portraits of Lesbians.* Washington, D.C.: Glad Hag Press, 1979.

Lyon, Phyllis, and Martin, Del. "The Older Lesbian." In *Positively Gay,* edited by Betty Berzon and Robert Leighton. Millbrae, California: Celestial Arts Press, 1979; pp. 134-145.

MacDonald, Barbara. "Do You Remember Me?" *Sinister Wisdom* 10 (Summer, 1979): 9-14. Special issue on being old and age.

Minnigerode, Fred, and Marcy Adelman. "Elderly Homosexual Women and Men: Report on a Pilot Study." *Family Coordinator,* October, 1978, pp. 452-456.

Pogoncheff, Elaine. "The Gay Patient," *R.N.* April, 1979.

Raphael, Sharon, and Mina K. Robinson. "Lesbian and Gay Men in Later Life," *Generations Journal of the Western Gerontological Society,* Fall 1981.

Robinson, Mina. "Lesbians in Later Life," *Sister* 9, no. 4, (August, 1978).

Robinson, Mina. *The Older Lesbian.* Unpublished Master's thesis, California State University, Dominguez Hills, California, July 1979.

Sarton, May. *House By the Sea.* New York: Norton, 1977.

Sarton, May. *Recovering*. New York: Norton, 1980.

Sinister Wisdom 10 (Summer, 1979). Special issue on being old and age.

Star, Susan Leigh. "Lesbians Over Sixty: Implications for Cohort Analysis and Minority Aging," Unpublished, November 1978.

Wolf, Deborah. *Growing Older: Lesbians and Gay Men* (tentative title). Berkeley, California: University of California Press, forthcoming.

Wolf, Deborah. "Life Cycle Change of Older Lesbians and Gay Men." Paper presented to the Gerontological Society of America, San Diego, California, November 1980.

Toward a Laboratory of One's Own: Lesbians in Science

H. Patricia Hynes

In late spring of 1979, I submitted an entry to *Matrices*[1] announcing that four women, lesbians[2] in science, had formed a study group. We were students in geology, environmental engineering, forestry, and general science at the University of Massachusetts, Amherst. Science students are notoriously short on time for everything except labs, research reports, and unsolved problems. A unique, microscopic subset of women, lesbians in science is the only class of feminists I have known who will reject a women's studies course for yet another science course and who will pass up a once-a-year women's event to do problem no. 6, one of thirty assigned that semester. The intense preoccupation with itself which science fosters is double-edged. The workload and demands on time require almost a fealty of students, and we must jealously guard our time for feminist reading, lectures, and cultural events. On the other hand, science is a context of learning in which discipline and the ability to focus and organize our work is, of necessity, quickly learned.

Eager to bring feminist passion to science, we four immediately set about to plan papers and field trips on those ideas and investigations which had originally sparked our passion for science. Our agenda spanned an exciting spectrum of subjects:

— a voyage via slides through the Yucatan in search of gynocentric myth and solar architecture in Mayan culture, and a discussion of the natural resources of this Mexican province.

— the sources, effects, and chemistry of acid rain in New England.

— a portrait of Ellen Swallow, founder of the science of ecology.

— the basics of rock-climbing, slides of rock formation, caverns, and the results of an extensive field study of Karst geology and cavern development.

— fundamental electronic theory of computers.

— an overview of conventional energy sources in the United States and the potential for alternative energy.

— a geological history of the Connecticut River Valley told from the vantage point of Skinner Park, overlooking the Connecticut River Valley in South Hadley.

— a walk through a forest to demonstrate the principles of woodlot management.

The diversity of ideas was deliberate: to reopen chambers of curiosity and passionate reason which are sealed off by the prohibition of science against venturing outside of one's field. If one moves on or beyond the compartmental boundary, one is suspect of being restless, intellectually immature, undisciplined, generalist, and dilettantish. One is expected to stand still and bore ever deeper, urged on by the omnipresent imperative to specialize or perish.

Ellen Swallow's ultimate failure at the Massachusetts Institute of Technology is paradigmatic of this dilemma. Swallow, the first woman to receive a degree from MIT and to teach there, distinguished herself as a water and industrial chemist, a metallurgist, a mineralogist, and expert in food and nutrition, and an engineer. In the late nineteenth century, she devised and taught the first interdisciplinary curriculum and science methods of ecology, leading students to test air, soil, water, and food. Her science of ecology which integrated the chemistry of soil, air and water, biology, and the scientific study of the human environment, was ultimately rejected at MIT. One biographer analyzes the failure of her new science accordingly: "It was, in spite of the validity of its parts, seen as an unpedigreed, mixed breed by the specialized science aristocracy."[3] He adds that "Swallow and most of her (ecology) friends were women and too few were scientists."

The idea of a lesbians in science study group came to me in my second year of graduate school. I had seen myself and other women in predominantly male sciences buffeted and demeaned in the scientific milieu:

— buffeted by the cruel rites of passage that characterize initiation into a male society: intense competition, always the threat of failure and expulsion, and willful obscuring of knowledge.

— demeaned by the sexual tension our anomalous presence catalyzed, by the invisibility of our talent and stamina, and by no recourse to women in power.

It was, though, the erosion of intellectual passion that I found to be the most appalling in science. I was and I remain confounded by the contradiction that the more advanced our study of science, the more remote becomes the subject of our intellectual passion: nature. It is absurd that field trips in botany courses for nonscience majors and lectures in "physics for poets" (so-called "pop-science") conjure up the dynamism, the variability, and the intelligence of nature, whereas fluid mechanics and advanced thermodynamics are arduous, mechanistic, and often spiritually dulling exercises in rote problem solving.

What, then, could be more appropriate for lesbians in science than to present to one another those ideas, those intellectual projects which had first fired our mental passion? With that one guide, we developed our agenda of presentations and field trips. Our meetings were thick with ideas and questions; they were always too brief. This unique collaboration created a background of pride and meaning altogether absent in science for woman-identified women.

Very simply I picture intellectual passion as a mind on fire: a fire whose metaphysical energy furiously gathers and creates ideas; a fire whose vital flames light the eyes; a fire whose heat warms the mind and expands the self. Patriarchal science has no passion. It has fractured passion into a chilling logic and pseudo-passion. Cold logic is all too familiar—it permits a nationally known toxicologist to stun his audience with larger-than-life pictures of thalidomide babies, drawing out clinical details of their deformities while bemoaning how difficult it was to do a valid statistical survey on the babies' mothers because the women were so suggestive that they could not be relied upon to know if they had taken thalidomide or not. "Furthermore," he added dryly, "women usually don't know when they get pregnant." Pseudo-passion has many guises. It is the tense excitement stirred up in students by pitting them against one another for grades, recommendations, and limited opportunities. Pseudo-passion is warmed by the prospect of inclusion in the high priesthood of science. It is the rush scientists have when doing research against time deadlines and budget constraints, in intense competition for grants, prizes, and publication. It is the bizarre fraternity and excitement men feel when they collaborate in a high-risk venture or in a climate of potential imminent tragedy. I heard one reserved chemist declare that the frenetic federal survey and cleanup operation of Love Canal in which he participated was "surprisingly exciting," one of the most exciting times in his life. In a commemorative article on Trinity Site at Los Alamos, New Mexico, where the first atomic bomb was exploded, *Time* magazine quoted two men who found the site and the event it conjured up "romantic."[4]

One wonders if the unique erasure of women in science—by erasure I mean both the cover-up of what women have done and the success of the lie that women cannot do science and mathematics—is really the erasure of passion from science. Nonetheless, it has imposed a silence so great that lesbian scientists have yet to imagine a history of lesbians in science. It does not occur to ask of the lone woman honored here and there in science: Was she a feminist? Were her mentors women? Did she dedicate her work to a woman? With whom did she live? It is so remarkable that she was honored in male history at all. All a woman need do is read the life of Ellen Swallow, Rachel Carson, or Rosalind Franklin to see the silencing and erasure of women by male "colleagues" for doing brilliant, passionate, and prodigious work. Their controversies unmask that face of patriarchy in which we read the disdain for, the envy of, and the hatred of women.

My mind still reels from the impact of H.J. Mozans's work, *Woman in Science*.[5] In one sweeping history of invention by women, Mozans unwittingly discloses the take-over of creative cultural work from women by men, the destruction of female power, and the effect of that violence on the character of male science. He cites the universal myths which record the creation by women of agriculture and agricultural implements, of dwellings which warm and cool naturally, of transport and sanitary storage of water, of the mechanical arts, in brief, of all vital systems. "Tradition in all parts of the world," he writes, "is unanimous in ascribing to woman the invention, in essentially their present form, of all the arts most conducive to the preservation and well-being of the human race." With great fervor, he then describes the brilliant work of hundreds of women scientists from classical Greece to the early twentieth century. The effect is like a great chain of lights being turned on, one by one, to illuminate female genius which, with the exception of one luminary, Mariè Curie,[6] has been systematically adumbrated by lies and silence.

None of us can measure or predict, I think, how it changes us to break the silence imposed by patriarchy. Presenting our ideas and projects to other women who welcome our intelligence and who know the woman-hatred in science, as in our study group, is much more than sharing ideas and gaining self-confidence. It is an act of rebellion against our own erasure. It is, too, exhilarating mental work which forges identity and meaning, identity and meaning which will never be given to a woman, no matter what degrees and prizes she achieves, by patriarchal science.

I have written this essay—as our study group proceeded—assuming that women who love science ought to study it. Why would a woman-identified woman study science when scarcely a grain of female genius is tolerated by male science, when the intention to preserve "the well-being of the human race" is only a fragile memory of the origins of science in prehistory, and when the petty passion of patriarchal science for splitting, splicing, and bombarding is so assaultive to nature? The scope of such a discussion goes beyond this short essay. I can only conclude with some open-ended remarks about women studying science.

The root of the word science is *scire*, to know, and *scientia*, knowledge. As I see it, the purpose of studying science for women is to know nature: because nature is fascinating, because we are part of nature and we depend on nature for our life, and because knowledge will guide our wise use of nature. Patriarchal science is no more what nature is about than the psychology of the female in Freud and the philosophy of female being in Jean-Paul Sartre is about women. As men assume that what they think about women is what women are, so they believe that what they theorize about nature is what nature is. I would suggest then that a woman who loves nature, who is intellectually curious and creative, would study science to identify precisely patriarchal science's definitions and construction of science. By studying and working in science, radical women can refuse to concede to men trained and degreed in science, the absolute power over nature that is assigned to and claimed by them. If, since a child, a woman has loved the theory and inner logic of numbers, or if she wants to learn about soil, pH, bacteria and organic matter, out of some ill-defined fascination, out of a desire to grow food and flowers, or become soil, like her own body—is in dynamic chemical balance with air, water, plants, animals, and stone—then where is she to go but books, laboratories, and schools where, despite the pathology of science, she can learn some language and ideas which she can use for "the preservation and well-being of the human race" and the planet? There is another reason for studying science. Without implying that nature is female or female is nature, I see extraordinary parallels between woman-centered being and dimensions of nature. The ideas of energy, motion, and power in physics and mechanical engineering, the image of an expanding universe and moving center in astronomy, the theory of charge in chemistry, the golden mean, continuum, and infinite series in mathematics, the cycling of energy, nutrients, and water in hydrology and geology, the vital signs of ecosystems in ecology[7]—all of these intuitions of dynamism in nature have obvious, exciting parallels in feminist theory. They may clarify dimensions of oppression. They may offer new images and, ultimately, new pathways of woman-centered being.

Notes

[1] *Matrices* is a lesbian feminist research newsletter which publishes subscribers' profiles, notes, queries, calls for papers, reviews, statements, etc. For a subscription, write to Julia Penelope (Stanley) c/o Dept. of English, University of Nebraska, Lincoln, NE 68588.

[2] I use the word lesbian interchangeably with woman-identified woman, woman-centered woman, and radical woman. All of these phrases have emerged from radical-feminist thinking. They imply a separation from patriarchal thinking and male parasitism. They describe the woman determined to search out the mystery of her own history and its connections with the lives of other women. In that same spirit, the lesbian in science searches out threads of connectedness between her own existence in this world and the subject of her intellectual passion, nature.

[3] Robert Clarke, *Ellen Swallow, The Woman Who Founded Ecology* (Chicago: Follett Publishing Co., 1973), pp. 152–53. Judy Gold, a member of Lesbians in Science, has written an extremely comprehensive paper on Swallow's life and work, with a radical-feminist analysis of the reaction of male science to Swallow's precocious work.

[4] *Time*, November 3, 1980, p. 6, 10. One man "had been looking forward to this thing for a long time . . . The whole atomic thing during my lifetime, and this is kind of romantic." The other man had worked at Los Alamos more than thirty-five years. Speaking of the development and the testing of the atomic bomb, he said, "It's very difficult to convey the special spirit of that time and place. Working toward a common goal, people formed a strong bond and sensed they were part of something romantic—as indeed they were."

[5] H.J. Mozans, *Woman in Science* (Cambridge: MIT Press, 1974; London: D. Appleton and Co., 1913).

[6] In *Ideology in/of the Sciences*, Monique Couture-Cherki, a French physicist, exposes the method by which even such a memorable woman as Marie Curie is mediated to history as a second sex, in the following incident. Leprince-Ringuet, a distinguished French physicist, when questioned by the French media about Marie Curie, replied: "Between Pierre and Marie Curie, Pierre Curie was a creator whose very genius established new laws of physics. Marie radiated other qualities: her character, her exceptional tenacity, her precision, and her patience." Leprince-Ringuet characterized Marie Curie as a superb laboratory technician. He cast her as a model of "feminine" research skills and denied her her genius. By polarizing her and Pierre Curie's abilities, he insinuated that she, on her own, was not an exceptional scientist, but that she was, however, a most desirable life partner for an eminent male theoretician.

[7] One example of drawing ideas from science for feminist analysis is the subject of a paper I wrote which was published in the *Heresies* issue on Feminism and Ecology, number 13. I have taken four principles of natural ecosystems and shown the parallels between the conditions of women under patriarchy and that of natural ecosystems under the stress of extreme pollution.

Lesbians in Physical Education and Sport

Linn ni Cobhan

In April, 1981, when the news broke that world-famous tennis star Billie Jean King was being sued for palimony by her ex-lover Marilyn Barnett, the media descended with slavering glee. A woman athlete had been "caught out" and put in a position where the curious seemed justified in asking about an ancient male fantasy: "Are all women in sports lesbians?" From the civilized voyeurism of Barbara Walters to those titillated and/or appalled by the thought that behind every tennis racket, golf club, or basketball might lurk a lesbian, women athletes in general, and Billie Jean King in particular, were fair game.

Not since *Time* magazine, in December 1970, announced in sixty-two languages that Kate Millett was "bi-sexual" has there been such a public brouhaha over one woman's sexual orientation. The exposé of Millett was, of course, primarily an attempt to discredit the women's movement, and there are those who would use King to the same end. But while Millett's "admission" was used to invalidate her scholarship in *Sexual Politics,* no one got busy stereotyping English literature or academic pursuits for women. Interviewers didn't ask "How many women in the English department are lesbians? Do you seduce young women over Shakespeare?" No one speculated that the pursuit of a Ph.D. would turn a woman into a lesbian. King's admission, on the other hand, is de facto evidence that sport is the province of lesbians, and will be used as ammunition by those who deny a woman's right to participate in athletics.[1]

Putting aside the question of whether King did and said the right things under public fire, it is worth noting that the use of Millett to dyke-bait movement women provoked, on the whole, a united stand among gay and straight feminists. No such thing has happened with King. Certainly she has received individual support from diverse people and organizations, and many privately applaud her courage. But we have not yet witnessed a uniting of feminists—lesbian and heterosexual, athlete and non-athlete—on the issue of lesbians in sport. Women athletes seem so far incapable of an action similar to the one used by the Dutch when Hitler asked them to hand over the Jews: they all put on yellow stars. And lesbian-feminists appear, in general, unwilling to forge a bond with public figures who feel it necessary to hide their lesbianism until forced out of the closet.

When the King news broke, it seemed that no one I knew could talk of anything else. Except in the physical education department of a large, prestigious university, where I worked as a secretary, no one could talk of anything else. In the P.E. department, no one said anything. Silence greeted the news which couldn't be missed as if it hadn't happened. Although one might expect the issues raised by the King publicity to be of vital interest to the women there, and although, of the women in the department, three of the seven professors, two emeritus professors, one of the three activity supervisors, and four of the nine graduate students were lesbians (not to mention three coaches and the head of the athletic department),[2] the silence was not surprising. It was one more symptom of a phenomenon I had become acquainted with in my year-and-a-half stint as a secretary in P.E.—that of an almost total disassociation and alienation of the women involved in academic physical education and/or intercollegiate sport from the issues of lesbianism, feminism, and women's studies, especially in places where it might change their own lives as women in sport.

I am not an athlete or a physical education major. Until two years ago, I was as ignorant of sports and P.E. as I am of nomadic life in the Sahara. High-school P.E. had been a horror of ugly gymsuits, dull calisthenics, arbitrary teams picked for games I didn't like, embarrassing displays of my lack of skill with round, flying objects, and a fear that I would be spotted as a lesbian the moment I entered a locker-room. Additionally, I had been dubbed early as "intellectually gifted" and raised in an academic hothouse. True to sex roles, no one thought it important that I viewed myself as physically inept except when in a ballet class. It isn't surprising that I believed every stereotype about sport: that people who played on teams weren't very bright; that athletes were a separate breed from the normal human; that a P.E. degree required only that one be able to run, catch, throw, and hit; that sport wasn't "feminine"; that women athletes were lesbians.

The time I spent in the P.E. department forced me to reexamine and discard those stereotypes, and in the process of so doing I found myself seriously wondering about the role of the physically educated woman in the feminist movement. Ultimately, the questions I raise will have to be answered by the women in sport and P.E. themselves.[3] Yet one does not need to be an athlete to notice the vast separation between lesbians involved in sport and the lesbians whose primary energies go to women's studies and feminist issues, or to observe that this mutual exclusion may be damaging to both groups. Nor need one be a sport psychologist to be aware that sport symbolizes and embodies several important cultural values,[4] that it is more than just entertainment or the vicarious release of aggression, or that those who are allowed to fulfill those roles have never been women.

To date, there has been no serious feminist analysis of the place of lesbianism—either actually or philosophically—in sport and physical education, or vice versa. No essays exist in anthologies of either feminism or lesbianism. With one exception, P.E. and sport have not been a concern of women's studies—let alone a course.[5] Few P.E. professors involve themselves in the liberal arts-dominated women's studies program, and there appears to be little participation by sports-oriented women in women's studies classes. Lesbian-feminists do not seem to want to have to do much with sport, except as spectators.[6] The Lesbian Periodicals Index has no entries on the subject of sport (beyond the local bar team) because there have been no articles in lesbian publications.[7] In lesbian fiction there are no women athletes, unless one includes the "variant" adolescent novels of R.R. Knudson.[8] The only nonfiction work on women in sport, *Out of the Bleachers: Writings on Women and Sport*, edited by Stephanie L. Twin (Feminist Press, 1979) does not mention lesbians at all, except in the index where it is listed under Homosexuality (female), and both references consist of one-liners about how a woman in sport might have her sexuality questioned.[9] Neither *Ms.* nor *womenSports* addresses the issue of lesbianism in their pages, except to acknowledge that dyke-baiting exists. In fact, the only place one is likely to find a discussion of lesbians and sport is in publications such as *Look, Newsweek, Sports Illustrated,* and the *Washington Star*—and it is not surprising that the prevalent attitude in these articles is "Gee, it's too bad women athletes have to put up with being called dykes—even though most of them are, heh, heh."[10]

If my experience in the P.E. department is not unusual, then it would be fair to characterize women in sport, and nonathletic lesbian-feminists, as two separate camps, each somewhat hostile, suspicious, and often ignorant of the other. The reasons for this are not as simple as "lesbian athletes have too much to lose by coming out," or the reason for nonsupport I've often heard from lesbian-feminists, "until those athletes are willing to come out publicly, we don't owe them anything."

This is not to say that every woman in P.E. or sport is a closet case with a consciousness of minus zero; two of the four lesbian graduate students I knew were feminists and reasonably open about their lesbianism. But for every feminist, there is a woman who will decline to state, or a woman who believes that no one does, or must, know about her lesbianism, as happened with a student who came into the office one day in tears. Joan and her major professor had fought, and the professor had said (among other things) that she "was tired of Joan's lesbian affairs interfering with her work." When I asked specifically what upset her, she sobbed at me "She says I'm a lesbian!" "But Joan," I said, "you *are* a lesbian. You've said so to me, and everyone knows that." (Her lover was standing right there, trying to be comforting.) "Did she threaten you about it?" "No... but she called me a lesbian! She can't prove it! I'll deny it!"[11] For every professor who admits that she's considered loving women, there are three more who will staunchly affirm that their private lives have nothing to do with their academic careers. For every coach who takes her team to a lesbian bar after the game (one I know was later reprimanded by the head of the athletics department) there is a coach like the one I talked to (who had been my high-school gym teacher) about someone in sport doing an article like this one—she admitted that people have gotten more open lately and changed the subject.

There are several reasons for the gulf which exists between physical education and women's studies, and for the unwillingness of women in sport to admit to lesbians in their own ranks, that bear examination. One is that it *is* very costly for professional athletes to come out. Athletes are not granted the "eccentricity" of other public figures and symbols (such as those in film, dance, drama, et cetera); sport is traditionally "pure" and "wholesome" and "all-American." Professional women athletes are grilled and bribed by male reporters who follow the sport circuits, in an attempt to discover who is a lesbian and lesbian athletes are under pressure from their straight counterparts to stay in the closet.[12] Under siege from without and within, faced with the probable horror of loss of sponsors and access to competition, no lesbian athlete is likely to volunteer her predilection on the Sunday afternoon sports program. Women in sport are vulnerable financially and socially. Sport occupies a peculiar niche of power in Western cultures, and it is perhaps the very last sacred male enclave—one that had been denied women for three thousand years—to hold out against women's liberation. Unless and until women athletes can overcome internalized homophobia, the notion that it's no one's business anyway, and a host of other roadblocks to unite against lesbian-baiting and its implications, any lesbian who comes out will do so alone and at great personal cost.

Does it matter whether a woman in sport is a lesbian? Is it enough to simply get women into sport and never mind their sexual preferences? A graduate student (who had "declined to state") did ask me once why it mattered. We were sitting in a bar when I mentioned that I'd considered doing research into lesbians in sport— were it possible to retreat while sitting in a booth, she would have done so. But she did manage to ask why I thought lesbianism important, why I was continually coming out when it wasn't anyone's business.

It matters because the label "lesbian" is effectively used to keep many women, lesbian and nonlesbian, from discovering whether they have any physical ability or talent. Women remain physically weak because to do otherwise is "abnormal." Also, women in sport *is* a feminist issue. Women who enter sport challenge deeply held beliefs about masculinity and femininity and the right of women to hold positions of social power. No thorough feminist analysis can avoid the fact of lesbianism, and as long as women attempt to challenge their exclusion from physical activity but deny the place of lesbians in their rebellion, the challenge will remain ineffective. Also, many women in sport and P.E. *are*, in fact, lesbians— some 30-60 percent, depending on who one listens to. As long as those women remain hidden, the reality of the kind of personality and lifestyle for a woman's success in a demanding profession that has been closed to her will remain unknown. We will maintain the myth that the cost of success is the insane ability to be one's own only source of strength unless a woman is "lucky" enough to find a supportive man. We will deny the lives and history of women who found success through the love and support of another woman. And last, as long as the lesbian athlete is ignored as a lesbian, the nonlesbian woman will not have to confront why she is continually asked to "prove" her femininity as an athlete, to understand how the male view of her as a "freak" gives them power over her.

But at least one factor in the reluctance of athletes to confront lesbianism is the primacy of an "athlete" identity. A woman who achieves athletic status has fought long and hard to get there. Not only has she overcome or ignored social approbation, she has challenged and trained herself physically to the limit of her potential—no mean feat. Given the difficulty of being where she is, she is likely to be proud of herself and to *identify as an athlete first.* Athletics is time-consuming, especially if one is also a student.[13] Simple circumstance is likely to keep athletes associating almost exclusively with other athletes, among whom the main issues are one's ability to cooperate on a team, the kind of competitor one is, how well one can stand up under pressure, how seriously one takes one's self and one's training. When one is running ten miles a day or practicing for a game, which gender one loves is a moot point. Further, like anyone else who has struggled for and achieved a difficult goal, a woman athlete is likely to be more comfortable with other women who have also done the same thing. Not unlike the way in which a Ph.D. views a high-school graduate, or the way in which a Third World woman regards a white woman who is unaware of her racism, the athlete is likely to regard the nonathlete with a certain air of condescension.

Another reason for a woman athlete's seeming disregard for feminist issues may well be that, by participating in athletic competition, she feels she has already done her part for women's rights. Even the most conservative athlete cannot avoid knowing that women are discriminated against in sport. A woman on a team may not feel she needs a CR group or a special feminist project in order to learn that camaraderie and support are possible between women. (This may be one of the reasons men are so threatened by women in sports, as it proves women can bond effectively in order to reach a goal.) A woman who can bench press 150 pounds does not need a women's self-defense class in order to learn that women can be strong. She may not feel she needs bars, dances, or meetings in order to find a sense of community among women because women athletes often form their own social groups. Her physical training has given her a self-confidence and instilled a sense of self-worth that is often alien to the nonathlete, and she may well view nonathletic feminists as timid and ineffective. Also, why should she publicly take on, in addition to the identity of athlete, a second socially unapproved status—that of a lesbian—particularly if her companions in sport are also lesbian or heterosexual women who are willing to acknowledge, accept, and then ignore her lesbianism. Last, she may feel that in becoming an athlete she has pushed the social limits of tolerance as far as she safely can; a public stance of lesbianism may just be too much.

On the academic side, physical education has traditionally been a somewhat defensive and conservative field for several reasons. One is that P.E. is *physical*, and in the best tradition of mind/body split in a technological, unphysical society, "physical" in the halls of academe smells just a bit badly. And students do tend to assume that a P.E. degree means one was on a team.[14] Other academic departments tend to look down on P.E. as an academic stepchild because it is multidisciplinary and combines hard science with social science.

Historically, physical education was at one time a place where women held a good deal of academic power. The profession began in the mid-1800s as an outgrowth of the medical concern for public health. The main emphasis, in the beginning, was primarily corrective calisthenics, but as theories of play and recreation developed along with the belief in the character-molding nature of P.E. (a form of social Darwinism), women were encouraged in the field so that they might supervise children and other females. By the 1880s, physical education was a very acceptable field for a middle-class woman left idle by urban society and industrialization, and by 1920, some 65 percent of the college graduates in P.E. were women. Because P.E. was sex-segregated, women in it were in a position to form a strong network of power in the field, similar to "the old boy" network that stretched from the football field to the senate.[15] By World War II, however, women's influence in the field was dying out. P.E. began to be desegregated, and many women discovered that separate was not equal, at least financially. One might logically suspect that the past influence of women in P.E. is partly responsible for P.E.'s conservative, defensive stand, especially now that the field is becoming increasingly science-oriented (there's money in exercise physiology), and hence, male-dominated. The women who have survived in P.E. are chary of their old power and aware that P.E. is now "unfeminine" in a way it had not been before. Few of them are likely to take a radical-feminist stand or declare themselves lesbians in the face of all that male hostility.

Last, the woman academic in P.E. may well feel she would be a minority in the humanities, literature, and social sciences-dominated area of women's studies. She may be uncomfortable with women who haven't a long tradition of participation in their fields, yet whose presence there is much more socially acceptable than hers in her field.

A feminist outside a P.E. department does not automatically acquire the label of lesbian from her colleagues.

The other side of the coin is the attitude of nonathletic lesbian-feminists who on the whole are exclusive toward women athletes. Despite the advances of feminism in breaking down sex-role categories, many of us still carry with us the views of sports we learned at an early age. Sport is *male*, an expression of power and sexuality and camaraderie (issues we have only begun to scratch the surface of) requiring strength, speed, endurance, courage, and independence. It is competitive, and it is big business—two things many feminists are wary of. From the day we were dressed in pink baby clothes we have been told we are physically weak, and years of unuse has left our muscles weak, thus reinforcing the belief.

The fact is, women have been so long and so well separated from sport that we don't even notice its absence in our lives, let alone in our politics. We have had no reason to examine our assumptions about sport and physical ability beyond a minimal level because for most of us, professional sport is something that happens on Mars. We have come just far enough to be able to openly admire and envy the Billie Jean Kings of the world, but not far enough to see them as anything but idols, not far enough to examine our subconscious expectations and assumptions toward them. King's achievement is wonderful, for her, we think, but it is not something we ourselves think we can do. In the time I've spent in Aikido classes (both a women's class and at a dojo), nearly two-thirds of the women I saw had no self-confidence in their physical selves, in their ability to fall, to block a punch, or even to duck. Is it a wonder we view physical ability as unattainable?

As a result, many of us are actually more comfortable confronting physical *disability* rather than physical *ability* in others. We are envious, admiring, and suspicious of women athletes. We talk a great deal about how women are strong, but usually we mean emotionally, or spiritually, or as a group, and we seem terribly unwilling to carry out that power in a physical dimension. A three-month rape-prevention course can be useful, but it does not produce the physical fitness and self-confidence of a trained athlete—the kind that projects "I am not a victim." We are ambivalent about women who sincerely perceive themselves as capable, especially physically. Some part of the subconscious can't help wondering how they escaped the "weak" conditioning, and I would suspect that some part of us perceives women athletes as superhumans who, by virtue of their strength, owe us something in return for our admiration. Many of us who are nonathletic feminists expect famous athletes to leap on the lesbian-feminist bandwagon, to confront power and sexuality and cultural values for us, despite the fact that we have more often than not ignored them, expected them to stand alone, and ourselves refused to become physically capable. Conversely, lesbian athletes seem to expect lesbian-feminists to fight all the nonsport-related battles for them, to expand the frontiers so that one day they may come out of the closet without risk.

The point here is that both sides are the victims of perceptions developed in isolation, and neither's viewpoint of the other is either practical, fair, or realistic. The general lack of communication between lesbian (and nonlesbian) athletes and lesbian-feminist nonathletes borders on the tragic. It is unnerving to spend a year and a half in a department with eight lesbians and never once hear anyone openly discuss lesbian or feminist issues. It is sad to see a capable lesbian drop out of graduate school, at least in part because her extreme openness in a closeted atmosphere got her treated as a pariah. It is difficult, if not impossible, to watch a lesbian cry that she will deny the undenial about herself, and it is totally ludicrous for a lesbian professor of sport history to confine her research to occasional articles about the early role of women in P.E. and exclude the fact that a fair number of those women appear to be lesbians. It is just as ridiculous to hear a woman in a bar say of Billie Jean King, "Well, it's too bad, but she *should* have come out years ago—*I* knew she was a lesbian." When an international athlete can be grilled about her sexuality by the media and then has to hear from the movement for which she's done so much that "she's set the women's movement back ten years," it's time to admit that both sides may be at fault, and that sincere analysis and dialogue are long overdue.

Notes

Linn ni Cobhan is, of necessity, a pseudonym whose purpose is to protect not the author but the women mentioned in the article. Nearly all of them are closeted to some degree, hence the university is unnamed and all names are fictitious.

[1] I forego the arduous task of documenting all the various media commentaries on King. As virtually every major magazine, newspaper, and TV station has made some sort of comment, I trust that the variety of media opinion, from the very nasty to the very supportive, is known to everyone. It is also to be understood that the "lesbian issue" for women's sports did not spring up overnight with the King affair. Although there was a time when the pursuit of a college degree was considered unnatural for a woman, hostility to women in sport hasn't changed despite women's strides in other areas, something I consider indicative of the importance we grant sport.

[2] In short, roughly 40 percent. Of the professors, only one discussed her orientation with me, saying "she thought she was probably bi-sexual," although to my observation she still functioned primarily as a heterosexual. She was, however, the only professor with even a rudimentary feminist consciousness. The two emeritus professors were discussed in the department as "life-long friends" who were essentially a couple. My identification of the two remaining professors, the activity supervisor and the Athletics department head is based on common belief and observation. Certainly none of them were likely to discuss their orientation with a secretary. The four graduate students were all women I became comfortably acquainted with, and were reasonably open about their lesbianism, with the exception of one woman, who is either truly bi-sexual or who has an excellent cover. She refuses to define herself as either gay or straight, though I view her as more lesbian than otherwise. The three coaches are known as lesbians, at least by their colleagues and to other lesbians. Among the graduate students and the coaches, lesbian-feminist consciousness varied enormously, but all would agree that women are discriminated against in sport. The professors were firmly in the closet, though their colleagues must know of their lesbianism. Additionally, I knew two women on the crew team, and one woman on the squash team who are lesbians. And rumor had it that the majority of the field hockey and softball teams

are lesbians, but this may be because these coaches are lesbians.

It should also be pointed out that all the women referred to here are white, and middle class, several upper middle or upper class. In the P.E. department, there was only one black woman, and perhaps seven Asian American women in the undergraduate program. On the teams I was aware of only one non-white woman, who was mulatto. The field hockey coach is Asian American.

[3]There is a distinction. P.E. is an academic discipline which does not require team competition. Sport, or athletics, is intercollegiate team competition in various games such as tennis, softball, field hockey, squash, crew, etc. The two usually have separate departments and budgets.

[4]I am referring here to what sport means to the spectator, and to the position it occupies in a culture. This has been sufficiently documented in sport psychology/sociology texts for my commentary to be unnecessary. But it should be pointed out that sport is universal and exists in all cultures.

[5]There was a women's studies course titled "P.E. Without Fear," taught in 1981 at San Francisco State.

[6]This is personal observation limited to two colleges. I hope to be proved wrong.

[7]Personal communication from Clare Potter.

[8]These are: *You Are the Rain* (Delacorte, 1974); *Zanballer* (Delacorte, 1972); and *Fox Running* (Avon, 1976). All three are slotted as "young adult" and can be read as "variant," i.e., they involve very strong female friendships that never become more explicit.

[9]Twin, *Out of the Bleachers*, pp. 167, 190-191.

[10]I have taken these references from Betty Hicks's "Lesbian Athletes" in *Christopher Street*, Oct./Nov., 1979. Hicks also makes reference to articles in *Ms.*, 1973, and *women-Sports*, 1978.

[11]It is interesting to note that Joan asked one of the lesbian professors to mediate the dispute she had with her own major professor. As it turned out, Joan's advisor was primarily concerned with Joan's work, and viewed her lesbianism as one more excuse for not meeting deadlines.

[12]Hicks, "Lesbian Athletes." From henceforth it should be clear that I will be talking about amateur collegiate athletes and athletics. I do not know anyone with a goal of professional competition; my observations of professional athletes are based on secondary sources.

[13]Not all women on teams are P.E. majors. But they must maintain a high grade point average to stay on the team, and women athletes, unlike men, must really work in their classes.

[14]A student who emerges from a P.E. department with a Bachelor's degree can be assumed to have a basic grounding in exercise physiology, biomechanics, kinesiology, motor development, sports medicine (and their prerequisites: biology, anatomy, chemistry, physics, physiology, various advanced mathematics, and statistics), sport psychology, sport history, sport sociology, recreation theory, and both practice and theory in teaching physical activities. Many, in addition, have Red Cross, Lifesaving, and Water Safety Instruction certifications.

[15]The history of P.E., and of the women in it in particular, is fascinating, and bears research from a lesbian-feminist viewpoint. Much of the history of P.E. I picked up as a secretary was a result of typing a professor's papers. Because of the necessity of keeping everyone anonymous in this article, I cannot cite this woman's work as it deserves, but I do wish to acknowledge her efforts.

Love between Women in Prison

Karlene Faith

The following article is adapted from a book in progress with the same title. Another version of this material, edited by Robin Linden, appeared in *Sinister Wisdom* 16 (1981): 2-10.

In the early 1970s, Karlene helped develop women's studies at the University of California at Santa Cruz. She later taught and coordinated women's studies at Sonoma State University.

Beginning in the late sixties Karlene was active in prisoner-support work, including teaching with men at Soledad prison. In 1972 she began to concentrate intensively on interviews and cultural support work with women at the California Institute for Women. At the urgings of women who wanted to know about the women's liberation movement, Karlene and her colleague Jeanne Gallick developed a cross-cultural prison classroom experience which focused on "Women in American Society." The fifty women who were in the class received university credit for their work, and the class became the starting point for the first college program for incarcerated women.

During the next four years hundreds of prisoners were involved in the educational programs and cultural events that evolved through the Santa Cruz Women's Prison Project[1] with sponsorship by the University of California Extension Division and the UC Santa Cruz History of Consciousness graduate program.

The interview material contained in this article was gathered primarily during the early stages of the contemporary women's movement, at a time when the links between feminism and lesbianism were just beginning to be articulated.

Women who live in rigid heterosexual environments have little opportunity to develop uninhibited feelings toward other women. But inside female communities— boarding schools, convents, prisons—a woman is virtually forced to confront herself relative to other females. In the absence of men, women are free to look to each other—for companionship, security, comfort, protection, and strength. And often they learn to love one another.

Every woman who had been deemed homosexual upon her admission to the prison carried an H on her jacket (the prisoner's administrative file), which makes her the historical kin to the colonial adulteress who was publicly stigmatized with a scarlet A on her breast.

It is commonly estimated by "corrections" officials that between 15 and 20 percent of women prisoners are "true homosexuals." This figure cannot be verified, since many women are falsely labeled homosexual and others who are lesbians go undetected.

Often a new prisoner is labeled homosexual if her clothing or mannerisms appear masculine, or a woman can be coerced into "confessing" to be homosexual if she is sufficiently harassed by the suspecting staff and/or psychiatrists.

RULES AND REGULATIONS OF THE DIRECTOR OF CORRECTIONS. TITLE 15 (CRIME PREVENTION AND CORRECTIONS), ARTICLE I. SECTION 3007 (SEXUAL BEHAVIOR).

"INMATES MAY NOT PARTICIPATE IN ILLEGAL SEXUAL ACTS. INMATES ARE SPECIFICALLY EXCLUDED IN LAWS WHICH REMOVE LEGAL RESTRAINTS FROM ACTS BETWEEN CONSENTING ADULTS. INMATES MUST AVOID DELIBERATELY PLACING THEMSELVES IN SITUATIONS AND BEHAVING IN A MANNER WHICH IS DESIGNED TO ENCOURAGE ILLEGAL SEXUAL ACTS."

Norma: The institutional policy on homosexuality is "Don't Get Caught." Otherwise you get a write-up and disciplinary action. They can't officially condone it even though it's no longer against the law on the outside. There's no such thing as rape in here, the way they play it up in books and movies. "Homosexuality in Prison!" They make it sound like prison invented it. If a woman cuts her hair, they figure she's turned gay. Sex is always the headliner.

Susan: I never felt threatened by it, nor did anyone ever express to me that they did. There were none of the horror stories you hear of or see in the movies. Stories of women being raped, having brooms stuck up them, held down, forced to do it. I never, never saw any intimidation to be involved sexually. I never saw or experienced it ever happening except between two consenting adult women who both wanted to become sexually close with another woman.

Angie: As a child I wanted so much to be a boy because they had so much freedom and adventure. Now I know I can exercise this same freedom, sexual included, as a woman.

Roberta: I never really liked women until I came here, I guess because I didn't like myself. We have so much time together, to really know each other. It's really something to have friends who know everything about you and still like you. Until I came here I was very ashamed of my body, but now I'm pretty damn proud of it. And I know now that there's nothing wrong with homosexuality. I'm a woman, and now I'm proud of it. It's time we all started listening to our own souls, instead of to all the perverted rules other people make up for us.

For such women, this process of reclaiming one's own identity is the great paradox of prison confinement.

Susan: A lot of women in here grew up always in subservient relationships— in relation to their families, to their jobs, to the men in their lives. Then all of a sudden they're ripped from all their connections, ripped off from their husbands, ripped off from their children, and placed in a prison on their own. Alone. They don't have these people, these men, to lean on or hide behind anymore. They're in interactions with people who are strangers. They don't know these other women. And they're forced to find out who they are. There's a whole lot of women who come to incredible realizations about who they are as people and where their strengths really are, untapped sources of strength within themselves.

Sometimes it's simple, basic stuff—finding out what kind of music you like for the first time, finding out what you like to do. What kinds of book will I read when I have a choice, and somebody's not telling me what I should read. What do I say to people when I'm not trying to please somebody else's image of me, when I'm being myself. I've seen a lot of women really develop, finding out who they are and becoming strong and really beautiful.

Annie: At the Los Angeles county jail they had a "Daddy Tank" where they put all the women they think are lesbians in the same cell block. They crowd two or three women into cells built for one. Women in the "Daddy Tank" can't have contact with any of the other women in jail, can't go anywhere without an escort, have to sit in the back row if there's a movie. All the "Daddy Tank" women are assigned to the laundry night shift. You're totally ostracized, night and day. And you always have to be careful not to have any physical contact with each other, not even holding hands.

Following the lead of federal corrections, most state prisons for women will no longer permit prisoners to receive any publications that advocate or openly discuss lesbianism. Thus women are denied the right to read about the growing strength of the lesbian community at the very time in their lives when it could have the most meaning for them.

Lobotomies, electroshock therapy, aversion therapy, and chemotherapy have all been employed as "cures" for the prisoner labeled homosexual. Efforts to prohibit such cruel and unusual punishments have met with limited success in the nation's courts; it is only slightly reassuring to know, for example, that psycho-surgery is not presently legal without the "informed consent" of the "patient." Extreme physical torture, performed as "treatment" for homosexuality, is currently less fashionable than psychological methods of control. At the California Institution for Women (CIW), the state prison, there is a pervasive attempt to pressure women into conforming to modern standards for femininity and to discourage habits or attitudes considered inappropriate to "ladylike" behavior. While the prisoners are breaking out of socially prescribed female roles, the people who keep them locked up are working hard to break their rebellious spirits.

Angie: I remember when the old warden decided she was going to clean up the campus and have a dress code. She didn't want anybody to look like a homosexual. The woman I was going with was a very masculine-looking woman who started wearing fake eyelashes and makeup and short skirts. It was a gas. Some women look ridiculous when they try to look femme. My friend didn't hate men or anything. She just didn't know how to put on lipstick. They tried to take her to rack (solitary confinement) because she wouldn't shave her legs. Then they realized that a lot of femmes didn't shave their legs, either. If they were going to take her, they were going to have to take us, too. We had to group on it, and then they let up on us, except for one "incorrigible" stud broad who they took off to a mental hospital.

So-called "stud broads" are women who, from physical appearance, might be easily mistaken for men. Less than 3 percent of all the women I observed in the prison over a three-year period fit the "stud-broad" stereotype, never more than twenty women in a population exceeding six hundred.[2] Contrary to media impressions, such women are no more likely to be aggressive than any other and in fact are often unusually quiet, gentle women. As a group these women do command a certain respect from other prisoners, as if they were men, and they are the target of a lot of attention. Some recoil from playing the "butch" in relationships, while others act out the role with confidence and flair, making the most of their desirability as partners to the femmes they attract.

Susan: When you go around here you see maybe four, five women in the whole prison who are righteous stud broads. Not very many. But those women really use sex to control other women. They perpetuate a lot of things that I don't think are good, like "You do the laundry, you get me a cup of coffee." They get these services by satisfying a woman sexually, which really trips me out. I struggle against that kind of role playing because I don't think it's positive.

"Jailhouse Turn-Out" (JTO) is prison vernacular for a woman who has her first sexual experience with another woman while she is incarcerated. Her unguarded enthusiasm and openness about her new sexual discoveries are often offensive and painful to older lesbians, who must live with the H stigma.

Kathryn: If you're unfortunate enough to have "homosexual" on your record your life is really miserable. I'm one of those with an H on my jacket, so I'm really considered a detriment to the prison society, even though I live very quietly in here. And yet they'll let these jailhouse turn-outs come in here and move in with their latest trick and carry on, conducting themselves in a disgraceful manner all over the campus. Yet someone who has been homosexual for years can come in here, and they're immediately set upon to change to a "better way of life."

They told me if I was ever caught in my room with a woman I'd go to rack. It would go with me to the board and hold up my [release] date. I'm not in here for being a lesbian, but you'd think I was because of the way they carried on about it when I went to the board for my time. They didn't talk to me at all about my crime, which involved a great deal of money. They talked to me about my homosexuality. I really don't think they understand about love. They don't understand two people just loving each other. It has to be something nasty, and it has to be physical. All love isn't physical.

Frances: It's hard to find privacy in prison. When you're locked up with people for years you just find yourself talking and listening. We'd have parties. A card game in one room, a Kool-Aid party in another room. And we had dances like they don't have anywhere else. They weren't romantic. They were a physical activity. They weren't a place to go with your girlfriend to dance. They were a place to go and just dance with other women who were also just dancing.

Sometimes we have live bands in the auditorium, and I used to dance with some of the women. They would come and get me to dance, and I loved it. I really loved it. I don't dance very well I don't think, but when you really feel good about dancing, just jumping up and down. . . . Well, it was fun. It wasn't a place for sexual stuff. The police thought so, but we knew it wasn't.

Rosanna: Homosexuality is technically against all the rules, and oral sex will get you three years tacked onto your time. But any PC [physical contact] can be considered homosexual by the staff. I'd been close to the same partner for over a year before they busted us one day for being in a "compromising" position. We were sitting on the steps talking, with our arms on each other's shoulders. If they'd been on the ball they could have caught us long ago in a real compromising situation. They're lazy about it, at least some of them are some of the time. It's like they wait till they're in a bad mood, and then they start busting everybody. We touch each other all the time, all of us. It's nice. But it's an easy thing for them to catch somebody in a PC, and it's a handy threat for them to be always holding over our heads.

The staff is instructed to write up a report each time a prison rule is broken by one or more prisoners. These "write-ups" are equivalent to a police arrest and, depending on the seriousness of the "crime," may be either a misdemeanor or a prison felony. Physical Contact in prison is a felony action. If a woman is written up she will face a disciplinary hearing where her punishment will be determined. There are many rules within a prison, and there are many prisoners. It is not possible for the harried staff to observe and write up every rule infraction. Arrests are made arbitrarily and erratically, not unlike arrests for traffic violations on the streets.

A woman's punishment for Physical Contact may be a scolding with a warning that the next time her punishment will be severe. She may be commanded to avoid any contact at all with her close friend. She may be sent to solitary confinement, i.e., rack. She may receive "counsel" from a chaplain or a psychologist who will attempt to understand her "sinfulness" or her "sickness," whether or not she wants to be "saved" or "cured." Male counselors, including chaplains, often gain reputations for offering "sex therapy" to a woman to help her overcome her "wickedness" or "deviance." The ultimate threat is loss of good time or time added to the original sentence.

Prison is fraught with double binds. It's hard to follow orders when the orders change from staff to staff and from day to day. If a woman strictly conforms to the rules against physical contact, she denies her need for intimate friendship, whether or not it includes sex. And every prisoner knows that even if she doesn't get involved sexually, she may be accused and punished for it nevertheless.[3] Arbitrary and inconsistent enforcements of ambiguous policies arouse a woman's nervous contempt for her jailers and reinforce her loyalty to women who share her vulnerable status.

Susan: Either you throw abandon to the wind and hope you don't get caught—you never know when the pig's gonna walk down the hall and make a surprise check—or you have a pinner. A pinner is somebody who sits out in the hall, and when the cop starts walking down the hall she whistles or gives some other high sign that tells you you have about twenty seconds to get up and be presentable. Which means you're never completely naked, you're never able to just relax in each other's arms, to get completely involved in making love. There is always the tension involved. But people manage in spite of it. Woman are able to comfort each other emotionally and physically. To hold each other, to touch and be gentle and listen and care. To love each other. In a prison situation that is a very beautiful thing.

Everybody knows what a relationship is, and sex is not the primary part of any relationship, and it isn't in prison either. Sex is a very important part of a relationship—when all the barriers are gone, and you're really exposed to another person. But what is more primary is the friendship, how you share dealing with the world. Somebody to face this madness with.

The madness is everywhere. Lesbians who leave prison today discover that to be a lesbian is to be implicated in one of the serious political struggles of this new decade. The woman who truly dares to love other women is not simply reacting against negative experiences with men. She is affirming her own womanhood. She is opening up to herself, in all her boundless possibilities. Empowered by her passion for personal freedom, she is implicitly, and often explicitly, challenging the authority of those who define and enforce codes for other people's behavior. It is from such individual courage that political movements are born and social change is possible.

Gino: Ten years ago I was thrown in jail three times for wearing men's clothes. Now I wear what I want, and no one's busting me for it, and I attribute the change to women on the street who have been fighting for women's rights, for lesbian rights. It was real hard when I first came out of prison, it's always real hard. But getting in touch with the women's movement has made a big difference to me, and I'm so happy it's come about. Job resources, health care, women's coffeehouses—there was never anyplace like that before. Now there's a whole community. I used to have to sneak around to be a lesbian, and it was just like being in prison. Now I can still be a lesbian and still deal with men at work, and it's great to be able to do that. Equal rights means that now I can get a job working with machinery, working with and beside men, and it's okay. I know we've got a long way to go, and whether you're a convict or a free sister, we've all got our work cut out for us. But the war's on, so fasten your seat belts.

During my second year of work at CIW I was called to an urgent meeting with the superintendent and her highest-ranking subordinates. Staff had reported to them that I'd been seen kissing women prisoners who greeted my arrivals at the institution, and the nervous administrators wondered if I realized the seriousness of such behavior. I tried to explain that where I come from kisses and embraces are healthy, natural exchanges of affection, but they reminded me of the institution's rules, and warned me to use better judgment in the future.

People die from not being loved, and from not loving, and unloved and unloving people become dead social weight long before they meet the grave. When such people are in positions of power they endanger our lives and our freedoms. As I listened to the prison authorities, I rejoiced in my heart for the hundreds of women I had known in their prison who would never be so firmly imprisoned as the keepers of the keys.

Notes

[1]Hundreds of people contributed to the overall success of the work of the Santa Cruz Women's Prison Project in initiating statewide support networks for women in (or coming out of) prison. There were several women, in the early days of this work, who gave me great personal encouragement, as well as making major contributions as teachers, community organizers, and advocates of prison rights. I would like to thank Jeanne Gallick, Catherine Angell, Debra Miller, Frances Reid, Mary K. Blackmon, Nancy Shaw, Laraine Goodman, Karen Rian, Leslie Patrick-Stamp, Jackie Christeve, and the women of the Legal Education Project. Likewise my gratitude extends to the women behind bars whose commitment to justice and whose generous willingness to share personal feelings and experiences have expanded our understanding of life in prison.

[2]During the 1970s, the prison population has grown to almost one thousand.

[3]The same is true of women in the military. In the summer and fall of 1980, for example, sixteen women crew members of the U.S.S. Norton were accused of being lesbians. Two were found guilty by a Navy board and discharged. See *Gay Community News*, September 6, 1980, p. 1.

A Lesbian Perspective on Women's Studies

Marilyn Frye

Looking at women's studies from my lesbian perspective and with my lesbian-feminist sensibility, what I see is that women's studies is heterosexual. The predominance of heterosexual perspectives, values, commitments, thought, and vision is usually so complete and ubiquitous that it cannot be perceived, for lack of contrast. (Like the air on a calm and moderate day; the way sexism still is for many people.) Sometimes, usually because of the interruption and contrast imported by my own presence, the basically and pervasively heterosexual character of women's studies is very clear and perceptible—overwhelming and deeply disappointing. It is also, usually, unspoken and unspeakable.

Some of my colleagues in women's studies say they cannot really tell the truth or "be radical" in their teaching because it would alienate the students. I tell them not to worry about alienating people; I say that the truth is challenging, interesting, compelling, and very effective in the classroom. I also say that when one attempts just to tell the truth, the responses, whether constructive or hostile, honest or dishonest, will be the best clues to one's errors. But in my dealings with my heterosexual women's studies colleagues, I do not take my own advice: I have routinely and habitually muffled or stifled myself on the subject of lesbianism and heterosexualism, feminism and women's studies, out of some sort of concern about alienating them. Some of these women are tangibly peculiar about lesbianism and are already offended by my being uncloseted and blatant; I do not think they have noticed that I avoid discussing lesbianism and heterosexuality with them for fear their already-nervous association with women's studies would become simply untenable for them. Much more important to me is the smaller number who are my dependable political co-workers in the university, the ones in the academic world with clearest and strongest feminist and antiracist politics, the ones with some commitment to not being homophobic and to trying to be comprehending and supportive of lesbians and lesbianism. If I estrange these women, I will lose the only footing I have, politically and personally, in my long-term work-a-day survival in academia. They are important, valuable, and respected allies. I am very careful, overcareful, when I talk about heterosexuality with them.

But the situation is asymmetrical, as it always is with minority or marginal people and majority or dominant people. What is *a topic* for them, which some can and some cannot attend to fruitfully, is a condition of life for me. I avoid "alienating" them, but they constantly and (usually) unconsciously alienate me by their mostly uncritical and apparently unalterable, to me unfathomable, commitment to heterosexuality—by which I mean deeply bound emotional and intellectual commitments to men, to reform, to integration, and to the centrality and natural necessity of heterosexual genital sex. The unwelcome weight of this heterosexualism is a salient fact of my life, and its manifestations in the politics of women's studies are coming very clear to me and should be stated.

In my experience with women's studies it seems common and characteristic for the women instructors to assume that widespread heterosexuality and the dominance of heterosexual conceptions have always been and will always be The Way It Is for humans on this planet, in particular, for women on this planet. Lesbianism is seen by most of them (but not all) as an acceptable, plausible alternative for some women and is understood (not by all) at least at a verbal level to be clearly coherent with feminism. But they all believe that it is only realistic to understand that most women are and most women will be heterosexual, at least for the duration of any era that our practical politics can concern itself with. Women's studies programming is grounded on the assumption that the vast majority of the students are and always will be heterosexual. Hence we give them almost entirely heterosexual women's literature, the history of heterosexual women,[1] and analysis of the roles of heterosexual women in work, business, the arts, and heterosexual domestic life. It is also assumed that we should support (not just tolerate) speakers, films, workshops, classes, whole courses, which encourage women to prepare themselves to cope with life in the "dual career marriage," teach how to be married and a feminist, and train them in the tricks of legislative reform so they can try to ensure that abortions will be available to them when they need them, since they obviously will not practice the only safe and sure method of contraception.[2] We presume the students are hopelessly heterosexual and cater to the interests and needs we assume heterosexual women to have, instead of assuming they are educable to other ways of living, different needs, and interests, and some non-or anti-heterosexist sensibility and politics.

Women's studies, as an institution, as I know it, actively and aggressively supports women in becoming and remaining heterosexual; it actively seeks to encourage women to believe that the personal, political, economic, and health problems associated with heterosexuality for women should be struggled with rather than avoided—that these problems are inevitable but more or less solvable (with great endurance and much work), rather than that they are unsolvable but definitely evitable.

I am notorious in my town for my recruitment of women to lesbianism and lesbian perspectives. But what I do is miniscule. Imagine a real reversal of the heterosexualist teaching our program provides. Imagine thirty faculty members at a large university engaged routinely and seriously in the vigorous and aggressive encouragement of women to be lesbians, helping them learn skills and ideas for living as lesbians, teaching the connections between lesbianism and feminism and between heterosexism and sexism, building understanding of the agency of individual men in keeping individual women in line for the patriarchy. Imagine us openly and actively advising women not to marry, not to fuck, not to become bonded with any man. Imagine us teaching *lots* of lesbian literature, poetry, history, and art in women's studies courses, and teaching out of a politics determined by lesbian perception and sensibility. Imagine all this going on as actively and openly and enthusiastically as the program now promotes the searching out of careers and "feminist men," the development of "egalitarian marriages," and the management of heterosexual sex and the family.[3]

But the politics which women's studies purveys, even when some material by or about lesbians is included in some courses, is heterosexual politics. And according to heterosexual politics, lesbianism could never be the norm, and promoting lesbianism for women generally is somewhere between unrealistic and abusive.

The people who are the primary agents in determining and promoting this politics in women's studies are the heterosexual feminists in academia. These women are (not without exception) quite good in their relations with the few lesbians they work with—supportive, tolerant, useful. But this friendly, open-minded, even appreciative attitude camouflages their continuing and firm commitment to our marginality. Their being friendly and supportive and respectful to a few lesbians (who inevitably serve as tokens) has obscured from me and from them the enduring fact that they never take seriously any idea that lesbians and lesbianism *should not be marginal.*

I want to ask heterosexual academic feminists to do some hard analytical and reflective work. To begin, I want to say to them:

I wish you would notice that you are heterosexual.

I wish you would grow to the understanding that you choose heterosexuality.

I would like you to rise each morning and know that you are heterosexual and that you choose to be heterosexual—that you are and choose to be a member of a privileged and dominant class, one of your privileges being not to notice.

I wish you would stop and seriously consider, as a broad and long-term feminist political strategy, the conversion of women to a woman-identified and woman-directed sexuality and eroticism, as a way of breaking the grip of men on women's minds and women's bodies, of removing women from the chronic attachment to the primary situations of sexual and physical violence that is rained upon women by men, and as a way of promoting women's firm and reliable bonding against oppression.

Some heterosexual women have said in response to these sorts of sayings, "I see the connection between lesbianism and feminism, but I cannot just decide to be a lesbian . . . I'm not sexually attracted to women: women just don't turn me on." And I want to ask, "Why not? Why don't women turn you on? Why aren't you attracted to women?" I do not mean these questions rhetorically. I am completely serious.

The suppression of lesbian feeling, sensibility, and response has been so thorough and so brutal for such a long time, that if there were not a strong and widespread inclination to lesbianism, it would have been erased from human life. There is so much pressure on women to be heterosexual, and this pressure is both so pervasive and so completely denied, that I think heterosexuality cannot come naturally to many women; I think that widespread heterosexuality among women is a highly artificial product of the patriarchy. I suspect that it is not true at all that we must assume that most women are and most women will forever be heterosexual. I think that most women have to be coerced into heterosexuality. I would like heterosexual women to consider this proposition *seriously*. I want heterosexual women to do intense and serious consciousness-raising and exploration of their own personal histories and to find out how and when in their own development the separation of women from the erotic came about for them.[4] I would like heterosexual women to be as actively curious about how and why and when they became heterosexual as I have been about how and why and when I became lesbian.

At this point it might seem that I am demanding of heterosexual women their respect for my choice but that I am unwilling to respect theirs. I think, though, that it is respectful of autonomy to genuinely inquire into the history and grounds of choices, and disrespectful or negligent of autonomy to let unfreedom masquerade as choice or let the declaration "It's my choice" close off rather than open up inquiry.

Millions of heterosexual women give no thought to what heterosexuality is or why they are heterosexual. Heterosexuality is understood by them to *be* sexuality, and they assume uncritically and unthinkingly that it is simply the way humans are; they do not perceive heterosexuality as *an* option. Where there are no perceived options, there can be no such thing as choice, and hence one cannot respect the choice. But well-educated, worldly, politically astute, thoughtful, analytical, feminist women do know perfectly well that there are options, and that lesbian life is an option that coheres very well with feminist politics. They do choose to be heterosexual. Respect for that choice (on my part and on their part) demands that they make that choice intelligible.

Many feminist lesbians have thought and reflected and written and worked very hard to demonstrate that our choice makes sense. We have gone forth and participated on panels and in workshops and appeared on television explaining ourselves. We have, over and over, at great personal risk and considerable cost, worked as hard as we knew how to make our choice intelligible to audiences ranging from the idle curious to the skeptical to the openly hostile. Respect for heterosexuals' choice demands equally that they show, within the gentle standards of rationality recommended by womanly sensibility, that their choice can be understood as a *reasonable choice*. Until this has been shown I will not grant the assumption that heterosexuality can make sense for feminists, and I am not willing to continue uncritical acceptance of women's studies programs promoting heterosexuality for women.

Unless many heterosexual feminists start working as hard at making their choice intelligible as lesbians have worked at making ours intelligible, they should refrain from teaching and publishing and other work which openly or implicitly encourages other women in becoming or remaining committed to heterosexuality, and lesbians should refrain from supporting women's studies.

Notes

I am grateful to Sarah Lucia Hoagland for organizing the panel "Lesbian Perspectives on Women's Studies" for the 1980 National Women's Studies Association conference; what is printed here is a revision of the speech I made. My thoughts reflect discussions with my lover Carolyn Shafer, and she gave help and suggestions in the revision process.

[1] . . . or the literature and history of woman *presumed* to be heterosexual. The evidence that many of the women we study were lesbians is generally overlooked—an erasure that builds in added security for the assumption of natural near-universal heterosexuality.

[2] By "the only safe and sure method," I do not mean only exclusive lesbianism, but whatever would add up to total female control of reproductive sexual intercourse.

[3] For a sense of magnitude of this, consider: at Michigan State the women's studies classes account for well over twelve thousand student-credit-hours each year.

[4] This phrase is due to Adrienne Rich. My thoughts on these things have benefited from my correspondence with her.

Resources

The purpose of this list is to give examples of the educational and cultural work lesbians are currently doing. It is not intended to be a complete guide.

Special Educational Projects

Lesbian Feminist Study Clearinghouse. Established in 1978 to foster and publicize study of lesbian experience from a feminist perspective. Seeks to represent voices of all segments of the community by making available to individuals, groups, and women's studies classes unpublished manuscripts, out-of-print articles, conference and workshop presentations, and course syllabi. Sample syllabi: "Lesbian Life and Literature," Bonnie Zimmerman; "Teaching Lesbian Novels, From Proposal to Reality," Julia Penelope (Stanley); "Lesbian Literature," Barbara Smith; "Lesbian Literature and Feminism," Cherríe Moraga; "The Lesbian Literary Tradition," Pamella Farley; Lesbianism: "An Historical, Cultural, and Political View," M. Davis, A. Michelson, M. Moloney, and S. Darrow. LFSC, Women's Studies Program, 1012 Cathedral of Learning, University of Pittsburgh, Pittsburgh, PA 15260.

Lesbian Perspectives. Educational program at Woman's Building in Los Angeles. Enables women to explore their lesbian identity and build community. Three terms. Fall: we examine personal and social issues of lesbianism; Winter: we articulate our experience through writing and art-making; Spring: we create a lesbian cultural event for the women's community. Terri Wolverton, c/o the Woman's Building, 1727 North Spring St., Los Angeles, CA 90012.

Womyn's Braille Press. Makes feminists and lesbian feminist material available to blind womyn. Offers tapes of *Sinister Wisdom* and *off our backs.* Subscribers pay between $5 and $15 to receive quarterly newsletter in large print, braille, or four-track cassette, and materials on loan. Box 8457, Minneapolis, MN 55408

Archives

The Canadian Gay Archives. National archives for lesbians and gay men. Founded in 1973 and incorporated in 1980. Largest collection in the country. Focus is primarily Canadian, but material is collected from around the world. Holdings include organization archives, personal archives, information files, gay and lesbian periodicals, articles from popular and learned journals, newspaper clippings, a library, photograph collection, video and audio tape collection, et cetera. Newsletter *Gay Archivist* issued periodically; three titles to date. Box 639, Station A, Toronto, Ontario, Canada M5W 1G2.

The Florida Collection of Lesbian Herstory. Nonprofit, nonpolitical, nonpartisan group of caring lesbians. Goals: to bring Florida lesbians closer together; to serve as an archive for books, magazines, photos, tapes, films, notices of events, bibliographies, and other lesbian related material; to form a communications network; and to sponsor educational and social events. Special emphasis on Florida communities, but donations encouraged from the entire country. FCLH, Box 5605, Jacksonville, FL 32207.

Kentucky Collection of Lesbian Her-story. An archive, a clearing house, and a network for lesbians throughout the country and especially the southeast. KCLH, Box 1701, Louisville, KY 40201. (502) 634-1869.

Lesbian Herstory Archives. Gathers and preserves records of lesbian lives and activities so that future generations of lesbians will have ready access to relevant material: Books, magazines, journals, news clippings (from establishment, feminist, and lesbian media), photos, bibliographies, manuscript collections, tapes, films, diaries, oral herstories, poetry and prose, biographies, autobiographies, notices of events, posters, graphics, other memorabilia, and obscure references to our lives. For several years, we have presented a slide show. LHA and Lesbian Herstory Educational Foundation, Inc., Box 1258, New York, NY 10116.

National Gay Archives. Natalie Barney, Edward Carpenter Library. A research collection of 10,000 books, periodicals, and clippings. Main collection gathered over thirty-six-year period by curator, Jim Kepner. Expanded with additional materials from friends and lesbian and gay organizations. Box 38100, Los Angeles, CA 90038. (213) 463-5450.

Tennessee Lesbian Archives. Small collection housed in cabin on working farm in Knoxville area. Particular interest in materials on Southern women, Jewish lesbians, and lesbians of color. TLA, Rt. 2, Box 252, Luttrell TN 37779. (615) 992-8423.

The West Coast Lesbian Collections. Community-based collection of oral herstory tapes, books, journals, newspapers, letters, photographs, posters, periodicals, leaflets, unpublished papers, and other artifacts which document lesbian lives, politics, culture. Plans for media presentations, newsletter, events, and tape library. WCLC, Box 23753, Oakland, CA 94623.

History Projects

Boston Area Lesbian and Gay History Project. c/o 75 Chandler St., #5, Boston MA 02118. See Slide Shows—Our Boston Heritage.

The Buffalo Women's Oral History Project. Madeline Davis, Liz Kennedy, and Avra Michelson. Our goals: to produce a comprehensive written history of the lesbian community in Buffalo, New York, using as the major source oral histories of lesbians who came out prior to 1970; to create and index an archive of oral history tapes, written interviews, and relevant supplementary materials; to give this history back to the community from which it derives. We question the dominant approach to lesbian history which portrays the lesbian as isolated or which tends to dismiss lesbian community prior to the women's movement as imitative, heterosexist, male-identified, and therefore inauthentic. Since the spring of 1978 we have collected narratives from many lesbians between the ages of 30 and 72. This group represents women of various classes, and though primarily white, includes Black, Native American, and Hispanic women. To complete our research, we intend to concentrate on Black lesbians and women over fifty. 255 Parkside Avenue, Buffalo, NY 14214.

Lesbian Heritage/D.C. Community group dedicated to collecting, preserving and making available to all women the history of women, especially lesbians, in the D.C. area. An affiliate of the Washington Area Women's Center. Collection includes organization and subject files, periodicals and newsletters, feminist pamphlets, tapes, posters, and T-shirts. Center address: 1519 P Street, N.W., Washington, D.C. 20005. (202) 347-5078.

Lesbian/Gay History Researchers' Network Newsletter. Network made up of both grassroots and university-affiliated historians and researchers. For newsletter information contact Lesbian Heritage/D.C., c/o Washington Area Women's Center.

San Francisco Lesbian History Project. Begun 1979. We read and discuss recent publications about lesbian and gay history; produce events to return our history to our communities; research San Francisco lesbian life, e.g., in bohemian North Beach; and take oral histories of lesbians who have been in San Francisco ten years or more. Box 42332, San Francisco, CA 94101. See also Slideshows—Lesbian Masquerade.

Slide Shows

Our Boston Heritage. Survey from the 1600s to the 1960s, focusing on important developments within each century, e.g., laws of the colonial period, same-sex relationships in the nineteenth century, and local bar scene in the mid-twentieth century. Continuing goal: to improve race and class representation of the slide show. Boston Area Lesbian and Gay History Project.

A Family of Friends: Portrait of a Lesbian Friendship Group, 1921-1973. Publishers of *The Little Review*, Margaret Anderson and Jane Heap; the *New Yorker's* Paris correspondent, Janet Flanner; Georgette Leblanc, writer, actress, singer, star of the Opera Comique and companion of Maeterlink; Solita Solano, writer and editor; and Dorothy Caruso, author and widow of Enrico Caruso. Uses letters and photographs from the Flanner-Solano collection in the Library of Congress. Frances Doughty, 192 St. John's Place, Brooklyn, NY 11217.

Lesbians in Fiction. Thirty-five minutes, 64 slides plus tape with four voices. Maida Tilchen and Fran Koski. Content: narration plus dramatized dialogue from lesbian novels in English, emphasizing the pulp novels of the 1950s. Made in 1975, ends with novels of that year.

Lesbian and Gay GIs in World War II. Based on letters, recently released government documents, photographs, and interviews. Allan Berube, San Francisco Gay and Lesbian History Project. See History Projects for address.

Lesbian Images in Photography: 1850-1980. JEB (Joan E. Biren). Presents work of more than thirty women, including Clementina Hawarden, Emma Jane Gay, Frances Benjamin Johnston, Alice Austen, and Berenice Abbott. Glad Hag Books, Box 2934, Washington, DC 20013.

Lesbian Masquerade. Passing women in San Francisco. San Francisco Lesbian and Gay History Project, Box 42332, San Francisco, CA 94101.

Lesbians in Paris, 1895-1930. Renée Vivien and Natalie Barney. Emphasis on Barney's circle. Gayle Rubin, Department of Anthropology, University of Michigan, Ann Arbor, MI.

Lesbian Sexual Imagery in the Fine Arts. Works from Asia Minor, Greece, India, China, Japan, Renaissance Europe, and contemporary America. Includes *A Sapphocentric Love Story,* a warm and gentle animation of lesbian lovemaking featuring two rag dolls. Tee Corinne. Rootworks, 2000 King Mountain Trail, Sunny Valley, OR 97497.

Preserving Our Lesbian Heritage. Lesbian Herstory Archives, New York City. See Archives for address.

The Public and Private: Lesbian Art and Artists. One hour. Part of a larger slide collection, *From Image to Image Maker: A Survey of U.S. and European Women's Art History.* Focuses on work of lesbian artists from nineteenth and early twentieth centuries, including Anna Klumpke, Rosa Bonheur, Romaine Brooks, and a group of U.S. lesbian and feminist sculptors in Rome constituting the "White Marmorean Flock." Andrea Weiss, Women Make Movies, Inc., 257 West 19th St., New York, NY 10011.

Straight Talk About Lesbians. Liz Diamond. Sixty-five minutes. Available in filmstrips for rental or purchase from Women's Educational Media, Inc., 36 Colwell Ave., Brighton, MA 02135. Three hundred and fifty color slides with commentary from lesbians, their parents, and their children. Diamond's book *The Lesbian Primer* available from Naiad Press.

Styles of Being Lesbian in Paris, 1890–1945. Includes lesbian bars, prostitutes, and entertainers as portrayed by Toulouse-Lautrec; working-class bars in the 1930s; the dancer Loie Fuller; bookstore owners Sylvia Beach and Adrienne Monnier; the wealthy circle around Natalie Clifford Barney; Colette's affair with Missy; the writers Stein and Hall and their mates Toklas and Troubridge. Frances Doughty and Tee Corinne. 192 St. John's Place, Brooklyn, NY 11217.

Woman-Loving Women. Patricia A. Gozemba and Marilyn L. Humphries. Twenty-five minute slide tape presentation with synchronized sound track for manual and automatic showing. Includes guide with discussion topics, typical questions and answers, a filmography, and a bibliography. Explores popular misconceptions about lesbians and the political, social, and economic oppression of lesbians. Shows the richness of lesbian culture and documents the contributions that lesbians of all ages, races, and classes make to society. Available from Lavender Horizons, Box 086, Marblehead, MA 01945. In slide-tape format or filmstrip format.

Art

The Blatant Image. A magazine of feminist photography. For women who use and appreciate photographic images as well as women who make them. Articles on practical and theoretical topics, e.g., what is a feminist or lesbian aesthetic? Box 56, Wolf Creek, OR 97497.

Great American Lesbian Art Show (GALAS). National project organized by six women in Los Angeles, with co-sponsorship of the Women's Building and the Gay and Lesbian Community Services Center. Major components: National network of lesbian art exhibits and events organized by women in their own communities; Invitational Exhibit at the Women's Building honoring ten artists' pioneering contributions to lesbian art and culture; and slide collection of art made by GALAS participants. Sets of this collection housed at the Women's Building Slide Registry (Los Angeles), Lesbian Herstory Archives (New York). *Guidebook* (illustrations of GALAS, with text by Terri Wolverton) available from Box 38777, Hollywood, CA 90038. (See "The Great American Lesbian Art Show Comes to Boston," *Gay Community News*, 2 August 1980, pp. 10–11.)

Lesbian Photography Directory, No. 1. Information about mailings, requests for work, and services available. Statements by artists about their work and geographical index. Morgan Gwenwald, Box 34, Port Jefferson, NY 11777

Films

See list by Andrea Weiss in "Lesbians and Films" issue of *Jumpcut: A Review of Contemporary Cinema*, No. 24/25 (1981). *Jumpcut*, Box 865, Berkeley, CA 94701.

Sappho, Dyketactics, Superdyke, Double Strength, Available Space, and other Barbara Hammer films available from Goddess Films, Box 2446, Berkeley, CA 94702. (415) 658-6959.

Jan Oxenberg films include *Home Movie, Comedy in Six Unnatural Acts*, and *I'm Not One of 'Em. Home Movie* available from Multi-Media Center, 1525 Franklin, San Francisco, CA.

Iris Films distributes lesbian films, including *In the Best Interests of the Children* (about lesbian mothers and their children). Box 5353, Berkeley, CA 94705. (415) 549-3192.

Lesbian films listed in *Women's Films in Print*. Booklegger Press, 555 29th St., San Francisco, CA 94131.

Word Is Out: Stories of Some of Our Lives portrays lesbians of different ages, classes, and ethnic groups. Mariposa Film Group, San Francisco 1978. Book version, edited by Nancy Adair and Casey Adair, gives complete interviews. (New York: Dell, 1978).

Susanna by Susanna Blaustein and *Luna Tune* by Carol Clement available from Women Make Movies, Inc., 257 West 19th St., New York, NY 10011.

Groups

Association of Lesbian and Gay Asians. Fosters communication and provides support and understanding within the gay Asian community and provides education about gay Asians to the local, national, and international communities. Five committees: Communications, Cultural, Social, Political Awareness (community outreach), and Business and Finance. Founded April 1981. ALGA, 55 Sutter St., Suite 97, San Francisco, CA 94104. (415) 861-4767.

Committee for the Visibility of the Other Black Woman: The Lesbian. New York City. Spring 1980, workshop on conflicts in the Black lesbian community. Winter 1981, First Annual Black Lesbian Conference for Eastern Regional States. Annual Hatshepsut awards (recognition for lesbians and gay men, named for Egyptian who crowned herself Pharaoh). July 1-8 1982, package tour to Haiti. Gail Johnson, 72-15 41st Avenue, Jackson Heights, NY 11377.

Disabled Lesbians. New York: The Lesbian Illness Support Group. Nancy Johnson, (212) 989-6587, or the Lesbian Herstory Archives, (212) 874-7232. San Francisco: call Operation Concern, Lesbian and Gay Counseling Center, 2483 Clay St., San Francisco, CA 94115, (415) 563-0202. For more information, see *off our backs* special issue on women and disability, vol. 2, no. 5, May 1981.

Dykes Against Racism Everywhere (DARE). Box 914, Stuyvesant Station, New York, NY 10009.

Fat Dykes. Fat Liberator Publications, Box 5227, Coralville, IA 52241.

Lavender Prairie Collective, Champaign-Urbana area. Publishes *The Lavender Prairie Newsletter* ten times yearly and sponsors monthly coffeehouses. Newsletter is $5 per year. Box 2096, Station A, Champaign, IL 61820.

*Lesbian Alumnae of Radcliffe College (LARC).*Sixty members. Formed to share thoughts and feelings about the experience of a Harvard education for a lesbian. Seeks to support lesbians currently on campus, including members of the Radcliffe Lesbian Association. Contact Radcliffe Alumnae Office, Cambridge, MA 02138 for current address of Renée Watkins or other representatives of LARC.

Lesbian Feminist Organizing Committee. 2104 Stevens Avenue S., Minneapolis, MN 55404. Monthly newsletter.

Lesbian and Gay Associated Engineers and Scientists. Founded 1980 to work for a new and better future for lesbians and gays in high-tech industries. Open to engineers, scientists, computer professionals, and technicians. Social activities, job lists, public education, and bibliographies (including a gay science-fiction bibliography). Documents cases of discrimination against lesbians and gays, and compiles them for future use. We are ready, *if requested by the victim,* to picket any discriminatory company. LGAES, Box 70133, Sunnyvale, CA 94086.

Lesbian Scholars Forum, Inc., 217 Pine St., Suite 2, San Francisco, CA 94115. (415) 346-9841

Lincoln Legion of Lesbians. Lesbian-feminist collective founded in November 1979 to provide cultural activities and programs about lesbianism for the local community. LLL publishes a newsletter for Nebraska, *Lesbian Community News.* LLL, Box 30137, Lincoln, NE 68503.

Quaker Lesbians. Annual East Coast and West Coast Conferences. Information in *Friends for Lesbians and Gay Concerns* newsletter, Box 222, Sumneytown, PA 18084.

SAGE: Senior Action in a Gay Environment. Organized in June 1978 by professionals in social work, gerontology, psychology, and health care to try to meet the special needs of older lesbians and gay men in various stages of their lives. SAGE, 487A Hudson St., New York, NY 10014. (212) 741-2247.

Salsa-Soul Sisters: Third World Gay Women's Organization. Begun 1976. Political, social concerns of the community. Meetings Thursday. c/o Washington Square Methodist Church, 133 West 4th Street, New York, New York 10014.

Younger Lesbians Support Group. For women between 15 and 20 who are lesbians or think they may be lesbians, who live in Rhode Island and nearby parts of Massachusetts. For more information contact Women's Growth Center (Providence), (401) 728-6023.

Centers

ALFA: the Atlanta Lesbian/Feminist Alliance. Formed in June 1972 to meet some needs of Atlanta's lesbian community. We house the Southeastern Lesbian Archives, do other educational work, hold social events, put out a monthly newsletter, and sponsor a lesbian softball team. ALFA, Box 5502, Atlanta, GA 30307.

The Lesbian Center. Madison, Wisconsin. Offers peer counseling, referrals, information line, drop-in counseling, and monthly nonalcoholic women's coffeehouse. 306 N. Brooks St. (the University Y), Madison, WI (608) 257-7378.

Lesbian Community Center. Chicago. Houses small lesbian library and archives. 3435 North Sheffield St., Chicago, IL 60657.

Lesbian Resource Center. Minneapolis. Information and referral service, speaker's bureau, monthly newsletter, and support groups, including coming-out groups, lesbian mothers, Amazon AA, and other topics as needed. Houses Lesbian Survival Center and *Lesbian Inciter* (newspaper). LRC, 2708 East Lake St., Suite 229/230, Minneapolis, MN 55406. (616) 721-4666.

Seattle Lesbian Resource Center. Multiservice organization offering peer counseling, drop-in center, group activities, lending library, and emergency services. Established in 1971. 4253 Roosevelt Way NE, Seattle, WA 98105. (206) 632-9631.

Several cities have gay community centers or gay counseling centers that offer special services to lesbians, eg., Operation Concern in San Francisco and Gay Community Services in Minneapolis. ED.

Conferences

Becoming Visible: The First Black Lesbian Conference. October 1980. Women's Building, San Francisco. Two hundred and fifty women from ten states attended. Keynote speakers: Pat Norman, Angela Davis, and Andrea Canaan. Workshops included: Black identity, imperialism, lesbians and the law, affirmative action, alcoholism, family issues, Black feminism, and white groups. Videotape film highlighting conference agenda was produced. Cassette recording of keynote addresses available from Marie Renfro, 11 Bucharelli, San Francisco, CA 94119. More information: Rose Mitchell, 773 Dolores, San Francisco, CA 94110 or Mary Mathis, 2814 Dohr, Berkeley CA.

Berkshire Conference on the History of Women. Vassar College, June 1981. Several papers on lesbian history were presented, including "Mary Ellicott Arnold, Mabel Reed, and the Karoks," by Judith Schwarz; "Buffalo Lesbian Bars 1930-1960," by Madeline Davis and Liz Kennedy, members of the Buffalo Women's Oral History Project; and "Politics of Lesbian Historiography and the History of Lesbians of Color," by Sabrina Sojourner, Mirthe Quintanales, and Angela Wilson. Two papers were read at a session titled "The Emerging Woman, 1880-1925: Alternative Institutions and Identity Crisis": "Male Mythologies and their Internationalization of Deviance from Krafft-Ebing to Radclyffe Hall," by Carroll Smith Rosenberg and Esther Newton; and "Students and Faculty in British Women's Colleges," by Martha Vicinus. Slide presentations on lesbian history included "Butch-Femme: Sexual Courage in the Fifties," by Joan Nestle and Deborah Edel of the Lesbian Herstory Archives in New York; "Styles of Being a Lesbian in Paris 1890-1945" by Frances Doughty; and "Lesbian Masquerade," by Estelle Freedman for the San Francisco Lesbian History Project.

England: National Lesbian Conference. c/o WAA, Io, Cambridge Terrace Mews, London NW1. Previous conferences held in 1981 and 1976.

First Annual Third World Lesbian Writers Conference. 24 February 1979. Sponsored by *Azalea,* a magazine by and for Third World lesbians. Second conference, 12 April 1980, Hunter College.

First Eastern Black Lesbian Conference. January 16–18, 1981, New York City. Sponsored by the Committee for the Visibility of the Other Black Woman: The Lesbian. See Groups.

First International Lesbian Conference. 27 December 1980–1 January, 1981, Amsterdam. Sponsored by International Lesbian Information Services (ILIS). Conference in Torino, Italy, April 1981. 1982 conference, USA. International address: ILIS, c/o COC, Frederidsplein 14, 1017 XM Amsterdam, The Netherlands. U.S. address: c/o Gay Community Center, 1469 Church St., Washington, D.C. 20010.

Modern Language Association Gay Caucus. Yearly Meeting, December. Publishes *Gay Studies Newsletter.*

National Women's Studies Association. National conferences. Lesbian panels and events at conferences in 1979, University of Kansas; 1980, University of Indiana; 1981, University of Connecticut; and 1982, Humboldt State University. Lesbian Caucus, NWSA, University of Maryland, College Park, MD 20742.

Periodicals

Azalea. A magazine by and for Third World Lesbians. We try to remain nonelitist, nontraditional, rotating the editor's spot with each issue. Box 200, Cooper Station, New York, NY 10276.

B.A.D. [Big Apple Dyke] News. A monthly New York City lesbian newspaper. 192 Spring St., #15, New York, NY 10012.

Common Lives/Lesbian Lives. Quarterly, collectively produced. Depicts lives of ordinary women, lesbians who have always struggled to survive and create a culture for ourselves. Especially committed to printing work of lesbians of color, fat lesbians, lesbians over fifty and under twenty, disabled lesbians, poor and working-class lesbians, and lesbians of varying cultural backgrounds. CL/LL, Box 1553, Iowa City, IA 52244.

Conditions. A magazine of writing by women with an emphasis on writing by lesbians. Publishes poetry, fiction, articles, journal entries, translations, drama, and reviews. Particularly concerned with publishing work by Third World, working-class and older women. Free to women in prison and mental institutions. Box 56, Van Brunt Station, Brooklyn, NY 11215.

Feminary. A feminist journal for the south. Emphasizes writing by lesbians. Box 954, Chapel Hill, NC 27514.

Focus. A journal for lesbians. 1151 Massachusetts Ave., Cambridge, MA 02138.

Gay Community News. Good coverage of lesbian issues and events. Nationwide circulation. Published weekly. Monthly Book Review section. GCN, Box 971, Boston, MA 02103.

Lesbian Connection. A nationwide forum of news and ideas by, for and about Lesbians. A publication of the Helen Diner Memorial Women's Center/Ambitious Amazons. Box 811, East Lansing, MI 48823.

Lesbian Insider/Insighter/Inciter. A space to celebrate and strengthen ourselves as lesbians. We report controversy, differences and connections among lesbians, and focus attention on the oppression of lesbians by lesbians and nonlesbians. We recognize that dyke oppression cuts across all class, geography, race, age, disability, appearance, and cultural/ethnic lines. Fourteen member collective. Box 7038, Powderhorn Station, Minneapolis, MN 55407.

Lesbian/Lesbienne. Bilingual, coast-to-coast publication for, by, and about lesbians. Began in Kitchener-Guelph and is now published in Toronto. Box 70, Station "F," Toronto, Ontario, Canada.

Lesbians Rising. Lesbian-feminist newspaper. Hunter College, 695 Park Avenue, Rm. 245, New York, NY 10021.

Lesbian Voices. We welcome differing points of view on controversial issues but request that ideas be expressed clearly. Founded 1974. Jonnik Enterprises, Box 2066, San Jose, CA 95109.

Matrices: A Lesbian-Feminist Research Newsletter. Begun in 1978 as vehicle for researchers to share information and communicate about their work. Each issue includes brief descriptions of readers' research interests and projects, notes and queries, and announcements. Published three times yearly. Julia Penelope, General Editor. Dept. of English, University of Nebraska, Lincoln, NE 68588.

Out and About. Seattle lesbian-feminist newsletter. Monthly. Collectively produced. Forum for sharing ideas, analysis, and information, 5434 Thackeray Pl. N.E., Seattle, WA 98105.

Sinister Wisdom. A Journal of Words and Pictures for the Lesbian Imagination in All Women. Quarterly journal devoted to analysis of our lives as women under patriarchy through fiction, poetry, art, and essays, and to the creation of new values and ethic which reflect our women-centeredness. *Sinister Wisdom,* Box 660, Amherst, MA 01004.

Third World Women's Gayzette. Newsletter of Salsa-Soul Sisters. Monthly. Information c/o C. McCray, editor, 41–11 Parsons Blvd. #616, Flushing, New York 11355.

Periodicals, Special Issues

Dyke: A Quarterly, No. 5 (Fall 1977). Ethnic lesbians.
Conditions: Five (1979). The Black women's issue.
Connexions: An International Women's Quarterly 3 (Winter 1982), Global Lesbianism. Special issue on global lesbianism; articles from Europe, Asia, South America.
Frontiers 4, no, 3 (Fall 1979). Lesbian history.
Heresies 3 (Fall 1977). Lesbian art and artists.
Heresies 8. Third World women.
Heresies 12 (1981). Sexuality.
Jumpcut, 24/25 (1981). Lesbians and films.
off our backs 9, no. 6 (June 1979). Women of color.
off our backs 11, no. 5 (May 1981). Women with disabilities.
Radical Teacher 17 (Spring 1981). Women's studies. Articles on Black women's studies and lesbian studies.
Sinister Wisdom 2 (Fall 1976). Lesbian writing and publishing.
Sinister Wisdom 10 (Summer 1979). On being old and aging.
Sinister Wisdom 13 (Spring 1980). Lesbian writing and publishing.

Publishers

Cleis Press. Committed to publishing serious woman-identified works, especially by lesbians and women of color. 1981 publications: *On Women Artists,* poetry and prose by Alexandra Grilhikes, and *Fight Back: Feminist Resistance to Male Violence.* Frédérique Delacoste, Felice Newman, and Mary Winfrey, Cleis Press, 3141 Pleasant Ave. S., Minneapolis, MN 55408. (612) 825–8872.

The Naiad Press, Inc. Founded 1973 to publish lesbian/feminist material. Genres include fiction, poetry, bibliography, biography, history. Titles include *Outlander, Black Lesbians: An Annotated Bibliography, A Woman Appeared to Me, The Black and White of It, Sapphistry, Lesbian Feminism in Turn-of-the-Century Germany, Anna's Country,* and *To the Cleveland Station.* Thirty-two titles by 1982. We do not accept grants or aid, and we do not pay employees. We use women typesetters and printers exclusively, and we pay royalties. Box 10543, Tallahassee, FL 32302.

Out and Out Books. 476 Second St., Brooklyn, NY 11215. Titles include *Amazon Poetry, On Strike Against God* and *The Lesbian: A Celebration of Difference.*

Persephone Press. Publications include *Wanderground,* by Sally Gearhart; *Choices,* a novel by Nancy Toder; *Lesbian Poetry: An Anthology,* edited by Elly Bulkin and Joan Larkin; *This Bridge Called My Back: Writings by Radical Women of Color,* edited by Cherríe Moraga and Gloria Anzaldúa; *Claiming an Identity They Taught Me to Despise,* by Michelle Cliff; and *The Coming Out Stories,* edited by Julia Penelope Stanley and Susan J. Wolfe. Box 7222, Watertown, MA 02172.

Spinsters, Ink. Feminist publishing company founded in 1978 by Maureen Brady and Judith McDaniel to make available literature by and about women which would not otherwise be published, the interest being in political material not usually described as "commercial." Titles include: *Bones and Kim* by Lynn Strongin; *The Cancer Journals* by Audre Lorde; *Give Me Your Good Ear* by Maureen Brady; and *Reconstituting the World: The Poetry and Vision of Adrienne Rich* by Judith McDaniel. RD 1, Argyle, NY 12809.

Bibliographies

Black Lesbians: An Annotated Bibliography compiled by JR Roberts, forward by Barbara Smith. Tallahassee, Florida: Naiad Press, 1981. Twenty illustrations, 112 pp., appendix, index, sources, organizations. $5.95. Partial contents: lives and lifestyles; oppression; resistance and liberation; music and musicians; periodicals.

"Black Lesbian Literature/Black Lesbian Lives: Materials for Women's Studies." Article by JR Roberts in *Radical Teacher* 17 (Spring 1981), pp. 11–17.

A Gay Bibliography, 6th edition. Gay Task Force of the American Library Association. $1 from Barbara Gittings, GTF, Box 2383, Philadelphia, PA 19103.

Lesbian Art and Artists. Special issue of *Heresies* 3 (Fall 1977). Bibliography pp. 115–117.

Lesbian Booklist. Womanbooks, a bookstore for women. 201 West 92nd St., New York, NY 10025. (212) 873–4121.

Lesbian Literature. Catalogue 2: old, rare, and out-of-print fiction, biography, poetry, and drama about lesbians and other independent women. 37 pp. Annotated. Christine Pattee, Independent Woman Books, 50 Forest Street, Apt. C 1, Hartford, CT 06105.

Lesbian Mothers and Their Children: An Annotated Bibliography of Legal and Psychological Materials. Edited by Donna Hitchens and Ann G. Thomas. San Francisco: Lesbian Rights Project, 1980. 45 pp. Sections on Cases, Law Review Articles, Miscellaneous Articles, Lesbians and Mental Health, Lesbian Relationships, Mothering Among Lesbians, and Mental Health of the Children.

The Lesbian in Literature, 3d edition, Barbara Grier, et al. Tallahassee, Florida: The Naiad Press, 1981. A one-hundred-and-sixty-page alphabetical listing by authors of all known works in the English language dealing with lesbians or lesbianism; extensively coded, cross-indexed, and partially annotated; contains approximately 7,000 works.

Third World Women in the United States—By and About Us, in *This Bridge Called My Back: Writings by Radical Women of Color*, edited by Cherríe Moraga and Gloria Anzaldúa, pp. 251–261. Includes sections on Third World Lesbians in the U.S., Afro-American Lesbians, Asian/Pacific American Lesbians, Latina Lesbians, and Native American Lesbians.

A Short Lesbian Reading List. Gay Task Force, ALA, see Gay Bibliography for address.

Dissertations

Attitudes Toward Lesbians. Explores how the various theories about the etiology of lesbianism (biological, psychodynamic, sociological) and the research on attitudes toward homosexuality have contributed to the development of stereotypes. Efforts will be made to measure how negative attitudes can be changed by supplying accurate information about lesbianism to counteract the effects of stereotypes. Includes feminist analysis of lesbianism and a critique of the empirical literature which has assessed attitudes toward lesbians. Chris Browning, Dept. of Psychology, University of Maine, Orono, ME 04469.

Institutionalized Heterosexism: The Social and Legal Aspects of Lesbian Parenting and Child Custody. Based on legal documents of child custody proceedings and actual observation of courtroom trials. Considers rationales for denying custody; manner in which lesbianism is addressed in court; assumption of fitness that dictates custody determination; and strategies used in cases. Researcher worked with feminist law collective which represented lesbian parents in custody disputes. Wendy Cutler, History of Consciousness Program, University of California, Santa Cruz, Santa Cruz, CA 95064.

Lesbian Origins: An Hystorical and Cross-Cultural Analysis of Sex Ratios, Female Sexuality and Homo-sexual Segregation Versus Hetero-sexual Integration Patterns in Relation to the Liberation of Women, Rutgers, Sociology, 1978. Believed to be the first lesbian feminist dissertation accepted by a U.S. university. Susan Cavin, Department of Sociology, Green Mountain College, Poultney, VT 05764; 192 Spring St. #15, NY, NY 10012.

The Problem of Gender and Subjectivity Posed by the New Subject Pronoun "j/e" in the Writing Of Monique Wittig, March 1981. Radical lesbian feminist study of *Le corps lesbien (The Lesbian Body).* Proposes a theory of "phallogocentrism" to explain dynamics of male oppression. Includes complete "Concordance of *Le corps lesbien.*" 825 pp. Available on microfilm. Namascar Shaktini, History of Consciousness, University of California, Santa Cruz, Santa Cruz, CA 95064.

A Whole New Poetry Beginning Here: Contemporary Themes of American Women Poets, Stanford University, 1981. A critical study of feminist poets, 1960–1980, including many lesbians. Extensive discussion of feminist and lesbian-feminist themes and aesthetics. Chapter on Black lesbian feminist poetry. Appendix: forty original essays by poets on their own work. Lynda Koolish, 4249 24th St., San Francisco, CA 94114.

Lifestyles of Never-Married Women Physical Educators in Institutions of Higher Education in the United States. (Ed.D. dissertation.) Bonnie Ann Beck (1976). University of North Carolina at Greensboro, Greensboro, NC. Available on microfilm.

Grants

Affectional Preference and Aging. Three year Continuing Education grant from the Center of Aging of the National Institute of Mental Health. 1979–1982. In the first two years, 6,000 individuals have attended workshops, seminars, graduate and undergraduate courses, and professional colloquia. Current foci: 1) Those who early in their development identify as lesbian or gay and grow old with that identity; 2) those who assume a gay identity as adults, often as result of life crisis; 3) those not lesbian- or gay-identified who experience same-sex relationships. Judith K. Scott, Director, Gay Community Services, 2855 Park Ave. South, Minneapolis, MN 55407.

Buffalo Women's Oral History Project. (See History Projects). Astraea Foundation grant, 1981. Group also received grant from SUNY/Buffalo Graduate School.

CUNY grant for New York City interviews of women who have changed their sexual identity in "mid-life" (ages 35 to 45) from a heterosexual to a lesbian one. Researchers aim to discover what social circumstances help make such a change possible. Subjects: women from all economic and ethnic backgrounds, mothers and nonmothers, previously married and never married. Claudette Charbonneau and Patricia Lander, Women's Studies Program, Brooklyn College, Brooklyn, NY 11210.

The Lives of One Hundred Lesbians and Gay Men: Three-year NIMH training postdoctorate in social gerontology. What supports and internal strengths have they developed for coping with aging? Results of the research will be published by the University of California Press, Deborah Wolf, Institute for the Study of Social Change, University of California, 2420 Bowditch, Berkeley, CA 94720.

Work in Progress

Against Sadomasochism: A Radical Feminist Analysis. Collection of essays edited by Robin Ruth Linden, Darlene Pagano, Diana E. H. Russell, and Susan Leigh Star. To be published by Frog in the Well Press, East Palo Alto, CA.

Anthology on Lesbian Separatism. For ourselves (separatists), asking our questions, focusing on our issues but challenging us, for example, with the problem of male children or the charge that separatism is only a white, middle-class issue. Analytical essays, personal stories, fiction, graphics, poetry, and transcribed tapes. Julia Penelope, Dept. of English, University of Nebraska, Lincoln, NE 68588 and Sarah Lucia Hoagland, Dept. of Philosophy, Northeastern Illinois University, 5500 N. St. Louis Ave., Chicago, IL 60625.

Biography of Margaret C. Anderson (1866-1973). Editor, musician, and autobiographer. Based primarily on unpublished letters, memorablia, a novella, and interviews. Mathilda M. Hills, Dept. of English, University of Rhode Island, Kingston, RI 02881.

Black Lesbians; Lesbians and the arts; Resources Directory for Newark NJ area. Terri Jewell, 70 Ellis Ave., #2, Irvington, NJ 07111.

Close Friends and Devoted Companions. Study of lesbian couples in nineteenth-century and early twentieth-century America. Based on mss. collection at Library of Congress; archives of women's history in Schlesinger Library, Radcliffe; National Archives; Lesbian Herstory Archives; and other sources. Judith Schwarz. Publisher: William Morrow, New York.

Identity and Work: Lesbian Mothers Survival on the Job. My research aims to identify what work means in our lives, how it has changed as we have changed, how we survive in the workplace, how we can create meaningful work. Based on interviews with lesbian mothers in a variety of work situations, of different ages, classes, races, political awareness, living with and not living with children. Sandra Rubaii, 28 Abdallah Ave., Cortland, NY 13045. (607) 756-8825.

Comapaneras. Latin American Lesbian Anthology. Stories, articles, songs, poems, transcribed tapes. Colectiva Lesbiana Latinoamericana. LALA, c/o D.L., 170 Avenue C, Apt. 4H, New York, NY 10009. (212) 473-6864.

Lesbian Mothers. Five-year research project by Ellen Lewin and Terrie A. Lyons. Compares adaptive strategies of lesbian and heterosexual mothers, including those who were married and those who had their children outside of a marital context. Ellen Lewin, Medical Anthropology Program, University of California, San Francisco, 1320 3rd Avenue, San Francisco, CA 94143.

Lesbians Over 65. Book based on 100 interviews. Monika Kehoe, Ph.D. C/o CERES, Psychology Building, San Francisco State University, 1600 Holloway, San Francisco, CA.

The Lesbian Periodicals Index, 1947-. Comprehensive author/subject index to some of the more than one hundred lesbian periodicals published in the United States. Will appear serially and provide access for the first time to contents of lesbian journals, including poems, visual art, short fiction, letters, news, analysis, and criticism. Goals include: to further creation of reference works in lesbian cultural studies and to struggle against erasure and invisibility. Circle of Lesbian Indexers, c/o Clare Potter, 2260 Yale St., Palo Alto, CA 94306.

Ongoing research on lesbian art and sensibility. Slides and archives. Book in progress will include chapter on lesbian art. Arlene Raven, Box 54335, Los Angeles, CA 90054.

Pre movement Lesbian Network. Oral history research. Toni Carcione and Pamella Farley, Lesbian Research Project of New York City. Pamella Farley, Women's Studies, Brooklyn College, Bedford Ave. and Avenue H, Brooklyn NY 11210.

Teaching and Learning about Lesbians and Gays. Two-hundred-and-fifty-page anthology with lesson plans for high-school and elementary classes. Will include personal experiences of lesbians and gay men during their school years and as teachers raising gay issues in their classrooms. Chapters for counselors, parents, and school activists. Grant from the MS. Foundation. Polly Kellogg, Director, Lesbian and Gay Curriculum Project, Education Exploration Center, Inc., Box 7339, Minneapolis, MN 55407. (612) 722-5705.

There's a Joker in the Menstrual Hut. Collection of lesbian-feminist anecdotes, aphorisms, stories, bumper stickers, et cetera. Unexpurgated anthology of our oral tradition. Cartoons and written or taped submissions welcomed.

Making Light. Collection of essays exploring radical lesbian feminist humor and examining use of humor as empowering and bonding force for women. Kate Clinton, 17 Williams St., Cazenovia, NY 13035. (315) 655–9591.

Book on Third World Lesbian Visual Artists. Robin Christian, 314 E. 91st St., New York, NY 10028.

Videotapes of Speeches for Symposia at AAAS Conference, (American Association for the Advancement of Science), January 1979: "Feminism and the Philosophy of Science" and "Women and Scientific Research." Speakers: Adrienne Rich, Mary Daly, Beverly Smith, Leigh Star, Janice Raymond, Barbara duBois, Pat Hynes, Lynda Birke, Denise Connors, Susan Cavin, Sandra Harding, and Sarah Hoagland. Robin Linden is seeking funding to make fifty-minute program from the videotapes. 121 B Corbett, San Francisco CA 94114.

Why Women Marry. Anthology. Edited by Julia Penelope and Susan J. Wolfe. Julia Penelope, Dept. of Enlgish, University of Nebraska. Lincoln, NE 68588.

Yantras of Womanlove. A book of erotica. Tee Corinne. Rootworks, 2000 King Mt. Trail, Sunny Valley, OR 97497.

Unpublished works

Existed, Resisted, Survived: Researching Lesbian Historiography. Five-chapter paper exploring different issues for lesbian historians, e.g., how and why historians have distorted lesbian history. Eight-page bibliography. Heidi Beth Kormyn, 1704 William and Mary Common, Hillsborough, NJ 08876, or Lesbian Herstory Educational Foundation Inc., Box 1258, New York, NY 10116.

The Making of a Deviant: A Model for Androgyny. 225-page biography of a lesbian in her seventies. Monika Kehoe C/o CERES, Psychology Building, San Francisco State University, 1600 Holloway, San Francisco, CA.

The Treatment of Lesbianism in Fiction about Girls' Schools. Book length ms. covering French, German, English, and American literature. Includes bibliography. Ilana Ozer, 38 Gramercy Park, Apt. 4B, New York, NY 10010.

Uranian Worlds: An Annotated Bibliography of Lesbian and Gay Images in Science Fiction. Lyn Paleo and Eric Garber. (Boston: G.K. Hall) 1982. Includes introductions by Joanna Russ and Samuel Delany.

Appendix

Sample Syllabi From Courses on Lesbianism

Lesbian Literature

Barbara Smith
University of Massachusetts, Boston
Fall 1980

This course will focus primarily on contemporary lesbian-feminist writing. Works by lesbians of color will be emphasized as well as the issues of racism and classism in the women's movement. The work for the course will be fairly extensive reading assignments, journal entries (two pages typewritten) due following each unit, and a final group project presented in class.

    Class 1:   Introduction to course.

I. **Coming Out**
    Class 2:   Peg Cruikshank, *The Lesbian Path*.
    Class 3:   *The Lesbian Path*. In class discussion, we share our own coming out stories.

II. **Some Definitions of Lesbian Literature**
    Class 4:   June Arnold and Bertha Harris, "Lesbian Fiction: A Dialogue," *Sinister Wisdom*, Fall 1976.
              Bertha Harris, "What We Mean to Say: Notes toward Defining the Nature of Lesbian Literature," *Heresies*, Fall 1977.
              Elly Bulkin, " 'Kissing/Against the Light': A Look at Lesbian Poetry," *Radical Teacher*, December 1978.
              Barbara Smith, "Toward a Black Feminist Criticism," *Conditions: Two*, October 1977.
              Journal Due

III. **Forerunners: Pre-Feminist Lesbian Writing**
    Class 5:   Stories from *The Lesbian's Home Journal*.
              Ann Shockley, *The Black and White of It*.
    Class 6:   Lesbian "pulp" fiction. Slide presentation by Maida Tilchen.

IV. (A.) **Between a Rock and a Hard Place: The Writing of Lesbians of Color**
    Class 7:   Joan Gibbs, *Between a Rock and a Hard Place.*
               Poetry by Third World Lesbian Writers, e.g., Paula Gunn Allen,
               Gloria Anzaldúa, Stephanie Byrd, Sandra Maria Esteves, Willyce
               Kim, Cherríe Moraga Lawrence, Naomi Littlebear, Audre
               Lorde, Barbara Noda, Pat Parker, Lorraine Sutton.
               Journal Due
    Class 8:   Poetry by Third World Lesbian Writers continues

IV. (B.) **Roadblocks and Bridges: Racism in the Women's Movement**
    Class 9:   Elly Bulkin, "Racism and Writing: Some Implications for
               White Lesbian Critics," *Sinister Wisdom* 13, Spring 1980.
               The Combahee River Collective Statement.
               Cherríe Moraga Lawrence, "La Güera," in *The Coming Out
               Stories.*
               Adrienne Rich, "Disloyal to Civilization: Feminism, Racism and
               Gynephobia," *On Lies, Secrets and Silence.*
    Class 10: Discussion of Bulkin, Combahee, Moraga Lawrence, and
               Rich continues.

IV. (C.) **Roadblocks and Bridges: Homophobia in the Black Community**
    Class 11: Charlotte Bunch, "Not for Lesbians Only," *Quest*, Fall 1975.
               Audre Lorde, "Scratching the Surface: Some Notes on Barriers to
               Women and Loving," *The Black Scholar*, April 1978.
               Cheryl Clarke, "Lesbianism as an Act of Resistance."
               "Keep Private Matters Private!" *Bay State Banner*, June 9, 1977.
               YeYe Akilimali Funua Olade, "Many A Lost Tomorrow: A Sister
               Speaks From Africa," *Black Male/Female Relationships.*
               Adrienne Rich, "Compulsory Heterosexuality," *Signs: Journal of
               Women in Culture and Society*, Fall 1980.
               Also see *The Black Scholar*, April 1978, March/April 1979, and
               May/June 1979.
               Proposal of Final Project Due

V. **The Power of the Erotic**
    Class 12: Amber Hollibaugh and Cherríe Moraga Lawrence, "What We're
               Rolling Around in Bed with: A Dialogue on Lesbian Sexuality."
               Becky Birtha, "Leftovers," *Sinister Wisdom*, Spring 1979.
               Becky Birtha, "Babies," *Azalea*, Winter 1979–80.
               Essays by Pat Califia and Gayle Rubin.
               Guest Speaker, Cherríe Moraga Lawrence: "Sexual Silences in
               Feminism."
               Journal Due
    Class 13: Susan D. Fleischmann, "Lesbian Erotica."
               Audre Lorde, *Uses of the Erotic: The Erotic as Power.*
               Poetry to be handed out.
    Class 14: Slide show by Lesbian photographers.

VI. **Roadblocks and Bridges: The Challenge of Difference**
    Class 15: Rosa Guy, *The Friends.*
               Journal Due
    Class 16: Guy, *The Friends.*
               Jo Sinclair, *The Changelings.*
    Class 17: Sinclair, *The Changelings.*

Class 18: Lorraine Bethel and Barbara Smith, eds., *Conditions: Five* (selections).

VII. **"What Will You Undertake?" The Ethical Vision**
Class 19: Judy Grahn, "A Woman is Talking to Death."
Adrienne Rich, "Hunger."
Adrienne Rich, "Power and Danger: Works of A Common Woman," from *On Lies, Secrets and Silence.*
Journal Due
Class 20: Grahn, "A Woman is Talking to Death."
Class 21: Audre Lorde, selected poems.
Pat Parker, "There Is a Woman in This Town" and "Where Will You Be?"
Adrienne Rich, "Women and Honor: Some Notes on Lying."
Assata Shakur, "Women in Prison: How We Are."
Class 22: Maureen Brady, "Grinning Underneath," *Conditions: One,* April 1977.
Birthalene Miller, "The Lonesomes Ain't No Spring Picnic," *Southern Exposure,* Generations of Women in the South, 4, no. 4.

VIII. **Visions: What Do We Want for the Future?**
Class 23: Discussion: How do we want to live; what do we dream of for ourselves; what kinds of cultural institutions do we need/want; what kind of lesbian literature do we want; what do we want to see happen in the women's movement?
Journal Due
Class 24: Catching up. Presentation of final projects.
Class 25: Final Projects.
Writing Assignment: Coming out Again, in What Ways Have We Changed?
Writing assignment due
Class 26: Final Projects.
Last day of class
Summing Up. Where we've been.

Books
Margaret Cruikshank, *The Lesbian Path.*
Ann Allen Shockley, *The Black and White of It.*
Joan Gibbs, *Between a Rock and a Hard Place.*
Audre Lorde, *Uses of the Erotic: The Erotic as Power.*
Rosa Guy, *The Friends.*
Lorraine Bethel and Barbara Smith, eds. *Conditions: Five.*

Lesbian Literature and Feminism

Cherríe Moraga Lawrence
San Francisco State University
Fall 1980

I. **Coming Out**

Class 1:   Group exercise—"Coming Out."
Class 2:   Modern Times book sales (bring checks).

II. Invisibility/Visibility in Lesbian Literature—Aesthetics and Criticism
Class 3:   Coming out stories due (three pages).
            Discuss Bulkin's "Some Implications for White Lesbian Critics."
            Discuss Smith's "Toward A Black Feminist Criticism."
Class 4:   Discuss Harris' "What We Mean to Say: Notes toward Defining the
            Nature of Lesbian Literature."
            Discuss Stanley and Wolfe's "Toward a Feminist Aesthetic."

III. Revolution in the Flesh—The Literature of Lesbians of Color.
Class 5:   Discuss selections from *Conditions: Five*
Class 6:   Introduce various Third World lesbian poets (Littlebear,
            Chrystos, Noda, Willyce, Tsui, Woo, Anzaldúa, et cetera)
First evening meeting—Poetry reading and discussion by lesbians of color
Class 7:   Discuss "Combahee River Collective Statement."
            Discuss "Hunger" by Adrienne Rich.
Class 8:   Discuss "Disloyal to Civilization: Feminism, Racism, and
            Gynephobia" by Rich.
            Discuss "Scratching the Surface: Some Notes on Barriers to
            Women & Loving" by Audre Lorde.
Class 9:   Group presentations on Third World lesbian writers.
            Class evaluations.
Class 10:   Same as previous class.

IV. If You're Poor, Then You're a Dyke—Class and Lesbianism.
Class 11:   Discuss "Our Right to Rebel" by Amber Hollibaugh.
            Selected poems from Karen Brodine's *Illegal Assembly.*
Class 12:   Selections from Judy Grahn's *The Work of A Common Woman.*

V. Feminism Is the Theory, Lesbianism Is the Practice
Class 13:   Discuss *The Dream of a Common Language* by Rich.
Class 14:   Continued previous class.
Class 15:   Discuss "Women and Honor: Some Notes on Lying" by Rich.
Class 16:   Discuss "Uses of the Erotic: The Erotic: The Erotic as Power" by
            Lorde.
Second evening meeting—Sexual Silences in Feminism. *Guest:* Amber
Hollibaugh on "Developing Sexual Theory." Erotic slide show.

VI. A Question of Ethics
"We left, as we have left all of our lovers/as all lovers leave all lovers/much
too soon to get the real loving done."—Judy Grahn.
Class 17:   "A Woman is Talking to Death" by Grahn.
Class 18:   Class panel on age and ablebodism. Selections from *Sinister
            Wisdom* 10.
Class 19:   Short Paper Due (3-5 pages): "Coming Out Again"—a response
            to "A Woman is Talking to Death"—class sharing and
            discussion.
Class 20:   Discussion on separatism versus coalition work.
Third evening meeting—*Sula.* Guest: Barbara Smith of Combahee River
Collective.
Class 21:   *Sula* continued.

VII. The Lesbian Utopia—The Function of Fantasy in Lesbian Literature
Class 22:   *The Wanderground.* Guest: Sally Gearhart

Class 23: *The Wanderground* continued.
Class 24: Day to spare.

VIII. **Not Somewhere Else, but Here—Toward a Redefinition of Feminist Lesbian Criticism.**
Class 25: Do class and color define people and politics?
What kind of lesbian literature do we need from here? What do you envision?
Class 26: Same as previous class.
Class 27: Group work for final papers.
Final evaluation.
Class 28: Same as previous class.
Fourth and last evening meeting—Party.
Friday, December 19: 10–15 page final critical paper due.

Work Expectations for the Course
To Read:
You are basically expected to read your brains out. Hopefully, how thoroughly you do so will be reflected by:
1) Class participation.
2) A Reader's Journal (which will be checked out by the instructor at least once during the semester).
And Write:
1) A two- to three-page "Coming Out" piece.
2) A three- to five-page "Coming Out Again" piece, in response to Grahn's poem.
3) A 10 to 15-page critical paper.

Required Texts
Lorraine Bethel and Barbara Smith, eds., *Conditions: Five.*
Toni Morrison, *Sula.*
Adrienne Rich, *The Dream of A Common Language.*
Judy Grahn, *A Woman Is Talking To Death.*
Sally Gearhart, *The Wanderground.*
Audre Lorde, *The Power of the Erotic.*

Required Articles
Zillah Eisenstein. "The Combahee River Collective Statement." In *Capitalist Patriarchy and a Case for Socialist Feminism* or *off our backs.*
Adrienne Rich. "Women and Honor: Some Notes on Lying." In *On Lies, Secrets and Silence.*
Barbara Smith. "Toward a Black Feminist Criticism." *Conditions: Two.*
Elly Bulkin, "Racism and Writing: Some Implications for White Lesbian Critics." *Sinister Wisdom* 13.
Julia Stanley and Susan Wolfe. "Toward a Feminist Aesthetic." *Chrysalis* 6.
Adrienne Rich. "Disloyal to Civilization: Feminism, Racism and Gynephobia." In *On Lies, Secrets and Silence.*
Monique Wittig. "One Is Not Born a Woman." Second Sex Conference 10/79.
Audre Lorde. "Scratching the Surface: Some Notes on Barriers to Women and Loving." *Black Scholar* 4/78.
Amber Hollibaugh. "Right to Rebel." Interview in *Gay Left* 9.
Bertha Harris. "What We Mean To Say: Notes Toward Defining the Nature of Lesbian Literature." *Heresies*, Fall 1979.

Adrienne Rich. "Compulsory Heterosexuality." *Signs* 5, no 4 (Summer 1980).
June Arnold and Bertha Harris. "Lesbian Fiction: A Dialogue." *Sinister Wisdom*
1, no. 2.

The Lesbian Novel

Joy Fisher
California State University, Long Beach
January 1978

Course Description

A survey course designed to introduce the student to novels from a literary and cultural tradition for which the basic research has only recently been accumulated. The novels are classics chosen for their importance in this tradition and for their depiction of a variety of lesbian lifestyles. Tracing the development of the genre in the Anglo-American tradition from the first decade of the twentieth century to the present, the course will examine the cultural and historical context out of which each novel developed. It will show how the portrayals of the lesbian experience changed from the early veiled representations (in Virginia Woolf, for example) to the more realistic depictions (in Rita Mae Brown) and will describe the social and political developments accompanying this change.

Lectures will also trace the publishing history of the genre, including the difficulty of finding publishers, the legal ramifications of publishing, and the reception of these novels by critics and the public. Information will also be provided about each author in order to understand the place of the novel in her personal history and the corpus of her work.

Knowledge of this tradition has hitherto been available to a small minority in academic circles. This course is an attempt to make this literary and cultural heritage accessible to a broader range of people in the university community. By participating in this lecture/discussion course, students will expand their understanding of a particular minority group and its literary history, and they will deepen their critical and analytical reading skills.

This one-semester course is aimed at upper division men and women students. It is an elective that could be used to fulfill requirements for the Women's Studies minor and Women's Studies option in American Studies. There are no prerequisites.

Course Outline

1. Introduction to the Course.
    The special role of fiction in transmitting experience; lesbian fiction, a definition; teaching methodology-studying literature within the context of its cultural history, getting to know the authors; structure of the course-lecture/discussion format; methods of evaluation; required and supplemental material.

2. The Lesbian Novel as Autobiography.
    Q.E.D., Gertrude Stein.

3. Fantasy as a Vehicle for the Lesbian Novel.
    The Treasure, Selma Lagerlof.
    Orlando, Virginia Woolf.

4. The Cause Célèbre—The Novel that Caused an Obscenity Trial.
    The Well of Loneliness, Radclyffe Hall.

5. The Novel Known as "The Novel With the Happy Ending."
The Price of Salt, Claire Morgan.

6. Jane Rule and The Critics.
Desert of the Heart, Jane Rule.

7. The Reluctant Publisher.
Patience and Sarah, Isabel Miller.

8. Interracial Lesbian Relationships.
Loving Her, Ann Shockley.

9. The Working-Class Lesbian in a Middle-Class Society.
Rubyfruit Jungle, Rita Mae Brown.
Yesterday's Lessons, Sharon Isabell.

10. Love After Menopause—The Aging Lesbian."
Sister Gin, June Arnold.

11. The Lesbian-Feminist Novel.
In Her Day, Rita Mae Brown.

Texts

Students will be required to read nine of the books cited above. Supplementary lecture material will be provided from the following books: *The Lesbian in Literature, A Bibliography*, Gene Dámon et al., eds.; *Radclyffe Hall at the Well of Loneliness*, Lovat Dickson; *Sex Variant Women in Literature*, Jeannette Foster; *Gay American History*, Jonathan Katz; *Woman + Woman*, Dolores Klaich; *Lesbian Images*, Jane Rule; *Focus: Lesbian Feminist Writing and Publishing*, a special issue of *Margins: A Review of Little Magazines and Small Press Books*; a special issue of lesbian writings and publishing, *Sinister Wisdom*, no. 13.

Additional supplementary material has been gathered by the instructor through interviews with contemporary authors.

Teaching methods: An introductory lecture will introduce each unit. A student discussion will follow the reading of each novel. From time to time lectures will be supplemented by guest speakers and tapes of authors speaking about their own writing.

Assignments and Evaluation

Students will be expected to read one of the selected novels each week. Small group discussions will focus on the reading, lectures, guest speakers, and tapes used to expand the material covered. At mid-term, students will be asked to turn in a written report analyzing an issue of interest to them arising out of the reading and discussions. The grade on this report will comprise 20 percent of the students' final grade. At the end of the course, the students will be expected to submit a term paper or a research paper approximately ten pages in length. In addition, there will be a final examination comprised of two essay questions of one hour each. The paper will receive a weight of 50 percent. The exam will receive a weight of 30 percent.

Course Purpose

This course represents an introduction to a relatively new body of knowledge for which basic research has only recently been accumulated. (See text list of supplemental books) Taken together, the novels selected are representative of a literary-cultural heritage which has hitherto been invisible to all but the most well-informed minority. The course is an attempt to make that literary tradition accessible to the general academic community. While similar courses are beginning to be taught elsewhere (the proposed instructor currently teaches this course in the extension program at the Women's Building in Los Angeles, and Dr. Judith McDaniel has taught a similar course at Skidmore College), no similar course currently exists at California State University, Long Beach.

Sample Lecture Outline

"The Cause Célèbre: Radclyffe Hall and the Obscenity Trials of *The Well of Loneliness*.

I. **Introduction.**
   A. Many people, gay and straight, have stories to tell that begin: "Well, when I read *The Well of Loneliness*..."
      1. Stories of the students who have previously read this novel.
      2. My story.
      3. Stories of other people:
         a. Barbara Gittings
         b. Del Martin
         c. Maya Angelou
         d. Anonymous, from a city in Florida.
   B. The reason this book became so well known.

II. **Radclyffe Hall.**
   A. Biographical information—similarities and differences between Radclyffe Hall and Stephen Gordon.
   B. Radclyffe Hall's literary work.
      1. Her poetry and songwriting.
      2. Her early novels, with emphasis on *The Unlit Lamp*, which is often called a "forerunner of *The Well of Loneliness*"
      3. Her literary honors:
         a. *The Prix Femina*
         b. *The James Tait Black Prize.*
   C. Radclyffe Hall's decision to write *The Well of Loneliness.*
      1. Tenor of the times—the post-World War I era and the emancipation of women in general and lesbians in particular.
      2. The literary climate—comparison with Virginia Woolf's *Orlando* and Compton MacKenzie's *Extraordinary Women.*
      3. The scientific models:
         a. Krafft-Ebing and Karl Heinrich Ulrichs.
         b. A forward to the book by Havelock Ellis.

III. **Publication and Reception of the Book.**
   A. Finding a publisher.
      1. Early rejections.
      2. Jonathan Cape.
   B. Complications.
      1. "A Book that Must be Suppressed"—the editorial in the *London Sunday Times.*
      2. The ruling of the Home Secretary.
      3. Seizure by customs officials.
   C. The obscenity trial in Great Britain.
      1. The law—the Obscene Publications Act of 1861.

        2. The trial and ruling of the court.
    D. The obscenity trial in the United States.
        1. Finding a publisher willing to defend the book.
        2. The complaint of John S. Sumner, secretary of the Society for the
            Suppression of Vice.
        3. The trial and appeal.
    E. Aftermath.
        1. Sales and translation of the book into other languages.
        2. The personal cost:
            a. Some examples of how Radclyffe Hall was held up to public
                ridicule.
            b. Development of stigmata on her hands during the writing of her
                next book.

Sample Topics for Short Papers

- Is *The Well of Loneliness* a "pro-lesbian" novel as Radclyffe Hall intended it to
  be, or an anti-homosexual book, as many modern readers judge it to be?
- What is the social cost to Therese in *The Price of Salt* of acting on her feelings
  for Carole? The social cost to Carole?
- What personal significance does the following quotation have for Evelyn in
  Desert of the Heart?

        Now I know why Eros,
        of all the progeny of
        Earth and Heaven, has
        been most dearly loved.

  Support your interpretation by references to other passages in the book.

Sample Topics for Critical Essays

- Interracial complications in *Loving Her*.
- Working-class perspectives: A comparison of Molly Bolt and Sharon Isabell.
- Lesbian love at seventy: An analysis of ageism in *Sister Gin*.
- The generation gap: as depicted in *The Price of Salt, The Desert of the Heart*
  and/or *In Her Day*.
- Toward a new vision: The feminist perspective in *Sister Gin* and/or *In Her
  Day*.

Sample Topics for Research Papers

- Natalie Barney and Other American Expatriate Lesbians in Paris during the
  1920s.
- Lesbian novels of the 1930s (1940s, or 1950s): An Overview.
- Lesbian Novels: The German (or French, or British) Tradition.
- Establishment Critics: Some Common Reactions to the Lesbian novel.
- Portraits of "The Old Butch" in American Lesbian Novels.
- An annotated bibliography of selected lesbian novels (including a content-
  analysis design for examination of printed materials).
- Toward a Feminist Theory of Criticism: Developing Standards for Judging the
  Lesbian novel.
- Changing Attitudes: The Impact of Reading Lesbian Novels on the Attitudes of
  Heterosexuals (or on the Attitudes of Lesbians).
- Alternative Publishers and Distribution Networks: Some Accomplishments,
  Some Needs.

Sample Final Exam Questions

Discuss the changing treatment of love scenes in the novels we have read; suggest reasons for the changes and postulate effects upon the heterosexual reader and importance to the lesbian reader. What is a lesbian? Discuss the diversity of lesbian lifestyles as revealed in the novels we have read.

Twentieth-Century Lesbian Novels

Julia Penelope
University of Nebraska
Spring 1981

[introductory paragraph omitted—ED.]

With some exceptions, e.g., *The Coming Out Stories*, the books listed will be read in the order in which they were published, to give a sense of the historical development of lesbian self-concepts.

Class 1:   Introduction to the course; bibliographical information; discussion of Toni McNaron's "Finding and Studying Lesbian Culture" in *Women's Studies Newsletter*; defining lesbian culture and the role of literature.
Introduction of the idea of asymmetrical reciprocity borrowed from Sandra Ott's "Blessed Bread, 'First Neighbors' and Asymmetric Exchange in the Basque Country," *Arch. europ. sociol.* 11 (1980): 40–58.

Class 2:   *The Coming Out Stories* (Persephone Press, 1980).
Establishing the lesbian community.
Jane Gurko's "The Shape of the Sameness," paper delivered at MLA, December 1980, Houston.
The lesbian as cultural hero.
Joan Larkin's "Coming Out." *Ms* magazine.
Letter written in July 1976 *Ms.* that started *The Coming Out Stories*; copies of four form letters sent to contributors to COS.

Class 3:   Lillian Faderman and Brigitte Eriksson, eds., *Lesbian-Feminism in Turn-of-the-Century Germany* (Tallahassee, Florida: Naiad Press, 1980).
The "discovery" of lesbianism in the late nineteenth century; the social and historical context of Hall's *The Well of Loneliness*.
Lecture on Lillian Faderman's *Surpassing the Love of Men* (Morrow 1981).

Class 4:   Radclyffe Hall, *The Well of Loneliness*, 1928.
Faderman's article in *Conditions* on *The Unlit Lamp*.
Gene Damon's (Barbara Grier) "'Tis Virtue, and not Birth, that makes us Noble: Radclyffe Hall."
Excerpts from male psychologists: Krafft-Ebing, Havelock Ellis, Frank Caprio

Class 5:   Arno reprint of Ann Bannon's *Journey to a Woman*, first published 1960. O.P. Excerpts xeroxed from: *Journey to A Woman*; Alain Abby, *Libido Beach*; Donna Richards, *Women Like Me*; Dale Greggsen, *Dark Triangle*; Claire Morgan, *The Price of Salt*; Anna E. Weirauch, *Of Love Forbidden* (orig. *The Scorpion*); Richard C. Robertiello, *Voyage From Lesbos: The Psychoanalysis of a Female Homosexual*.

Essays: "Some Pulp Sappho" by Maida Tilchen and Fran Koski, in *Margins* (June 1975) and in *Lavender Culture* (eds. Jay and Young); "The Realistic Novel" by Valerie Taylor and "The Lesbian Paperback" by Barbara Grier, both in *The Lesbian's Home Journal* (eds. Grier & Reid).

Class 6:   Paula Christian, *Edge of Twilight*, reprinted Timely Books, first published 1959.

Joan Nestle's "Butch-Fem Relationships: Sexual Courage in the 1950s," *Heresies* (Spring 1981).

Class 7:   Rita Mae Brown, *Rubyfruit Jungle* (Daughters, 1974). Now published by Bantam (1977) and sold in airports.

Bonnie Zimmerman's "Exiting from Patriarchy: The Lesbian Novel of Development." In *Formation/Deformation/Transformation: The Female Novel of Development*, edited by Elizabeth Abel, Marianne Hirsch, and Elizabeth Langland (forthcoming).

Class 8:   Kate Millett, *Flying*, 1974.

Class 9:   *Flying* continued. Introduction to *Flying*; Annette Kolodny's "The Lady's Not for Spurning," in Jelinek's *Women's Autobiography*; Penni Stewart's "He Admits...But She Confesses," *WSIQ* 3 (1980); and my "Fear of *Flying*?" in *Sinister Wisdom* 2.

Class 10:   Sharon Isabell, *Yesterday's Lessons*, 1974. First published by The Women's Press Collective, now distributed by Diana Press.

Judy Grahn's "Murdering the King's English" in *True to Life Adventure Stories*, vol I.

Class 11:   Ann Shockley, *Loving Her*, first published 1974.

Class 12:   June Arnold, *Sister Gin* (Daughters 1975).

As a "bridge" between *Sister Gin* and *The Wanderground* the students read Ti-Grace Atkinson's "Strategy and Tactics" from the collection of her essays *Amazon Odyssey* (New York: Link Books, 1974), pp. 135–189.

Class 13:   Sally Gearhart, *The Wanderground*, (Persephone Press, 1979).

Class 14:   Donna Camille, *The Bra-Strap Bar and Grill*, (self-published, 1979).

Class 15:   Monique Wittig, *Lesbian Peoples: Material for a Dictionary* (Avon, 1979).

Class 16:   Wrap-up; defining lesbian community; ten-page term paper due; journals due; take home final.

The Lesbian in Literature, Honors Tutorial

Joan Nestle
Queens College, CUNY, Flushing, NY
1975

An appreciation, a cherishing, a sharing, an understanding, a touch, a thought, a battle, a growing.

Descriptions of Literature
A book a book telling why when at once and at once
A book which mentions all the people who have had individual chances to come again.
A book describing Edith and Mary and flavouring fire.
A book which chanced to be the one universally described as energetic.
A book more than ever needed.
A book of dates and fears.
A book which asks questions of everyone.
A book more than ever a description of happiness and as you were.
A book which makes a play of daughter and daughters.
A book which plans homes for any of them.
All of this is a beginning and a continuing.

—Gertrude Stein

Bibliographies

1. Damon, Gene; Jordan, Robin; and Watson, Jan; eds. *The Lesbian in Literature*. Reno, Nevada: 1975. All known novels, short stories, short novels, poetry, drama, nonfiction work since 1907. [Third edition published 1981 by the Naiad Press—ED.]

2. Foster, Jeannette. *Sex Variant Women in Literature*. New edition comes out from Diana Press in 1975. A pioneer work.

3. Kuda, M.J. *Women Loving Women: A Bibliography*. Chicago: Lavender Press, 1974.

4. Rule, Jane. *Lesbian Images*. New York: Doubleday, 1975.

Class Readings

Class 1: *Patience and Sarah*, Isabel Miller.

Class 2: *Rubyfruit Jungle, Songs to a Handsome Woman, The Hand that Cradles the Rock*, Rita Mae Brown.

Class 3: *Lavender Papers 2: An Analysis of Lesbian Oppression*, New York Women's School; *Well of Loneliness*, Radclyffe Hall (discussion will include reviews, biography, trial).

Class 4: *This Is Not For You*, Jane Rule; *The Price of Salt*, Claire Morgan *Carol in a Thousand Cities*, Ann Aldrich; *Diana*, Diana Fredericks.

Class 5: A selection of lesbian poetry, including:
      a. Sappho (Barnard Translation).
      b. Pat Parker.

    c. Judy Grahn (*Edward the Dyke*).
    d. May Sarton.
    e. Audre Lorde.

Class 6:   *Les Guérilleres, Lesbian Body*, Monique Wittig; "When It Changed,"
    Joanna Russ (in *Dangerous Visions*); selection from *The Ladies Alma-
    nack*, Djuna Barnes.

Class 7:   *Yesterday's Lessons*, Sharon Isabell; *Mrs. Stevens Hears the Mermaids
    Singing* (read intro.) May Sarton.

Class 8:   *Loving Her*, Ann Shockley; *Lesbians Speak Out; Loving Women; Fly-
    ing*, Kate Millett; *The World is Round*, Gertrude Stein; selection of
    letters from Alice B. Toklas' *Staying on Alone;* if desired, *The Autobiog-
    raphy of Alice B. Toklas*, Gertrude Stein; selections from *Gullible's
    Travels*, Jill Johnston.

Class 9:   *Lesbianism and the Women's Movement*, edited by Nancy Myron and
    Charlotte Bunch; sharing of archive tapes, a gift to the future.

Class 10: Future visions: ritual, myth, power.

Everyone will be expected to contribute to the Lesbian Herstory Archives in the
form of tapes, poems, papers, bibliographies, graphics, photographs.

[The syllabus also includes a supplementary reading list and a list of periodicals—
ED.]

Lesbian Culture

Evelyn Beck
University of Wisconsin
1980

This course will explore lesbian culture(s) in Europe and the United States, with
an emphasis on the contemporary lesbian-feminist scene. We will raise such
theoretical questions as: What is lesbian culture? By whom is it created? For whom?
How has it been distributed and made known? What is its relationship to "mainstream" culture and to the culture of other minority groups? Can we meaningfully
speak of a lesbian aesthetic? A lesbian sensibility? If so, how have these changed in
varying social and political contexts? We will apply these theoretical questions to
the productions of lesbian artists in the genres of fiction, poetry, film, biography,
the visual arts, and music.

I. Historical Backgrounds and Theoretical Questions
    Week 1: *Why study lesbian culture? What is lesbian culture?* To what
    extent can we speak of a unfied lesbian culture disregarding
    factors of race, class, religion, ethnicity, education, age, and other
    differentiations among lesbians? Where and when has lesbian
    culture thrived? How has survival been possible?
    Readings in: Sidney Abbot and Barbara Love, *Sappho Was A Right-
    On Woman*. Vida, *Our Right to Love*.

Week 2: *The Past in the Present.* The myths about lesbians: What are they? How do they function? How do they affect lesbian creativity and productivity? The impact of feminism on lesbian culture; the impact of lesbian culture of feminist theory.
Readings in: Julia Stanley and Susan Wolfe, *The Coming Out Stories.* Adrienne Rich, *Women and Honor: Some Notes on Lying.*
Slide-tape show: Lavender Horizons, *Woman-Loving Women.*

II. Backgrounds to Contemporary Lesbian Culture
Week 3: *Female Friendships and the Paris groups/Passing Women in the United States. Coded Tests.*
Readings in: Gertrude Stein, *Tender Buttons.* Djuna Barnes, *Ladies Almanack.* Preface to *Miss Marks and Miss Wooley.* Doris Faber, *The Life of Lorena Hickok, E.R.'s Friend*
Week 4: *The visual arts:* The work of Romaine Brooks, Harriet Hosmer, and Mary Ann Willson.
Readings in Jonathan Katz, *Gay American History.*
Week 5: *Breaking Silence:* 1928, Radclyffe Hall, *The Well of Loneliness.*

III. Contemporary Lesbian Culture
Week 6: *Breaking Silence Again:* 1973, Rita Mae Brown, *Rubyfruit Jungle.*.
Week 7: *Lesbian Images in Photography.*
Slides of work by Beenice Abbott, Alice Austin, JEB, Tee Corinne.
Readings in: *Heresies* (Lesbian art issue). *The Blatant Image,* issue #1.
Week 8: *Lesbian Film-makers and Their Films.*
Jan Oxenberg, *Home Movie; A Comedy in Six Unnatural Acts.*
Barbara Hammer, *Dyketactics, Superdyke.*
Week 9: *The lesbian contribution to "women's" culture.*
Music and lyrics by Alix Dobkin; Linda Shear; Meg Christian; Holly Near.
Humor by Maxine Feldman; Robin Tyler.
Spirituality and women's music: Kay Gardner.

IV. Issues in Lesbian Culture
Week 10: *Class.*
Readings: Sharon Isabell, *Yesterday's Lessons.* Judy Grahn, *True to Life Adventure Stories* Vol-1.
Week 11: *Race.*
Readings in: Ann Shockley, *The Black and White of It.* Poetry by Audre Lorde, Pat Parker; essay by the Combahee River Collective; music by Sweet Honey in the Rock.
Week 12: *Anti semitism.*
Readings in: Evelyn Beck, *Nice Jewish Girls: A Lesbian Anthology.* Poetry by Martha Shelley; Irene Klepfisz.
Week 13: *Lesbian Motherhood.*
Film: *In the Best Interests of the Children*
Readings in: Jan Clausen, *Mother, Daughter, Sister, Lover.*
Week 14: *Aging:* June Arnold, *Sister Gin.*
Poetry by Elsa Gidlow; May Sarton.
SAGE Writings; Film: *A World of Light:* portrait of May Sarton.
Week 15: *The Erotic and Relationships.*
Readings: Audre Lorde, "The Erotic as Power." Poetry by Rich, Lorde, Larkin, Parker.

Texts

Sidney Abbott and Barbara Love, *Sappho Was A Right-On Woman*
Ginny Vida, *Our Right to Love.*
Julia P. Stanley and Susan J. Wolfe, eds., *The Coming Out Stories.*
Adrienne Rich, *Women and Honor.*
Jonathan Katz, *Gay American History.*
Radclyffe Hall, *The Well of Loneliness.*
Rita Mae Brown, *Rubyfruit Jungle.*
The Blatant Image: A Magazine of Feminist Photography.
Sharon Isabell, *Yesterday's Lessons.*
Ann Shockley, *The Black and White of It.*
Evelyn Beck, *Nice Jewish Girls.*

Recommended

Lillian Faderman, *Surpassing the Love of Men.*
Nancy Toder, *Choices.*
Paula Christian, *The Other Side of Desire.*
Conditions: Five. The Black woman's issue.

Films

Home Movie.
Dyketactics.
Superdyke.
A Comedy in Six Unnatural Acts.
In the Best Interests of the Children.
A World of Light.

Women's Studies College 265: Lesbianism

Madeline Davis
State University of New York At Buffalo,
Fall, 1972

Introduction
> Class 1: Introductions.
> > Term projects.
> > Syllabus.
> Class 2: Coming Out: Guilt, Fear, Joy.
> > "It Just Happened"—Womankind.
> > "As it was in the beginning"—Davis.
> > "Section II, Section IV" Ellen Chambers "Lesbianism, a political, cultural, and personal view" from *Notes from a personal journal.*

Literature
> Class 3: Radclyffe Hall, *The Well of Loneliness.*
> Class 4: Novels from the 1950s.
> > Ann Aldrich, *Take A Lesbian to Lunch.*
> Class 5: Isabel Miller, *Patience and Sarah.*

Lifestyles
> Class 6: Myths and Theories of Lesbianism.
> > Charlotte Wolff, *Love Between Women.* Chapter 3.

Radicalesbians, "Woman Identified Woman."
Hope Thompson, "Sex & Sexuality" *The Ladder* March, 1972.
Ellen Chambers, Part 1.
Class 7: Role Playing, Sexuality, the Bar.
Del Martin and Phyllis Lyon, *Lesbian/Woman*. Chapter 3
Ellen Chambers, Part 3
Katz, "Macho & Monogamy"
"Up from the Butch Trip"
Class 8: Class Differences.
Furies 3 and 4
Class 9: The Black Lesbian.
Class 10: The Lesbian Mother.
Martin and Lyon, *Lesbian/Woman*. Chapter 5.

The Movement
Class 11: History and Development.
Martin and Lyon, *Lesbian/Woman*. Chapter 3.
Sidney Abbott and Barbara Love, *Sappho Was A Right-On Woman*
chapter 5

Toward a Women's Culture
Class 12: Poems, music, art, submitted by class.

Male Supremacy and Sexual Repression
Class 13: Abbott and Love, *Sappho Was A Right-On Woman* Chapters 8 and 9
Articles.
Pornography.
Class 14: Term projects.
Evaluation.

Heterosexism and the Oppression of Women

Melanie Kaye
University of New Mexico
Spring 1981

Texts
Del Martin and Phyllis Lyon, *Lesbian/Woman*.
Blanche Cook, *Women and Support Networks*.
Jonathan Katz, *Gay American History*.
Toni Morrison, *Sula*.
Karla Jay and Allen Young, *Out of the Closets*.
June Arnold, *Sister Gin*.
Plus handouts.

Week 1: Introduction: definitions, assumptions, explanations, et cetera.

History
Week 2: Burial and Excavation.
Read: Katz—Introduction, Trouble, and Native Americans/Gay
Americans, sections marked ♀, and pp. 139-160. Bass, Faderman,
Duggan, Schwartz (2), Smith, Grahn, Roberts, Grier, Lorde.

Week 3: Female Bonding (women's culture)
   Read: Cook; Smith-Rosenberg, Corinne, Smith, Lorde; start *Sula.*
Week 4: Making Taboo.
   Read: Finish *Sula*, Katz—treatment (sections marked   esp.);
   Faderman, Eriksson, Dworkin, Birtha.

Lesbian Possibility
Week 5: Experience Before the Liberation Movements.
   Read: Katz—Resistance & Love (sections marked ♀), Start
   Lesbian/Woman; Bulkin & Lunden, Lorde, Miller, Taylor.
Week 6: Women's Liberation/Gay Liberation.
   Read: *Closets*, pp. 4-34; 170-250; 290-93; Myron & Bunch (intro.),
   Berson, Reid, Cornwell, Parker.
Week 7: Coming Out.
   Read: *Sister Gin, Lesbian Woman*; Smith, Malinowitz, Pratt, and
   other handouts (later).
Week 8: Lesbian/Woman.
   Read: finish *Lesbian/Woman, Closets*, pp. 122–41; Mays, Martin.
Week 9: Lesbian/Feminist Culture;
   Read: *Closets* pp. 284-87; Rich, "Silence" panel, Hull, Shockley, Kaye
   (2), Schive & Becker, Hagen, Hodges, Nestle and Edel.

Normative Effects of Heterosexism
Week 10: Dykebaiting & Suppression of Women.
   Read: "Normative status. . . . " Deevey, Wughalter, & other handouts.
   (later).
Week 11: Heterosexism, Science & Ecology.
   Read: *Closets* pp. 157-65; handouts (later).

Themes
Week 12: Roles & Costumes.
   Read: Katz—*Passing Women*; Cliff.
Week 13: Mothers, Sisters.
   Read: Smith, Rich, Lorde, Michaels, Raymond, other handouts.
Week 14: Love & Sexuality
   Read: Koedt, Hite, Rule, Kaye, other handouts.

Strategies
Week 15: Lesbian/Heterosexual Conflict.
   Read: Cornwell, Zita, Frye, Koedt; in class; role play.
Week 16: Future Projections.
   To be decided.

Assignments Due Each Week
2—Bring a clue from your family history.
3—Make a list in the form: "With women (a woman), I . . . "
4—When/how did you learn fear/shame about love between women, about
   "queers"?
5—What did you know about lesbians before the late sixties? What did you
   think?
6—What were you doing? What did you hear, know, think?
7—Fantasize coming out: to yourself; friends, family; at work; school; et cetera.
8—Go through a day "as" a lesbian, or as a heterosexual (whichever you
   aren't); keep notes.
9—To be decided.
10—To be decided.

11—Imagine the world you want; go as large as you can.
12—Bring to class two sets of clothing, 1 "female," 1 "male."
13—To be decided.
14—Write up "How I went straight" or "How I went gay," whichever.
15—List issues of conflict or difference.

Relationships Between Women

Ann Schroeder, Niki Rockwell
Goddard/Cambridge
Spring 1980

"the crucial test of feminism in a work is the presence of at least two women who are friendly. Not one, and not two who are rivals. Male works which try (sometimes honestly) to be feminist almost invariably focus on the woman-man couple or the one woman among male colleagues. The secret of feminism is what happens when women talk to women, advise women, love women. The two may be lovers, friends, or friendly strangers, or friendly colleagues, but this is the absolute precondition for (a) feminism and (b) truth."

—Joanna Russ
"Feminist Science Fiction"
Sojourner—July 1979.

Class 1: Introduction.
Discussion about class, expectations, et cetera.
Go over reading list.
Discuss readings.

Unit One: Love and Ritual
Carroll Smith-Rosenberg. "The Female World of Love and Ritual: Relations between Women in Nineteenth Century America, An Ethnohistorical Inquiry." *Signs*: 1 no. 1, 1975.
"Friendship Among Women." In *What Can Women Do?*, 1893. Written by Alice E. Ives; edited by Mrs. M.L. Rayne.
Class 2: Sarah Orne Jewett. "Martha's Lady." In *Country of the Pointed Firs*.
Isabel Miller. *Patience and Sarah*. Chapters 1–3,
Jeanette Lee. "The Cat and the King." *Lesbian Home Journal*.
Olga Broumas. "Song for Sanna."
Amy Lowell. "A Sprig of Rosemary," "Madonna of the Evening Flowers," and "In Excelsius." In *Selected Poems of Amy Lowell*.
Class 3: Sarah Orne Jewett, "Miss Tempy's Watchers."
Sally Miller Gearhart. "The Telling of the Days of Artilidea." In *The Wanderground*.
Judith Katz. "This is About How Lesbians Capture Straight Women & Have Their Way With Them," In *Coming Out Stories*.
Sandy Boucher. "Mountain Radio." In *Assaults and Rituals*.

Unit Two: Lies and Silences
Class 4: Michelle Cliff. "Speechlessness." *Sinister Wisdom*.
Sandy Boucher. "Retaining Walls."
Mary Wilkins Freeman "A Gala Dress." In *The Revolt of the Mother and Other Stories*.
excerpt—Lillian Smith, *Killers of the Dream*.

Class 5: Tillie Olsen. "I Stand Here Ironing." In *Tell Me A Riddle.*
Gabrielle Vivian Bertrand "Betty George." In *Lesbian Home Journal.*
Maureen Brady. "Grinning Underneath," *Conditions: One.*
Class 6: Adrienne Rich. "To A Dead Woman in her Forties." In *A Dream of a Common Language.*
Maureen Brady, excerpt—*Give Me Your Good Ear.*
Kate Chopin. "Lilacs." In *American Voices: American Woman.*

Unit Three: Struggles

Class 7: Cherríe Moraga Lawrence. "La Guera." *Coming Out Stories.*
Becky Birtha. "Leftovers." *Sinister Wisdom 9.*
Zora Neale Hurston. *Their Eyes Were Watching God.* Chapter 2.
Toni Morrison. "Winter." In *The Bluest Eye.*
Class 8: Alice Walker. "Everyday Use." *In Love and Trouble.*
Willa Cather. "Old Mrs. Harris." *Obscure Destinies.*
Mary Wilkins Freeman. "Louisa." *The Revolt of Mother.*
Class 9: Tillie Olsen. "O Yes."
Rosa Guy. *Friends.* Chapters 6, 7, 9, 13, 14.
Esther Newton and Shirley Walton. *Womenfriends: A Soap Opera,* pp. 13–20.
Louisa May Alcott. "The Servant." In *Work.*

Unit Four: Truthtelling

Class 10: Adrienne Rich. "Women and Honor: Some Notes on Lying."
Audre Lorde. "Silence." *Sinister Wisdom 6.*
Lorraine Bethel. "What Chou Mean We, White Girl?" *Conditions 5,*
Birthalene Miller. "Lonesomes Ain't No Springtime Picnic." In *Generations.*
Susan Glaspell. "Jury of Her Peers." In *American Voices: American Woman.*
Class 11: Sherry Thomas. "The Shape of Things to Come." *Sinister Wisdom 8.*
June Arnold. *Sister Gin.* Chapter 12.
Hadley Irwin. "Afraid." *Sinister Wisdom.*
Becky Birtha. "Babies." *Azalea.*
Olga Broumas. "Artemis."
Class 12: Agnes Smedley. "Silkworkers." In *Portraits of Chinese Women.*
Sally Miller Gearhart. "Gatherstretch." In *The Wanderground.*
Olga Broumas. "Calypso," *Beginning With O.*
June Arnold. *Sister Gin.* Chapter 13,
Adrienne Rich "Phantasia for Elvira Shatayev." In *Dream of a Common Language.*
Final Evaluation

Bibliography

Books

Lyndall MacCowan

The following bibliography is intended as a guide to instructors who wish to teach a course on lesbianism—whether it is a literature, history, theory, or culture/aesthetics course. It is by no means a complete or exhaustive review of the books by or about lesbians or lesbianism. I have limited it to books which are 1) Written by women, with the exception of the biography section and a few books co-edited by men and women; 2) Books which are currently in print, although this status may change for a few works by the time *Lesbian Studies* is available. I have tried to avoid some of the screamingly negative or stereotypical works; however, this quickly becomes a matter of personal taste and politics. Even "negative" books can be of use if taught in the proper context; when in doubt, I have tried to be inclusive rather than exclusive. Further, I have limited this bibliography to works which are primarily lesbian in content or viewpoint, although, again, there are a few exceptions when the work is of value in a lesbian course for other reasons (e.g., Cecelia Holland's *Floating Worlds*, while not primarily lesbian, has exceptional potential for use in a feminist science fiction/fantasy course).

Only the fiction section has annotations, due to space limitations, and then only brief ones. In lieu of extensive commentary I have organized books into sections so as to be as self-explanatory as possible. I did not have a chance to review works which appeared as *Lesbian Studies* was going to press, or books which are self-published and sporadically available. The publication data with each book is that of the *most recent edition.* Books with two publishers indicate a hardback and a paperback edition; books with one indicate a paperback (although a hardback edition may have preceded it), or a hardback edition that was followed by a paperback from the same publisher the following year. Early works that have been recently reprinted are listed with the latest edition first, and the original publication date is given in parentheses.

Although the lesbian presses are beginning to print works which include Third World women, racism is still inherent in our movement, and this is reflected by the scarcity of available books. Teachers and students should refer to JR Roberts's *Black Lesbian: An Annotated Bibliography* (Naiad Press); *This Bridge Called My Back,* edited by Cherríe Moraga and Gloria Anzaldúa (Persephone Press); the special issues of *Conditions* and *off our backs; Azalea*; and to Barbara Smith's and Cherríe Moraga's article and syllabi in this book. Teachers and students should also see Lillian Faderman's *Surpassing the Love of Men*, an overview of lesbian literature in an historical context and Jeannete Foster's *Sex Var-*

iant Women in Literature, which reviews every known work through 1954. Barbara Grier's third edition of *The Lesbian in Literature* is invaluable to anyone doing detailed research on lesbian literature. In some entries, I use Foster's term "variant," to mean relationships that are not sexual or explicitly sexual, or characters who do not consciously identify themselves as lesbians.

All the books listed here should be available from the local women's bookstore. Some of the rarer works can be obtained by mail from Woman-Books (201 West 92nd Street, New York, NY 10025), Old Wives Tales (1009 Valencia St., San Francisco, CA. 94110), or A Woman's Place (4015 Broadway, Oakland, CA 94611). Women's publications such as *Conditions, Signs, Frontiers, Chrysalis, Sinister Wisdom, off our backs,* and *Plexus* carry reviews of recent lesbian works, or materials of use in lesbian studies classes. Updates of new books, archival material, and academic papers can be obtained from WomanBooks, the Lesbian Herstory Archives in New York, and the Lesbian-Feminist Study Clearinghouse. For further material, see the Resources section in this book.

This bibliography is divided into Fiction and Nonfiction sections. Fiction includes: Mystery/Suspense/Occult, Romance, Young Adults, Short Stories, Early Books (before 1950), Paperback Originals from the 1950s and 1960s, Mainstream Novels (since 1950), New Feminism/Experimental Work, and Drama. Nonfiction comprises: Bibliographies and Resource Books, Anthologies from Lesbian Magazines, Sexuality and Erotica, Art, Poetry, Poetry Anthologies, Biography and Autobiography (by subject), Biography and Autobiography (by author), and Essays, Theories, and Analysis. If you cannot locate a book in one section, try another. See, too, the bibliographies in other sections of this book, in the articles by Poor, Hickok, Roberts, and Zimmerman.

FICTION

Science Fiction/Utopian Fiction

Bradley, Marion Zimmer. *The Ruins of Isis.* New York: Pocket, 1978. A woman anthropologist and her husband visit a matriarchal planet.

Bryant, Dorothy. *The Kin of Ata Are Waiting for You.* San Francisco: Moon Books, 1971. A feminist (not lesbian) alternate-reality utopia.

Charnas, Suzy McKee. *Walk to the End of the World.* New York: Ballantine, 1974. A chilling vision of a post-holocaust future where men are the literal masters and women literal slaves.

Charnas, Suzy McKee. *Motherlines.* New York: Berkley, 1978. Sequel to *Walk.* A slave woman escapes her country and finds two societies of free women living in the desert. No male characters.

Gearhart, Sally. *The Wanderground.* Watertown, Massachusetts: Persephone Press, 1978. A lesbian-feminist utopian vision of a woman's society existing on the border of hostile partriarchal territory. A breakthrough.

Gilman, Charlotte Perkins. *Herland.* New York: Pantheon, 1979. (First published 1915.) An early feminist utopia (not lesbian) written at the turn of the century.

Gould, Lois. *A Sea Change.* New York: Avon, 1976. A woman is raped at gunpoint; in order to cope she metamorphoses into a man and perpetuates the same violence on other women. Controversial.

Holland, Cecelia. *Floating Worlds.* New York: Knopf, 1976; Pocket, 1977. A woman ambassador from anarchist Earth is sent to a dynastic Saturn which plans to rule the solar system. Lesbian content is minor, but explicit and crucial. Well written and challenging.

Lynn, Elizabeth A. *Watchtower.* New York: Berkley, 1979. First in the Chronicles of Tornor fantasy series. Supporting characters include two women lovers, disguised as men who serve as messengers.

Lynn, Elizabeth A. *The Northern Girl.* New York: Berkley, 1980. Third in the Tornor trilogy. Main character is a lesbian, as are several others in a matrilineal society three hundred years after *Watchtower.*

Lynn, Elizabeth A. *The Woman Who Loved the Moon and Other Stories.* New York: Berkley, 1981. Short-story collection, including title story, "Jubilee's Story," "Gods of Reorth," and "The Man Who Was Pregnant."

Piercy, Marge. *Woman On the Edge of Time.* New York: Fawcett, 1976. Is this incarcerated woman really crazy, or is she able to visit an alternate future? Searing indictment of patriarchal racism, classism, and psychiatric abuse of women.

Russ, Joanna. *The Female Man.* New York: Bantam, 1975. Three women from alternate times come together through the action of a fourth woman who lives on a planet engaged in a literal battle of the sexes. Major.

Russ, Joanna. "When It Changed." In *Again Dangerous Visions,* edited by Harlan Ellison. New York: Doubleday, 1972. Available in several feminist science fiction anthologies. The precursor to *Female Man.* Set on a women-only planet where the men are not missed.

Singer, Rochelle. *The Demeter Flower.* New York: St. Martin's, 1980. A heterosexual couple arrives at an all-woman settlement that has survived twentieth-century partriarchy and exacerbates an already existing conflict.

Wittig, Monique. *Les Guérilleres.* New York: Viking, 1971. Heavily impressionistic, symbolic, mythological story of a community of women living without men.

Young, Donna J. *Retreat! As It Was.* Tallahassee, Florida: Naiad Press, 1979. A feminist utopian fantasy.

Mystery/Suspense/Occult

Beal, M.F. *Angel Dance.* New York: Daughters, 1977. Lesbian-feminist suspense thriller featuring a Chicana detective.

Chambers, Jane. *Burning.* New York: Jove, 1978. Exceptional suspense tale of two women who find themselves reliving the lives of two women lovers who died during the Salem witch mania.

Christie, Agatha. *Nemesis.* New York: Dodd, Mead, 1971; Pocket, 1973. Content here is variant and somewhat negative. Woman guardian murders her ward rather than see her marry.

Cross, Amanda (pseudonyn of Carolyn Heilbrun). *Death in a Tenured Position.* New York: Dutton, 1981. Murder mystery with two lesbian characters.

Jackson, Shirley. *Hangsaman.* New York: Farrar, 1951; Ace, 1964. Horror story. Natalie is mad, but is the woman seducing her really another woman, or just a fragment of her own personality?

Jackson, Shirley. *The Haunting of Hill House.* New York: Viking, 1959; Popular Library, 1966. Four people are invited to solve the mystery of a haunted house. Strong lesbian overtones in two of the three women characters.

Jackson, Shirley. *We Have Always Lived in the Castle.* New York: Viking, 1962; Popular Library, 1963. A lesbian allegory of two sisters shut away in their house. Suspenseful.

Moyes, Patricia. *Many Deadly Returns.* New York: Holt, Rinehart & Winston, 1970; Dell, 1981. (Published in England as *Who Saw Her Die?*) An aging socialite is murdered for her inheritance. She has a life-long companion.

Rendell, Ruth. *From Doon With Death.* London: Long, 1964; Arrow, 1979. A woman takes revenge on the lover who spurned her for a man.

Sayers, Dorothy. *Unnatural Death.* London: NEL, 1977. (First published 1928 as *The Dawson Pedigree.*) An early "variant" novel. The lesbian is the murderess. Typical of its time.

Tey, Josephine. (pseudonym of Elizabeth McIntosh). *Miss Pym Disposes.* New York: Macmillan, 1947; Berkley, 1964. Devotion between two schoolgirls leads to murder.

Tey, Josephine (pseudonym of Elizabeth McIntosh). *To Love and Be Wise.* New York: Macmillan, 1950; Berkley, 1962. A mystery of attempted murder. Lesbian content is minor but central to the plot.

Yorke, Margaret. *Grave Matters.* London: Arrow, 1976. Murder occurs in a small English town. Central characters include a lesbian couple.

Zaremba, Eve. *A Reason To Kill.* Markham, Ontario: Paperjacks, 1978. A lesbian detective is hired to solve the murder of a gay male college student.

Romance

(All published by Naiad Press, Tallahassee, Florida)

Aldridge, Sarah (pseudonym of Anyda Marchant). *The Latecomer.* 1974. An older professor and a younger film editor find each other against a backdrop of international intrigue.

Aldridge, Sarah. *Tottie.* 1975. Set in the sixties.

Aldridge, Sarah. *Cytherea's Breath.* 1976. A period piece set in turn of the century Baltimore. A woman doctor and her patroness achieve a relationship only after much struggle.

Aldridge, Sarah. *All True Lovers.* 1978 To teenager women, living during the depression, remain raithful despite poverty and parental pressure.

Gapen, Jane. *Something Not Yet Ended.* Pagoda Press; distributed by Naiad Press, 1981. Autobiographical love story; sketches of Maine island life.

Ramstetter, Victoria A. *The Marquise and the Novice.* 1981. Lesbian gothic.

Taylor, Valerie. *Love Image.* 1977. A Hollywood star deserts fame and fortune for the woman she loves.

Young Adults

Guy, Rosa. *Ruby.* New York: Bantam, 1976.
Two black women in New York City, one native to Harlem, the other from the West Indies, become lovers while in high school. Traditional ending.

Hautzig, Deborah. *Hey, Dollface!* New York: Bantam, 1978. Two high school women explore the meaning of their "best friendship," including its lesbian implications. Best "young adults" book yet written. Highly recommended.

Knudson, R.R. *You Are the Rain.* New York: Delacorte, 1974.
Variant. Two high-school women, complete opposites, become attached to each other while lost in the Florida swamps.

Knudson, R.R. *Fox Running.* New York: Avon, 1975. Two women training for the Olympics develop a deeper-than-average friendship.

Levy, Elizabeth. *Come Out Smiling.* New York: Delacorte, 1981.

Reading, J.P. *Bouquets for Brimbal.* New York: Harper & Row, 1980.
Two best friends go to a summer theater workshop together. One is straight and somehow remains oblivious to her friend's lesbian lover. Lacks a certain plausibility.

Russ, Joanna. *Kittatinny.* New York: Daughters, 1978. A young woman embarks on an adventure and meets, among others, the Woman Warrior, the Little Mermaid, and Sleeping Beauty. Excellent fantasy.

Scoppettone, Sandra. *Happy Endings Are All Alike.* New York: Dell, 1978.
Two high school women are lovers. One is raped because she is a lesbian, and her lover leaves her rather than publicly acknowledge her love. Controversial.

Short Stories

Boucher, Sandy. *Assaults and Rituals.* Oakland: Mama's Press, 1975.

Brown, Linda J. *jazz dancin wif mama.* New York: Iridian Press, 1981.

Brown, Linda J. *The Rainbow River.* New York: Iridian Press, 1980.

Bulkin, Elly, ed. *Lesbian Fiction.* Watertown, Massachusetts: Persephone Press, 1981.

Clausen, Jan. *Mother, Sister, Daughter, Lover.* Trumansburg, New York: The Crossing Press, 1980.

Covina, Gina, and Galana, Laurel, eds. *The Lesbian Reader.* Oakland, California: Amazon Press, 1975.

Dinesen, Isak. *Seven Gothic Tales.* New York: Vintage, 1974. (Originally published 1934.)

Dinesen, Isak. *A Winter's Tale*. New York: Random, 1942. Other editions available.

Dworkin, Andrea. *The New Woman's Broken Heart*. East Palo Alto, California: Frog in the Well Press, 1980.

Geller, Ruth. Pictures from the Past. Buffalo, New York: Imp Press, 1980.

Grahn, Judy, ed. *True to Life Adventure Stories*. Vol. 1. Oakland, CA: Diana Press, 1978. Vol. 2 co published with Crossing Press, Trumansburg, New York, 1981.

Grier, Barbara, and Reid, Coletta eds. *The Lesbians Home Journal*. Oakland, California: Diana Press, 1976.

Kleinberg, Seymour, ed. *The Other Persuasion*. New York: Random, 1977.

Luce, Hadden. *After the Prom*. Atlanta: Vanity Press, 1977.

Rule, Jane. *Theme for Diverse Instruments*. Vancouver: Talonbooks, 1976.

Rule, Jane. *Outlander*. Tallahassee, Florida: Naiad Press, 1981.

Shockley, Ann. *The Black and White of It*. Tallahassee, Florida: Naiad Press, 1980.

Straayer, Amy Christine. *Hurtin and Healin and Talkin It Over*. Chicago, Illinois: Metis Press, 1980.

Stockwell, Nancy. *Out Somewhere and Back Again*. Washington, DC: Self-published, 1978.

Swansea, Charleen, and Campbell, Barbara, eds. *Love Stories by New Women*. New York: Avon, 1978.

Early Books (before 1950)

Barnes, Djuna. *The Ladies Almanack*. New York: Harper & Row, 1972. (First published privately 1928 in France.) Delightful spoof/tribute to Natalie Barney's Paris lesbian circle.

Barnes, Djuna. *Nightwood*. New York: Harcourt, 1937; New Directions, 1961. Complex and haunting story of an affair between two women. Set in Left-Bank Paris and New York City during the 1920s.

Barnes, Djuna. *Selected Works of Djuna Barnes*. New York: Farrar, 1962. Relevant stories include "The Grand Malade," and "A Little Girl Tells a Story to a Lady."

Bowen, Elizabeth. *The Little Girls*. New York: Avon, 1978. (First published 1963.) Three childhood friends come together again in later life; two find each other as lovers.

Bowen, Elizabeth. *The Hotel*. New York: Popular Library, 1966. (First published 1928.) A Widow and a college student become interested in each other while vacationing at a Riviera hotel.

Bowles, Jane. *My Sister's Hand in Mine*. New York: Viking, 1978. Two relevant works here. "Camp Cataract" (first published 1966) is a variant tale of obsessive love between two sisters. "Two Serious Ladies" (first published 1943) is a comedy in which a woman leaves her husband for a prostitute.

Colette. *The Complete Claudine*. New York: Farrar, 1976. (Includes *Claudine at School,* 1900; *Claudine in Paris,* 1901; *Claudine Married,* 1902; *Claudine and Annie,* 1904) *At School* tells of sixteen-year-old Claudine attending a rural school and of the many lesbian intrigues there; *In Paris* is mostly a retrospective of the events in the first book; *Married* tells how to save one's marriage by having an affair with a woman; *And Annie* tells how Claudine rescues Annie from her husband, only to fall in love with her herself.

Colette. *The Other One*. New York: Farrar, 1970. (First published 1929.) Wife and mistress ally against husband.

Colette. *The Pure and the Impure*. New York: Farrar, 1976. (First published 1932.) Descriptive of Colette's friends' affairs; portraits of the Ladies of Llangollen and Renée Vivien.

de Beauvoir, Simone. *She Came to Stay*. New York: Fontana, 1975; 1979. (First published 1943.) Semi autobiographical account of a ménage à trois consisting of the author, Jean-Paul Sartre, and Violette Leduc. Lesbian emotion is made clear but not expressed physically.

Frederics, Diana. *Diana: A Strange Autobiography*. New York: Arno Press, 1975. (First published 1939.) Story of a young woman's struggle to accept her lesbianism.

Hall, Radclyffe. *The Unlit Lamp*. New York: Dial, 1981. (Originally 1924.) Teacher/Student love story.

Hall, Radclyffe. *The Well of Loneliness*. New York: Avon/Bard, 1981. (First published—and banned—in 1928.) A classic. An autobiographical plea for the acceptance of lesbians as people.

Lehmann, Rosamund. *Dusty Answer*. New York: Harcourt, 1975. (First published 1927). Autobiographical first novel. Lesbian love forces young woman to leave college.

Lehmann, Rosamund. *The Ballad and the Source*. New York: Harcourt, 1975. (First published 1945.) Romantic attachment between two English schoolgirls.

Nin, Anais. *Ladders to Fire*. Chicago: Swallow, 1966. (First published 1945.) Explores the erotic relationship between two women.

Olivia (pseudonym of Dorothy Strachey Bussey.) *Olivia*. London, Hogarth Press, 1949; New York: Arno Press, 1975. Autobiographical account of English girl's stay in French boarding school, her love for the headmistress, and the headmistress' relations with two other women.

Renault, Mary. *The Middle Mist*. New York: Popular Library, 1972. (First published 1945.) Young woman leaves home to live with her sister who is a lesbian.

Renault, Mary. *Promise of Love*. New York: Pyramid, 1974. (First published 1939.) Young nurse has affair with female colleague.

Richardson, Dorothy. *Dawn's Left Hand*. In *Pilgrimage*. Vol. 4 New York: Popular Library, 1976. (First published 1931.) One in a series of twelve autobiographical novellas. Details her relationship with a young woman.

Schreiner, Olive. *Story of An African Farm*. New York: Penguin, 1979. (First published 1883.) Variant. Strong feminist account of a woman's search for an ideal outside of marriage.

Sinclair, Jo (pseudonym of Ruth Seid). *The Wasteland*. New York: Harper, 1946; Lancer, 1961. A young man, first generation American Jew, struggles to reconcile two conflicting cultures. His sister is a lesbian.

Stein, Gertrude. *Fernhurst, Q.E.D. and Other Early Writings*. New York: Norton, 1973. "Fernhurst" is a fictionalized account of Stein's involvement in a love triangle of three women. "Q.E.D." is the story of her first affair with a woman.

Stein, Gertrude. *Matisse, Picasso and Gertrude Stein*. Millerton, New York: Something Else Press, 1972. Includes "A Long Gay Book," "Many Many Women," and "G.M.P."

Vivien, Renée. *A Woman Appeared to Me*. Tallahassee, Florida: Naiad Press, 1976. (First published 1904 in France.) Fictionalized account of the author's relationship with Natalie Clifford Barney.

White, Antonia. *Frost in May*. New York: Dial, 1980. (First published 1933.) Variant. Set in a repressive Catholic girl's school; four girls defy the rules and form loving "couples."

Wierauch, Anna Elisabet. *The Scorpion*. New York: Arno Press, 1975. (Published 1919 in Germany.)

Wierauch, Anna Elisabet. *The Outcast*. 2 vols. New York: Arno Press, 1975. (Published 1921 in Germany.) The story of a woman in the Berlin lesbian underground. She has several tragic relationships and finally renounces her lesbianism.

Wilhelm, Gale. *We Too Are Drifting*. New York: Arno Press, 1975. (First published 1938.) Two women fall in love despite enormous pressures. A classic.

Wilhelm, Gale. *Torchlight to Valhalla*. New York: Arno Press, 1975. (First published 1935.) A woman artist lives with her father until his death. Offered marriage as "comfort" she instead chooses to live with and love another woman.

Winslow, Christa. *The Child Manuela*. New York: Arno Press, 1975. (First published 1933 in Germany.) Schoolgirl falls in love with her teacher. Reprimanded, she attempts suicide. Basis for the play and film, *Maedchen in Uniform*.

Wollstonecraft, Mary. *Mary: A Fiction*. New York: Schocken, 1977. (First published 1788.) Thinly disguised account of the author's relationship with Fanny Blood. First known lesbian novel by a woman in English.

Woolf, Virginia. *Orlando*. London: Hogarth Press, 1928. Woolf's fantasy tribute to her lover Vita Sackville-West. Story spans three hundred years; the protagonist changes sex every hundred years or so. Sheer delight.

Woolf, Virginia. *Mrs. Dalloway*. London: Hogarth Press, 1925. Lesbian content is minor in this complex novel. A mature, wealthy woman reflects on her life, including the passion she once felt for another woman.

Paperback Originals from the 1950s and 1960s

Paperback originals were published by the hundreds during this period. These two authors are listed because their books are currently available.

Bannon, Ann. *Odd Girl Out* (1957); *I Am a Woman* (1959); *Women in the Shadows* (1959); *Journey to a Woman* (1960). All reprinted by Arno Press, New York, 1975. Four books in a series. In *Odd Girl Out* Laura goes to college and falls in love and bed with Beth, her roommate. Beth eventually rejects her for a man and marriage; Laura flees to New York City. In *I Am a Woman*, Beth, in New York, falls in love with her straight roommate but can't help bedding with Beebo, butch of Greenwich Village, who loves her. After drama and trauma she moves in with Beebo. *Women in the Shadows* occurs two years after *Woman*, and Laura and Beebo are breaking up. Overly negative. *Journey* finds Beth, after nine years of marriage, unable to live without a woman. She leaves husband to move to New York in search of Laura. But first she meets Beebo. A "who gets the girl?" story. The Bannon books are classics of the "pulp" genre of lesbian fiction, and, on the whole, are some of the more positive and accurate portrayals of lesbian love for their time.

Christian, Paula. *Edge of Twilight* (1959); *Another Kind of Love* (1961); *Love Is Where You Find It* (1961); *This Side of Love* (1963); *Amanda* (1965); *The Other Side of Desire* (1965). All reprinted by Timely Books, New Milford, Connecticut, between 1978 and 1981. All these books vary with regard to presentation of stereotypes and "straight" endings, although Christian wrote with an awareness of class issues which many of her contemporaries lacked. In *Edge*, Val, a stewardess, is seduced by Toni and discovers a lesbian life. In its sequel, *This Side of Love*, Toni becomes overly possessive of Val, and Val has a nervous breakdown. Ending is ambiguous as to whether Val will remain a lesbian or try to go straight. *Another Kind of Love* finds Laura, a Hollywood publicity agent, trying to unravel the question of whether she really is straight and has just had a bad affair with a woman, or gay and has had a bad affair with a woman. Lesbian ending. *Love Is Where You Find It* is the story of a photographer trying to cope with being in the closet. *Amanda* is about a straight writer of lesbian fiction, with much the same sort of plot as *Another*, but with a straight ending this time. *Other Side of Desire* is in the same vein as the previous books, also with a heterosexual ending.

Mainstream Novels (since 1950)

Alther, Lisa. *Kinflicks*. New York: Signet, 1975. Young woman from the South progresses from an acceptable "straight" life to a lesbian commune in Vermont.

Bedford, Sybille. *A Compass Error*. New York: Ballantine, 1970. Seventeen-year-old girl has an affair with the ex-wife of her mother's lover.

Blais, Marie-Claire. *Nights in the Underground*. Don Mills, Ontario: Musson Books, 1979. Story of a lesbian group of friends as they move from a closeted bar scene to a politically aware state of lesbian oppression and love. Experimental style.

Boyd, Blanche. *Mourning the Death of Magic*. New York: Macmillan, 1977. Story of a modern family in the South. Focuses on two sisters, one of whom is a lesbian. Blockbuster of an ending.

Crawford, Linda. *In a Class by Herself*. New York: Popular Library, 1978. Woman journalist is an alcoholic, and seemingly a lesbian, but keeps falling in with men who abuse her. Long on violent, destructive and drunken scenes; short on analysis and love.

De Lynn, Jane. *Some Do*. New York: Macmillan, 1978; Pocket, 1979. Seven women from different backgrounds meet in Berkeley in the late sixties. Most become feminists, a few explore lesbianism both personally and politically.

French, Marilyn. *The Women's Room*. New York: Jove, 1977. Long saga of an older mother's struggle to survive divorce and a return to college. Several of the younger women she meets are lesbians.

Futcher, Jane. *Crush*. Boston: Little Brown, 1981. Boarding school setting.

George, Sally. *Frog Salad*. New York: Charles Scribner's Sons, 1981.

Grumbach, Doris. *Chamber Music*. New York: Button, 1979. The widow of a famous composer finds love with another woman.

Hiller, Cathy. *An Old Friend From High School*. New York: Pocket, 1978. A lesbian visits an old school friend, now married. They fall in love.

Howard, Elizabeth Jane. *Odd Girl Out*. New York: Dell, 1973. No relation to the Bannon book of the same title. Arabella comes to stay with a married couple, has an affair first with him, then with her. Traditional ending, but Arabella is portrayed as the only honest and loving character in the book.

Koertge, Noretta. *Who Was That Masked Woman?* New York: St. Martin's, 1981. Comic adventure.

Leduc, Violette. *Ravages*. New York: Farrar, 1967; London: Panther, 1972. (Originally titled *Therese and Isabel*.) Autobiographical account of the author's love for another school girl and its consequences for her later life. Depressing but very good.

Leduc, Violette. *La Bâtarde*. New York: Farrar, 1965; London, Panther, 1973. Account of the author's life, early deprivation, and eventual acceptance of her lesbianism.

Leduc, Violette. *Mad in Pursuit*. New York: Farrar, 1974. More autobiography. An account of unrequited loves, both lesbian and heterosexual.

Lindau, Joan. *Mrs. Cooper's Boardinghouse*. New York: McGraw Hill, 1980. A young tomboy learns about life and love through her job at a boardinghouse run by an older lesbian. Very positive.

McCarthy, Mary. *The Group*. New York: Signet, 1964. A story that follows the lives of eight women graduates of Vassar from the class of '33. One of them is a lesbian.

Mallet, Françoise. *The Illusionist*. New York: Arno Press, 1975. (First published 1951 in France.) A young French girl has an affair with her father's mistress and comes to maturity.

Miller, Isabel (pseudonym of Alma Routsong). *Patience and Sarah.* New York: Fawcett, 1973. (First published 1969 as *A Place for Us.*) Love story of two women who make a life together in the rural America of the 1800s.

Morgan, Claire (pseudonym of Mary Patricia Highsmith). *The Price of Salt.* New York: Arno Press, 1975. (First published 1952.) Early story of a mother forced to choose between her child and her woman lover. A classic.

Pass, Gail. *Zoe's Book.* New York: Avon, 1976. An old woman tells a younger researcher of her lesbian love among the Bloomsbury set.

Pass, Gail. *Surviving Sisters.* New York: Atheneum, 1981.

Piercy, Marge. *Small Changes.* New York: Doubleday, 1973; Fawcett, 1974. Two women from different backgrounds move through the early feminism of the sixties and seventies. One becomes trapped in a destructive marriage, the other finds fulfillment with a woman lover.

Piercy, Marge. *The High Cost of Living.* New York: Harper & Row, 1978; Fawcett, 1979. A lesbian graduate student finds herself in a triangle with a gay male prostitute and a manipulative teenage woman who seems neither lesbian or heterosexual.

Piercy, Marge. *Vida.* New York: Summit, 1980; Fawcett, 1981. A woman radical's life after ten years in the Left underground. The main character is bisexual, another character is lesbian. Powerful book.

Rule, Jane. *Desert of the Heart.* New York: World, 1965; Vancouver: Talonbooks, 1978. Set in Reno in the 1950s. A young woman who works in a casino finds love with an older woman professor who has come to Reno for a divorce. Naiad ed., 1982.

Rule, Jane. *This Is Not For You.* New York: McCall, 1970. Kate loves Esther but refuses to consummate their relationship. Esther's relations with men are destructive; she joins a convent. Kate keeps her lesbian affairs separate from the rest of her life, becoming a sad older woman. Excellent book, despite Kate's self-hate. Naiad ed., 1982.

Rule, Jane. *Against the Season.* New York: McCall, 1971; Manor, 1975. An unwed mother comes to a small town and falls in love despite herself. Some of the minor characters are lesbians.

Rule, Jane. *The Young in One Another's Arms.* New York: Doubleday, 1977. Residents of a boardinghouse band together when they are forced to move. Several characters are lesbians.

Rule, Jane. *Contract with the World.* New York: Harcourt, 1980. Portrait of a group of artists in Vancouver and their effects on each other's life, work and politics. Several gay men and lesbian characters.

Sarton, May. *The Small Room.* New York: Norton, 1961. An older professor and a wealthy trustee struggle to maintain their relationship of many years in a small college town.

Sarton, May. *The Fur Person.* New York: Rinehart, 1967; Signet, 1970. A cat's life story, told from the viewpoint of the cat, who lives with a lesbian couple.

Sarton, May. *Mrs. Stevens Hears the Mermaids Singing.* New York: Norton, 1974. An older writer reflects on her past loves, both male and female, and concludes that women are her primary source of strength and inspiration.

Sarton, May. *A Reckoning.* New York: Norton, 1978. A widowed editor, dying of cancer, struggles to help a young lesbian writer complete her first novel about coming out. As she worsens, she reflects that her strongest ties have been to women friends, not to husband or children.

Shockley, Ann. *Loving Her.* Indianapolis: Bobbs-Merrill, 1974; New York: Avon, 1978. The first novel about an interracial lesbian relationship written by a Black lesbian.

Stimpson, Kate. *Class Notes.* New York: Times, 1979. A young woman grows up in the 1950s as a "good" girl, but in college she falls in love with a woman.

Suyin, Han. *Winter Love* (with *Cast But One Shadow*). New York: Putnam, 1962; London: Panther, 1973. A married woman pines for her lost lesbian lover from college.

Yankowitz, Susan. *Silent Witness.* New York: Avon, 1976. A deaf-mute woman is imprisoned for a murder she did not commit. In jail she finds a woman lover and the first accepting and loving community she has known.

New Feminism/Experimental Work

Aidoo, Ama Ata. *Our Sister Killjoy or Reflections from a Black-Eyed Squint.* Self-published, 1979. A black African woman traveling through Europe finds love with a German housewife.

Arobateau, Red Jordan. *The Bars Across Heaven.* Self-published, 1975.

Arnold, June. *The Cook and the Carpenter.* New York: Daughters, 1973. Experimental novel of a woman's commune. Uses no gender-specific pronouns.

Arnold, June. *Sister Gin.* New York: Daughters, 1975. About age, love, sex, power, drinking, and menopause. A celebration of women's strength.

Arnold, June. *Applesauce.* New York: Daughters, 1977. (First published 1966.) A novel of sexual transformation. An early androgynous vision.

Brown, Rita Mae. *Rubyfruit Jungle.* New York: Daughters, 1973; Bantam, 1977. The classic novel of the lesbian from the wrong side of the tracks who will let no one stand in her way.

Brown, Rita Mae. *In Her Day.* New York: Daughters, 1976. Two women from vastly different backgrounds try to reconcile those differences in their relationship. Explores many issues relevant to feminism.

Brown, Rita Mae. *Six of One.* New York: Harper & Row, 1978; Bantam, 1979. The story of three generations of Southern women.

Brady, Maureen. *Give Me Your Good Ear.* Argyle, New York: Spinsters, Ink, 1979. Growing-up novel; mother-daughter relationship central.

Camille, Donna. *Bra-Strap Bar and Grill.* Self-published, 1979. Melodrama set in a lesbian bar.

Causse, Michele. *Lesbian: 7 Portraits*. Paris: Le Nouveau Commerce, 1981.

Dykewoman, Elana. *They Will Know Me by My Teeth*. Northampton, Massachusetts: Megaera Press, 1976. A collection of stories, prose, and poems about lesbian love and struggle.

Geller, Ruth. *Seed of a Woman*. Brooklyn, New York: Imp Press, 1979.

Gingerlox. *Berrigan*. Tallahassee, Florida: Naiad Press, 1978. Lesbian woman's lover dies in an accident. A fine story about their love and about picking up the pieces afterward.

Harris, Bertha. *Confessions of Cherubino*. New York: Harcourt, 1972; Daughters, 1978. Two long-time friends never consummate their love; both become insane with sexual oppression implied as the cause. Experimental style.

Harris, Bertha. *Lover*. New York: Daughters, 1976. Stories of women's lives, told as creation rather than as history.

Hauser, Marianne. *The Talking Room*. New York: Fiction Collective, 1976. Told by a pregnant thirteen-year-old. Her mother is a lesbian and an alcoholic. Experimental style.

Isabell, Sharon. *Yesterday's Lessons*. Oakland, California: Women's Press Collective, 1974. Autobiographical story of a working-class lesbian.

Jones, Sonya. *The Legacy*. Atlanta: Vanity Press, 1976. A young lesbian academic finds her love mixed up with an episode from her mother's past. Set in the South.

Kunz, Alesia. *Shangrila and Linda*. New York: Prickly Pear Press, 1981. A love story?

McCauley, Carole Spearin. *Happenthing in Travel on*. New York: Daughters, 1975. The survivors of a plane crash try to survive the winter. Includes a lesbian couple.

Marie, Linda. *I Must Not Rock*. New York: Daughters, 1977. A young lesbian as battered child, thief, and whore. A story of survival.

Nachman, Elana. *Riverfinger Women*. New York: Daughters, 1974. A tale of radical lesbian-feminism from the viewpoint of women in their teens during the late sixties.

Riis, Sharon. *The True Story of Ida Johnson*. Toronto: Women's Press. 1976.

Russ, Joanna. *On Strike Against God*. Brooklyn, New York: Out and Out Books, 1980. A college professor comes out with one of her graduate students.

Snow, Karen. *Willo*. Ann Arbor, Michigan: Street Fiction press, 1981.

Strongin, Lynn. *Bones and Kim*. Argyle, New York: Spinsters, Ink, 1980.

Taylor, Sheila Ortiz. *Faultline*. Tallahassee, Florida: Naiad Press, 1982. Comic adventure story involving lesbian mothers.

Toder, Nancy. *Choices*. Watertown, Massachusetts: Persephone Press, 1980. A story about finding one's love with women.

Wilson, Anna. *Cactus*. London: Only Women Press, 1980. A lesbian love story.

Wittig, Monique. *The Opoponax.* New York: Simon & Schuster, 1966;
Daughters, 1976. Experimental novel of the day-to-day life of a
French schoolgirl and her first relationship with another girl.

Wittig, Monique. *The Lesbian Body.* New York: Morrow, 1975. A tribute to
the specifically lesbian body, done within the framework of several
lesbian relationships.

Wittig, Monique, and Zeig, Sande. *Lesbian Peoples: Material for a
Dictionary.* New York: Avon, 1979. A dictionary done from the
standpoint of lesbian-feminist language and history.

Drama

Boesing, Martha. *Journey Along the Matrix.* Vanilla, 1978.

Griffin, Susan. *Voices.* New York: Feminist Press, 1975.

Hellman, Lillian. *The Children's Hour* (in *Collected Plays of Lillian
Hellman*). New York: Little, Brown, 1979. (First published 1934.)

Hoffman, William M., ed. *Gay Plays: The First Collection.* New York: Avon,
1979. (See plays by Susan Miller and Jane Chambers.)

Terry, Megan. *Couplings and Groupings.* New York: Avon, 1972.

NONFICTION
Bibliographies and Resource Books

Faderman, Lillian. *Surpassing the Love of Men: Romantic Friendship and
Love Between Women from the Renaissance to the Present.* New
York: Morrow, 1981.

Foster, Jeannette. *Sex Variant Women in Literature.* Oakland, California:
Diana Press, 1975. (First published 1956.)

A Gay Bibliography. Sixth Edition, March 1980. Philadelphia: Gay Task
Force, American Library Association. Nonfiction.

Grier, Barbara, et al. *The Lesbian in Literature: A Bibliography.* Tallahassee, Florida: Naiad Press, 1981.

Grier, Barbara. *Lesbiana: Book Reviews from the Ladder.* Tallahassee,
Florida: Naiad Press, 1976.

Hitchens, Donna, and Thomas, Ann, eds. *Lesbian Mothers and Their
Children: An Annotated Bibliography of Legal and Psychological
Materials.* San Francisco: Lesbian Legal Rights Project, 1980.

Katz, Jonathan. *Gay American History: Lesbians and Gay Men in the U.S.A.*
New York: Crowell, 1976; Avon, 1978.

Kuda, Marie. *Women Loving Women.* Chicago: WomanPress, 1976.

Paleo, Lyn, and Garber, Eric. *Uranian Worlds: Lesbian and Gay
Images in Science Fiction, An Annotated Bibliography.* Boston:
G.K. Hall, 1982.

Roberts, J.R. *Black Lesbians: An Annotated Bibliography.* Tallahassee,
Florida: Naiad Press, 1981.

Anthologies from Lesbian Magazines

Bunch, Charlotte, et al., eds. *Building Feminist Theory.* New York: Longman, 1981. Essays from *Quest.*

Covina, Gina, and Galana, Laurel, eds. *The Lesbian Reader.* Oakland, California: Amazon Press, 1975. Essays, poems, and short stories from *Amazon Quarterly.*

Grier, Barbara. *Lesbiana.* Tallahassee, Florida: Naiad Press, 1976. Book reviews from *The Ladder.*

Grier, Barbara, and Reid, Coletta, eds. *The Lavender Herring.* Oakland, California: Diana Press, 1976. Essays from *The Ladder.*

Grier, Barbara, and Reid, Coletta, eds. *The Lesbians Home Journal.* Oakland, California: Diana Press, 1976. Short fiction from *The Ladder.*

Grier, Barbara, and Reid, Coletta, eds. *Lesbian Lives.* Oakland, California: Diana Press, 1976. Short biographies from *The Ladder.*

Myron, Nancy, and Bunch, Charlotte, eds. *Women Remembered.* Oakland, California: Diana Press, 1975.

Myron, Nancy, and Bunch, Charlotte, eds. *Lesbianism and the Women's Movement.* Oakland, California: Diana Press, 1975. Essays from the *Furies.*

Myron, Nancy, and Bunch, Charlotte, eds. *Class and Feminism.* Oakland, California: Diana Press, 1975. Essays from the Furies.

Sexuality and Erotica

Balliett, Bev, and Patton, Patti. *Graphic Details.* Phoenix, Arizona: Star Publications, 1979.

Califia, Pat. *Sapphistry: The Book of Lesbian Sexuality.* Tallahassee, Florida: Naiad Press, 1980.

Cedar and Nelly. *A Woman's Touch.* Eugene, Oregon: Womanshare Books, 1979.

Corinne, Tee. *The Cunt Coloring Book.* San Francisco: Pearlchild Productions, 1975. Reissued as *Labiaflowers* in a slightly revised edition by Naiad Press in 1981.

Gayle, Marilyn. *What Lesbians Do.* Portland: Godiva Press, 1975.

Harris, Bertha, and Sisley, Emily. *The Joy of Lesbian Sex.* New York: Crown, 1977.

Hite, Shere. *The Hite Report.* New York: Macmillan, 1976.

Nin, Anais. *Delta of Venus.* New York: Bantam, 1978.

Nin, Anais. *Little Birds.* New York: Bantam, 1979.

Nomadic Sisters. *Loving Women.* 1976.

Odette. *Pleasures: The Secret Garden of Sexual Love between Women.* New York: Warner, 1978.

Art

Abbott, Berenice. *Berenice Abbott: Photographs.* New York: Horizon, 1970.

Brooks, Romaine. *Portraits, Tableaux, Dessins.* New York: Arno Press, 1975.

Chicago, Judy. *The Dinner Party.* New York: Anchor/Doubleday, 1979.

Chicago, Judy, *Through the Flower.* Garden City, New York: Doubleday, 1975.

Harris, Ann Sutherland, and Nochlin, Linda. *Women Artists, 1550–1950.* New York: Knopf, 1976.

JEB. *Eye to Eye: Portraits of Lesbians.* Glad Hag, 1979. Distributed by Naiad Press, Tallahassee, Florida.

Lippard, Lucy, ed. *From the Center: Feminist Essays on Women's Art.* New York: Dutton, 1976.

Poetry

Allen, Paula Gunn. *A Cannon between My Knees.* New York: Strawberry Press, 1981.

Allen, Paula Gunn. *Coyote's Daylight Trip.* Albuquerque: La Confluencia, 1978.

Bissert, Ellen Marie. *The Immaculate Conception of the Blessed Virgin Dyke.* New York: 13th Moon, 1977.

Broumas, Olga. *Beginning with O.* New Haven: Yale University Press, 1977.

Brown, Rita Mae. *The Hand that Cradles the Rock.* New York: New York University Press, 1971; Oakland, California: Diana Press, 1974.

Brown, Rita Mae. *Songs to a Handsome Woman.* Oakland, California: Diana Press, 1973.

Byrd, Stephanie. *25 Years of Malcontent.* Boston: Good Gay Poets Press, 1976.

Clausen, Jan. *After Touch.* Brooklyn, New York: Out & Out Books, 1975.

Clausen, Jan. *Waking at the Bottom of the Dark.* Brooklyn: Long Haul, 1979.

Courtot, Martha. *Journey.* Santa Rosa: Pearlchild, 1977.

Courtot, Martha. *Tribe.* Santa Rosa: Pearlchild, 1977.

Davenport, Doris. *It's Like This.* Los Angeles: Self published, 1981.

Dickinson, Emily. *The Complete Poems,* edited by T. Johnson. Boston: Little, Brown, 1960.

Doolittle, H. D. *Helen in Egypt.* New York: Grove, 1961.

Doolittle, H.D. *Hermetic Definitions.* New York: New Directions, 1972.

Foster, Jeannette, and Taylor, Valerie. *Two Women.* Chicago: Woman-Press, 1976.

Gibbs, Joan. *Between a Rock and a Hard Place.* Brooklyn: February 3rd Press, 1979.

Gidlow, Elsa. *Sapphic Songs: Seventeen to Seventy.* Oakland, California: Diana Press, 1976. (Includes work from *Moods of Eros* [1970] and *On a Grey Thread* [1923]).

Gidlow, Elsa. *Sapphic Songs: Eighteen to Eighty.* Mill Valley, California: Druid Heights Press, 1982.

Grahn, Judy. *The Work of a Common Woman.* Oakland, California: Diana Press, 1978. (Includes work from *Edward the Dyke, She Who, A*

Woman is Talking to Death, and the "Common Woman" poems.)
Greenspan, Judy. *To Lesbians Everywhere.* New York: Violet Press, 1976.
Griffin, Susan. *Like the Iris of an Eye.* New York: Harper & Row, 1976.
(Includes work from *Dear Sky* [1971], *Let Them Be Said* [1973], and *Letter* [1973].)
Hacker, Marilyn. *Taking Notice.* New York: Knopf, 1981.
Hacker, Marilyn. *Separations.* New York: Knopf, 1976.
Hacker, Marilyn. *Presentation Pieces.* New York: Viking, 1974.
Hopkins, Lea. *I'm Not Crazy, Just Different.* Kansas City: Womyn, 1977.
Hopkins, Lea. *Womyn I Have Known You.* Kansas City: Womyn, 1978.
Jordan, June. *Passion: New Poems, 1977-1980.* Boston: Beacon Press, 1980.
Kaye, Melanie. *We Speak in Code.* Pittsburgh: Motheroot Publications, 1980.
Kim, Willyce. *Eating Artichokes.* Oakland: Women's Press Collective, 1972.
Kim, Willyce. *Under the Rolling Sky.* Berkeley: Maud Gonne Press, 1976.
Klepfisz, Irena. *Periods of Stress.* Brooklyn: Out and Out Books, 1976.
Lallo. *Into a Pegasus Dream.* San Francisco: Prosciutto Press, 1977.
Lapidus, Jacqueline. *Ready to Survive.* Brooklyn: Hanging Loose Books, 1975.
Lapidus, Jacqueline. *Starting Over.* Brooklyn: Out & Out Books, 1977.
Larkin, Joan, *Housework.* Brooklyn, New York: Out & Out Books, 1975.
Lonider, Lynn. *A Lesbian Estate: Poems 1970-1973.* San Francisco: ManRoot, 1977.
Lorde, Audre. *Between Ourselves.* Point Reyes, California: Eidolon Editions, 1976.
Lorde, Audre. *Coal.* New York: Norton, 1968.
Lorde, Audre. *From A Land Where Other People Live.* Detroit: Broadside Press, 1973.
Lorde, Audre. *The Black Unicorn.* New York: Norton, 1978.
Millay, Edna St. Vincent. *Collected Poems.* New York: Harper & Row, 1956.
Noda, Barbara. *Strawberries.* Berkeley, California: Shameless Hussy, 1979.
Parker, Pat. *Movement in Black.* Oakland, California: Diana Press, 1978.
(Includes work from *Child of Myself* [1972] and *Pit Stop* [1973].)
Parker, Pat. *WomanSlaughter.* Oakland, California: Diana Press, 1978.
Pratt, Minnie Bruce. *The Sound of One Fork: Poems.* Durham, North Carolina: Night Heron Press, 1981.
Rich, Adrienne. *Poems: Selected and New 1950-1974.* New York: Norton, 1974.
Rich, Adrienne. *The Dream of a Common Language, Poems 1974-1977.* New York: Norton, 1978.
Rossetti, Christina. *Goblins' Market.* First published 1859. Available in many anthologies.
Sappho. *Works.* The translation by Mary Barnard, University of California Press, 1958, is recommended.
Sarton, May. *Collected Poems, 1930-1973.* New York: Norton, 1974.

Segrest, Mab. *Living in a House I Do Not Own.* Durham, North Carolina: Night Heron Press, 1981.

Sexton, Anne. "Rapunzel." in *Transformations.* Boston: Houghton Mifflin, 1971.

Shelley, Martha. *Crossing the DMZ.* Oakland, California: Women's Press Collective, 1974.

Shelley, Martha. *Lovers and Mothers.* Oakland, California: Sefir Publishing, 1981.

Sherman, Susan. *Woman Poems Love Poems.* New York: Two and Two, 1975.

Vivien, Renée. *The Muse of the Violets.* Tallahassee, Florida: Naiad Press, 1977. (Originally published in France between 1903-1909.)

Vivien, Renée. *At the Sweet Hour of Hand in Hand.* Tallahassee, Florida: Naiad Press, 1979. (First published 1906 in France.)

Waters, Chocolate. *To the Man Reporter from the Denver Post.* Denver: Big Mama Rag, 1975.

Waters, Chocolate. *Take Me Like a Photograph.* Denver: Eggplant Press, 1977.

Winant, Fran. *Dyke Jacket.* New York: Violet Press, 1976

Winant, Fran. *Looking At Women.* New York: Violet Press, 1971.

Wood-Thompson, Susan. *Crazy-Quilt: Poems.* Self-published, 1980. Distributed by Crossing Press, Trumansburg, New York.

Poetry Anthologies

Bernikow, Louise, ed. *The World Split Open: Four Centuries of Women Poets in England and America, 1552-1950.* New York: Random House, 1974; Vintage, 1975.

Bulkin, Elly, and Larkin, Joan, eds. *Lesbian Poetry: An Anthology.* Watertown, Massachusetts: Persephone Press, 1981. (Revised edition of *Amazon Poetry*, 1975.)

Howe, Florence, and Bass, Ellen, eds. *No More Masks.* Garden City, New York: Doubleday, 1973.

Iverson, Lucille, and Ruby, Kathryn, eds. *We Become New.* New York: Bantam, 1975.

Lesbians Speak Out. Oakland, California: Women's Press Collective, 1974.

Biography, Autobiograpy, Part I

The following section is alphabetized by the *subject's* last name.

Mercedes de Acosta

Acosta, Mercedes de. Here Lies the Heart. New York: Arno Press, 1975. (First published 1960.)

Margaret Anderson (Jane Heap, Georgette Leblanc, Dorothy Caruso)

Anderson, Margaret. *My Thirty Years War.* New York: Horizon, 1970.

Anderson, Margaret. *The Fiery Fountains.* New York: Horizon, 1970.

Anderson, Margaret. *The Strange Necessity.* New York: Horizon, 1970.

Natalie Clifford Barney
Chalon, Jean. *Portrait of A Seductress*. New York: Crown, 1979. (First published in France.)
Wickes, George. *Natalie Barney: Amazon of Letters*. New York: Popular Library, 1976.
See also: *Romaine Brooks, Liane de Pougy, and Renée Vivien*
Elizabeth Bowen
Glendenning, Victoria. *Elizabeth Bowen*. New York: Avon, 1978.
Jane Bowles
Dillon, Millicent. *A Little Original Sin: The Life and Work of Jane Bowles*. New York: Holt, Rinehart and Winston, 1981.
Romaine Brooks
Secrest, Meryle. *Between Me and Life*. New York: Doubleday, 1974.
Willa Cather
Lewis, Edith. *Willa Cather Living*. Lincoln, Nebraska: University of Nebraska Press, 1976. Orig. pub. 1953.
Colette
Colette. *Earthly Paradise*. Edited by Robert Phelps. New York: Penguin, 1974.
Crosland, Margaret. *Colette: The Difficulty of Loving*. Indianapolis: Bobbs-Merrill, 1973; NY: Dell, 1975.
See also: *Paris*
Liane de Pougy
de Pougy Liane. *My Blue Notebooks*. New York: Harper & Row, 1979.
Emily Dickinson
Patterson, Rebecca. *The Riddle of Emily Dickinson*. Boston: Houghton Mifflin, 1951.
Sewell, Richard B. *The Life of Emily Dickinson*. New York: Farrar, Straus & Giroux, 1974 (2 vols.); 1980 (1 vol.).
Radclyffe Hall
Dickson, Lovat. *Radclyffe Hall at the Well of Loneliness*. New York: Scribner's, 1975.
Troubridge, Lady Una. *The Life and Death of Radclyffe Hall*. New York: Citadel, 1973.
Both of these biographies are highly unsatisfactory, for very different reasons; however, they are the only existing works on Hall.
Lorena Hickok, Eleanor Roosevelt
Faber, Doris. *The Life of Lorena Hickok: E.R.'s Friend*. New York: Morrow, 1980.
Alice James
James, Alice. *The Diary of Alice James*. Edited by Leon Edel. New York: Dodd, Mead,1964.
Strouse, Jean. *Alice James: A Biography*. Boston: Houghton Mifflin, 1980.
Sarah Orne Jewett
Donovan, Josephine. *Sarah Orne Jewett*. New York: Frederick Unger, 1980.

Janis Joplin

Caserta, Peggy. *Going Down With Janis.* New York: Dell, 1974.

Two other biographies make some mention of Joplin's "bisexuality," but this is the most explicit title. It is also the most trashy and exploitative.

The Ladies of Llangollen

Gordon, Mary. *Chase of the Wild Goose.* New York: Arno Press, 1975. (First published 1936.)

Mavor, Elizabeth. *The Ladies of Llangollen.* New York: Penguin, 1971.

Amy Lowell

Gould, Jean. *Amy.* New York: Dodd, Mead, 1975.

Carson McCullers

Carr, Virginia Spencer. *The Lonely Hunter: A Biography of Carson McCullers.* New York: Doubleday, 1976.

Anais Nin

Nin, Anais. *The Diary of Anais Nin.* Vols. 1–5 New York: Harcourt Brace, 1966–1975.

Vol. 1 contains the most lesbian material.

Paris 1920s

Beach, Sylvia. *Shakespeare and Co.* New York: Harcourt Brace, 1959; Lincoln, Nebraska: University of Nebraska Press (Bison), 1980.

Flanner, Janet. *Paris Was Yesterday.* New York: Popular Library, 1973.

Flanner, Janet. *Janet Flanner's World: Uncollected Writing 1932–1975.* New York: Harcourt Brace, 1979.

Monnier, Adrienne. *The Very Rich Hours of Adrienne Monnier.* New York: Scribner's 1976.

Vita Sackville West, Virginia Woolf, and Violet Trefusis

Jullian, Philippe, and Phillips, John. *The Other Woman: A Life of Violet Trefusis.* Boston: Houghton Mifflin, 1976.

Nicholson, Nigel. *Portrait of A Marriage.* New York: Bantam, 1974.

Trautmann, Joan. *The Jessamy Brides: The Friendship of Virginia Woolf and Vita Sackville West.* University Park, Pennsylvania: Pennsylvania State Studies, 1973.

George Sand

Barry, Joseph. *Infamous Woman.* New York: Doubleday, 1977.

Maurois, André. *Lelia.* New York: Penguin, 1979. (First published 1953.)

Gertrude Stein and Alice B. Toklas

Mellow, James R. *Charmed Circle: Gertrude Stein and Company.* New York: Avon, 1974.

Simon, Linda. *The Biography of Alice B. Toklas.* New York: Doubleday, 1977; Avon, 1978.

Steward, Samuel M., ed. *Dear Sammy: Letters from Gertrude Stein and Alice B. Toklas.* Boston: Houghton Mifflin, 1977.

Toklas, Alice. *What Is Remembered.* New York: Holt, Rinehart and Winston, 1963.

Toklas, Alice. *Staying on Alone.* New York: Liveright, 1973.

Renée Vivien
  Vivien, Renée. *A Woman Appeared to Me.* Tallahassee, Florida: Naiad Press, 1976.
  This is actually a fictionalized account of Vivien's relationship with Natalie Barney. Published 1904 in France.

Virginia Woolf
  Bell, Ann Olivier, ed. *The Diary of Virginia Woolf.* Vols. 1–6. New York: Harcourt Brace, 1977–. Vols. 3 and 4 contain the most lesbian material.
  Bell, Quentin. *Virginia Woolf: A Biography.* New York: Harcourt Brace, 1972.
  Nicholson, Nigel, and Trautman, Joan, eds. *The Letters of Virginia Woolf.* Vols. 1–6. New York: Harcourt Brace, 1975-1980. The letters are a gold mine. Vol. 1 contains her letters to Violet Dickinson; Vols. 3 and 4 her letters to Vita Sackville-West; Vol. 5 letters to Ethel Smyth.

Autobiography, Biography, Part II

Adair, Nancy, and Adair, Casey. *Word Is Out.* New York: Delta, 1978.
Baetz, Ruth. *Lesbian Crossroads: Personal Stories of Lesbian Struggles and Triumphs.* New York: Morrow, 1980.
Brittain, Vera. *Testament of Friendship.* New York: Wideview, 1981. (First published 1940 in England.)
Casal, Mary. *The Stone Wall.* New York: Arno Press, 1975. (First published 1930.)
Cliff, Michelle. *Claiming an Identity They Taught Me to Despise.* Watertown Massachusetts: Persephone Press, 1980.
Country Lesbians. *Country Lesbians.* Eugene, Oregon: Womanshare Books, 1976.
Cruikshank, Margaret, ed. *The Lesbian Path.* Monterey, California: Angel Press, 1980. Second edition, 1981; distributed by Naiad Press.
Falk, Ruth. *Women Loving.* New York: Random House, 1975.
Galana, Laurel, and Covina, Gina. *The New Lesbians.* San Francisco: Moon Books, 1977.
Gibson, Gifford. *By Her Own Admission: A Lesbian Mother's Fight to Keep Her Son.* New York: Doubleday, 1977.
Grier, Barbara, and Reid, Coletta, eds. *Lesbian Lives.* Oakland, California: Diana Press, 1976.
Johnston, Jill. *Lesbian Nation.* New York: Touchstone, 1973.
Johnston, Jill. *Gullibles Travels.* New York: Links, 1974.
Meigs, Mary. *Lily Briscoe: A Self-Portrait.* Vancouver: Talonbooks, 1981.
Millett, Kate. *Flying.* New York: Knopf, 1974; Ballantine, 1975.
Millett, Kate. *Sita.* New York: Farrar, Straus & Giroux, 1977.
Myron, Nancy, and Bunch, Charlotte, eds, *Women Remembered.* Oakland, California: Diana Press, 1975.
Newton, Esther, and Walton, Shirley. *Womenfriends.* N.p., 1976.
Perrin, Elula. *Women Prefer Women.* New York: Bantam, 1980.

Perrin, Elula. *So Long As There Are Women.* New York: Morrow, 1980.
Sanders, Marion K. *Dorothy Thompson: A Legend in Her Time.* New York:
    Avon, 1974.
Sarton, May. *I Knew a Phoenix.* New York: Norton, 1979.
Sarton, May. *Recovering.* New York: Norton, 1980.
Sarton, May. *A World of Light.* New York: Norton, 1976.
Sarton, May. *Journal of a Solitude.* New York: Norton, 1977.
Stanley, Julia P., and Wolfe, Susan J., eds. *The Coming Out Stories.*
    Watertown, Massachusetts: Persephone Press, 1980.
Stewart-Park, Angela, and Cassidy, Jules. *We're Here.* London: Quartet,
    1977; New York: Horizon.
Sanders, Marion K. *Dorothy Thompson: A Legend in Her Time.*
Van Deurs, Kady. *The Notebooks that Emma Gave Me.* 1978. Distributed
    by Naiad Press.
Wells, Anna Mary. *Miss Marks and Miss Woolley.* Boston: Hougton Mifflin,
    1978.
Wolff, Charlotte. *Hindsight.* London: Quartet Books, 1982.

ESSAYS, THEORY, ANALYSIS
Anthologies

Beck, Evelyn Torton, ed. *Nice Jewish Girls: A Lesbian Anthology.* Water-
    town, Massachusetts: Persephone Press, 1982.
Birkby, Phyllis, et al., eds. *Amazon Expedition.* New York: Times Change
    Press, 1973.
Building Feminist Theory. Essays from Quest. New York: Longman, 1981.
    Essays by Janice Raymond, Joanna Russ, Ginny Apuzzo, Betty Powell,
    Marilyn Frye. Charlotte Bunch, and Lucia Valeska.
Crew, Louie, ed. *The Gay Academic.* Palm Springs, California: ETC Press,
    1978.
Gibbs, Joan, and Bennett, Sara, eds. *Top Ranking: A Collection of Articles
    on Racism and Classism in the Lesbian Community.* Brooklyn, New
    York: February 3rd Press, 1980.
Jay, Karla, and Young, Alan, eds. *Out of the Closets.* New York: Jove, 1972.
Jay, Karla, and Young, Alan, eds. *After You're Out.* New York: Jove, 1975.
Jay, Karla, and Young, Alan, eds. *Lavender Culture.* New York: Jove, 1978.
Lesbians Speak Out. Oakland, California: Women's Press Collective, 1974.
Moraga, Cherríe, and Anzaldúa, Gloria, eds. *This Bridge Called My Back:
    Writings by Radical Women of Color.* Watertown, Massachusetts:
    Persephone Press, 1981. Bibliography includes works by Afro-
    American lesbians, Asian/Pacific American lesbians, Latina lesbians,
    and Native American lesbians.

General Works

Abbott, Sidney, and Love, Barbara. *Sappho Was a Right-On Woman.* New
    York: Stein & Day, 1972.
Alyson, Sasha, ed. *Young, Gay and Proud.* Boston: Alyson Publications,
    1980.

Blackmon, Mary K. *In the Best Interests of the Children*. Iris Publications, 1977.

Bowles, Juliet, ed. *In the Memory and Spirit of Frances, Zora, and Lorraine: Essays and Interviews on Black Women and Writing*. Washington, District of Columbia: Howard University Press, 1979. Interviews with Audre Lorde, Barbara Smith, and June Jordan.

Cordova, Jeanne. *Sexism: It's a Nasty Affair*. Los Angeles: New Ways Books, 1974.

Deming, Barbara. *Remembering Who We Are*. East Palo Alto: Frog in the Well Press, 1981. Distributed by Naiad Press.

Deming, Barbara. *We Cannot Live without Our Lives*. New York: Viking, 1974.

Diamond, Liz. *The Lesbian Primer*. Women's Educational Media, 1979.

Faderman, Lillian, and Eriksson, Brigette, eds. *Lesbian-Feminism in Turn-of the-Century Germany*. Tallahassee, Florida: Naiad Press, 1980.

Faderman, Lillian. *Surpassing the Love of Men: Romantic Friendship and Love Between Women from the Renaissance to the Present*. New York: William Morrow, 1981.

Goodman, Bernice. *The Lesbian: A Celebration of Difference*. Brooklyn, New York: Out and Out Books, 1977. Essays by a psychologist. Introduction by Adrienne Rich.

Hanscombe, Gillian, and Forster, Jackie. *Rocking the Cradle*. London: Peter Owen, 1981. On lesbian mothers.

Hughes, Nym, Johnson, Yvonne and Perreault, Yvette. *Stepping Out of Line*. A Workship Manual and Resource Guide on Lesbianism/Feminism. Vancouver: Press Gang Publishers, 1981.

Klaich, Dolores. *Woman Plus Woman*. New York: Morrow, 1974.

Lorde, Audre. *The Cancer Journals*. Argyle, New York: Spinsters, Ink, 1980.

Audre, Lorde. *Uses of the Erotic: The Erotic as Power*. Brooklyn, New York: Out and Out Books, 1978. Reprinted by Lesbian-Feminist Study Clearinghouse, University of Pittsburgh.

Martin, Del, and Lyon, Phyllis. *Lesbian/Woman*. San Francisco: Glide Publications, 1972; Bantam, 1973.

Molloy, Alice. *In Other Words: Notes on the Politics and Morale of Survival*. Oakland: Women's Press Collective, 1977.

Newman, Felice, and Frederique Delacoste, eds. *Women Fight Back*. Feminist Resistance to Male Violence. Minneapolis: Cleis Press, 1981.

O'Donnell, Mary, et al. *Lesbian Health Matters!* Santa Cruz: Santa Cruz Women's Health Collective, 1979.

Schwarz, Judith. *Close Friends and Devoted Companions: A History of Lesbian Relationships in America*. New York: Morrow, 1982.

Schwarz, Judith. *Radical Feminists of Heterodoxy*. Greenwich Village 1912-1940 Lebanon, New Hampshire: New Victoria Publishers, Forthcoming. Distributed by the Crossing Press. About a club for creative and unconventional women, some of whom were lesbians.

Simpson, Ruth. *From the Closets to the Courts*. New York: Viking, 1975.

Tannenhaus, Beverly. *To Know Each Other and Be Known: Women's*

Writing Workshops. Brooklyn, New York: Out & Out Books, 1978.

Vida, Ginny, ed. *Our Right to Love: A Lesbian Resource Book.* Englewood Cliffs, New Jersey: Prentice-Hall, 1978.

Wysor, Bettie. *The Lesbian Myth.* New York: Random, 1974.

Social Sciences

Brooks, Virginia. *Minority Stress and Lesbian Women.* Lexington, Massachusetts: D.C. Heath, 1981.

Ettore, E.M. *Lesbians, Women and Society.* London: Routledge & Kegan Paul, 1980.

Lewis, Sasha Gregory. *Sunday's Women.* Boston: Beacon Press, 1979.

Moses, Alice E. *Identity Management in Lesbian Women.* New York: Praeger, 1978.

Ponse, Barbara. *Identities in the Lesbian World: The Social Construction of Self.* Westport, Connecticut: Greenwood, 1978.

Ruth, Barbara. *The Politics of Relationships.* New York: Seven Woods Press, 1979.

Tanner Donna M. *The Lesbian Couple.* Lexington, Massachusetts: D.C. Heath, 1978.

Wolf, Deborah. *Aging Lesbians and Gay Men.* Berkeley: University of California Press, forthcoming.

Wolf, Deborah. *The Lesbian Community.* Berkeley: University of California Press, 1979.

Wyland, Francie. *Motherhood, Lesbianism, and Child Custody.* Toronto: Wages Due Lesbians and Falling Wall Press, 1977.

Theory

Atkinson, Ti-Grace. *Amazon Odyssey.* New York: Links, 1974.

Brown, Rita Mae. *A Plain Brown Rapper.* Oakland, California: Diana Press, 1977.

Chesler, Phyllis. *Women and Madness.* New York: Avon, 1972.

Daly, Mary. *Beyond God the Father.* Boston: Beacon Press, 1973.

Daly, Mary. *Gyn/Ecology: The Metaethics of Radical Feminism.* Boston: Beacon Press, 1978.

Gearhart, Sally, and Johnson, William. *Loving Women/Loving Men: Homosexuality and the Church.* San Francisco: Glide, 1974.

Griffin, Susan. *Woman and Nature: The Roaring Inside Her.* New York: Harper & Row, 1978.

Raymond, Janice. *The Transsexual Empire: The Making of the She-Male.* Boston: Beacon Press, 1979.

Rich, Adrienne. *Of Woman Born.* New York: Bantam, 1976.

Rich, Adrienne. *On Lies, Secrets and Silence.* New York: Norton, 1979.

Rule, Jane. *Lesbian Images.* New York: Doubleday, 1975.

Articles

Margaret Cruikshank

Most of these articles appear in easily accessible sources, for example women's studies periodicals such as *Signs: Journal of Women in Culture and Society* and *Feminist Studies*, books from mainstream publishers, and widely circulated lesbian periodicals such as *Conditions* and *Sinister Wisdom*. Other articles, which may be difficult for students and teachers to find, are taken from local periodicals such *Out and About* in Seattle and those having a small circulation but a regional or national audience, such as *Focus* in Boston. For descriptions of these and other lesbian publications see Resources: Periodicals. A few articles listed here appeared in periodicals no longer in existence: *Chrysalis, The Lesbian Tide, Gai Saber: Gay Academic Union Journal*, and *Dyke: A Quarterly*. The less accessible articles are included because of their historical importance and because reliable work on lesbians and lesbianism must consider grassroots sources. Most of the articles here were published in the last five years.

Abbitt, Diane, and Bobbie Bennett, "Being a Lesbian Mother." In *Positively Gay*, edited by Betty Berzon and Robert Leighton. Millbrae, California: Celestial Arts, 1979.

Adelman, Marcy. "A Comparison of Professionally Employed Lesbians and Heterosexual Women on the MMPI." *Archives of Sexual Behavior* 6 (1977): 193-201.

Allen, Paula Gunn. "Lesbians in American Indian Cultures." *Conditions: Seven* (1981), pp. 67-87.

Allison, Dorothy. "The Billie Jean King Thing." *The New York Native*, 18-31 May 1981, p. 10.

Allison, Dorothy. "Confrontation: Black/White." In *Building Feminist Theory: Essays from* Quest. Edited by Charlotte Bunch et al. New York: Longman, 1981.

Allison, Dorothy. "I am Working on My Charm." *Conditions: Six* (1980), pp. 15-21.

Annas, Pamela J. "Feminist Utopian Fiction: *Herland* and *The Wanderground*." *Women's Studies International Quarterly* 4 (Fall 1981), pp. 385-87.

Annas, Pamela J. "'My Lady Ain't No Lady': Teaching the Poetry of Pat Parker and Audre Lorde." Presentation at NWSA (June 1981), University of Connecticut.

"Anti-Semitism in the Lesbian Community." *Out and About*, April 1979, pp. 4-6. See also April 1980 issue, pp. 8-9.

Armaro, Hortencia, Maria Diaz, and Irma Perez-Cordova, "Lesbians Dance at Hispanic Conference." *Lesbian Tide* 9 (May/June 1980): 13.

Bennett, Paula. "The Language of Love: Emily Dickinson's Homoerotic Poetry." *Gai Saber: Gay Academic Union Journal* 1 (Spring 1977): 13-17.

Bennett, Paula. Review of *The Coming Out Stories* and *The Lesbian Path*. *Focus*, September-October 1980, pp. 25-26.

Bentley, Caryl. "Meeting Lisa." *Lesbian Insider* 1 (August 1980):30 Conference of Fat Dykes.

Berube, Allen. "Lesbian Masquerade." *Gay Community News*, 17 November 1979, pp. 8-9. On women who passed as men.

Bethel, Lorraine, and Barbara Smith, eds. *Conditions: Five* (1979). The Black women's issue.

Bethel, Lorraine. Review of Audre Lorde's *The Black Unicorn*. *Gay Community News*, 10 February 1979, Book Supplement, pp. 1, 5, 6.

Birtha, Becky. "Becoming Visible: The First Black Lesbian Conference." *New Women's Times*, 7 January 1981, pp. 3-4

Birtha, Becky. "A Mother-Daughter Victory: An Interview." *Azalea* 3 (Winter 1979-80), pp. 17-23. Julie Blackwomon's successful child custody court case.

Birtha, Becky. "For Those Who Would Be Sisters." *Feminist Review of Books* 7 (November 1979). Review of Pat Parker's *Movement in Black*.

Brady, Maureen, and McDaniel, Judith. "Lesbianism in the Mainstream: Images of Lesbians in Recent Commercial Fiction." *Conditions: Six* (1980): 82-105.

Brady, Maureen. Review of Michelle Cliff's *Claiming an Identity They Taught Me to Despise*. *Feminist Review of Books*, (Spring 1981). p. 10.

Brown, Linda. "Dark Horse: A View of Writing and Publishing by Dark Lesbians." *Sinister Wisdom* 13 (Spring 1980): 45-50. Entire issue devoted to lesbian writing and publishing.

Brownworth, Victoria. "Lesbian Nuns; Closeted in the Cloister?" *Philadelphia Gay News*, May 2-15, 1980, p. 9; May 30-June 12, 1980, p. 12.

Broumas, Olga. "Excerpts from a Talk," *Trellis* 3 (Summer 1979): 15-17.

Bulkin, Elly. "Heterosexism and Women's Studies." *Radical Teacher* 17 (Winter 1981): 25-31.

Bulkin, Elly. "Racism and Writing: Some Implications for White Lesbian Critics." *Sinister Wisdom* 13 (Spring 1980): 3-22.

Bulkin, Elly. "Teaching Lesbian Poetry." *Women's Studies Newsletter* 8 (Spring 1980): 5-8.

Bullough, Vern, and Bonnie Bullough. "Lesbianism in the 1920s and 1930s: A Newfound Study." *Signs* 2, no. 4 (Summer 1977): 895-904.

Bunch, Charlotte. "Learning from Lesbian Separatism." *MS*, November 1976.

Bunch, Charlotte. "Not for Lesbians Only." In *Building Feminist Theory: Essays from* Quest. Edited by Charlotte Bunch et al. New York: Longman, 1981.

Canaan, Andrea. "Brownness." In *This Bridge Called My Back: Writings by Radical Women of Color.* edited by Gloria Anzaldúa and Cherríe Moraga. Watertown, Massachusetts: Persephone Press, 1981.

Cavin, Susan. "Lesbians Have Natural Rhythm." *Majority Report*, 15-29 November 1975, p. 10. Lesbians in nineteenth-century voodoo ceremonies in New Orleans.

Clark, Jil. "Activist Lesbian Mother Wins N.J. Custody Battle." *Gay Community News*, 16 August 1980, pp. 1, 6.

Clark, Jil. "Becoming Visible: Black Lesbian Conference in New York City." *off our backs*, March 1981, pp. 13-14. Reprinted from *GCN*, 31 January 1981.

Clark, Jil. "Nice Jewish Girls." *Gay Community News*, May 1, 1982, 8-9. Interview with publishers of a lesbian anthology by Jewish women.

Clarke, Cheryl. Review of Pat Parker's *Movement in Black. Conditions: Six* (1980): 217-225.

Cliff, Michelle. "Notes on Speechlessness," *Sinister Widom* 5 (Winter 1978): 5.

Cook, Blanche. "Female Support Networks and Political Activism: Lillian Wald, Crystal Eastman, Emma Goldman." In A *Heritage of Her Own: Toward a New Social History of American Women.* Edited by Nancy F. Cott and Elizabeth H. Peck. New York: Simon and Schuster, 1980, pp. 60-65.

Cook, Blanche. "The Historical Denial of Lesbianism." *Radical History Review*, no. 20 (Summer 1979).

Cook, Blanche. Review essay on *The Life of Lorena Hickok, ER's Friend* by Doris Faber. *Feminist Studies* 6 (Fall 1980): 511-516.

Cook, Blanche. "Women Alone Stir My Imagination: Lesbianism in the Cultural Tradition." *Signs: Journey of Women in Culture and Society* 4 (Summer 1979): 718-739.

Cornwell, Anita. "The Black in a Malevolent Society." *Dyke: A Quarterly* 5 (1977): 14-17.

Cornwell, Anita. Interview with Audre Lorde. *Sinister Wisdom* 4 (Fall 1977): 15-21.

Cornwell, Anita. "Three for the Price of One: Notes from a Gay Black Feminist." In *Lavender Culture,* edited by Karla Jay and Allen Young. New York: Harcourt, Brace, Jovanovich, 1978.

Corinne, Tee. "Clementina Hawarden, Photographer." *Sinister Wisdom* 5 (Winter 1978): 45-49.

Cross, Tia. Freada Klein, Barbara Smith and Beverly Smith. "Face-to-Face, Day to Day, Racism CR." *Women's Studies Newletter* 8 (Winter 1980): 27-28.

Cruikshank, Cathy. "Probably Not My Last Essay on Feminism." *Out and About,* December 1980, pp. 19-20, 23. Reflections of a former separatist. Response by Joanna Russ, January 1981 issue.

Cruikshank, Cathy. "Random Thoughts on Lesbian Literature." *Margins,* August 1975, pp. 40-41. Special issue on lesbian writing and publishing edited by Beth Hodges.

Cruikshank, Margaret. "Lesbian Studies: Some Preliminary Notes." *Radical Teacher* 17 (Spring 1981): 18-19.

Cruikshank, Margaret. "Lesbians in the Academic World." In *Our Right to Love: A Lesbian Resource Book,* edited by Ginny Vida. Englewood Cliffs, N.J.: Prentice-Hall, 1978.

"Cuban Lesbians Arrive in Seattle." *Out and About,* January 1981, pp. 3-6.

Daniels, Gabrielle. "First Black Lesbian Conference." *off our backs* 10 (December 1980). pp. 4-5, 8. Report on conference held in San Francisco, October 1980. Reprinted *Lesbian Insider* 3 (April 1981): 10.

Davenport, Doris. "The Pathology of Racism: A Conversation with Third World Wimmin." In *This Bridge Called My Back,* edited by Gloria Anzaldúa and Cherríe Moraga. Watertown, Massachusetts: Persephone Press, 1981.

Davies, Rosalie. "Representing the Lesbian Mother." *Family Advocate* 21 (Winter 1979).

Davis, Madeline, Elizabeth Kennedy, and Avra Michelson. "Notes on Release Forms in Lesbian and Gay Oral History." Article #125, Lesbian-Feminist Study Clearinghouse, University of Pittsburgh, Pittsburgh, Pennsylvania.

Deming, Barbara. "Remembering Who We Are." *Quest* 4 (Summer 1977): 52-74. Open letter to Susan Saxe. Book by Deming has same title. Published 1981 by Frog in the Well Press, East Palo Alto, California.

Desmoines, Harriet; Bertha Harris,; and Irena Klepfisz, "Lesbian Literary Criticism." *Sinister Wisdom* 9 (Spring 1979): 20-30.

Doughty, Frances. "Doing Lesbian Herstory." Paper presented at the Forum, Mid-Decade Conference for International Women's Year, Copenhagen, July 1980.

Doughty, Frances. "Homophobia and the New Right." Paper presented to regional NOW conference, Moorhead, Minnesota, June 1980.

Doughty, Frances. "The World of Women: A Lesbian-Feminist Perspective on Female Sexuality." Paper presented at Fourth World Congress of Sexology, Mexico City, December 1979.

Escamilla-Mondanaro, Josette. "Lesbians and Therapy." *Psychotherapy for Women.* In *Treatment Toward Equality,* edited by Edna Rawlings and Dianne Carter. Springfield, Illinois: Charles Thomas, 1977. Also contains Barbara Sang's essay "Psychotherapy for Lesbians: Some Observations and Tentative Generalizations."

Faderman, Lillian. "Emily Dickinson's Letters to Sue Gilbert." *The Massachusetts Review* 18 (Summer 1977): 197-225.

Faderman, Lillian. "Lesbian Magazine Fiction in the Early Twentieth Century. *Journal of Popular Culture* 11 (Spring 1978): 800-817.

Faderman, Lillian. "Warding Off the Watch and Ward Society: Amy Lowell's Treatment of the Lesbian Theme." *Gay Books Bulletin* 1 (Summer 1979): 23-27.

Farley, Pamella. "Lesbianism and the Social Function of Taboo." In *The Future of Difference,* edited by Hester Eisenstein and Alice Jardine. Boston: G.K. Hall, 1980.

Fiorenza, Mary. "Persephone: Revolution in Process." *Sojourner* 6 (August 1981): 15, 26. Interview with Persephone Press women.

Frontiers, A Journal of Women's Studies 4 (Fall 1979). Lesbian history issue.

Frye, Marilyn. Review of *The Coming Out Stories. Sinister Wisdom* 14 (Summer 1980), pp. 97-98.

Frye, Marilyn. "Some Thoughts on Separatism and Power." *Sinister Wisdom* 6 (Spring 1978), pp. 30-39.

Frye, Marilyn. "To Be and Be Seen: Metaphysical Misogyny." *Sinister Wisdom* 17 (Summer 1981): 57-70.

Gearhart, Sally. "The Lesbian and God the Father or All the Church Needs is a Good Lay—on Its Side." In *Persuasion: Understanding, Practice and Analysis,* edited by Herbert W. Simons. Menlo Park, California: Addison-Wesley, 1976. Used as an example of militant rhetoric. Also appears in *Radical Religion* 1 (Spring 1974).

Gearhart, Sally. "The Spiritual Dimension: Death and Resurrection of a Hallelujah Dyke." In *Our Right to Love,* edited by Vida. Englewood, Cliffs, New Jersey: Prentice-Hall, 1978.

Gennoy, Mary. "Thoughts of a Disabled Dyke." *Lesbian Voices* 3 (Winter 1976-1977): 13.

Gibbs, Joan, and Sara Bennett. "Racism and Classism in the Lesbian Community: Towards the Building of a Radical, Autonomous Lesbian Movement." In *Top Ranking: A Collection of Articles on Racism and Classism in the Lesbian Community.* Brooklyn, New York: February 3rd Press, 1980.

Gidlow, Elsa. "Lesbianism as a Liberating Force." *Heresies* 1 (May 1977): 94-95.

Gidlow, Elsa. "Memoirs." *Feminist Studies* 6 (Spring 1980): 103-127.

Gidlow, Elsa. "On Control and Lizards at Sea." *WomanSpirit* 7 (1981): 21. Short essay on nature and technology.

Green, Richard. "Sexual Identity of 33 Children Raised by Homosexual or Transsexual Parents." *American Journal of Psychiatry* 135 (1978): 692-97. Used to support lesbian mothers in custody cases.

Grier, Barbara. "The Lesbian Paperback." Article #130 of Lesbian-Feminist Study Clearinghouse, University of Pittsburgh, Pittsburgh, Pennsylvania. Reprinted from *Tangents,* 1966.

Griffin, Susan. "Thoughts on Writing: A Diary." In *The Writer and Her Work: Contemporary Women Writers Reflect on Their Art and Situation,* edited by Janet Sternburg. New York: Norton, 1980.

Gurko, Jane. "The Shape of Sameness: Contemporary Lesbian Autobiographical Narratives." Paper presented to MLA, December 1980, Houston.

Gurko, Jane, and Sally Gearhart. "The Sword and the Vessel Versus the Lake-on-Lake: A Lesbian Model of Nonviolent Rhetoric." *Bread and Roses* 2 (Spring 1980) pp. 26-34. Excerpt from MLA paper, December 1979, San Fransicso.

Guttag, Bianca. "Homophobia in Library School." In *Revolting Librarians,* edited by Celeste West and Elizabeth Katz. San Francisco: Booklegger Press, 1972.

Hall, Marny. "Lesbian Families: Cultural and Clinical Issues." *Social Work* 23 (September 1978): 380-385.

Hammer, Barbara. "Lesbian Aesthetics." *The Blatant Image: A Magazine of Feminist Photography* 1 (1981).

Hammer, Barbara. "Lesbian Space." *Discourse: Berkeley Journal for Theoretical Studies in Media and Culture* 4 (Fall 1981).

Hammer, Barbara. "Women's Images in Film." In *Women's Culture,* edited by Gayle Kimball. Metuchen, New Jersey: Scarecrow Press, 1981.

Harris, Barbara. "Lesbian Mother Child Custody: Legal and Psychiatric Aspects." *Bulletin of the American Academy of Psychiatry and Law* 75 (1977).

Harris, Bertha. "The More Profound Nationality of Their Lesbianism: Lesbian Society in Paris in the 1920's." In *Amazon Expedition,* edited by Phyllis Birkby. New York: Times Change Press, 1973.

Henry, Alice. "Women's History: A Report from the Berkshire Conference." *off our backs* 11 (August-September 1981), pp. 2-7. Includes accounts of lesbian presentations.

Heresies 3 (Fall 1977). Lesbian art and artists issue.

Hoagland, Sarah. "Androcentric Rhetoric in Sociobiology." *Women's Studies International Quarterly* 3 (1980). Reprinted in *The Voice and Words of Women and Men.* Edited by Cheris Kramarae. Oxford: Pergamon Press, 1981.

Hoagland, Sarah. "Lesbian Ethics." *Lesbian Insider* 2 (January 1981): 3, 9, 15, 26-29.

Hoagland, Sarah. "Re-membering Lesbian Lives." *Sinister Wisdom* 14 (Summer 1980), pp. 52-56.

Hodges, Beth. Interview with Joan and Deborah of the Lesbian Herstory Archives. *Sinister Wisdom* 11 (Fall 1979): 3-13. Part 2, *Sinister Wisdom* 13 (Spring 1980), pp. 101-105.

Hodges, Beth. Interview with Michelle Cliff. *Gay Community News* 7 (7 February 1981): 8-9.

Hodges, Beth, ed. *Margins,* no. 23 (August 1975). Special issue on lesbian-feminist writing and publishing.

Hodges, Beth, ed. *Sinister Wisdom* 13 (Spring 1980). Lesbian writing and publishing. See also *Sinister Wisdom* 2 (Fall 1976).

Hollibaugh, Amber. "Right to Rebel." In *Homosexuality: Power and Politics,* edited by Gay Left Collective. London: Allison and Busby, 1980.

Hull, Gloria. "'Under the Days': The Buried Life of Angelina Weld Grimké." *Conditions: Five* (1979): 17–25.

Hull, Gloria. Review of Audre Lorde's *Between Ourselves. Conditions: One* (1977): 97–100.

"In Amerika They Call Us Dykes." In *Our Bodies, Ourselves: A Book by and for Women,* by the Boston Women's Health Collective. New York: Simon and Schuster, 2d ed., 1979.

Israel, Laura. Review of *Sunday's Women* by Sasha Gregory Lewis. *Gay Books Bulletin* 4 (Fall 1980): 6–8.

Jumpcut, no. 24/25 (1981). Special issue on lesbians and film. Articles on lesbian vampires; Barbara Hammer; Jan Oxenberg; *Maedchen in Uniform*; filmography by Andrea Weiss.

Kaye, Melanie. "Anti-Semitism, Homophobia, and the Good White Knight." *off our backs* 12 (May 1982), 30-31. Experiences of a lesbian women's studies teacher at a university in the Southwest. This special education issue of *off our backs* includes other lesbian articles.

Kaye, Melanie. "Culture Making: Lesbian Classics in the Year 2000?" *Sinister Wisdom* 13 (Spring 1980): 23–34.

Kaye, Melanie. "Women and Violence." *Fight Back!: Feminist Resistance to Male Violence,* edited by Felice Newman and Frederique Delacoste. Minneapolis: Cleis Press, 1981.

Kearns, Martha. "Making the Invisible Visible: The Lesbian Imagery of Arleen Olshan." *The Lesbian Tide* 8 (July/August 1978): 12.

Klepfisz, Irena. "Women Without Children/Without Families/Alone." *Womanews,* May 1981, p. 7. Reprinted in *Why Children,* edited by Stephanie Dowrick and Sibyl Grundberg. New York: Harcourt Brace Jovanovich, 1981.

Kolodny, Annette. "The Lady's Not for Spurning: Kate Millett and the Critics." In *Women's Autobiography: Essays in Criticism,* edited by Estelle C. Jelinek. Bloomington, Indiana: Indiana University Press, 1980.

Koolish, Lynda. "Choosing Ourselves, Each Other, and This Life." *Sinister Wisdom* 10 (Summer 1979). pp. 94-102. On Rich, Lorde, Glück, and Plath.

Koolish, Lynda. "The Incendiary Feminism of Lesbian Poetry." *San Francisco Bay Guardian,* 23 March 1978 p. 11.

Kort, Michelle. "Is She or Isn't She? Women Athletes and Their Gender Identity." *Chrysalis* 9 (Fall 1979): 76–80.

Langer, Sandra. "Fashion, Character and Sexual Politics in Some Romaine Brooks' Lesbian Portraits." Article #131, Lesbian-Feminist Study Clearinghouse, University of Pittsburgh, Pittsburgh, Pennsylvania.

Larkin, Joan. "Nothing Safe: The Poetry of Audre Lorde. *Margins* 23 (August 1975): 23-25.

Lehman, Lee. "Sappho Moves into Astrology." *WomanSpirit* 7 (Spring 1981): 42-43.

"Lesbians of the World Unite." *Connexiôns,* Spring 1981, pp. 12-13. Report on international lesbian conference, Amsterdam 1980.

Loewenstein, Andrea. "Sad Stories: A Reflection on the Fiction of Ann Bannon." *Gay Community News,* 24 May 1980, pp. 8-9, 12.

Lorde, Audre. "Man Child: A Black Lesbian-Feminist's Response." *Conditions: Four* (Winter 1979) pp. 30-31 Reprinted by Lesbian-Feminist Study Clearinghouse.

Lorde, Audre. "An Open Letter to Mary Daly." In *Top Ranking: A Collection of Articles on Racism and Classism in the Lesbian Community,* edited by Joan Gibbs and Sara Bennett. Brooklyn: February 3rd Press, 1980.

Lorde, Audre. "Poems are not Luxuries." *Chrysalis* 3 (1977): 7-9.

Lorde, Audre. "Scratching the Surface: Some Notes on Barriers to Women and Loving." *Black Scholar* 9 (April 1978): 31-35.

Lottman, Loretta. "I Was the Dyke at My High School Reunion." In *Lavender Culture,* edited by Karla Jay and Allen Young. New York: Harcourt Brace Jovanovich, 1978.

Lunden, Doris. "Class." In *Our Right to Love,* edited by Vida. Englewood Cliffs, New Jersey: Prentice-Hall, 1978.

McCray, Chirlane. "I Am a Lesbian." *Essence,* September 1979, p. 90.

McDaniel, Judith. "A Conversation with Jan Clausen." *Motheroot* 1, no. 3 (Summer 1979). p. 2.

McDaniel, Judith. "A Conversation with Muriel Rukeyser." *Feminist Review of Books* 10 (Spring 1980): 4-5.

McDaniel, Judith. "Is There Room for Me in the Closet: My Life as the Only Lesbian Professor." *Heresies* 7 (Fall 1979): 36-39. Reprinted in *The Lesbian Path,* edited by Margaret Cruikshank.

Macdonald, Barbara. "The Development of the Contemporary Lesbian Short Story." *Feminist Review of Books,* June 1981, pp. 8-9.

Macdonald, Barbara. "Look Me in the Eye." *Sinister Wisdom* 16 (Spring 1981): 11-19. Combatting stereotypes of older women.

Macdonald, Barbara, and Cynthia Rich,. "Coming Out With Culture." *Sojourner* 6 (August 1981): 17, 27. Interview with Joan Larkin and Elly Bulkin, editors of *Lesbian Poetry: An Anthology.*

McNamara, Devon. Interview with Adrienne Rich. *Trellis* 3 (Summer 1979): 46-51.

McNaron, Toni. "Finding and Studying Lesbian Culture." *Radical Teacher* 6 (December 1977): 14-20. An excellent early article on the subject.

Maenad 6 (Winter 1981-1982). Special issue on the lesbian/heterosexual split.

Manahan, Nancy. "Lesbian Books: A Long Search." *Mother Jones* 1 (April 1976) pp. 63-65. Reprinted in *The Lesbian Path,* edited by Margaret Cruikshank.

Manahan, Nancy. "The Lesbian: A Survey." *Sexism in Education.*

Minneapolis: The Emma Willard Task Force on Education, 1972.

Marks, Elaine. "Lesbian Intertextuality." In *Homosexualities and French Literature,* edited by Elaine Marks and George Stambolian. Ithaca: Cornell, 1979. Collection also includes Monique Wittig's essay, "Paradigm."

Martin, Del. "Concerns of Lesbian Parents." In *Matrifocal Family: Its Effects on Mothers and Children*, p. 58. Edited by Dee Graham and Edna Rawlings. In press.

Martin, Del. "If That's All There Is." *Vector,* November 1970. A good-bye to gay male liberation. Reprinted by KNOW, Pittsburgh.

Martin, Del, and Phyllis Lyon,. "The Older Lesbian." In *Positively Gay*, edited by Betty Berzon and Robert Leighton. Millbrae, California: Celestial Arts, 1979).

Martin, Del, and Sally Gearhart,. "Afterthought: Lesbians as Gays and as Women." *We'll Do It Ourselves: Combating Sexism in Education,* edited by David Rosen, Steve Werner, and Barbara Yates. Lincoln, Nebraska: University of Nebraska Press, 1974.

Meyers, Janet. "Diaspora Takes a Queer Turn: A Jewish Lesbian Considers Her Past." *Dyke* 5 (Fall 1977): 12–14. Issue devoted to ethnic lesbians.

Motive (1972). Lesbian feminist issue.

"National Lesbian Conference—London 1980." *Gay News* [London], no. 213, 16–29 April 1981, pp. 6–7.

Nestle, Joan. "Butch/fem and sexual courage." *The Body Politic*, September 1981, pp. 29-31. On roles in the 1950s.

Nestle, Joan. "I Didn't Go Back There Anymore: Mabel Hampton Talks About the South." *Feminary* 10 (1977): 7-17. Interview with seventy-seven-year-old Black lesbian.

Nestle, Joan. "The Lesbian Herstory Archives." *Focus*, February-March 1979, pp. 8-9.

Nestle, Joan. "Surviving and More: Interview with Mabel Hampton. *Sinister Wisdom* 10 (Summer 1979): 19-24.

Nicholson, Catherine. "Notes on Deafness." *Sinister Wisdom* 8 (Winter 1979): 63-66.

Niemi, Judith. "Jane Rule and the Reviewers." *Margins* 23 (August 1975): 34-37.

Noda, Barbara; Kitty Tsui, and Z Wong,. "Coming Out: We are Here in the Asian Community. A Dialogue with Three Asian Women." *Bridge: An Asian-American Perspective* 7 (Spring 1979): 22-24. Reprinted by Lesbian-Feminist Study Clearinghouse.

"Observations of a Black Lesbian Feminist: an Interview with Marie Dennis." *Dinah* [Lesbian Activist Bureau, Cincinnati], March 1977, pp. 1-6.

off our backs 11, no. 5 (May 1981). Special issue on women and disability. Several articles by and about disabled lesbians.

Orenstein, Gloria Feman. "The Salon of Natalie Barney: An Interview with Berthe Cleyreruge." *Signs: Journal of Women in Culture and Society* (1979): 484-496.

Pagelow, Mildred. "Heterosexual and Lesbian Single Mothers: A Comparison of Problems, Coping, and Solutions." *Journal of Homosexuality* 5 (September 1980): 189-204.

Parker, Pat. "Revolution: It's Not Neat or Pretty or Quick." In *This Bridge Called My Back,* edited by Cherríe Moraga and Gloria Anzaldúa.

Paz, Juana Maria. Review of *This Bridge Called My Back. Lesbian Insider,* no. 6 (February 1982), p. 14.

Paz, Juana Maria. "Womyn and Colour: A Puerto Rican Dyke Examines Her Roots." *off our backs* 9 (June 1979).

Potter, Clare. "Black Lesbian Herstory." *Plexus,* July 1981, p. 14. Review of JR Roberts's *Black Lesbians: An Annotated Bibliography.*

Potter, Sandra, and Trudy Darty. "Social Work and the Invisible Minority: An Exploration of Lesbianism." *Social Work* 26 (May 1981): 187-198.

Pratt, Minnie Bruce, and Mab Segrest,. "Conversations with Barbara Deming." *Feminary* 11 (1981): 71-85.

Quintanales, Mirtha. "The Politics of Lesbian Biography: Cross-Cultural Perspectives on Lesbian Historiography." Paper presented at NWSA, Bloomington, May 1980. Other panelists: Sabrina Sojourner, Angela Wilson, and Frances Doughty.

Radical Teacher 17 (Spring 1981). Special issue on women's studies: Black women's studies and lesbian studies. Edited by Pam Annas.

Raven, Arlene. "The Eye of the Be*Hold*Her: The Lesbian Vision of Romaine Brooks." *Sinister Wisdom* 16 (Spring 1981): 35-42.

Raven, Arlene, and Ruth Iskin,. "Though the Peephole: Lesbian Sensibility in Art." *Chrysalis* 4 (1977): 19-31.

Reagan, Patty. "Lesbian Women and their Relationship to Health Professionals." *Patient Counseling and Health Education* 3 (1st Quarter 1981): 21-25.

Refractory Girl 5 (Summer 1974). Special issue on lesbians. Australian periodical.

Rich, Adrienne. "Compulsory Heterosexuality and Lesbian Existence." *Signs: Journal of Women in Culture and Society* (Summer 1980): 631-657.

Rich, Cynthia. "Reflections on Eroticism." *Sinister Wisdom* 15 (Fall 1980): 59-63.

Riddle, Dorothy, and Barbara Sang,. "Psychotherapy with Lesbians." *Journal of Social Issues* 34 (1978): 84-100. Special issue on psychology and the lesbian/gay community.

Roberts, JR. "Lesbian Hoboes: Their Lives and Times." *Dyke* (Fall 1977). pp. 36-49. Reprinted by Lesbian-Feminist Study Clearinghouse.

Roth, Audrey. "Assaults on Lesbians—More Brutal and on Rise." *Womanews,* May 1981, p. 3.

Sabaroff, Nina. "Lesbian Sexuality: an Unfinished Saga." In *After You're Out,* edited by Karla Jay and Allen Young. New York: Harcourt Brace Jovanovich, 1975.

Sahli, Nancy. "Smashing: Women's Relationships Before the Fall." *Chrysalis* 8 (Summer 1979): 17-27.

Sand, Cy-thea, "Radclyffe Hall: A Feminist Analysis." *Maenad* 1 (Winter 1981): 78-90.

Schuster, Marilyn R. "Strategies for Survival: The Subtle Subversion of Jane Rule." *Feminist Studies* 7 (Fall 1981): 431-50.

Schwarz, Judith. "E. Jane Gay (1830-1919)." *The Blatant Image: A Magazine of Feminist Photography* 1 (Summer 1981): 28-29.

Schwarz, Judith. "On Being Physically Different." *Sinister Wisdom* 7 (Fall 1978): 41-50.

Schwarz, Judith. "Researching Lesbian History." *Sinister Wisdom* 5 (Winter 1978): 55-59.

Seajay, Carol. "The Class and the Closet." In *Top Ranking*, edited by Joan Gibbs and Sara Bennett.

Secor, Cynthia. "Lesbian—The Doors Open." *Change Magazine* 7 (February 1975): 13-17.

Segrest, Mab. "Lines I Dare to Write: Lesbian Writing in the South." *Southern Exposure* 9 (Summer 1981). p. 53.

Segrest, Mab. "Southern Women Writing: Toward a Literature of Wholeness." *Feminary* 10 (1980): 28-43.

Shabazz, Naeemah. "Homophobia: Myths and Realities." *Heresies* 8 (1979): 34-36. Issue on Third World Women: the Politics of Being Other.

Shockley, Ann Allen. "The Black Lesbian in American Literature: an Overview." *Conditions: Five* (Autumn 1979): 133-142.

Shockley, Ann Allen. "Third World Lesbian/Feminist Writing and Publishing: a Pragmatic View." Paper read to Third World Lesbian Writers Conference, Hunter College, April 1980, by Audre Lorde.

Sheldon, Caroline. "Lesbians and Films: Some Thoughts." In *Gays and Films*, edited by Richard Dyer. London: British Film Institute, 1977.

Smith, Barbara. "The Other Black Women." *Gay Community News*, 28 February 1981, p. 5. Keynote address at first Eastern Black Lesbian conference, New York, Janaury 1981.

Smith, Barbara. "Racism and Women's Studies. *Frontiers*, Spring 1980, pp. 48-49.

Smith, Barbara. "Towards a Black Feminist Criticism." *Conditions: Two* (1977): 25-44.

Smith, Beverly. "Surviving These Hard Times." *Gay Community News*, 11 July 1981, p. 5. Keynote speech to the New England Lesbian and Gay Conference, Boston University, June 1981.

Smith, Beverly. and Barbara Smith,. "I am Not Meant to be Alone and Without You Who Understand: Letters from Black Feminists." *Conditions: Four* (1979), 62-77.

Smith, Beverly; Judith Stein,; and Priscilla Golding., "The Possibility of Life Between Us: A Dialogue Between Black and Jewish Women." *Conditions: Seven* (1981), pp. 25-46.

Sojourner, Sabrina. "On Gender and Color." *Coming Up* [San Francisco], October 1980, p. 1.

Snow, Jennifer. "All We Really Are Is Open." *Country Women*, April 1975, pp. 22-26. Sexuality issue.

Stanley, Julia. "Homosexual Slang." *American Speech* 45 (1970): 45-49.

Stanley, Julia. "The Lesbian Perspective: Pedagogy and the Structure of Human Knowledge." Paper presented to the National Council of Teachers of English, Chicago, November 1976.

Stanley, Julia. "Lesbian Separatism: The Linguistic and Social Sources of Separatist Politics." In *The Gay Academic*, edited by Louie Crew. Palm Springs, California: ETC Publications, 1978.

Stanley, Julia. "Teaching Lesbian Novels: From Proposal to Reality." Article #114, Lesbian-Feminist Study Clearinghouse.

Stanley, Julia, and Susan Wolfe, "Crooked and Straight in Academia." In *Pulling Our Own Strings: Feminist Humor and Satire,* edited by Gloria Kaufman and Mary Kay Blakely. Bloomington: University of Indiana Press, 1980.

Star, Susan Leigh. "The Politics of Wholeness: Lesbian Feminism as an Altered State of Consciousness." *Sinister Wisdom* 5 (Winter 1978), pp. 82-102.

Star, Susan Leigh. Review essay on Deborah Wolf's *The Lesbian Community. Journal of Homosexuality* 5 (Summer 1980): 415-417.

Stracher, Carol. "Choosing Lesbian Life at 73," *The Boston Globe*, 2 February 1981. Interview with Elizabeth Dunker.

Stein, Judith, and RaeRae Sears, "Fat, Lesbian, and Proud." *Gay Community News,* 28 March 1981, pp. 8-9.

Steward, Samuel. M. "France and Gertie and Sam and Alice." *The Advocate,* 14 May 1918, pp. 19-22. Recollections of Gertrude Stein and Alice B. Toklas.

Tilchen, Maida. "Ebb Tide: The Editor and Publisher of *The Lesbian Tide* Discuss Beginnings and Endings." *Gay Community News,* 28 February 1981, pp. 8-9.

Urbanska, Wanda. "Conversation with Rita Mae Brown." *California Living. Los Angeles Herald Examiner,* 3 May 1918, p. 5.

Valeska, Lucia. "The Future of Female Separatism." In *Building Feminist Theory,* edited by Charlotte Bunch et al. New York: Longman, 1981.

Van Deurs, Kady. "The Notebooks that Emma Gave Me." *Sinister Widsom* 7 (Fall 1978): 84-91. Excerpt from autobiography.

Wechsler, Nancy. "Sadomasochism: Fears, Facts. Fantasies." *Gay Community News*, 15 August 1981, pp. 6-8. Interview with Pat Califia and Gayle Rubin.

White, Toni. "Lesbian Studies Flourish at National Women's Studies Conference." *off our backs*, July 1980, pp. 16-19.

"Women Loving Women." Special issue of *Women: A Journal of Liberation* 5 (1977).

Wood-Thompson, Susan. Review of Adrienne Rich's *Dream of a Common Language. Feminary* (Autumn 1979), pp. 68-70.

W.S. "Notes from Just Over the Edge: a New Lesbian Speaks Out." *The Second Wave* 6 (1981): 10-26.

Zimmerman, Bonnie. "Exiting from Patriarchy: The Lesbian Novel of Development." *In Formation/Deformation/Transformation: The Female Novel of Development,* edited by Elizabeth Abel, Marianne Hirsch, and Elizabeth Langland. In press.

Zimmerman, Bonnie. "Lesbianism 101." *Radical Teacher* 17 (Spring 1981): 20-24. Reprinted by Lesbian-Feminist Study Clearinghouse.

Zimmerman, Bonnie. "What Has Never Been: an Overview of Lesbian Feminist Literary Criticism." *Feminist Studies* 7 (Fall 1981): 451-76.

INDEX

[Index covers text and footnotes; see Resources, Appendix, and Bibliography for author, subject, and title listings.]

Constitution of, 54
Negroes of New York 1936-41, 104
The New Woman's Theater, 67, 139-40
The New York Times, 53
The New York Times Index, 162-164
Newman, Felice, 146
Nicholson, Katherine, 167
Nightwood, 137-38
Nin, Anais, 135
No More Masks!, 32-33, 51
Noda, Barbara, 38-39, 52
NOW, 13, 167

Of Woman Born, ix, 79
Offir, Carole, 80
O'Keefe, Joan, 144
Olsen, Tillie, 83, 128, 131
  "One Out of Twelve", 128
  "Tell Us A Riddle", 83
Olson, Karen, 151
Operation *Concern*, 169
Orpheus, 35
Ottley, Roi, 104
Our Right To Love: A Lesbian Resource Book, 52, 53, 79, 80, 104-5, 130
Owens, Rochelle, 145

Parker, Pat, 36, 37
Parsons, Jacqueline, 80
Pearson, Carol, 138
Peery, Patricia, 80
Penelope, Julia, xvii, 58, 79, 80, 99, 131, 226
Peretz, I. I., 82
Perry, Marjean, 139
Philips, Katherine, 50, 144, 146
Philosophy and Women, 99
Pierce, Christine, 99
Piercy, Marge, 135, 141, 145
Pinson, Luvenia, 104
The Poetry of the Blues, 106
Poets Press, 37
Pogoncheff, Elaine, 172
Poor, Matile, 165-173
Pope, Katherine, 138
Potter, Clare, 152-161, 186

Queen Christina of Sweden, 67, 139-40

Radicalesbians, 71, 79, 93, 128
  "Woman Identified Woman", 71
Radical History Review, xvii
Radical Teacher, xv, xviii, 52, 53
Rainey, Carol, 146
Rainey, Ma, 106
Raphael, Sharon, 172
Rapone, Anita, 79
The Readers' Guide to Periodical Literature, 162-164
Rebirth of Feminism, 130
Red Clay Books, 143
Red, Ida VSW, xv, 162-64
Redmond, Fergus, 106
Reid, Coletta, 51, 67, 129, 130
Rich, Adrienne, x, xiii, xvi, xvii, 13, 30, 31, 37, 38, 44-46, 51-53, 59-60, 64-65, 71, 79, 99, 135-37, 144-46, 167.
  Adrienne Rich's Poetry, 45
  Diving into the Wreck, 45
  The Dream of a Common Language, 31, 45, 53, 59, 65
  "For Judith, Taking Leave,", 45-46
  Of Woman Born, x, 79
  Poems: Selected and New, 45
  Twenty-One Love Poems, 44, 53
Rising Tides, 32-33, 144
Roberts, Joan L., 131
Roberts, JR, xv, xviii, 103-109, 113, 153
  Black Lesbians: An Annotated Bibliography, 103
Robinson, Mina K., 172
Rockwell, Niki, 234
Roles Women Play: Readings Toward Women's Liberation, 129
Rosaldo, Michelle K., 30
Rose, Suzanne, 80
Rosebrook, Jacqueline Higgins, 52
Rosenberg, B. G., 80
Rosetti, Christina, 50, 143
Rotter, Pat, 142
Rubin, Gayle, 112
Ruble, Diane, 80
Ruby, Kathryn, 51, 145
Rubyfruit Jungle, x, 55, 66-67
Rukeyser, Muriel, 3, 7, 32, 35-36, 143
  "The Conjugation of the Paramecium," 35, 36
  "Käthe Kollwitz," 143
  "The Poem as Mask," 35, 36
  "The Speed of Darkness," 32, 35
  "The Transgress,", 35, 36

Contributor's Notes

EVELYN TORTON BECK is a movement activist and an academic. She teaches courses on "Lesbian Culture," "The Jewish Woman," and "Women in the Arts" at the University of Wisconsin, Madison. She is co-editor of an interdisciplinary feminist anthology, *The Prism of Sex* (University of Wisconsin Press, 1979), and an anthology about Jewish lesbians, *Nice Jewish Girls*, published by Persephone Press.

PAULA BENNETT raises kids, pets, and vegetables in Lincoln, Massachusetts. She edits *FOCUS: A Journal for Lesbians*, serves as treasurer and membership secretary for the gay caucus of the Modern Language Association, and teaches at Northeastern University. She was elected to a three-year term on the Lincoln School Committee. If she had it to do over she would count loons in northern Canada.

BECKY BIRTHA. A Black lesbian-feminist writer of short stories, poetry, and reviews, she has been taking herself seriously as a writer since she was sixteen. She is now thirty-two. Her work has appeared in *Azalea, Sinister Wisdom, Conditions, The New Women's Times Feminist Review*, and in the anthologies *A Woman's Touch* and *Lesbian Poetry*.

CLARE BRIGHT teaches women's studies at Mankato State University. Feminist philosophy represents the intersection of her intellectual, political, and personal interests. Besides women, she loves softball, Italian food, banjo music, and her feet.

ELLY BULKIN, co-editor of *Lesbian Poetry: An Anthology* and editor of *Lesbian Fiction: An Anthology* (Persephone Press), is a founding editor of *Conditions*. She has written about teaching lesbian poetry in *College English, Radical Teacher*, and *Women's Studies Newsletter*, about racism and writing in *Sinister Wisdom*; and about heterosexism and women's studies in *Radical Teacher*. A Jewish lesbian whose father and maternal grandparents emigrated from Eastern Europe, she lives in Brooklyn with her lover and their 11-year-old daughter.

MARGARET CRUIKSHANK edited *The Lesbian Path*, a collection of autobiographical writing. She lives in San Francisco and reviews lesbian books.

DORIS JUANITA DAVENPORT likes yoga, saunas, jogging, and camping trips and believes that the potential and power of wimmin is Unlimited, once we get our shit together. She is working on hers, with the help of Yemaye.

MADELINE DAVIS is a member of the Buffalo Women's Oral History Project, a singer, guitar player, songwriter, quilter, and an ardent cat person. She is the only "out" librarian in the Buffalo and Erie County Library system and was the first open lesbian elected delegate to a national convention (Democratic, McGovern, 1972).

FRANCES DOUGHTY. Quicksilver and roots. The play of form *and* content: interactions. Someday: a therapist/artist/writer living in light, air, birds, and trees in the deepness of a rich and long partnership. She was a founding board member and chair of the women's caucus of the National Gay Task Force.

LILLIAN FADERMAN has published *Lesbian-Feminism in Turn-of-the-Century Germany* (Naiad Press, 1980); *Surpassing the Love of Men: Romantic Friendship and Love between Women from the Renaissance to Present*; and numerous articles on love between women. She is presently at work on a book about the early nineteenth century Scottish trial on which Lillian Hellman based *The Children's Hour.*

KARLENE FAITH is a mother, writer, teacher, and community organizer with special interests in music, cross-cultural alliances, and women in prison. She has completed her Ph.D. in the History of Consciousness, University of California at Santa Cruz.

CORALYN FONTAINE lives and works in Pittsburgh, Pennsylvania, and coordinates the Lesbian Feminist Study Clearinghouse. The martial arts are her love, and she currently holds a brown belt in Shorin-Ryu Karate after studying with Karate Women of Pittsburgh for the past four and a half years. Her other love is the outdoors, especially backpacking, kayaking, and cross-country skiing.

ESTELLE FREEDMAN lives in San Francisco and teaches women's history at Stanford. She is the author of *Their Sisters' Keepers: Women's Prison Reform in America 1830–1930* (University of Michigan Press, 1981).

MARILYN FRYE is a writer, teacher, philosopher, and lifelong constant companion to an artist. She likes good food and wine and intelligent conversation.

JANE GURKO is Professor of English and Associate Dean of Humanities at San Francisco State University. She was a founder of women's studies on her campus and teaches courses in women's literature (including lesbian literature) and women's writing skills. She writes articles on contemporary gay, feminist, and lesbian-feminist literature.

KATHLEEN HICKOK is an assistant professor of English and women's studies at Iowa State University. She is just finishing a book on the image of women in women's poetry in nineteenth-century England. She has been a feminist activist for many years, holding various local and state positions in the National Organization for Women, and she seldom misses a march or demonstration.

PAT HYNES is an environmental engineer who works in the enforcement of hazardous waste regulations. She has designed a two-story passive solar greenhouse. She was a founder of Bread and Roses, a woman's vegetarian restaurant and feminist cultural center in Cambridge.

LYNDALL MACCOWAN is a bibliographer (*Word is Out*, Delta/New Glide Publications, 1978). She taught the first "Lesbian in Literature" course at San Francisco State, and is a member of the San Francisco Lesbian and Gay History Project. She lives in Oaklad with her love and their menagerie.

TONI A.H. MCNARON. At forty-four she struggles to integrate being a transplanted Southerner, a tenured university professor, a poet, a recovering alcoholic, and an incest survivor.

NANCY MANAHAN teaches part time at a San Francisco Bay Area College. She has published articles in *Mother Jones, Plexus, Lesbian Voices, Focus, American Notes and Queries,* and in two books: *The Lesbian Path* and *First Person Female American: An Annotated Bibliography of Autobiographies of American Women Living After 1950.* Nancy also backpacks, gardens, does therapeutic massage, and is a part-time parent.

CHERRÍE MORAGA is a L.A.-born Chicana turned Brooklyn-based writer and cultural worker. She is the co-editor of *This Bridge Called My Back: Writings By Radical Women of Color* and is presently working on a play about "the life."

LINN NI COBHAN is the pseudonym of a lesbian writer who is opposed to pseudonyms. She often has to work as a secretary but nonetheless puts the experience to good use. A pacifist, she lives on the West Coast, studies Aikido and raises cats (seven).

MATILE POOR is a therapist who does organizing and consciousness raising in the gay and lesbian community and for service workers concerning the needs of older lesbians. She is also a university administrator.

CLARE POTTER coordinates the Index to Lesbian Periodicals Project. She lives in Palo Alto.

IDA VSW RED writes and performs with Mothertongue, a feminist readers' theater in San Francisco and edits, researches funding, and manages a research library for the Aging Health Policy Center at the University of California. *The Lesbian Path* includes her autobiographical sketch "Naming," and she is co-editor of *The Nation's Health*, a Courses by Newspaper reader. Ida is searching for the ideal doctoral program in women's literature, fairly compensated work in women's research, and the great feminist theater of her dreams.

JR ROBERTS is a trained librarian (MLS, State University of New York, Geneseo, 1976). Formerly a rural woman, she has lived in cities for the last eight years. Her articles on lesbian culture and history have appeared in *Lavender Woman, Dyke Magazine, Sinister Wisdom,* and *Radical Teacher.* Her bibliography, *Black Lesbians: An Annotated Bibliography,* was published by Naiad Press in 1981. Currently she is enjoying researching her family's history.

MAB SEGREST is a lesbian poet who works on *Feminary: A Feminist Journal for the South*. She may be unemployed by the time her article comes out.

BARBARA SMITH is a Black feminist writer and activist. Recent work has appeared in *Lesbian Poetry: An Anthology* and *This Bridge Called My Back: Writings by Radical Women of Color*. She is the co-editor of *Conditions* 5 (The Black Women's Issue) and *All the Women Are White, All the Blacks Are Men, But Some of Us Are Brave: Black Women's Studies* (The Feminist Press, 1981).

SUE STURTZ is a psychologist who counsels with lesbians and sells books in Tucson, Arizona. She can be found climbing mountains, playing banjo and bongos, and writing outrageous essays and the great lesbian romance.

BONNIE ZIMMERMAN teaches women's studies at San Diego State University. She has published widely in academic and movement journals. She loves being a lesbian and says so every chance she gets.

THE FEMINIST PRESS offers alternatives in education and in literature. Founded in 1970, this nonprofit, tax-exempt educational and publishing organization works to eliminate sexual stereotypes in books and schools and to provide literature with a broad vision of human potential. The publishing program includes reprints of important works by women, feminist biographies of women, and nonsexist children's books. Curricular materials, bibliographies, directories, and a quarterly journal provide information and support for students and teachers of women's studies. In-service projects help to transform teaching methods and curricula. Through publications and projects, The Feminist Press contributes to the rediscovery of the history of women and the emergence of a more humane society.

Feminist Classics from the Feminist Press

Brown Girl, Brownstones, a novel by Paule Marshall. Afterword by Mary Helen Washington. $6.95 paper.

Call Home the Heart, a novel of the thirties by Fielding Burke, Introduction by Alice Kessler-Harris and Paul Lauter and afterwords by Sylvia Cook and Anna W. Shannon. $8.95 paper.

Cassandra by Florence Nightingale. Introduction by Myra Stark. Epilogue by Cynthia Macdonald. $2.50 paper.

The Convert, a novel by Elizabeth Robins. Introduction by Jane Marcus. $5.95 paper.

Daughter of Earth, a novel by Agnes Smedley. Afterword by Paul Lauter. $10.00 cloth, $5.50 paper.

Guardian Angel and Other Stories by Margery Latimer. Afterwords by Louis Kampf, Meridel Le Sueur, and Nancy Loughridge. $16.95 cloth. $7.95 paper.

I Love Myself When I Am Laughing...And Then Again When I Am Looking Mean and Impressive by Zora Neale Hurston. Edited by Alice Walker. Introduction by Mary Helen Washington. $16.95 cloth, $7.95 paper.

Life in the Iron Mills by Rebecca Harding Davis. Biographical interpretation by Tillie Olsen. $4.50 paper.

The Living is Easy, a novel by Dorothy West. Afterword by Adelaide M. Cromwell. $6.95 paper.

The Maimie Papers. Edited by Ruth Rosen and Sue Davidson. Introduction by Ruth Rosen. $15.95 cloth, $6.95 paper.

Portraits of Chinese Women in Revolution by Agnes Smedley. Edited with an introduction by Jan MacKinnon and Steve MacKinnon. $4.50 paper.

Ripening: Selected Work, 1927-1980 by Meridel Le Sueur. Edited with an introduction by Elaine Hedges. $14.95 cloth, $7.95 paper.

The Silent Partner, a novel by Elizabeth Stuart Phelps. Afterword by Mari Jo Buhle and Florence Howe. $6.95 paper.

These Modern Women. Edited with an introduction by Elaine Showalter. $4.95 paper.

Weeds, a novel by Edith Summers Kelley. Afterword by Charlotte Goodman. $6.95 paper.

The Woman and the Myth: Margaret Fuller's Life and Writings by Bell Gale Chevigny. $8.95 paper.

Women Working: An Anthology of Stories and Poems. Edited and with an introduction by Nancy Hoffman and Florence Howe. $6.95 paper.

The Yellow Wallpaper by Charlotte Perkins Gilman. Afterword by Elaine Hedges. $2.25 paper.

Other Titles from The Feminist Press

Antoinette Brown Blackwell: A Biography by Elizabeth Cazden. $7.95 paper.

But Some of Us Are Brave: Black Women's Studies. Edited by Gloria T. Hull, Patricia Bell Scott, and Barbara Smith. $14.95 cloth, $8.95 paper.

Complaints and Disorders: The Sexual Politics of Sickness by Barbara Ehrenreich and Deidre English. $2.95 paper.

Everywoman's Guide to Colleges and Universities. Edited by Florence Howe, Suzanne Howard, and Mary Jo Boehm Strauss. $12.95 paper.

Moving the Mountain: Women Working for Social Change by Cantarow with Susan Gushee O'Malley and Sharon Hartman Strom. $5.95 paper.

Reconstructing American Literature: Courses, Syllabi, Issues. Edited by Paul Lauter. $8.95 paper.

Witches, Midwives, and Nurses: A History of Women Healers by Barbara Ehrenreich and Deirdre English. $2.95 paper.

Women Have Always Worked: A Historical Overview by Alice Kessler-Harris. $14.95 cloth, $5.95 paper.

Women's Studies in Italy by Laura Balbo and Yasmine Ergas. A Women's Studies International Monograph. $5.95 paper.

When ordering, please include $1.00 for postage and handling for one hardcover or one or two paperback books and 35¢ for each additional book. Order from: The Feminist Press, Box 334, Old Westbury, NY 11568. Telephone (516) 997-7660.